*Jo-Anne Schmitzer ▪ Karl Ostertag ▪ Ernestine Prachner ▪
Beate Siegel ▪ Herbert Wiesner ▪ Sibylle Vogel*

English for Hotels and Restaurants

Dieses Buch gehört:

*Liebe Schülerin, lieber Schüler,
dieses Schulbuch dient Ihrer Ausbildung.
Bücher helfen nicht nur beim Lernen,
sondern sind auch Freunde fürs Leben.*

Jo-Anne Schmitzer
Karl Ostertag
Ernestine Prachner
Beate Siegel
Herbert Wiesner
Sibylle Vogel

English for Hotels and Restaurants

Trauner Schulbuch Verlag
Linz
www.trauner.at

Die Autorinnen und Autoren:
Jo-Anne Schmitzer, Landesberufsschule für das Gastgewerbe in Obertrum am See
Karl Ostertag, Landesberufsschule für Tourismus in Waldegg
Ernestine Prachner, Berufsschule für Tourismus in Wien
Beate Siegel, Landesberufsschule für Tourismus in Bad Gleichenberg
Herbert Wiesner, Landesberufsschule für Tourismus in Bad Gleichenberg
Sibylle Vogel, Berufsschule Erfurt, Deutschland

Approbiert für den Unterrichtsgebrauch
- an Berufsschulen für die Lehrberufe Koch, Restaurantfachmann/frau sowie Koch und Restaurantfachmann/frau im Unterrichtsgegenstand Berufsbezogenes Englisch, Bundesministerium für Unterricht und Kunst, GZ 42.478/1-I/9/91 vom 25. Februar 1992;
- an Hotelfachschulen für die 1. bis 3. Klasse im Unterrichtsgegenstand Englisch, Bundesministerium für Unterricht und Kunst, GZ 42.478/7-V/2/94 vom 30. Mai 1994;
- an Tourismusfachschulen für die 1. bis 3. Klasse im Unterrichtsgegenstand Englisch, Bundesministerium für Unterricht und Kunst, GZ 42.478/9-V/2/95 vom 17. Juli 1995.

Schulbuch-Nr. 3.667 (D)
Schmitzer ua., English for Hotels and Restaurants
Trauner Schulbuch Verlag, Linz
7. überarbeitete Auflage 2003

Dieses Buch wurde auf umweltfreundlichem Papier gedruckt:
Holzhaltiges Druckpapier, satiniert, umweltfreundlich Gruppe A laut Greenpeace (C-Stoff)

Dieses Schulbuch wurde auf der Grundlage eines Rahmenlehrplans erstellt; die Auswahl und die Gewichtung der Inhalte erfolgen durch die LehrerInnen.

**Wir weisen darauf hin, dass das Kopieren zum Schulgebrauch aus diesem Buch verboten ist –
§ 42 Absatz (3) der Urheberrechtsgesetznovelle 1996:
„Die Befugnis zur Vervielfältigung zum eigenen Schulgebrauch gilt nicht für Werke, die ihrer Beschaffenheit und Bezeichnung nach zum Schul- oder Unterrichtsgebrauch bestimmt sind."**

© 2003 by Trauner Schulbuch Verlag, Köglstraße 14, A 4021 Linz
Alle Rechte vorbehalten
Nachdruck oder sonstige Vervielfältigung, auch auszugsweise, nur mit ausdrücklicher Genehmigung des Verlages
Schulbuchvergütung/Bildrechte: © VBK Wien
Lektorat: Dr. Sieglinde Korab
Umschlag und Layout: Mag. Wolfgang Kraml
Satz: Adelheid Hinterkörner
Grafiken: Adelheid Hinterkörner, Gertud Kirschenhofer, Arnulf Kossak
Gesamtherstellung: Trauner Druck, Linz
ISBN 3-85487-352-2

Vorwort

Das vorliegende Buch wurde didaktisch und grafisch völlig neu gestaltet, inhaltlich aktualisiert und ist auf die mündliche Verständigung in Alltags- und Berufssituationen ausgerichtet. Es wurde als Arbeits- und Lehrbuch so aufgebaut, dass es einerseits Grundkenntnisse vermittelt, andererseits aber auch zur selbstständigen Weiterbildung und Anwendung im Beruf geeignet ist.

Die in den Texten verwendeten grammatikalischen Strukturen werden auf leicht verständliche Weise erläutert. Ohne einen Anspruch auf Vollständigkeit erheben zu wollen, ist die Grammatik jedoch nur so weit erklärt, als es in der jeweiligen Situation erforderlich ist. Im Anhang finden Sie eine gesammelte Übersicht der Grundzüge der englischen Grammatik.

Der Anhang rundet dieses Buch weiters mit Originaltexten, Rezepten, Menükarten und einem Verzeichnis von gastronomischen Vokabeln ab (einmal nach Speisengruppen geordnet und einmal in alphabetischer Reihenfolge). Dieses umfassende gastronomische Fachvokabular stellt eine wertvolle Stütze nicht nur im Unterricht, sondern auch in Ihrem späteren Berufsleben dar.

Alle Dialoge sowie andere kommunikative Beispiele sind auf der dazugehörigen CD in englischer Originalsprache zu hören. Die betreffenden Texte sind im Buch mit einem eigenen Symbol und der entsprechenden Tracknummer gekennzeichnet.

Querverbindungen zu den anderen Pflichtgegenständen helfen, Gesamtzusammenhänge zu erfassen. Dies führt zu einer selbstständigen Anwendung der erworbenen Fertigkeiten und Kenntnisse und motiviert zu deren Weiterentwicklung.

Am Anfang jeder Lektion, die mit einem englischen Einstiegstext beginnt, befinden sich auch die Lehr- und Lernzielformulierungen. Um das Lernen zu erleichtern, werden zu jeder Lektion die neuen Vokabeln übersichtlich angeführt.

Folgende Piktogramme haben wir für die verschiedenen Aufgaben gewählt:

 unsere Ziele   Sprachübung auf CD

 mündliche Übungen, Rollenspiele   Rätsel

 zum Nachdenken, Arbeitsaufgaben   für Schreibaufgaben

 Hinweis auf Besonderheiten

Zur leichteren Lesbarkeit wurde bei den personenbezogenen Formulierungen manchmal auf das Nebeneinander von männlicher und weiblicher Form verzichtet. Jede Bezeichnung gilt jedoch für die weibliche und die männliche Form in gleicher Weise.

Die Autorinnen und Autoren hoffen, dass alle, die mit diesem Buch arbeiten, viel Freude am Lernen und selbstständigen Arbeiten haben werden!

Vorwort für die Ausgabe für Deutschland

Da gerade im gastronomischen Bereich, zB bei Speisen- und Produktnamen, Sprachunterschiede zwischen Österreich und Deutschland bestehen, hat sich der Verlag entschlossen, diese Unterschiede zu berücksichtigen.
Frau Sibylle Vogel, Lehrerin an der deutschen gastronomischen Berufsschule in Erfurt, hat alle österreichspezifischen Begriffe durch die in Deutschland üblichen ersetzt. Weiters wurden bekannte Spezialitäten der deutschen Küche aufgenommen.
Wir wünschen den SchülerInnen und LehrerInnen viel Freude beim Arbeiten mit diesem Buch.

Contents – Inhaltsverzeichnis

1st Lesson:
Introducing 9
Vorstellung, Begrüßung, Vorlieben und Abneigungen

2nd Lesson:
Phoning 12
Telefonieren, Grundzahlen, Adressgestaltung

3rd Lesson:
Welcoming Guests 16
Begrüßung eines Gastes, Tageszeiten

4th Lesson:
Apologizing 20
Beschwerden, richtiges Reagieren auf Reklamationen

5th Lesson:
Telling the Time 24
Uhrzeit, lokale Feiertage, Datum (Tag, Monat, Jahreszeit), Ordnungszahlen, Tischreservierung

6th Lesson:
In the Kitchen 28
Küchenpersonal und seine Aufgaben, Küchengeräte, Vor- und Zubereitungsarten in der Küche, Lebensmittelbestellungen, Fisch, Fleisch, Gemüse, Früchte

7th Lesson:
Service Staff and Serving Utensils 34
Servierpersonal und seine Aufgaben, Serviergegenstände, korrektes Tischdecken

8th Lesson:
Breakfast 38
Serviergegenstände, Frühstücksarten, Frühstückskarte

9th Lesson:
In the Restaurant 40
Speisenkarte, europäische Länder und ihre Spezialitäten

10th Lesson:
Hotel Staff 44
Hotelpersonal und seine Aufgaben, richtiges Buchstabieren

11th Lesson:
A Day at a Hotel 46
Zimmerarten, Hoteltypen, Entgegennahme von Reservierungen, Online-booking, Wege im Hotelbereich erklären

12th Lesson:
Shopping – Working Clothes 52
Einkaufen, Berufskleidung

13th Lesson:
Family 54
Verwandtschaftsverhältnisse, Freizeitbeschäftigungen

14th Lesson:
Cafés 58
Typische Kaffeehausspezialitäten

15th Lesson:

Front Office 60
Empfang an der Rezeption, Formalitäten, Auskünfte, Wegbeschreibungen anhand eines Stadtplans

16th Lesson:

Hotel Facilities 66
Zimmer- und Etagenservice, Zimmereinrichtung, Hotelausstattung

17th Lesson:

In the Kitchen 72
Zubereitung, Zutaten, Tätigkeiten, Rezepte

18th Lesson:

In the Restaurant 77
Menügänge, Nationalgerichte, Restaurantrechnung

19th Lesson:

Dealing with Complaints 82
Beschwerden im Restaurant, Reaktionen

20th Lesson:

In the Bar 84
Bargeräte, -getränke, -personal, Cocktailrezepte

21st Lesson:

Sightseeing in Germany 88
Besichtigungsprogramme in Deutschland, Tickets für öffentliche Verkehrsmittel

22nd Lesson:

Hotels in Germany 94
Hotelangebote und Einrichtungen

23rd Lesson:

Brunch 100
Typische Gerichte und Serviergegenstände

24th Lesson:

Dinner 104
Speisen- und Getränkekarte, Weinempfehlungen

25th Lesson:

Austrian and German Cooking 108
Österreichische und deutsche Spezialitäten

26th Lesson:

Cooking all around the World 112
Britische Spezialitäten, Systemgastronomie, große Speisenfolge, Küchenpersonal, Anforderungen für Bankette und Konferenzen

27th Lesson:

Eating Habits 120
Essgewohnheiten von Gästen unterschiedlicher Nationalitäten und Religionen

28th Lesson:

Payment 124
Zahlungsarten, Währungen

29th Lesson:

The Bar 126
Erweiterung der Barkenntnisse, Bargeräte und -gläser

30th Lesson:

Complaints 130
Beschwerden im Hotel, Reaktionen

31st Lesson:

Looking for a Job   132
Bewerbungsschreiben, Lebenslauf, Bewerbungsbogen

32nd Lesson:

Correspondence   139
Form eines englischen Briefs, elektronische Post, Reservierungsbestätigung, -ablehnung, Stornierung

33rd Lesson:

Weather   144
Wettervorhersagen

34th Lesson:

Regional Studies   146
Besichtigungsprogramme in London, Großbritannien und Amerika

Appendix

Solutions	157
Menus	170
Recipes	176
Reading Exercises	181
Grammar	188
Phrases	199
Measures, Weights and Sizes	207
Cooking Terms	210
Gastronomic Vocabulary	
German – English	211
English – German	219
Vocabulary	
German – English	228
English – German	237
Books Consulted	246
Photo Credits	247

1. Lektion

Introducing

? *Do you know how people greet each other in other countries?*

Think of greeting habits you have already heard of.

English people rarely shake hands, except when being introduced to someone for the first time. They hardly ever shake hands with their friends, except when seeing them after a long interval or saying goodbye before a journey. Whether to shake hands or not in England is sometimes a problem, even for the English people.
In much of the world today, people do not shake hands when they meet. They may hug formally or kiss one another on the cheek, as in eastern Europe and Arab states or they may bow softly, eyes turned to the ground, as in Japan and China.

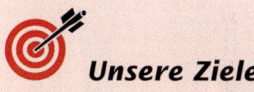 **Unsere Ziele**

Nach Bearbeitung dieses Kapitels sollten Sie

- sich selbst und andere vorstellen können;
- wissen, wie man Fragen richtig formuliert und beantwortet;
- Vorlieben und Abneigungen ausdrücken können.

1st Lesson

Introducing yourself:

May I introduce myself?
My name is ...
Hello. I'm ...
How do you do?

I'm ...
How do you do?
Pleased to meet you.

Introducing other people:

Let me introduce you to ...
This is ...
Hello.
Pleased to meet you.

I'd like you to meet Mr. / Mrs. ...
How do you do?
How do you do?

Asking for professions:

What do you do / are you?
I'm an apprentice.
- a waiter / waitress.
- a cook.
- a hotel assistant.
- a systems caterer.
- a stewardess.
- a travel agent.

Find out who is who:

What's your name?
Where are you from?
What are you?
What is your profession?

Dialogues 1–6

Listen and fill in the missing words.

1

Mary: Hello, I'm Mary.

Gary: _____ Gary.

Mary: _____ , Gary.

2

Gary: Here comes my girlfriend, Anna.

Anna, _____ Mary.

Mary: _____?

Anna: How do you do? Nice to meet you.

3

Mary: _____ from?

Anna: _____ New York.

4

Mary: And what _____?

Anna: I'm _____ in my father's restaurant. My mother is _____ . My father is a waiter and my brother is _____ . My sister is _____ .

5

Anna: What do you do?

Mary: I'm _____ and Gary is a _____ .

6

Mary: _____ your job?

Anna: Yes, _____ .

Exercises

1. Introduce yourself to your classmates.
2. Introduce your neighbours.
3. Introduce your family (to your boss).
4. Introduce your working place (hotel / inn / restaurant).

Practise

**Work with a partner. Ask each other about your choices and say what you like and what you are not so fond of.
Change partners and discuss your choices again.**

Example:

A: *Do you like drinking tea?*
B: *Yes, I really like drinking tea.*
   No, I don't like drinking tea.

Now ask two classmates. Tick the words and tell the results.

Words:	Name:		Name:	
	likes	doesn't like	likes	doesn't like
tea				
coffee				
chocolate				
juice				
milk				
beer				
wine				
steaks				
chicken				
fish				
salad				
listening to music				
dancing				
watching TV				
skiing				
swimming				
cooking				
travelling				
shopping				
reading books				
working				
going out				
phoning				
writing letters				
playing games				
sleeping				
talking with friends				

Expressing likes:

I really like ...ing
I'm very fond of ...
   ... interested in ...
   ... keen on ...

I find travelling

   ... exciting.
   ... enjoyable.
   ... fascinating.
   ... relaxing, etc.

Expressing dislikes:

I don't (really) like ...
I hate ...
I can't stand
I can't bear ...ing.
I find ...ing (rather)
   ... boring.
   ... tiring.
   ... dull etc.

 Compare "listen" and "hear":

To **listen** is to make a conscious or active effort to hear something.

To **hear** is to receive a sound by chance or in a passive way with your ears.

Example:

I love listening to music.
I always wake up when I hear my alarm clock.

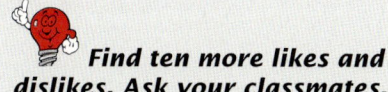 **Find ten more likes and dislikes. Ask your classmates.**

Phoning

Very frequently our first and sometimes only contact with guests or international business partners is on the phone. That's why it's so important to sound confident and credible.

Many people get nervous when phoning. We have an eight-point plan with some of the key phrases you will possibly need when calling someone for the first time.

But do remember one thing: We can hear a smile on the phone!

Phoning in Austria and Germany

There are telephone booths in almost all post offices where you can make calls without having to insert coins. You can pay directly at the Post Office counter.

All other public telephones can be used by inserting coins or with telephone cards, which are available at every Post Office. Mobile telephones on the international GSM network can be used in Austria and Germany in accordance with the "Roaming" agreement.

 Unsere Ziele

Nach Bearbeitung dieses Kapitels sollten Sie

- *die Grundzahlen kennen;*
- *Telefonnummern korrekt notieren können;*
- *Informationen über persönliche Daten einholen können;*
- *sich beim Telefonieren höflich und richtig verhalten können sowie*
- *Adressen im Schriftverkehr richtig gestalten können.*

2. Lektion

Phoning the correct and polite way

 Ask your classmates

What's your ...
- name?
- address?
- telephone number?
- profession?

1. Get service at the switchboard
Tell the operator it's an international call, which often speeds up the process.
"Good morning. I'm calling from Austria / Germany."

Give your name if it's appropriate. "This is ..."

Say who you want to speak to. "I'd like to speak to Mr. / Mrs. ..., please."
"I'd like to speak to your manager, please."

2. Greet your telephone partner and introduce yourself
Mention his or her name. "Good morning, Mr. / Mrs. ..."
Mention your hotel name first. "I'm calling from Hotel ... in ..."
Mention your own name. "Hello, this is ... speaking."
"My name is ... ." (repeat full name)

3. Say what you want
Get straight to the point. "The reason I'm calling is ..."
"I'm returning your call ..."
"I'm calling in reply to your e-mail ..."

Then you can go into the details of the call.

4. Control the call
If your partner is speaking too quickly. "Could you speak a bit more slowly?"
too quietly. "... up a bit, please?"

If you don't understand: "I'm sorry, I didn't catch that."
"I'm sorry, I didn't get that."
"Sorry, could you repeat that, please?"

5. Confirm the information
Make sure you've both understood the same thing by summarizing.
"So, we agree ..."
"May I just repeat that?"
"Could we go over this one more time?"

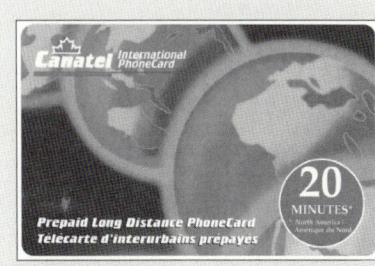

6. End the call
You can signal to your partner that you want the call to end.
"Right. I think that was all."
"Good. I think that's all I need to know."
"OK. Is there anything else we need to discuss?"

7. Be polite
End on a positive, polite note.
"Thanks a lot for your help."
"We'll be in touch soon."
"Hope to see you over here in ... sometime."

8. Last words
Show you are hanging up. "Goodbye."
"Bye."
"Bye then."

2nd Lesson

British Telecom Payphones

zero
one
two
three
four
five
six
seven
eight
nine

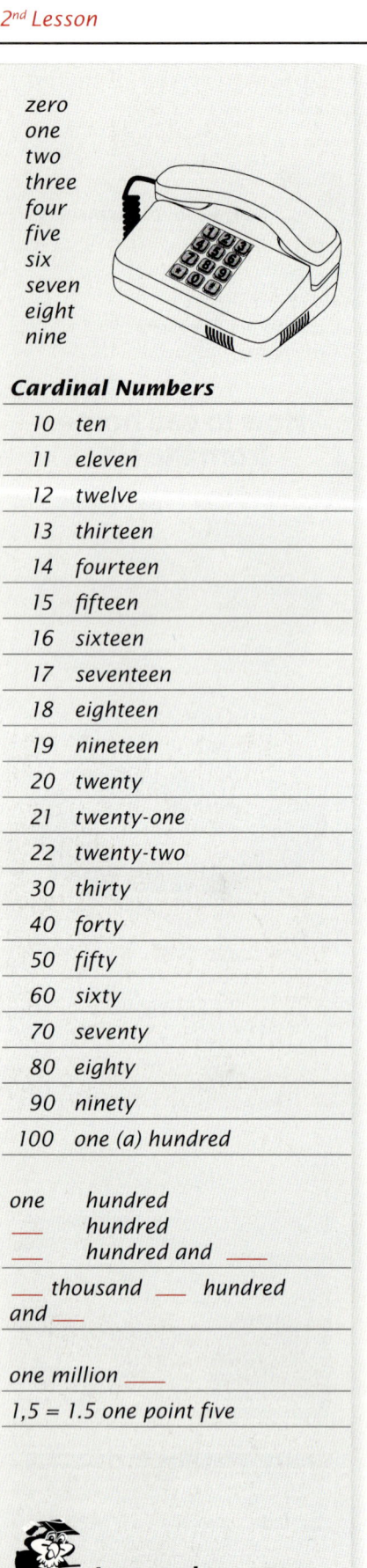

Cardinal Numbers

10	ten
11	eleven
12	twelve
13	thirteen
14	fourteen
15	fifteen
16	sixteen
17	seventeen
18	eighteen
19	nineteen
20	twenty
21	twenty-one
22	twenty-two
30	thirty
40	forty
50	fifty
60	sixty
70	seventy
80	eighty
90	ninety
100	one (a) hundred

one ___ hundred
___ hundred
___ hundred and ___
___ thousand ___ hundred and ___

one million ___

1,5 = 1.5 one point five

Aussprache:
01-982 77 53
(phonetic "0", "double seven")

Payphone
Collect / Telephone credit card / Coins
You can usually call Collect or charge to your telephone credit card from a payphone – even if it is flashing „999 calls only". Payphones accept coins to the value of £ 1, 50p, 20p, 10p, 5p and 2p. You'll need at least £ 1 to make an International Direct Dialled Call. British Telecom payphones are widely available throughout the UK.

Phonecard payphone
Phonecard / Collect / Telephone credit cards
This looks similar to a payphone, but only accepts pre-paid green Phonecards, which vary in value and are available at Post Offices and shops displaying a green Phonecard sign. However, you can also make Collect or telephone credit card calls from one of these phones, without inserting a green Phonecard.

British
TELECOM

Fill in

 7

Listen and note the telephone numbers.

a) What's your telephone number?

   My number is _____ .

b) Please call me. My mobile telephone number is _____ .

c) Call Gary, his mobile number is _____ .

d) May I give you the telephone number of our hotel?

   The international dialling code is _____ , the area code is _____ ,

   omit the _____ when dialling from a foreign country, the telephone number

   is _____ .

Postal Addresses

When a Briton or an American gives you an address over the phone, you might have trouble putting each piece of the address in the right place. Here is some help:

A typical British address

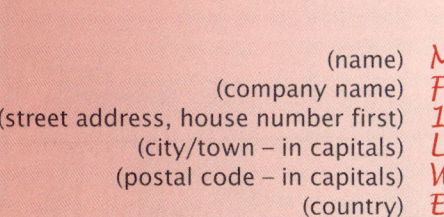

(name)	Mr. Peter Grey
(company name)	Four Seasons Hotel
(street address, house number first)	1 Hamilton Place, Park Lane
(city/town – in capitals)	LONDON
(postal code – in capitals)	W1A 1AZ
(country)	ENGLAND

A typical US address

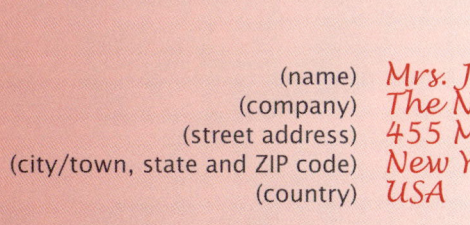

(name)	Mrs. Jennifer Carlton
(company)	The New York Palace
(street address)	455 Madison Avenue
(city/town, state and ZIP code)	New York, NY 10022-6809
(country)	USA

ZIP code (postcode):

("Zone improvement plan")

In the USA the ZIP code consists of five or nine numbers. The first three numbers give information about the region, the other numbers about the local post office.

SASE = Self Addressed Stamped Envelope

SARP = Self Addressed Response Postcard

Exercise

Write the following addresses in the correct way.

1. Happy HolidayTours, Alberta, Box 137, North Star, Canada, T0H 2T0
2. Alton, LON 1 AO, Canada, Ontario, 55 John Street, The Millcroft Inn
3. 8671 Odlin Crescent, Richmond International High School, Richmond, B.C., V6 X 1G1, Canada
4. Canada, N.F., 17 Dawe Crescent, Amazing Adventures Inc., Grand Falls, A2A 2T2

3rd Lesson

Welcoming Guests

A friendly and polite greeting gives the guests a feeling of a warm and heartily welcome. A courteous and knowledgeable staff is able to provide high standards of attentive and personalized service and so reflect the hospitality at its best.

 Unsere Ziele

Nach Bearbeitung dieses Kapitels sollten Sie

- Gäste richtig anreden und unter Berücksichtigung der Tageszeiten korrekt begrüßen können;
- Zeitangaben machen können;
- die Frageform mit den Hilfszeitwörtern "be", "do", "have" anwenden sowie
- die Gegenwart (Present Tense) und die Mitvergangenheit (Past Tense) verwenden können.

3. Lektion

Dialogues

Listen and fill in.

(a)

Waiter: Good _____, sir. _____?

Guest (gentleman): Yes, please. A table _____, please.

Waiter: Please _____.

(b)

Waiter: Good _____, madam. _____?

Guest (lady): A table for three, please.

(c)

John Miller: I'm John Miller. _____?

Bill Brown: How do you do? I'm Bill Brown and this is my wife Ellen.

John Miller: _____, Mrs. Brown.

(d)

Guest (man): _____.

Waiter: Goodbye. _____ day.

(e)

Bill: _____, John. _____ today?

John: Not _____. I didn't sleep last _____.

(f)

Waitress: _____, sir. A table for _____?

Guest (man): Yes, I phoned _____. My name is Johnson.

Waitress: _____, please.

Answer

1. How are you today?
2. How do you do? My name is …
3. Do you work at a hotel?
4. Are you an apprentice?
5. Do you live in …?
6. Do you like dancing?
7. How is your friend?
8. How do you greet guests in the morning?
9. How do you greet a guest in the evening?
10. When do you begin to work?

To learn

in the	morning
	afternoon
	evening
on	holidays
	Monday
at	five o'clock
	quarter to seven
	half past twelve
	quarter past ten
	the weekend

Greeting

Hello, Mary.
    Gary.
Can I help you?
What can I do for you?

Good morning, Mrs. …
… afternoon, Mr. …
… evening, Miss …

How do you do?
Nice to meet you.

Asking about one's state of health

How are you?
Fine (I'm fine), thank you.

How is John?
(He's) very well, thanks.
Not so / too bad, thanks.

3rd Lesson

Play the scenes with your partner.

Choose the right answer

Then listen and correct.

(a)

Guest:
Good evening.

You:
○ Good evening.
○ Good evening, sir. Can I help you?
○ Good night.

(b)

American guest:
My name is John Miles. How do you do?

You:
○ Thank you, fine and you?
○ My name is _____ .
○ How do you do? I am _____ .

(c)

You:
How are you, sir?

Guest:
○ Fine, thanks.
○ How are you?
○ How do you do?

(d)

English girl:
This is my mother.

You:
○ Nice to meet you, madam.
○ How are you?
○ Hello.

(e)

Canadian guest:
How are you?

You:
○ How are you?
○ Not so bad, thanks.
○ Can I help you?

(f)

American lady:
Good morning.

You:
○ Hello.
○ Nice to meet you.
○ Good morning, madam.

(g)

American guest:
How is your girlfriend?

You:
○ She is not well today.
○ I'm fine, thanks.
○ I'm not fine.

(h)

Mr. Miller:
How do you do? I am Mike Miller.

You:
○ I'm fine, thanks.
○ I am _____ . How do you do?
○ I am _____ .

IDIOM MAGIC

the welcome mat is out

Spotlight

The welcome mat is out is an expression that means "you are welcome to visit at any time". A welcome mat is the mat that lies in front of most people's front doors.

"It would be wonderful to see you. You know the welcome mat is always out for good friends like you."

Welcome the guest at …

7.10	(ein Herr)	Good morning, sir.
11.40	(eine Dame)	_____ .
14.20	(Mr. Miller)	_____ .
21.30	(Mrs. Smith)	_____ .
20.00	(Damen und Herren)	_____ .

Fill in

Complete the dialogues below using following expressions.

Good evening, sir. Can I help you?
Nice to meet you.
How do you do? (2x)
Hello, John.
How do you do? I'm Ronald Burns.
I am fine, thanks.

(a)

John: Hello, Mike.

Mike: _____

John: How are you?

Mike: _____

(b)

George: Mike, this is my friend Alan.

Mike: _____

(c)

Tom Miller: Good evening.

Waiter: _____

Tom Miller: A table for two, please.

(d)

Richard: How do you do?

Ronald: _____

And this is Miss Bailey from Manchester.

Richard: _____

Miss Bailey: _____

Translate

1. Guten Morgen, meine Damen und Herren. Was kann ich für Sie tun?

_____

2. Wie heißen Sie bitte?

_____

3. Es tut mir sehr Leid, ich habe Ihren Namen nicht verstanden.

_____

4. Woher kommen Sie?

_____

5. Hatten Sie eine angenehme Reise?

_____

6. Ich wünsche Ihnen einen schönen Tag.

_____

Do you shy away from introducing people, or feel embarrassed while being introduced?

If you do, practice in making correct introductions will help you to overcome this social handicap.

Whenever you find yourself with a stranger at a social gathering, introduce yourself.

The Changing of the Guard

This happens every day at Buckingham Palace, the Queen's home in London. Soldiers stand in front of the palace. Each morning these soldiers (the "guard") change. One group leaves and another arrives. In summer and winter tourists stand outside the palace at 11.30 every morning and watch the Changing of the Guard.

4th Lesson

Apologizing

How do you react to complaints made by guests?
Complaints are a very delicate matter. It is part of a good service and it is in the hotel's interest to handle complaints in a calm, quick and generous way.
All aspects of guest's comfort and convenience are of the highest concern.

 Unsere Ziele

Nach Bearbeitung dieses Kapitels sollten Sie

- die Fragewörter kennen;
- auf Fragen und Reklamationen der Gäste höflich reagieren können;
- sich richtig entschuldigen können.

4. Lektion

Dialogues

Listen and answer the question to each picture.

 10

(a) How many?

(b) How long?

(c) Where?

(d) Who?

(e) When?

(f) What?

To learn

How many?
How long?
Where?
Who?
When?
What?

Apologizing

I'm sorry, …
    … we don't take foreign money.
    … the line is engaged / busy.
    … we haven't any tables left on …

Please forgive me for not …
I'm terribly sorry.
I really must apologize for …
Can you forgive me for …
I greatly regret.
We regret to inform you …
Please accept our apologies.

 Attention

I'm afraid we are fully booked.
Wir sind **leider** vollkommen ausgebucht.

to be afraid **of**
sich fürchten **vor**

To learn

I'm afraid we're fully booked.

I'm sorry, there are only rooms with hot and cold water left.

I'm sorry, we don't take foreign money.

I'm sorry, the line is engaged.

I'm afraid we haven't any tables left on Monday.

I'm sorry, the machine is broken.

Match

1. I'd like to book a single room for next Monday. — I'm sorry, we are fully booked. (1)
2. I'd like to reserve a table for tomorrow. — I'm afraid we have no tables free tomorrow.
3. My soup is cold. — I'm sorry, I'll bring a hot one.
4. Please put me through to Mr. Smith in room number 201. — Sorry, he's not in his room.
5. I'd like to reserve a table for breakfast at 6:00. — We aren't open before 8:00.
6. My napkin is dirty. — I'm sorry, I'll change it.

Zukunft mit „will / shall"

In der Alltagssprache verwenden die Briten in allen Personen „will". In der 1. Person Einzahl und Mehrzahl (I, we) hört man gelegentlich noch „shall", besonders in der gehobenen Sprache.
Die Amerikaner verwenden ausschließlich „will".

I'll = I will
we'll = we will
won't = I will not

Which is right?

Delete the wrong part.

1. I phone / I'll phone you tomorrow, madam.
2. I haven't written the menu yet. I do / I'll do it later.
3. I would like some more coffee. I bring / I'll bring it right away.
4. Bring me another towel. Just one moment, sir. I see / I'll see to it right away.
5. This is for my wife. I give / I'll give it to her.
6. It's very warm here. Shall I / will I open the window?
7. It's a nice day. Shall you / will you go for a walk?
8. I think I go / I will go to bed early today.

Translate

1. Guten Abend, meine Damen und Herren. Einen Tisch für vier?
2. Ich möchte gerne einen Tisch für Dienstag Abend reservieren.
3. Es tut mir Leid, wir sind völlig ausgebucht.
4. Dieser Kaffee ist kalt.
5. Es tut mir Leid, ich werde Ihnen einen anderen bringen.
6. Möchten Sie eine Nachricht hinterlassen?
7. Wir nehmen bedauerlicherweise keine Kreditkarten.
8. Wie lange werden Sie bleiben?
9. Möchten Sie eine Tasse Kaffee oder Tee?
10. Es tut mir Leid, wir haben heute geschlossen.

Choose the right answer

Then listen and correct.

(a)

Guest (man):
I'd like to reserve a table for tomorrow evening.

You:
○ I'm sorry, there is only one table for six persons.
○ I'm sorry, we are fully booked.
○ We haven't any tables left the day after tomorrow.

(b)

Guest (lady):
My coffee is cold.

You:
○ I'll speak to the head waiter.
○ I'm sorry, would you like to have a cup of tea?
○ I'm sorry, I'll bring you a hot one.

(c)

Guest (man):
My knife is dirty.

You:
○ I'll clean it.
○ I'm sorry, I'll get you another one.
○ Sorry, I'll speak to the chef.

(d)

Guest (lady):
I'd like to book a double room for next Sunday.

You:
○ I'm afraid we are fully booked.
○ I'm sorry, we are fully booked today.
○ We only have single rooms.

Do you remember?

today
tomorrow
yesterday
the day after tomorrow
the day before yesterday
next week / month / year
last week / month / year

Remember to react friendly and polite.

Practise

Work with a partner. Play the following situations.

Example:

Guest:
I'd like to book a double room for next week.

You:
I'm afraid we are fully booked next week.

a) single room with private bath / next week   fully booked
b) dirty tablecloth   change it
c) change money   at the reception
d) small espresso   machine out of order
e) speak to Mr. Johnson / room 407   no answer / leave a message
f) table for lunch / tomorrow   closed tomorrow
g) plate is not clean   bring another one
h) meat dish is not done   speak with the chef
i) coffee cup is broken   change it
j) wrong connection   put through again

Telling the Time

Asking for the time

At what time ...?
When ...?
How long ...?

from ... to ...
till / until
approximately

The solar time is different from place to place according to its meridian. A time zone is approximately 15° longitude wide and extends from pole to pole. Each 15° indicates an hour time difference. This means that while Elizabeth in England is taking afternoon tea at 3 p.m., Helmut is playing handball in Germany whereas Billy Joe is just getting up for a Los Angeles breakfast at 7 a.m. of that same morning.

Time zones have been known to be detrimental to the long-distance traveller's health causing fatigue, disorientation, dehydration and broken sleeping patterns. This condition, commonly known as jet lag, occurs because our bodies are not programmed for these, sometimes crass, time differences and therefore react adversely to the changes in routine. NASA has estimated that for every time zone crossed you need a day's sleep to get back to normal. So a 4 hour time difference will require you to sleep for four days to recover!

It can be quite confusing when you fly long-distance over a number of time zones and end up in a different country hours before you even have left home.

 Unsere Ziele

Nach Bearbeitung dieses Kapitels sollten Sie

- die Uhrzeit und das Datum verstehen und übersetzen können;
- die wichtigsten Mahlzeiten kennen;
- dem Gast Auskunft über Essenszeiten geben können;
- die lokalen Feiertage kennen;
- Redewendungen über Alter und Geburtstag anwenden können.

Dialogues

Listen and note the time.

a) _____

b) _____

c) _____

d) _____

e) _____

f) _____

g) _____

h) _____

Opening hours

Restaurant	
Breakfast buffet	7.30 – 10.00
Continental breakfast (for late risers)	10.00 – 11.00
Lunch	12.00 – 13.30
Coffee bar	15.00 – 21.00
Dinner	19.00 – 21.00

Swimming pool	7.00 – 20.00
Sauna	16.00 – 19.00
Solarium	8.00 – 20.00
Tennis	7.00 – 22.00

Practise

When do you serve ...?

Example:

When do you serve breakfast?
Breakfast is served from 7.30 a.m. to 10 a.m.

Breakfast	is served from	_____	to	_____ .
Brunch	is served from	_____	to	_____ .
Lunch	is served from	_____	to	_____ .
Coffee / tea	is served from	_____	to	_____ .
Dinner	is served from	_____	to	_____ .
Supper	is served from	_____	to	_____ .

To learn

 It's four o'clock.

 It's five minutes **past** four.

 It's quarter **past** four.

 It's twenty-five minutes **past** four (four twenty-five).

 It's half **past** four.

 It's twenty minutes **to** five (four forty).

 It's quarter **to** five.

 It's ten minutes **to** five (four fifty).

`10.00` ten a.m.

`22.00` ten p.m.

 Work with a partner. A guest wants ...

- to know when meals are served.
- to know when the ticket office opens.
- to know the opening hours of the restaurant / the bar / banks.
- to know how long public transport runs.
- to order an airport-taxi for the next day.
- to be woken up at seven a.m. in the morning.

5th Lesson

Days of the week

Monday
Tuesday
Wednesday
Thursday
Friday
Saturday
Sunday

Months

January
February
March
April
May
June
July
August
September
October
November
December

Thirty days have September, April, June and November; all the rest have thirty-one, except February alone which has twenty-eight days clear and twenty-nine each leap year.

Seasons

spring
summer
autumn / fall
winter

 How to say important dates:

My birthday is on the ...
- John / 2nd February
- Ann / 27th March
- Mary / 30th June
- Tom / 23rd November
- Phil / 21st December

Exercise

Form questions and answer.

Example:

What time do you serve lunch?
We serve lunch from 12.00 to 14.00 o'clock.

1. open/every day//closed Mondays
   _____
   _____

2. time/dinner//seven to eleven
   _____
   _____

3. open/evening//seven o'clock
   _____
   _____

4. have/single room/Friday//certainly/name
   _____
   _____

Take a calendar

Date the local holidays of this year.

	20..		20..
New Year's Day	_____	Assumption	_____
Epiphany	_____	National Holiday	_____
Good Friday	_____	All Saints' Day	_____
Easter Monday	_____	Immaculate Conception	_____
Labour Day	_____	Christmas Eve	_____
Ascension Day	_____	Christmas Day	_____
Whitsun	_____	Boxing Day	_____
Corpus Christi	_____		

Ordinal numbers

1st the first	11th the eleventh	20th the twentieth
2nd the second	12th the twelfth	21st the twenty-first
3rd the third	13th the thirteenth	22nd ...
4th the fourth	14th ...	23rd ...
5th the fifth	.	24th ...
6th ...	.	.
.		

5. Lektion

Prepositions of time

in	2002 (a year)	**on**	Monday (a day of the week)
	July (a month)		my birthday (a particular day)
	(the) summer (a season)		24th December (a date)
at	Easter (a religious period)	**in**	the evening (part of a day)
	4 o'clock / midday (time)		

Exercise

Fill in the right preposition.
at, in, on

Mr. Clark will arrive _____ 7th September.

The meeting ends _____ 8 o'clock _____ the evening.

Our restaurant is closed _____ August.

We are always fully booked _____ winter.

We will be very busy _____ Christmas.

The company was founded _____ 1992.

Are you open _____ Sunday?

The new apprentice will start _____ Monday _____ 8 o'clock _____ the morning.

To learn

I'd like to reserve / book a table.
Do you have a reservation?
I've got a reservation for …
What day / date?
What time?
How many persons?

Dialogues 🎵 13–15

Listen and complete.

13
Name: _____
Persons: _____
Time: _____
Day: _____

14
Name: _____
Persons: _____
Time: _____
Day: _____

15
Reservation   ○ yes   ○ no
Name: _____
Persons: _____

Make table reservations. Play the scenes with your partner.

1.
for 2 / tomorrow evening / 9 p.m.

2.
for 4 / next Wednesday / 12.30 p.m.

3.
for 6 / Sunday / brunch / 11 a.m.

4.
for 3 / dinner / Saturday / 8 p.m.

5.
for a party of 10 / birthday celebration / the day after tomorrow / 7 p.m.

6th Lesson

In the Kitchen

The **kitchen staff** do not only prepare dishes, they should also know about personal hygiene and sources of infection. The food hygiene regulations should be known and compiled with by all people involved in the handling of food. Cooks must also know about nutriments like carbohydrates, proteins and fats.

Kitchen equipment is expensive so initial selection is important, and may be divided into three categories:
1. Large equipment – ranges, steamers, boiling pans, fish-fryers, sinks, tables etc.
2. Mechanical equipment – peelers, mincers, mixers, refrigerators, dishwashers etc.
3. Utensils and small equipment – pots, pans, whisks, bowls, spoons etc.

Unsere Ziele

Nach Bearbeitung dieses Kapitels sollten Sie

- *das Küchenpersonal und seine Aufgaben nennen können;*
- *Lebensmittel und einfache Speisen übersetzen können;*
- *wichtige Zubereitungsarten erklären können;*
- *Küchenutensilien und deren Verwendung kennen;*
- *einige Fische, Fleischarten, Gemüse- und Obstsorten bezeichnen können;*
- *einfache Lebensmittelbestellungen aufgeben sowie*
- *die Bestellung des Küchenchefs verstehen können.*

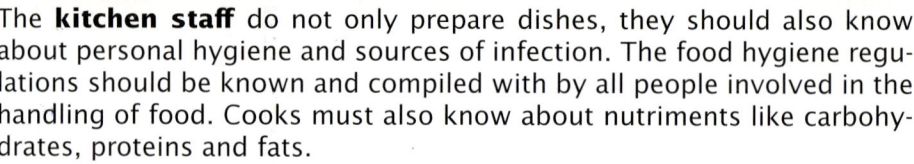

6. Lektion

Kitchen Staff

food and beverage manager / manageress

second chef — head chef — chefs de partie 1

sauce cook 6 — fish cook — pastry cook / baker — larder / butcher — staff cook 9

roast cook / grill cook / carver ✗ — vegetable cook / soup cook 4 — relief cook / duty cook / night cook ✗ 8

assistant cook 3

apprentice

dishwasher ✗ 10

Answer

1. Who organizes and supervises the kitchen?
2. Who organizes and is in charge of a section?
3. Who assists the cook?
4. Who prepares the vegetables?
5. Who prepares the cold dishes?
6. Who prepares the soups and sauces?
7. Who prepares the sweets?
8. Who is on duty in the night?
9. Who prepares the meals for the staff?
10. Who cleans the kitchen?

Fill in the cooking terms

fry, bake, braise, slice, whip, boil, grill, roast, poach, gratinate, steam, sauté

Cook by dry heat in an oven, e.g. bread: bake

Cook in water or other liquid at 100°C: boil

Beat with regular movements, e.g. the egg whites until they become stiff: whip

Cook in hot fat or oil in a frying pan: fry

Brown the top of a sauced dish: gratinate

Cook in a little fat for a short time: sauté

Cook under or over direct heat: roast

Cook in gently boiling water or other liquid, e.g. fish: poach

Cook (especially meat) by dry heat either over an open fire or in an oven: grill

Cut into slices: slice

Brown meat or vegetables in fat, then cook slowly in a small amount of liquid: braise

Cook in steam generated by boiling water: steam

Find the twelve cooking terms.

```
G B R A I S E L U
B R D E S L I C E
E F A M I O L R O
P A Y T B A K E Y
O R G R I L L A W
F U R O M N U S H
U P O A C H A C I
R O E S C U S T P
L T B T T B R O E
S A L E N O C A L
```

29

6th Lesson

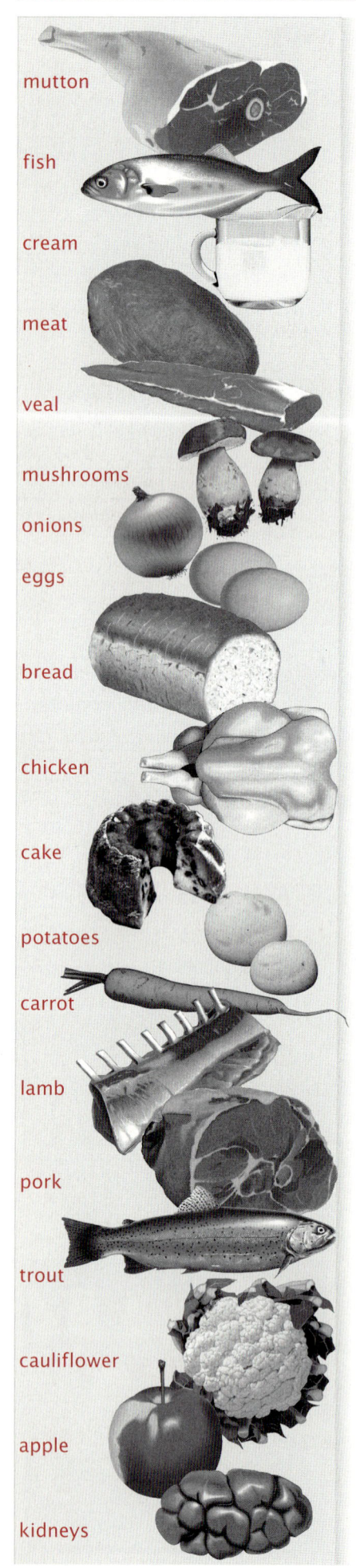

mutton
fish
cream
meat
veal
mushrooms
onions
eggs
bread
chicken
cake
potatoes
carrot
lamb
pork
trout
cauliflower
apple
kidneys

Kitchen Utensils

Exercise

Match the kitchen utensils and their functions. Then form sentences.

Example:

I use a mincer to mince meat.
When I mince meat I use a mincer.

Kitchen utensils   **Functions**

	Kitchen utensils			Functions
1.	mincer *Fleischwolf*			keep food hot
2.	chopping board *Schneidebrett*			peel potatoes
3.	grill (salamander) *grill*		1	mince meat
4.	potato peeler *Kartoffelschäler*			chop and cut
5.	fridge (refrigerator) *Kühlschrank*		10	weigh the portions
6.	fryer *Fritöse*			cool
7.	steamer *Dämpfer*			bake and roast
8.	range *Herd zado*		6	fry
9.	oven *Ofen*			warm up dishes
10.	table weighing-machine *Tischwaage*		7	steam
11.	microwave oven *Mikrowelle*			boil and braise in pots and pans
12.	convection oven *Centomat*			grill and cook quickly
13.	hot cupboard (bain marie) *Warmhalteschrank*			cook and heat food

Practise

Use your notebook.

Example:
How can you prepare vegetables?
I can boil vegetables. Vegetables can be boiled.

Fill in

Put the _____ (Kartoffeln) in the _____ (Pfanne).

Mix the _____ (Eier) with the _____ (Schneebesen).

Weigh the _____ (Hühner) on the _____ (Waage).

Bake the _____ (Gemüse) in the _____ (Rohr).

Store the _____ (Fleisch) in the _____ (Kühlschrank).

Serve the _____ (Suppe) with the _____ (Schöpfer).

6. Lektion

Dialogue

Listen and name the pictures using the words below.

weighing machine / scales, cook's knife, refrigerator (fridge / freezer), stock pot, mixer, frying-pan, whisk, kitchen-range

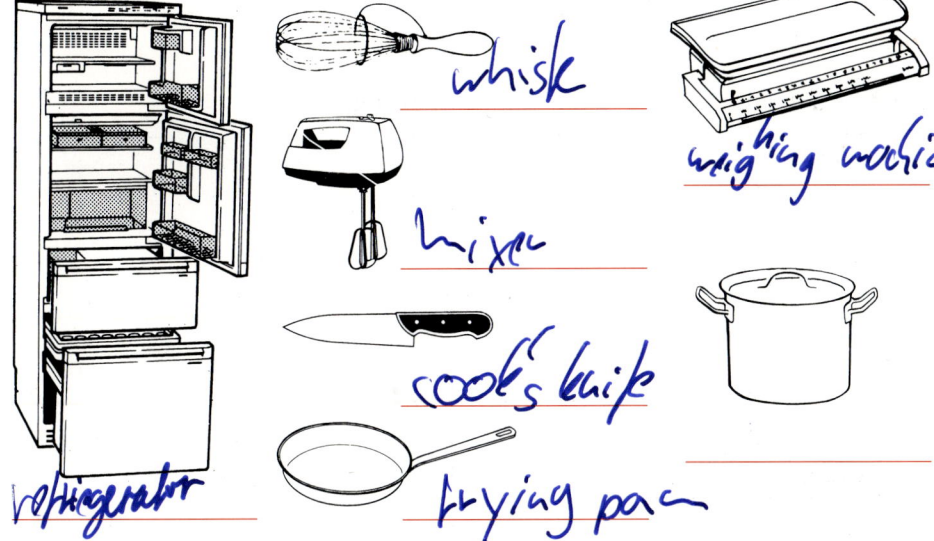

- whisk
- weighing machine
- mixer
- cook's knife
- refrigerator
- frying pan

Form sentences with the utensils in the picture.

Examples:

Bring me the frying-pan.
I need a frying-pan for frying fish.
When I fry fish I need a frying-pan.

Fill in

Name the utensils. Then form sentences with them and explain their functions.

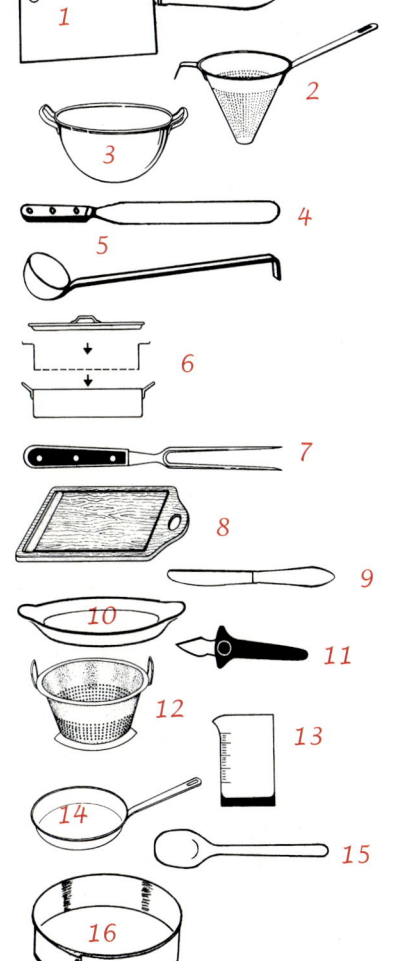

1. _____
2. _____
3. _____
4. _____
5. _____
6. _____
7. _____
8. _____
9. _____
10. _____
11. _____
12. _____
13. _____
14. _____
15. _____
16. _____

To learn

carving fork
metal spatula
sauté pan
measuring jug
fish kettle
small fruit knife
cleaver
oyster knife
colander
conical strainer
ladle
chopping board
flanring
mixing bowl
(wooden) spoon
oval eared dish

6th Lesson

Ordering Food

Dialogues   17–19

Listen what the chef is ordering by phone. Tick the orders.

Fish are valuable, not only because they are a good source of protein, but because they are suitable for all types of menus and can be cooked and presented in a wide variety of ways. The oily fish, such as sardines, mackerel, herrings and salmon contain vitamins A and D in their flesh. In white fish, such as halibut and cod, these vitamins are present in the liver.

Fish (17)

turbot, trout, eel, carp, pike, herring, sole, haddock, plaice, salmon

To cook **meat** properly it is necessary to know and understand the structure. Cattle, sheep and pigs are reared for fresh meat and certain pigs are specifically produced for bacon.

Animal	Meat
calf	veal
cattle (bull, cow, ox)	beef
pig, swine	pork
sheep	lamb, mutton
hen, cock	chicken

Meat (18)

cattle (bull, cow, ox), fillets of beef, calf, veal, pig, swine, loins of pork, lamb chops, sheep, chickens, hen, cock

6. Lektion

Vegetables (19)

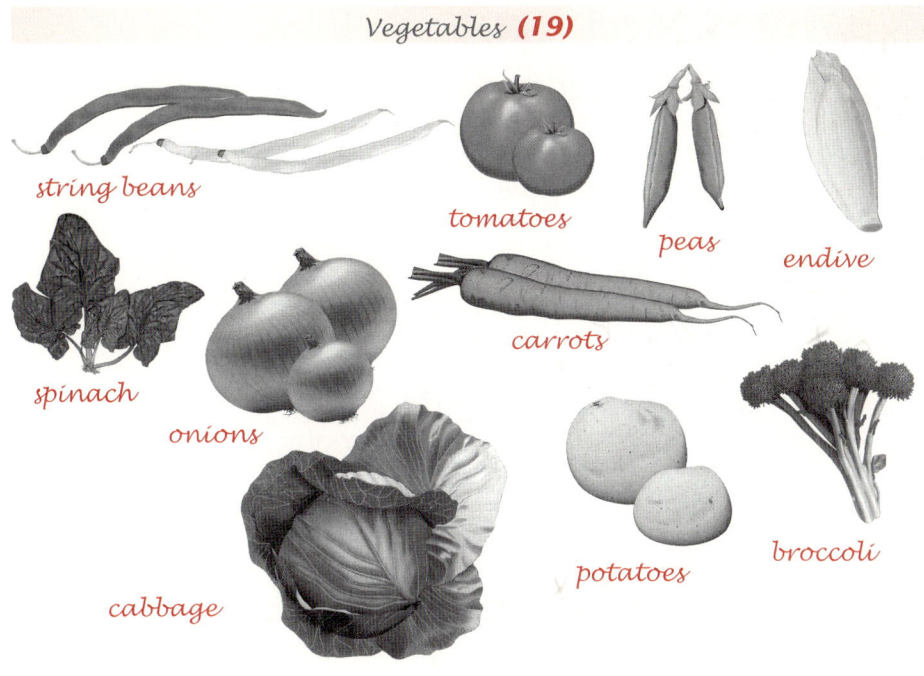

string beans, tomatoes, peas, endive, spinach, onions, carrots, broccoli, cabbage, potatoes

Fresh **vegetables** and **fruits** are important foods both from an economic and nutritional point of view. The purchasing of these commodities is difficult because of the highly perishable nature of the products, changes in market practice owing to varying supply and demand, the effect of preserved foods, e.g. frozen vegetables. Experience and sound of judgement are essential for the efficient buying and storage of all commodities, but none probably more so than fresh vegetables and fruits.

HACCP: **H**azard **A**nalysis and **C**ritical **C**ontrol **P**oints

Fruits (19)

lemon, orange, strawberry, apple

Sources of infection

Food-poisoning bacteria live in:
- the soil
- humans – intestines, nose, throat, skin, cuts, sores, spots etc.
- animals, insects and birds – intestines and skin etc.

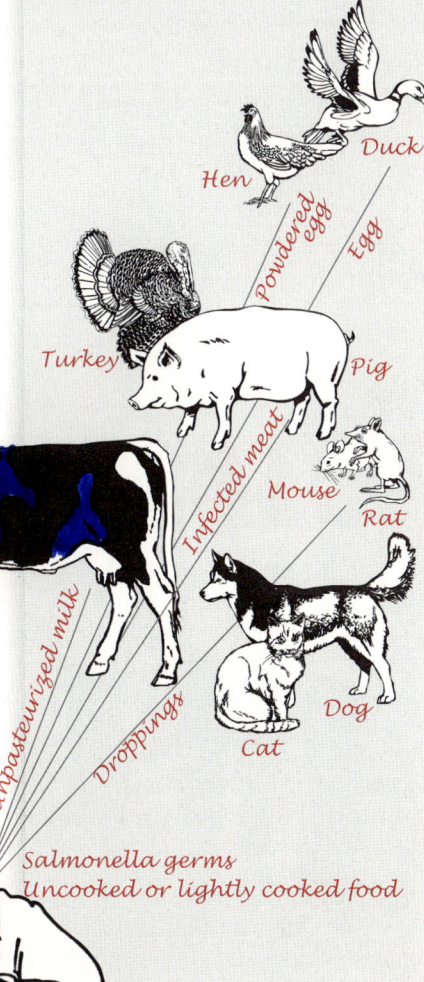

Read

Personal hygiene
The practice of clean habits in the kitchen is the only way to achieve a satisfactory standard of hygiene.

1. Hands must be washed frequently and always after using the toilet.
2. Bathing must occur frequently.
3. Hair must be kept clean and covered.
4. Nose and mouth should not be touched with the hands.
5. Cough and sneeze in a handkerchief.
6. Jewellery, rings and watches should not be worn.
7. Smoking and spitting must not occur where there is food.
8. Cuts and burns should be covered with a waterproof dressing.
9. Clean clothing.
10. Food should be tasted with a clean tea spoon.
11. Don't sit on tables.
12. Only healthy people should handle food.

7th Lesson

Ask your partner:

**Who works in your restaurant?
What does he / she do?**

Example:

Mr. Mayer is the head waiter at my restaurant. He welcomes and receives the guests.

Service Staff and Serving Utensils

Waitresses and waiters are very important persons in restaurants and dining rooms. Everybody who chooses the profession of a waiter should know that this profession requires certain qualities. In the first place, waitresses and waiters are expected to be neat and spotlessly clean. They must also be honest, sober and reliable. They should have a good appearance, should be well and neatly dressed and always show a cheerful expression, even if a guest is hard to please. Waitresses and waiters must do their duties patiently in a polite and obliging manner. The service in a hotel or restaurant is as important as the cooking and forms part of the reputation of a place. They must not lose their nerve when their place of work is crowded and, even in the greatest rush, they should remember the words: "Keep smiling"!

 Unsere Ziele

Nach Bearbeitung dieses Kapitals sollten Sie

- *das Servierpersonal und seine Aufgaben kennen;*
- *Serviergegenstände kennen;*
- *einen Tisch korrekt decken können.*

Service Staff

food and beverage manager / manageress

restaurant manager / maître d'hôtel

bartender (barman / barlady)	head waiter	section captain (chef de rang)
barwaiter / barwaitress	**waiter / waitress / server**	**wine butler sommelier wine waiter / waitress**	**assistant section captain (commis de rang)**

apprentice waiter / waitress trainee

busboy, cleaning staff

Answer

Who ...?
- ... receives and welcomes guests?
- ... supervises the service?
- ... is in charge of a section?
- ... mixes cocktails?
- ... sets the tables?
- ... assists the wine butler?
- ... is responsible for wine service?
- ... trains to be a waiter / server?
- ... is in charge of food and beverage purchase and sale?
- ... serves food and beverages?
- ... clears tables?

Describing professions:
What is his / her job?
What does he / she do?
What is his / her responsibliity?
What is his / her task?
She mixes cocktails.
He assists the wine butler.
She is in charge of food and beverage purchase and sale.
She trains to be a waitress.

Fill in

quickly, mention, seconds, fun, deliver, contact, present, pride, tasted, suggest, thank, greet, wine, offer, minutes

1. Have _fun_ !
2. Make eye _contact_ and smile!
3. _Greet_ every guest – not just your own – within 90 _seconds_ !
4. _Offer_ a specific cocktail, _wine_ and/or starter!
5. Offer to take the order. _Mention_ a salad or soup, and _____ the price!
6. _____ the drinks within three minutes!
7. Deliver the food within 12 to 18 _minutes_ !
8. Once the guests have _____ their food, check back immediately!
9. _____ the check in a check presenter! Process all payments _____ !
10. _____ the guests and invite them back!
11. Take _pride_ in everything you do!

Ask your partner what he / she especially likes / dislikes about his / her job.

7th Lesson

 **Crossword puzzle**

Across

1. She serves drinks at the bar.
2. He cleans the dishes.
3. He learns to become a cook or a waiter.
4. He prepares fish dishes.
5. He serves wine.
6. She serves food and beverages.
7. He supervises the service.
8. She prepares cakes.

Down

9. He is responsible for all the restaurant service.
10. She prepares the meals.
11. He supervises the preparation of the food.
12. He carries away dirty dishes from the table.
13. She makes soups and sauces.

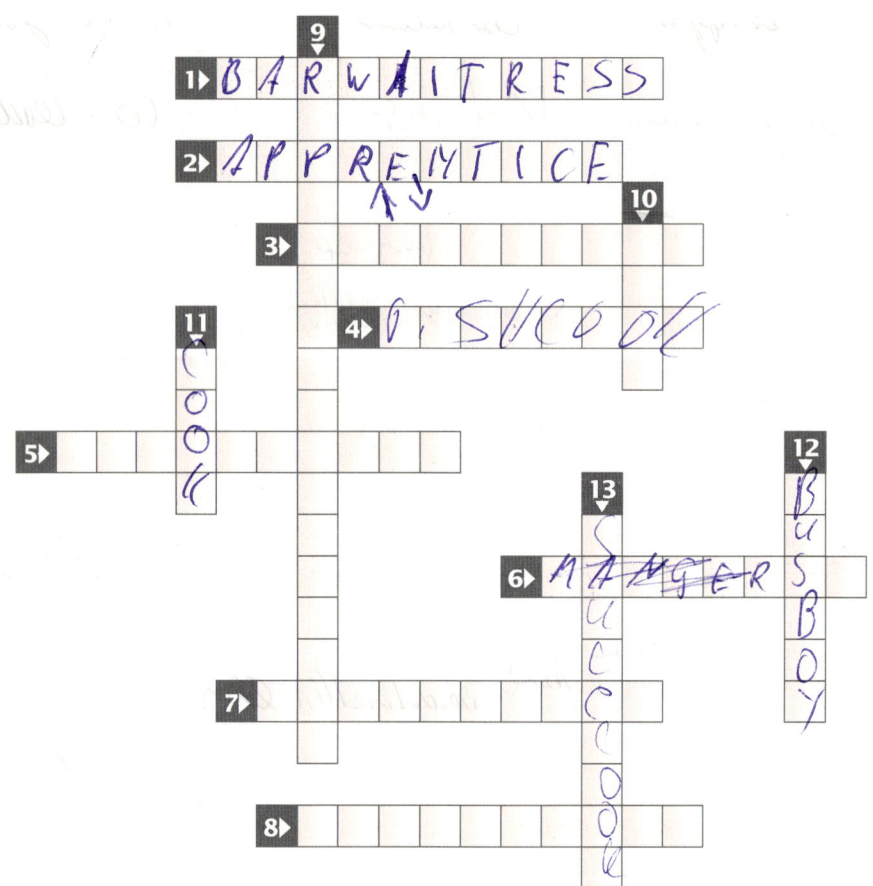

A waitress or waiter must never forget that she / he is a representative of her / his country and that it is she / he from whom foreign guests often gather their first impression of the country they visit. The work of a waitress / waiter is not easy, though interesting. She / he will get acquainted with all kinds of people and their habits. Most waitresses / waiters often change their places of work in order to improve their knowledge of foreign languages and to see other countries.

Waiting staff offend upset guests, if they ...

- ... forget to say "Thank you" or fail to acknowledge a tip.
- ... are bad tempered or indifferent.
- ... talk too much to table guests when these are talking to each other: in other words they are tactless.
- ... ignore guests by talking among themselves.
- ... hurry customers to get their stations clear in order to leave earlier.
- ... offer bad service (usually on the wrong side of the diner) spill soup or other foods.
- ... add up bills wrongly (against the customer) – this is dishonest.
- ... have an unpleasant smell.
- ... have dirty or untidy hair.
- ... have dirty hands and fingernails.
- ... have spotted or greasy clothes.
- ... have unpolished shoes.
- ... wear jewellery (wedding rings and watches allowed).
- ... quarrel or are noisy on duty.

See how many of these faults you notice when you are a customer. By avoiding these faults you will please your customer and satisfy your employer.

7. Lektion

Serving Utensils
How to lay a table
First listen and then tick the items in the picture according to the dialogue.

Dialogue
Listen again and name the items.

1. _____ 2. _____ 3. _____
4. _____ 5. _____ 6. _____
7. _____ 8. _____ 9. _____
10. _____ 11. _____ 12. _____

Fill in
Give orders with:
to lay, to put (2x), to bring, to get (2x), to be, to greet, to take

Be _____ careful with the glasses, please!

_____ the tablecloth on the table!

_____ the milk to table number 15!

_____ the salt from the kitchen!

_____ the basket and _____ it on the table!

_____ the table for dinner, please!

_____ the order for table number seven!

_____ the guests who just entered the restaurant!

Tell your partner how to lay the table.
Use the following words:
- napkin (serviette)
- dinner knife
- dinner fork
- tablespoon
- dessert fork
- side knife
- side plate
- water glass
- wine glass
- butter dish
- bread basket
- ashtray
- salt and pepper
- tablecloth

Giving commands:
Always be polite!
Use **"please"** before or after a command!

Example:

Please bring me a cup!
Put it on the table, please!

8th Lesson

Breakfast

Match words and numbers.

- ○ dessert knife
- ○ teaspoon
- ○ sugar
- ○ jam
- ○ milk pot
- ○ cup
- ○ napkin
- ○ coffee pot
- ○ saucer
- ○ bread / rolls
- ○ breakfast menu
- ○ butter
- ○ dessert plate

? *What kind of breakfast is served at your restaurant / hotel?*

What did you have for breakfast today? Ask your partner what he / she had for breakfast.

Continental breakfast: It consists of coffee, tea or hot chocolate, rolls or crescents, butter, and jam or honey.
Original Viennese breakfast: It consists of rolls or crescents, butter, apricot jam, one soft-boiled egg, and a cup of coffee with milk (Melange).
English or American breakfast: It is more substantial; a continental breakfast with fruit, juice, cereal (dry or cooked), fish/egg/meat dish, pancakes, French toast.
Breakfast buffet: A variety of items: fruits, juices, cereals, eggs, bacon, sausage, pancakes, French toast, and much more.

Unsere Ziele

Nach Bearbeitung dieses Kapitals sollten Sie

- das Frühstücksgedeck kennen;
- die verschiedenen Frühstücksarten kennen;
- Frühstückskarten verstehen und einem Gast erklären können;
- Höflichkeitsformen (Verkaufsgespräch) verwenden können sowie
- die höfliche Frageform beherrschen.

Dialogue

What does the guest order? Listen and tick the order.

- ○ tomato juice
- ○ English breakfast
- ○ orange juice
- ○ cereal
- ○ continental
- ○ juice
- ○ honey
- ○ coffee
- ○ butter
- ○ jam
- ○ fried eggs
- ○ tea
- ○ bread
- ○ ham
- ○ cornflakes
- ○ roll
- ○ hot chocolate
- ○ scrambled eggs

Taking an order:
Would you like ...?
May I take your order?
Do you prefer?

Form questions and answers.

Example:

May I take your order?
Yes, please.

take / order
like / juice
want / cereal
prefer / fried or scrambled eggs
like / honey
prefer / tea or coffee

BREAKFAST

Available 6:30 a.m. to 11:00 a.m. For Room Service Dial 3211.

FRUITS & JUICES
V-8, Tomato, Apple or Cranberry Juice
Fresh Orange or Grapefruit Juice
Half Florida Grapefruit
Fresh Seasonal Melons
Fresh Strawberries with Cream

CEREALS
Cold Cereals
Granola with Cream
Oatmeal or Grits**
With Fresh Fruit

FROM THE BAKERY
Fresh Baked Danish or Croissant
Muffins
White, Rye or Raisin Toast
Toasted Bagel with Cream Cheese

OFF THE GRIDDLE
Buttermilk Pancakes, Belgian Waffles or French Toast
With Powdered Sugar and Maple Syrup
With Bacon, Ham or Sausage
With Seasonal Fruit

EGGS & OMELETTES
All Eggs are served with Hashed Brown Potatoes, Toast, Butter and Preserves.
Single   In Pairs
Three Egg Omelette
Ham, Cheese, Bacon, Mushroom, or Any Combination

BREAKFAST SPECIALITIES
American Continental
Choice of juice, basket of breakfast pastry, coffee, tea or milk.
European Continental
Fresh fruit, cheese wedges, toast and coffee, tea or milk.
Country Breakfast
Choice of juice, two eggs, ham, bacon or sausage, basket of breakfast pastries and coffee, tea or milk.

Eggs Benedict
Two eggs on a toasted English muffin with Canadian bacon and hollandaise sauce.
Corned Beef Hash
A poached egg on corned beef hash with a grilled tomato and toast.
Steak 'n Eggs
Fresh eggs, fried or scrambled, with a grilled steak, hashed brown potatoes and toast.

BEVERAGES
Hot Chocolate   Herbal Teas
Coffee or Brewed Decaffeinated Coffee
Two Cups   Four Cups   Eight Cups

**Low Cholesterol Margarine and Lowfat Milk available upon request.

Write a breakfast menu for English speaking guests.

Discuss different kinds of breakfast foods.

Which of the items on the menu do you serve at your restaurant / hotel?

You are the guest and your partner is the waiter / waitress. Then change roles.

Guest: Choose your breakfast and order it.
Waiter / waitress: Take the order.

Find more breakfast menus on p. 170.

9th Lesson

In the Restaurant

When dining out in Germany or Austria, you'll get the best value for your money at the simpler restaurants. Most of them post menus with the prices outside. If you begin with the Würstelstand (sausage vendor) on the street, the next category would be the Imbissstube, for simple, quick snacks. You'll find a lot of them at city markets, serving soups and daily specials at noon. Another reasonably priced way to get a quick, but delicious meal are butcher's shops, which offer a variety of meals from their "hot buffets". A lot of cafés are also open for lunch, but watch the prices; some can turn out more expensive than restaurants. Gasthäuser are simple restaurants or country inns with no pretensions. Mostly they offer their guests a good choice of specialities from the region.

German and Austrian hotels have some of the best restaurants in these countries and they have hired outstanding chefs to attract the paying customers.

Wine cellars and wine gardens in Austria that offer a type of young wine (Heuriger means from that particular year) are a special category among the Austrian eateries. In Germany the Biergarten has become more and more popular. Originating in Bavaria they have spread all over the country and seem to be everybody's favourite in summertime.

Fast food restaurants are becoming popular all over the world. They serve dishes that can be prepared quickly, such as Hamburgers, hot dogs, sandwiches and fried chicken. So if you travel abroad and you are not familiar with the cooking in a country you can go there and feel at home everywhere in the world.

Ask a partner

What kind of restaurant do you work at?
What kind of restaurant do you prefer?

Which of the dining places are you familiar with? What is offered there?

Unsere Ziele

Nach Bearbeitung dieses Kapitals sollten Sie

- mit einfachen Speisenkarten arbeiten können;
- Bestellungen aufnehmen können;
- europäische Länder und ihre Spezialitäten kennen
- sowie Nationalitäten bezeichnen können.

9. Lektion

Exercise

Read the text (page 40) and tick the sentences that are true.

○ Most Austrian or German restaurants post their menus outside.
○ Hamburgers and hot dogs are usually served in Gasthäuser.
○ Cafes are known for their food and wines.
○ At an Imbissstube you can get a simple, quick snack.
○ Fast food restaurants are popular in Austria and Germany.

Dialogues

🄲 22–26

22 Listen and answer the questions.

What does the waiter bring first? _____

Which aperitif does the gentleman order? _____

What does the lady drink? _____

What is the soup of the day? _____

Which starters do they order? _____
_____

Listen to the orders and note them.

23 _____
24 _____
25 _____
26 _____

Menu

Starters
Smoked Salmon
Melon with Raw Ham
Chicken Salad Waldorf
Shrimp Cocktail
Soup of the Day
Tomato Soup
Fried Mushrooms
Fresh Asparagus

Menu

Main Dishes
Poached Trout
Fried Carp
Roast Pork
Grilled Lamb Chops
Chicken in Paprika Sauce
Braised Beef
Fillet Steak

Side Dishes
Baked Potato
String Beans
Fried Potatoes
Bread Dumplings
Sauerkraut
Spinach
Tomato Salad
Potato Salad

Desserts
Apple Strudel
Chocolate Cake
Fresh Fruit Salad
Ice Cream

❓ What would you order from the menus?

9th Lesson

? Where do you come from?

Make sentences like:

He was born in Bavaria.
He is Bavarian.
He comes from Saxony.
He is Saxon.

? What regional dishes do you know from ...?

- Baden-Würtemberg
- Bavaria
- Brandenburg
- Bremen
- Hamburg
- Hesse
- Lower Saxony
- Mecklenburg-Westpomerania
- North Rhine-Westphalia
- Rhineland-Palatinate
- Saarland
- Saxony
- Saxony-Anhalt
- Schleswig-Holstein
- Thuringia

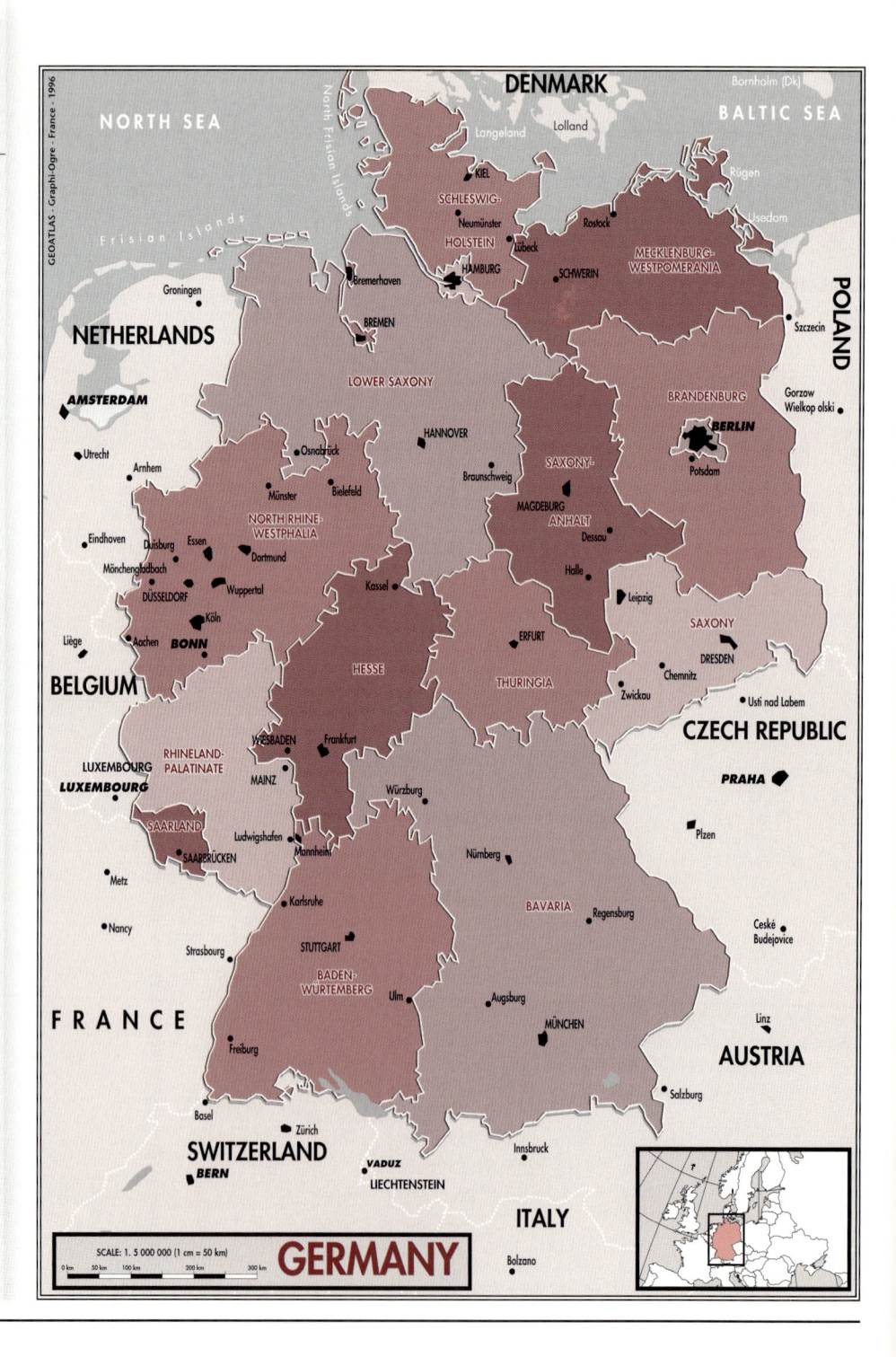

Dialogue

Listen and take the orders. (Use the menu.)

27

9. Lektion

Fill in

Where are these dishes and beverages from?

Spaghetti _____   Tafelspitz _____

Mussaka _____   Beaujolais _____

Cevapcici _____   Sherry _____

Goulash _____   Portwine _____

Fondue _____   Vodka _____

Eisbein _____   Gin _____

Using the map explain to a partner where these dishes and beverages come from.

Example:

Fondue is a Swiss dish. It is from Switzerland.

? What other European dishes and beverages are you familiar with?

? Which of the countries on the map have you visited and what did you eat there?

Exercise

Where do these guests come from? Fill in the names of the countries.

A		PL	
D		H	
F		GB	
I		CZ	

Form sentences like:

Mrs. Huber comes from Austria. She is Austrian.

? Can you think of other examples?

10th Lesson

Hotel Staff

? Remember their duties?

Kitchen staff
F & B manager
head chef
second chef
chef de partie
sauce cook
roast cook
fish cook
soup cook
pastry cook
baker
larder
butcher
staff cook
relief cook, duty cook
assistant cook
dishwasher
apprentice

Service staff
restaurant manager
bartender
barwaiter / barwaitress
head waiter / waitress
waiter / waitress
winebutler
section captain
assistant section captain
apprentice waiter / waitress
trainee
busboy
cleaning staff

All members of staff, who work at the **front desk** of a hotel, have direct contact with the guests. The front desk is located in the lobby near the main entrance of the hotel. In large hotels, the reception is divided into sections. At the reception the guests ask for and book hotel rooms. At the registration desk, the **room clerk** welcomes and registers the arriving guests. When guests check in, they fill in a registration form. It is used to record the full name, nationality, home address and the signature of the guest. In many countries, the guest's passport or identification card must also be checked. The **bellman** shows the guests to their room. Bellmen also answer questions about the hotel's services and run errands for the guests. The **porter** carries the luggage up to the rooms.

Another section is where the guests pick up and return their keys, mail and messages. The **information clerk** provides information about entertainment, events and sights of interest. He may also arrange for transportation. The **doorman** is stationed at the hotel entrance and helps guests in and out of cars and taxis. Often he gives directions for places guests wish to visit. The **cashier** settles accounts, exchanges foreign money and cashes traveller's and bank cheques. The **telephone operator** receives messages and takes care of wake-up calls. She also passes on reservation requests to the receptionist.

Unsere Ziele

Nach Bearbeitung dieses Kapitels sollten Sie

- die einzelnen Berufe des Hotelpersonals nennen können;
- die Aufgaben des Personals beschreiben können;
- Gästenamen buchstabieren können.

10. Lektion

Hotel Staff and their Duties

Hotel Staff	Duties
general manager/ess *(hotel manager)* *assistant*	runs the hotel
resident manager	is responsible for the day to day running

head housekeeper
    chambermaid
        cleaner
	is responsible for the tidiness in the hotel

front office manager	is responsible for the reception, reservation, cashier and lounge
receptionist	supports the front office manager, welcomes and registers the guests

Exercise

Read the text (page 44) again and complete the chart.

Hotel Staff	Duties
room clerk	
bellman	
day and evening porter	
information clerk	
doorman	
cashier	
telephone operator	

The Alphabet

a	b	c	d	e	f	g	h	i
[eɪ]	[biː]	[siː]	[diː]	[iː]	[ef]	[dʒiː]	[eɪtʃ]	[aɪ]

j	k	l	m	n	o	p	q	r
[dʒeɪ]	[keɪ]	[el]	[em]	[en]	[əʊ]	[piː]	[kjuː]	[ɑː]

s	t	u	v	w	x	y	z
[es]	[tiː]	[juː]	[viː]	['dʌbljuː]	[eks]	[waɪ]	[zed]

Listen and find out the names 🔊 28

a) *Estrich*
b) _____
c) _____

Attention

staff
 Personal

to stuff
 fest füllen

stuff
 Ding, Zeug

To learn

is responsible for
is in charge of
looks after
comes / works under
supervises

👫 *Think of any job in the hotel and pretend you do the job. Do not tell your partner which one it is.*

Your partner asks questions which you only answer with yes or no. He / She must try to guess your job within ten questions.

Spelling on the phone →
Appendix p. 206

👫 *Ask your partner for his / her name. Ask him / her to spell it.*

11th Lesson

A Day at a Hotel

To learn

I've got a reservation for a

    single room

    double room

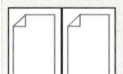

    twin-bedded room

with shower / bath
room number
type of room
length of stay
name of guest
What's the price for ...?
We are looking for ...
What would you like?
What can I do for you?
Fill in this registration form, please.

Staying at a hotel can be a very exciting experience, especially if you have never been to that country before. There is much to see and do in large hotels and you can spend a whole day enjoying yourself without even leaving the hotel. You can relax by the swimming pool, have a drink at the bar, buy souvenirs in the shops or just have a cup of coffee in the lounge and watch other people strolling by. A nice way to spend a rainy day.

Unsere Ziele

Nach Bearbeitung dieses Kapitels sollten Sie

- *Zimmerarten unterscheiden und erklären können;*
- *Reservierungen aufnehmen*
- *sowie geeignete Zimmer für diverse Anlässe aussuchen können.*

Room Types

Junior Suite	one large room separated into a sleeping and a sitting area
Duplex	two-storey suite
Exhibition Room	room used for showing merchandise
Adjoining Rooms / **Connecting Rooms**	rooms side by side with connecting doors
Studio Room	room with a convertible sofa
Parlour	sitting room, also called salon
Function Room	used for entertaining or conference

Exercise

Read the enquiries of these guests who need rooms in a hotel. Which rooms would you offer them?

1
Lady: I'd like to book a room for my husband and myself as well as for our two children aged twelve and sixteen. Have you anything suitable?

2
Gentleman: Good morning. I'm from the Nashville Bank and we're looking for a place to meet with our European partners, approximately 30 persons. Have you got any suitable rooms?

3
Gentleman: I'm the manager of the famous saxophone player Kenny G. I'm organizing accommodation for him. He only wants the best and privacy is an absolute must.

4
Lady: I'm the secretary of Lord and Lady Southern. They want to hold an engagement reception for their daughter at the end of July. Just one or two hundred guests are expected. Most of them would also want to stay over night.

5
Lady: I'm Mr. Longsome's assistant. Our company is looking for a place to show some of our products and meet customers. We are expecting about 300 persons, do you have any suitable rooms?

6
Gentleman: I'll be in town for business the day after tomorrow and would need a quiet room with a large desk and an internet connection because I have to work at night. My wife will also meet me for a few days.

Make short dialogues.

- a double room with bath / 1 week / Mr. and Mrs. Brown / 205
- a single room with bath / 2 nights / Miss. Irene Lindström / 107
- a twin-bedded room with shower / 3 nights / Mr. and Mrs. Jozef Blida / 115
- a single room without bath and shower / 1 night / Mrs. Vera Dubcek / 209

What rooms do you offer at your hotel?

11th Lesson

Where would you like to spend your holiday?

Fill in the request.

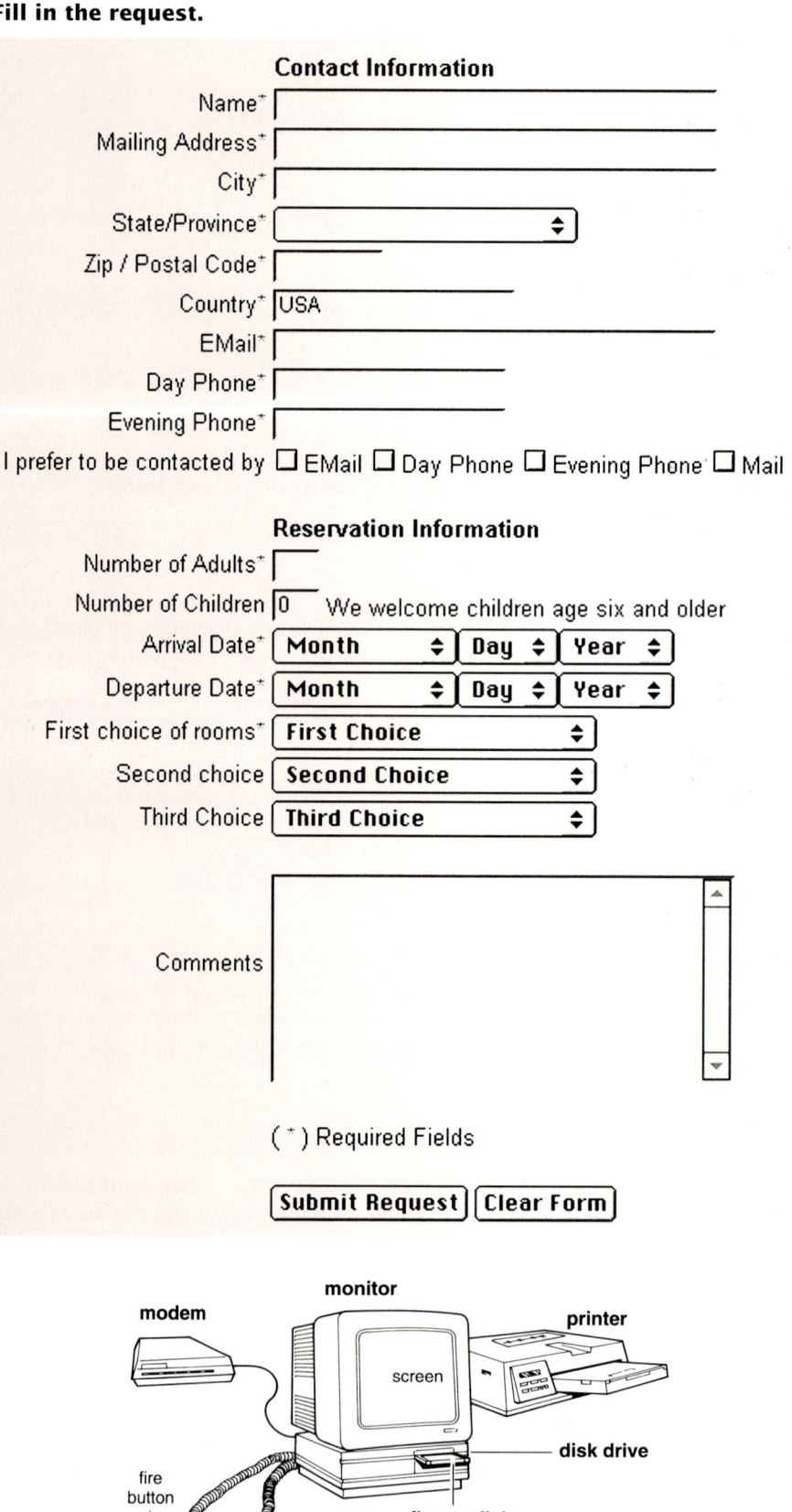

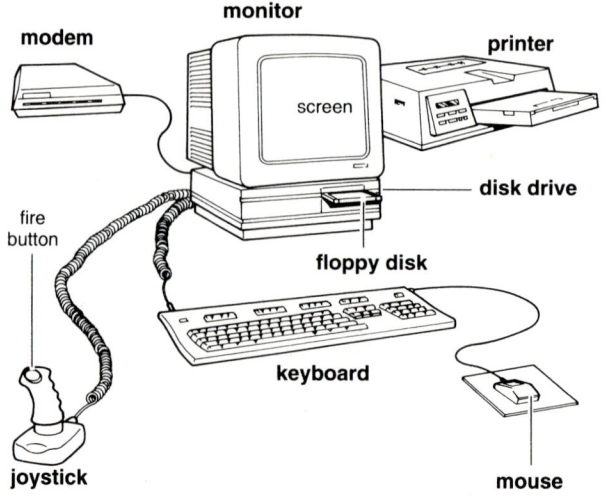

Nowadays online bookings are getting very popular. People choose a suitable hotel in the internet and send their requests by e-mail or fill in a reservation request like shown beside.

Contact Information

- Name*
- Mailing Address*
- City*
- State/Province*
- Zip / Postal Code*
- Country* USA
- EMail*
- Day Phone*
- Evening Phone*

I prefer to be contacted by ☐ EMail ☐ Day Phone ☐ Evening Phone ☐ Mail

Reservation Information

- Number of Adults*
- Number of Children 0   We welcome children age six and older
- Arrival Date*   Month | Day | Year
- Departure Date* Month | Day | Year
- First choice of rooms*   First Choice
- Second choice   Second Choice
- Third Choice   Third Choice

Comments

(*) Required Fields

[Submit Request] [Clear Form]

Here are some of the special words that are used in computing.

The information that you put into a computer is called **data**. If you **enter** or **key** in data, the computer will **process** it. The list of instructions that the computer follows in order to process data is called a **program**.

If you want to store a program or data onto a disk or tape, you **save** it. You can organize the data by saving it into different **files** or **folders**. When you put the disk or tape back into the computer, you **load** it.

A **byte** is a unit of computer memory. It is usually made up of a series of eight smaller units called **bits**.

Hardware means the computer and any equipment that is connected to it. The programs that are used in a computer are called **software**.

Labels: modem, monitor, screen, printer, disk drive, floppy disk, fire button, keyboard, joystick, mouse

11. Lektion

Hotel Types

Match the hotels with the explanations.

Resort Hotel	situated by the sea or in the mountains, used by tourists who stay for a longer period of time
Summer Hotel	open only during the summer months, often used as student dormitory during wintertime
Commercial Hotel	situated in town centre, used by businessmen who stay for a few nights
Hostel	modest, moderately priced, normally with sleeping and breakfast facilities only
Airport Hotel	near an airport, used by airport staff or passengers who stay for one night
Motor hotel	hotel with parking facilities and other services for motorists, first class restaurant
	hotel offering medical treatment, physical exercise and other recreational facilities
	parking and other services for motorists, on a highway, simple restaurant or cooking facilities
Holiday Village	small individual cottages or bungalows, cooking facilities
Congress Hotel	meeting and exhibition facilities, audio-visual equipment and banquet rooms for large and small groups

- Airport Hotel
- Commercial Hotel
- Congress Hotel
- Health Spa
- Holiday Village
- Hostel — Jugendherberge
- Motel
- Motor Hotel
- Resort Hotel — Ferien Hotel
- Summer Hotel

facilities
Einrichtungen, Annehmlichkeiten

To learn

situated in
... minutes from
near the sea
close to
located in
with views of
surrounded by
overlooking
famous for

Exercise

What type of hotel would you recommend to the following persons?

Mr. Brown:	I'd like to do business in your town and try to sell this new coffee-machine.	Commercial Hotel
Mrs. Jones:	I'm flying from London to Vienna in the evening and would like to continue to Athens early in the morning.	Airport Hotel
Peter:	I've been hitchhiking from Munich to Salzburg. Are there any cheap places where I could stay overnight?	Hostel
Miss Roberts:	I'm arranging the Annual Conference of Austrian Barkeepers.	Congress Hotel
Family Smith:	We are going by car to Klagenfurt and would like to stop somewhere for one night.	Motel
Mrs. Baker:	I have bad rheumatism and would like to get some treatment in pleasant surroundings.	
Mr. and Mrs. Friers:	We'd like to spend a week's holiday at the seaside.	Summer Hotel

11th Lesson

full board
Vollpension

half board / part board
Halbpension

bed and breakfast (BB)
Zimmer mit Frühstück

Food Plans

AP	Full American Plan	3 full meals + pension = **full board**
MAP	Modified American Plan	breakfast, dinner + room
	Demi Pension	breakfast, lunch or dinner + room = **half board**
EP	European Plan	room, no meals
CP	Continental Plan	breakfast + room = **bed and breakfast**

Telling the Way

Dialogues 29

Listen and circle the parts of the hotel they are talking about. Write them below.

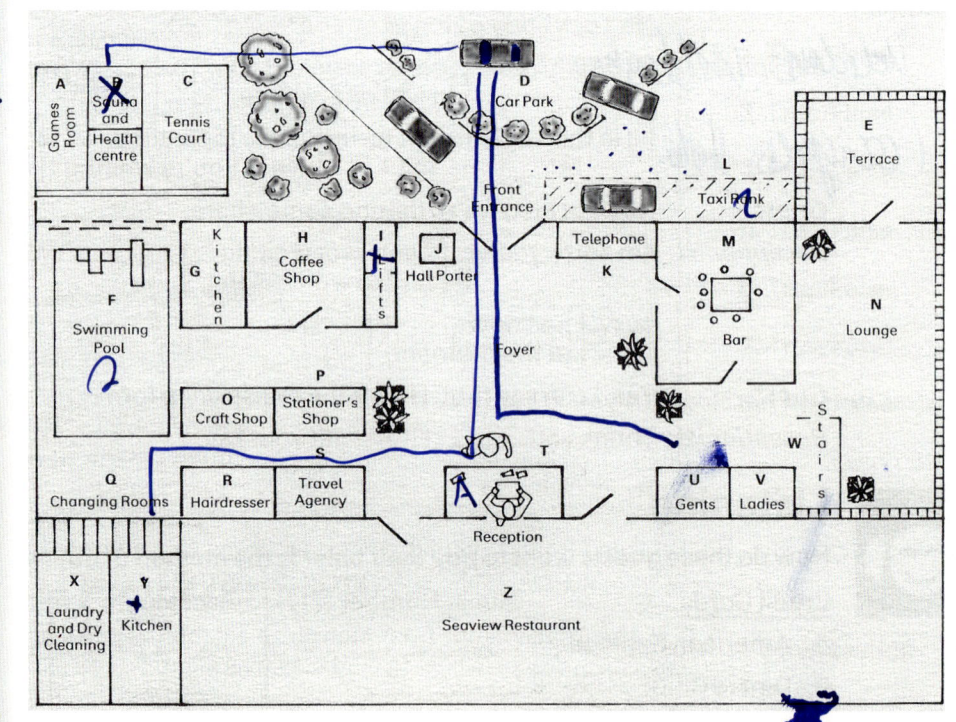

To learn
- on the left / right
- opposite
- in front of
- walk along
- go past / across
- on the left-hand side
- on the first floor
- beside
- at the end of

Give directions from the reception to these places.
- swimming pool
- telephone
- toilets
- craft shop
- tennis court
- bar
- lifts
- hairdresser
- health centre
- stairs

a) _____

b) _____

c) _____

d) _____

11. Lektion

💡 Find seven parts of the hotel you also find on the plan.

C	T	E	R	R	A	C	E
O	F	G	E	N	T	S	I
F	I	S	T	W	D	H	R
F	L	A	R	G	S	O	A
E	L	U	O	N	C	P	B
E	B	N	P	T	F	I	E
F	C	A	R	P	A	R	K
L	O	U	N	G	E	T	S

Exercise

Match the places on the left with the words on the right.

1. where guests make reservations, check in and out
2. where guests eat
3. where guests drink alcoholic or soft drinks
4. where food is cooked
5. where bills are added up and money matters dealt with
6. department that makes sure the hotel and rooms are clean, and that everything in the rooms is in order

[ ] housekeeping
[ ] kitchen
[*1*] front office or reception
[ ] restaurant
[ ] bar
[ ] cashier's office

Read

It is very important for the hotel staff to be polite and helpul to their guests. This is not difficult when the guests are also polite and easy to deal with. But what happens when a guest is rude and abusive? Only well trained staff is able to handle such situations with care. You must listen to the guest and sympathize with his or her problems. If the guest feels that the problem is handled to his or her satisfaction in a friendly way, he will always come back and recommend the hotel to others. A complaint handled properly can then become a compliment. Besides, if you can handle difficult guests it will give you a lot of satisfaction.

12th Lesson

Shopping
Working Clothes

Shopping in Great Britain

Overseas visitors account for 6 per cent of total consumer spending in Britain and for 17 per cent of all spending in London's Oxford Street. The specialist shops and department stores in London's Knightsbridge, Regent Street, Bond Street and Oxford Street attract many overseas visitors. Leading mixed retail businesses like Marks & Spencer and prestige brands such as Wedgwood china and Burberry clothing and accessories are also popular.

Clean whites (protective clothing) and clean underclothes should be worn at all times. Dirty clothes enable germs to multiply and if dirty clothing comes into contact with food the food may be contaminated.

Cloths used for holding hot dishes should be kept clean, as the cloths are used in many ways, such as wiping knives, dishes and pans. All these uses could carry over germs on to food. Always wear suitable clothing and stout footwear.

Suitable clothing must be:
1. protective
2. washable
3. of a suitable colour
4. light in weight and comfortable
5. strong
6. absorbent

Footwear should be stout and kept in good repair so as to protect and support the feet.

Unsere Ziele

Nach Bearbeitung dieses Kapitels sollten Sie

- die einzelnen Kleidungsstücke benennen können;
- nach bestimmter Berufskleidung fragen
- sowie die im Gastgewerbe üblichen Bekleidungen erklären können.

12. Lektion

Practise
Which uniform pieces can you find in the pictures?

To learn

waistcoat
long apron
short apron
chef's hat
chef's kerchief
jacket buttons
catering clogs
traditional dress
tie, bow tie
black skirt
chef's trousers
white shirt
black shoes

Buy three new uniform pieces with your friend. Make a dialogue.

To learn

I'm looking for ...
Can you help me?
Do you have ...?
What about ...

(too) small
(too) large
(too) cheap
(too) expensive
(too) short
(too) long
a smaller / larger / cheaper one
a shorter / longer one

small
medium
large
extra – large
extra extra – large

International sizes: page 207

Make short dialogues.

Example:

I like this black skirt. It's too small. I'll look for a larger one.

- *white blouse / too long*
- *black socks / too small*
- *chef's jacket / too short*

Dialogues 30

What does the costumer want to buy? **Where are these articles?**

a)		
b)		
c)		
d)		

Answer

When was the last time you went shopping, with a friend or alone, in your favourite shopping center? Tell your partner which shopping center it was, describe him or her the shops, what you can get there, what you were looking for and what you finally bought.
Would you recommend this shopping center to a guest?
If not, where could guests go shopping in your town?

13th Lesson

Family

This is Sarah's family tree. All the people in the picture are Sarah's relatives.

grandmother grandfather

aunt uncle mother father mother-in-law father-in-law

cousin cousin sister-in-law brother SARAH husband sister-in-law brother-in-law

niece nephew daughter-in-law son daughter son-in-law

*granddaughter grandson
(grand children)*

Other relationships

If you have a girlfriend or boyfriend, you say you are **going out with** him / her. If you want to be married to somebody, you **get engaged** first and then **get married.** If you decide that you want to end your marriage, you **get divorced.** Some people decide **to live** with somebody without getting married.

If your parents get divorced, your mother may decide to marry again, and her new husband will be your **stepfather.** If your stepfather or **stepmother** already has children from an earlier marriage, those children become your **stepsisters** and **stepbrothers,** and your mother's and father's **stepchildren.** If your mother and stepfather (or father and stepmother) then have children together, they are your **half-brothers** and **half-sisters.**

🎯 Unsere Ziele

Nach Bearbeitung dieses Kapitels sollten Sie

- die Bezeichnung der verschiedenen Familienmitglieder nennen können;
- Sätze über Vorlieben und Abneigungen formulieren können;
- einfache Berufsbezeichnungen und Hobbys nennen können.

13. Lektion

Dialogue
Listen and fill in.

1 is Mr. Johnson's _____

2 is his _____

3 is his _____

4 is his _____

5 is his _____

6 is his _____

Fill in
Fill in the relationship.

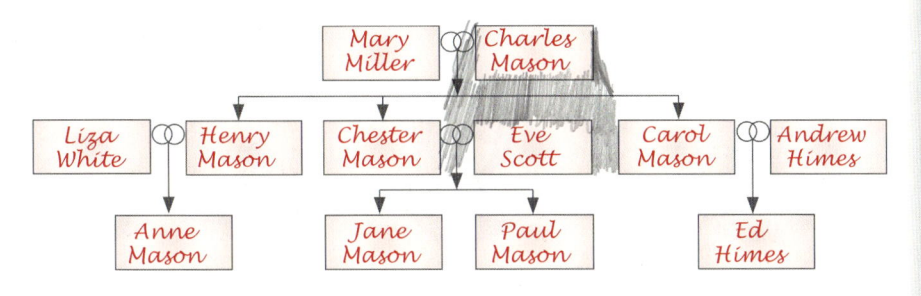

Carol Mason is Andrew Himes' _____ and Ed Himes' _____.

Ann Mason is Charles Mason's _____.

Mary Miller is Jane Mason's _____ and Liza White's _____.

Charles Mason is Andrew Himes' _____ and Ed Himes' _____. Jane Mason is Andrew Himes' _____ and her brother is his _____.

Henry Mason is Chester Mason's _____ and Eve Scott's _____.

Jane Mason is Paul Mason's _____ and Ann Mason's _____.

Liza White is Jane Mason's _____ and Chester Mason's _____.

Carol Mason is Mary Miller's _____ and Eve Scott's _____.

Chester Mason is Paul Mason's _____ and Ed Himes' _____.

Members of families

grandmother
grandfather
mother
father
daughter
son
aunt
uncle
cousin
sister
brother
sister-in-law
brother-in-law
niece
nephew
mother-in-law
father-in-law
daughter-in-law
son-in-law
granddaughter
grandson
grandchild / grandchildren
wife
husband
stepdaughter
stepson

55

13th Lesson

Jobs

bank clerk
barkeeper
chef
doctor
electrican
hairdresser
houseman
housewife
journalist
nurse
policeman / policewoman
receptionist
shop assistant
teacher
typist
waiter / waitress
cook
travel agent
hotel assistant
caterer

Exercise

Work in pairs: These family trees seem to be similar. Try to find out the differences by asking your partner questions like:

Is Peter's wife called Alice? or: *Is Pamela a teacher?*

Student A

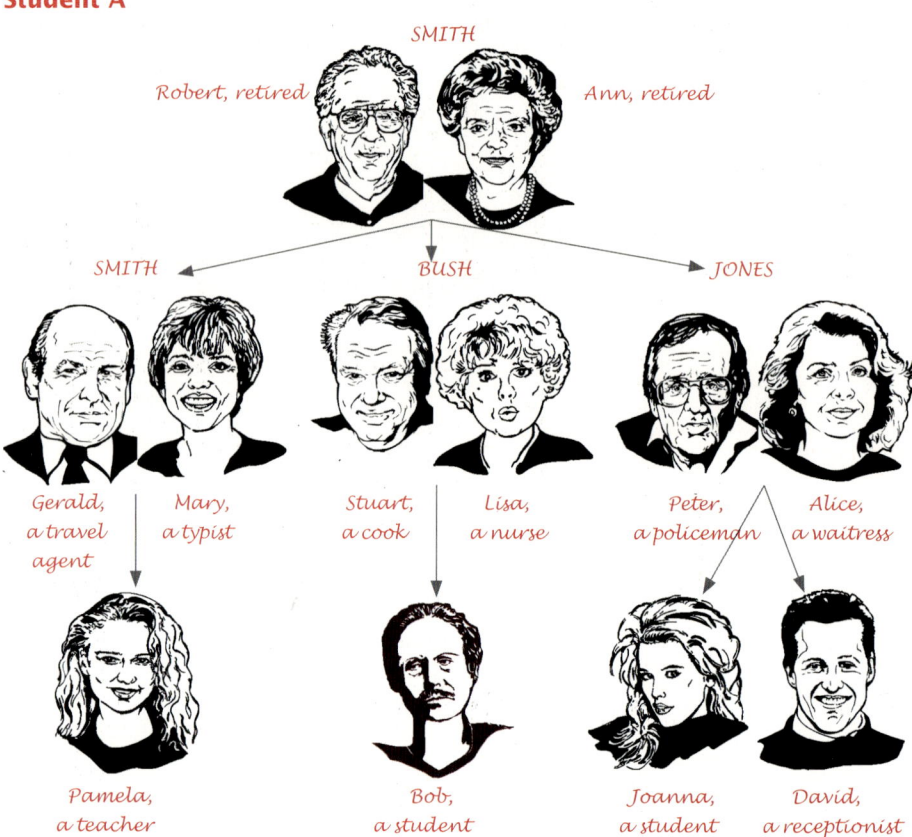

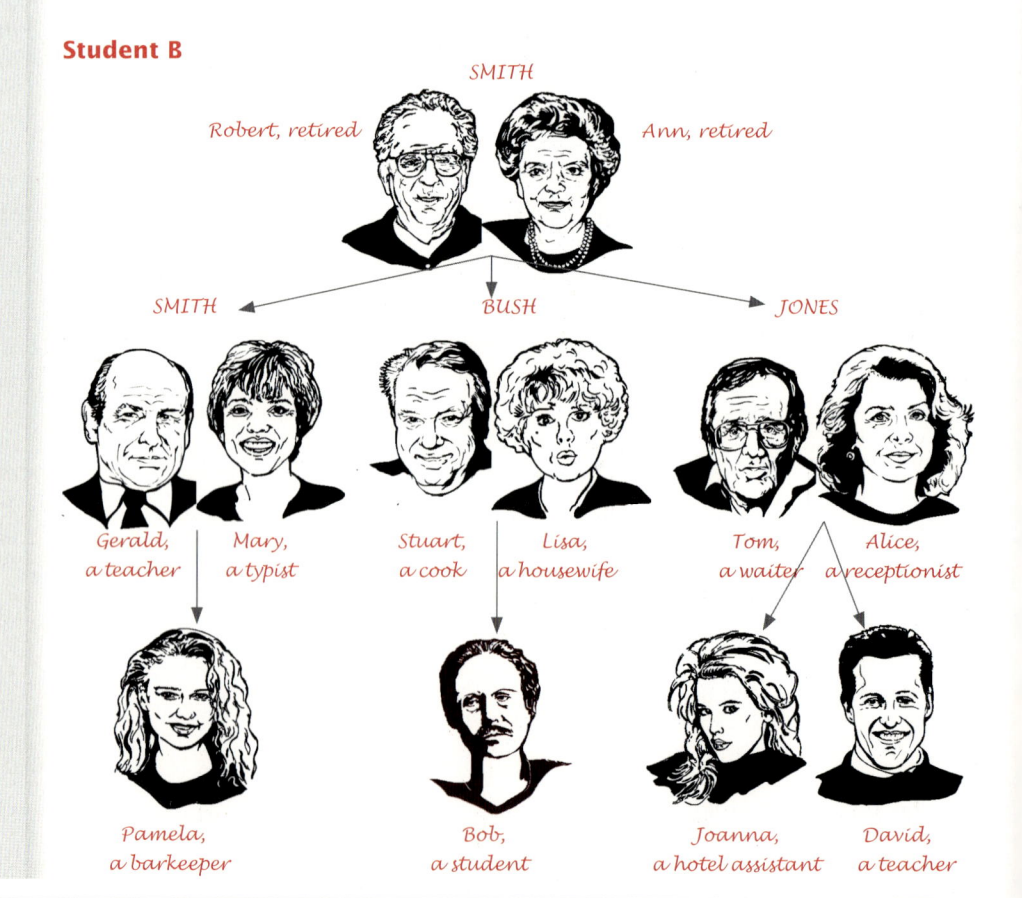

SMITH
Robert, retired — Ann, retired

SMITH — BUSH — JONES

Gerald, a travel agent — Mary, a typist | Stuart, a cook — Lisa, a nurse | Peter, a policeman — Alice, a waitress

Pamela, a teacher | Bob, a student | Joanna, a student | David, a receptionist

Student B

SMITH
Robert, retired — Ann, retired

SMITH — BUSH — JONES

Gerald, a teacher — Mary, a typist | Stuart, a cook — Lisa, a housewife | Tom, a waiter — Alice, a receptionist

Pamela, a barkeeper | Bob, a student | Joanna, a hotel assistant | David, a teacher

13. Lektion

Mark your answer with a cross

I love	I like	I quite like	I don't care about	I don't really like	I don't like	I hate	
							skating.
							listening to Hip-Hop music.
							writing letters.
							skiing.
							watching TV.
							going to the movies.
							cooking.
							horse-riding.
							going to the theatre.
							singing.
							watching football.
							listening to the radio.
							hiking.
							classical music.
							rock music.
							my job.
							travelling by boat.
							going to discos.
							visiting relatives.
							sailing.
							travelling by plane.

How can you express likes and dislikes?

I love / he / she loves
I like / he / she likes
I quite like
I do not / I don't
I don't care about
I don't like
I don't really like
He / she does not / doesn't like
I hate
I like more / he /she likes more
I like best /he / she likes best

Find other expressions; use your dictionary.

When you have finished, talk about your likes and dislikes with your classmates.

Example:
A: *I quite like writing letters.*
B: *Yes, so do I.*
or: *Oh, I hate it.*

Take turns at starting.

Exercise

**Test your knowledge of sport terms.
Every sport has its own vocabulary. Each set of words is associated with a certain sport.**

1. racket, court, love, match, serve _____

2. free kick, header, corner, penalty, field _____

3. diamond, base, steal, home run, short stop _____

4. half-pipe, grip tape, wheels, deck, kickflip _____

5. quarterback, touchdown, field goal, blitz, first down _____

6. free throw, court, foul, dunk, jump-ball, dribble _____

7. scrum, fly-half, try, drop-kick, tackle _____

The sports are:

- skateboarding
- basketball
- tennis
- baseball
- football
- American football
- rugby

14th Lesson

Cafés

Did you know that an Original Sacher-Torte produced at Hotel Sacher in 1998 with a diametre of 2.5 meters is even included in the "Guiness Book of Records 2000"?

Hotel Sacher Wien
The History of the Sacher

The Hotel Sacher has become world famous as an Austrian institution and is probably comparable with no other. The Sacher offers great tradition and atmosphere, its long history can be felt in each room. A splendid collection of old oil paintings and valuable etchings serves to make the guest feel particularly at home.

When Eduard Sacher, son of the inventor of the Original Sachertorte, opened his hotel in 1876, he had no idea of the fame it would eventually acquire. His wife Anna, with her legendary cigar, formed the style of the house with her strong and resolute personality and her heart-warming charm. At this time, the Sacher became the meeting place of the Austrian nobility, performers and business magnates.

It has always been the concern of the management to carry on the old tradition, to keep the history, the ambiente of the house, in evidence, and still offers its guests all that comfort and luxury that is today expected from a hotel of this class.

The sale and dispatch of the Original Sachertorte throughout the world has certainly helped to make the Sacher as famous in Austria as the St. Stephan's Cathedral, the Viennese Boys Choir and the Spanish Riding School.

The Sacher is situated directly behind the Viennese State Opera, in the heart of the century-old cultural city; only a few minutes walk from the hotel are the elegant Ringstraße, the much-praised museums, the Hofburg and the unique Spanish Riding School.

The tradition of the Austrian "Kaffeehaus" finds here its true reality. Water-colour portraits of famous conductors who are so connected with the musical town of Salzburg, the Original Sachertorte from Vienna, the variety of Austrian "Kaffeehaus" specialities, home-made cakes and international newspapers provide for the typical atmosphere only found in Austria.

In the Sacher Confiseries the Original Sachertorte is exclusively sold and dispatched all over the world.

The "Kaffeehaus" is typical for Vienna. Furnished in the period of the 19th century, with portraits of the former Royal Family. Here began the triumphant crusade of the Original Sachertorte, and until this very day the Viennese and guests from all over the world enjoy this unique speciality.

Read the text and try to find out the words you don't know with your dictionary.

Unser Ziel

Nach Bearbeitung dieses Kapitels sollten Sie

- *dem Gast typische Kaffeehausspezialitäten erklären können.*

14. Lektion

Tick the right answers

	true	false
Eduard Sacher invented the Sachertorte.		
The hotel was opened in the 19th century.		
Anna Sacher smoked cigars.		
The Sachertorte is sold all over the world.		
The hotel is directly behind St. Stephan's Cathedral.		
The café offers home-made cakes, specialities of Demel's and international newspapers.		
The Sachertorte is sold only in Vienna.		
The Hotel Sacher is one of the newest hotels in Vienna.		

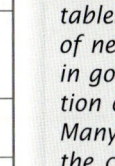

The typical Viennese café, with polished brass or marble-topped tables, bentwood chairs, supplies of newspapers, and tables outside in good weather, is a fixed institution of which there are hundreds. Many people take breakfast in the cafés, students do homework, businesspeople conclude deals, billiards is played, and bridge clubs meet. Everybody has his favourite; some people even have a regular table that is reserved for them every day. All cafés serve pastries and light snacks in addition to beverages; many offer a set lunch at noon.

Listen and connect 32

Kaisermelange   Viennese yeast cake

Pharisäer   coffee with a small amount of cream

Kapuziner   half coffee and half milk with egg liqueur

Guglhupf   coffee with rum and whipped cream

Connect

1. *Brauner* — 5 small or large strong coffee
2. *Einspänner* — half coffee and half milk
3. *Kaffee Maria Theresia* — coffee with little milk
4. *Melange* — hot black coffee in a glass with a knob of whipped cream
5. *Mokka / Espresso* — cold coffee with vanilla ice cream and whipped cream
6. *Wiener Eiskaffee* — coffee with orange liqueur and whipped cream
7. *Cappuccino* — hot coffee, brown sugar and Irish Whisky, topped with cream
8. *Rüdesheimer Kaffee* — hot strong coffee with foamed milk, sprinkled with cocoa powder
9. *Irish Coffee* — hot coffee, poured over sugar lumps flambéed with "Asbach"

To learn

amount
sprinkled with …
topped with …
poured over …
flambéed with …
sugar lumps

Work with a partner:

An English guest wants a cup of coffee. Offer him / her some specialities and explain them to him / her.

15th Lesson

Front Office

The hotel receptionists are very often the first and last members of the staff guests will see. They have to reflect the hotel's atmosphere and convey a sincere welcome to all customers.
In larger hotels, the front office job is often split into four – that of receptionist, cashier, reservation clerk and concierge. In smaller hotels, however, the receptionist could be performing the duties of all four.

Personal qualities needed:
- Pleasant appearance and warm personality to create a good first impression;
- tactful and patient;
- able to communicate clearly and willing to help others;
- eye for accuracy for checking reservations, processing room requests and so on;
- flexible and diplomatic when dealing with demanding and unreasonable guests;
- aptitude for numbers and good at handling cash and accounting machines.

POLITENESS
How would you translate the following?

Sie wünschen?

a) You wish?
b) What do you want?
c) What can I do for you?

Spotlight

The correct answer is c):

"What can I do for you?"

Alternative (a) is not possible in English, and (b) is impolite. "What is your pleasure?" used to be common, but it is now considered old-fashioned.

talent

Unsere Ziele

Nach Bearbeitung dieses Kapitels sollten Sie

- *ein Anmeldeformular ausfüllen können;*
- *einen Check-in bzw. eine Reservierung durchführen können;*
- *anhand eines Stadtplans verschiedene Wege erklären können.*

15. Lektion

Dialogues

Listen and fill in the missing words.

🎵 33–34

33

Receptionist:	_____ , sir. Welcome to Hotel Hope. _____ ?
Guest:	Yes, I phoned last week to book a double room.
Receptionist:	_____ ?
Guest:	Barry Benson. B-E-N-S-O-N.
Receptionist:	Yes, Mr. Benson, _____ for three nights.
Guest:	That's right.
Receptionist:	_____ this registration form, please?
Guest:	Is it necessary to fill in the passport information?
Receptionist:	Yes, if you would. _____ key. It's room number 22 ____ the second floor. I'll ask _____ to help you with your luggage.
Guest:	By the way, what time's breakfast?
Receptionist:	Breakfast _____ 7.30 to 10.30 a.m.

34

Receptionist:	Good evening, madam. _____ ?
Guest:	I have a booking for tonight. The name is Jones.
Receptionist:	One moment, madam. Yes, that was a _____ _____ .
Guest:	That's right.
Receptionist:	Would you like _____ , please? Just put your _____ _____ here on the first line, then your _____ below. Here, put your _____ , and next to that, put your _____ . Write your _____ _____ on the next line, and please sign here. Could I see your _____ , please?
Guest:	Here you are.
Receptionist:	Thank you. You have room number 12 _____ floor. The porter will _____ to your room. _____ a nice evening, madam.

To learn

Can / May I help you?

Do you have a reservation?

Who's the reservation for?

I'd like to book a …

I'd like to make a reservation.

What's your name, please?

Can you give me your name, please?

How long will you be staying?

When for? For how long?

Would you fill in this registration form?

Would you like to register?

Here's your key.

Here's your key card.

Please sign here.

Breakfast is served from … to …

May I see your passport, please?

Have you got any identification?

Do you want …?

Would you like …?

I can confirm your booking.

You have room number ….

Your room number is ….

How will you be paying?

How will you be settling your account?

Can you give a deposit, please?

The porter will show you to your room.

The porter will carry your luggage.

Have a pleasant stay in …, sir / madam.

first name / surname

date of birth

nationality

15th Lesson

Exercise 35–42

What does the receptionist ask the guest?

35

May I _____?

How _____?

Would you _____?

Can you _____?

36

Would you _____?

May I _____?

37

What kind _____?

38

Who's _____?

Would _____?

39

Do _____?

40

Would you _____ a room in another hotel?

What does the guest ask?

41

Do you _____?

How _____?

42

Could I _____?

Vacation Time in Great Britain

The word "vacation" is used in American English for what British people call "holiday" (Urlaub). However, "vacation" is not exclusively American. The word is also used in British English for the fixed holiday period between terms in universities (Semesterferien) and law courts (Gerichtsferien). The word is sometimes shortened to "vac". The "long vacation" or "long vac" is the three-month summer holiday taken at British universities, as in: "Jane plans to spend the long vac with her parents in Devon."

15. Lektion

Would you fill in this registration form, please?

GUEST REGISTRATION FORM

*SURNAME .... ROOM No. ....
(in capitals) Mr./Mrs./Miss.

*FORENAME(S)..

HOME ADDRESS ....

....

*NATIONALITY ....

CAR REGISTRATION No. ....

*DATE OF ARRIVAL ....

DATE OF DEPARTURE ....

METHOD OF PAYMENT ....

*This information is required for every guest aged 16 years and over.

The following additional information must be given by a guest who is neither a British nor Commonwealth citizen.

NUMBER OF PASSPORT, CERTIFICATE OF REGISTRATION, or other document establishing identity and nationality

....

ISSUED AT ....

NEXT DESTINATION, and full address there, if known

....

SIGNATURE ....

Fill in

Complete the sentences below spoken by a hotel staff trainer. Use the words listed below.

reservation form, reservation, date, corrected, reservation diary, room, arrive, hand, advance (2x), reservation chart, types, computer terminals

As soon as a guest makes a _____ we write the details on

the _____ .

Next, we can enter all reservations into a _____ under the

_____ when guests are due to _____ .

It's useful to know the _____ occupation of each _____ especially in hotels with many different _____ of rooms.

We record the _____ reservations in a _____ .

Even though most hotels have _____ reservations

may still be written by _____ .

Be sure to use a pencil, so mistakes can be _____ easily.

Make up your own dialogues. Work in pairs.

Ask the guest to fill in the registration form. Give the guest the key. Tell the guest the room number. The porter will help with the luggage.

single room / 3 nights
shower?
telephone?
PC?
price?

double room / 4 nights
bath?
television set?
price?

apartment / 2 weeks
balcony?
car park?
price?

15th Lesson

Telling the Way

Dialogues 43–45

Take a look at the map of Salzburg. We are at the Hotel Stein (x) and the receptionist is giving directions to the places the guests want to visit. Listen and complete the conversations.

To learn

- about ten minutes walk — *10 Minuten zu Fuß (ungefähr)*
- at the back of — *Auf der Rückseite*
- away from — *weg von*
- behind — *dahinter*
- between — *dazwischen*
- by car / bus / train / boat — *mit dem*
- carry on — *etwas fortfahren*
- cross / across — *überqueren*
- from
- get on / off — *einsteigen aus Steig*
- go down
- go straight on
- in front of
- inside / outside
- it's too far
- next to
- not far — *nicht weit*
- on foot — *zu Fuß*
- on the corner of
- on the left
- on the right
- onto / off
- opposite — *hier aus hinei*
- out of / into
- roundabout — *Kreisverkehr*
- straight ahead — *geradeaus*
- traffic lights
- turn left
- turn right
- turn round — *umdrehen*
- under / over — *unter / über*
- Follow the signs for — *folge silen zeichen*
- Can you tell me the way to …?
- How do I get there?
- Where can I catch the bus to …? — *wo ist der bus*
- at the crossroad — *an der kreuzung*

43

Guest: Have you got a map of the city centre?
Porter: Yes, madam. _here you are_.
Guest: I'd like to go to the cathedral this morning. Is it within walking distance?
Porter: Take _____ at the map. We are here. When you go _how_ _____ the hotel, go _over_ the bridge, go _down_ to the traffic lights, then _turn right_. Go _across_ the Mozartplatz. You'll see the cathedral _in front of_ you.
Guest: Fine, thank you very much.

44

Guest: Excuse me, could you tell me how to get to the zoo, please?
Porter: Well, it's _too far_ to walk. You can _take_ the bus number 55. You _get_ _____ right outside the zoo.
Guest: And where's the bus stop?
Porter: It's just _across the road_, madam.
Guest: That sounds easy. Thank you.

45

Guest: Excuse me, can you tell me if the theatre is far from here?
Receptionist: It's only a _15 minutes walk_.
Guest: How do I get there?
Receptionist: _Turn right_ outside the hotel, go straight _across_ _____ the traffic lights, _follow_ this street, and go down to the roundabout. You'll see the theatre _in front of_ you.
Guest: Thank you.

Practise

Give directions from the hotel to the:

- cathedral / church
- museum
- information office
- Mozart's birthplace
- Fortress Hohensalzburg
- Mirabell Palace
- Festival Houses

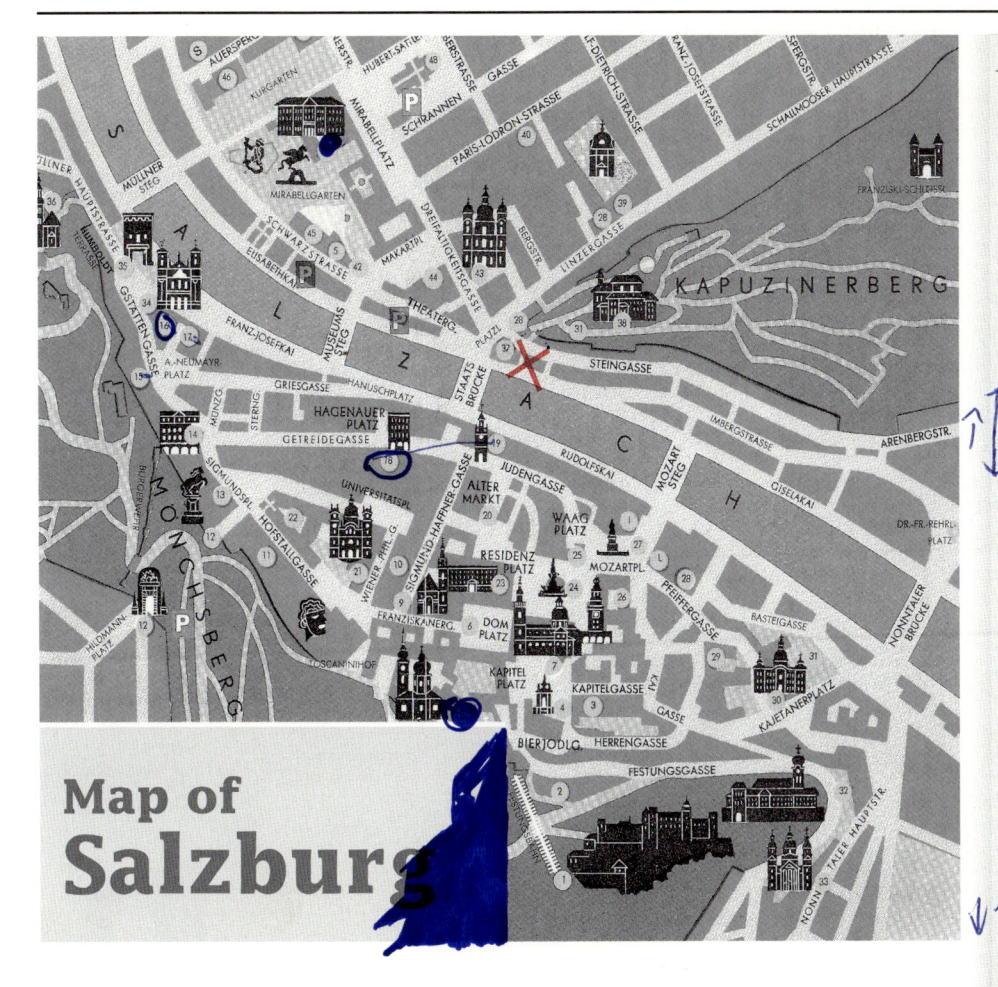

15. Lektion

Salzburg

1. Fortress Hohensalzburg
2. Stieglkeller, beergarden
3. Archbishop's Palace
4. Neptune Fountain
5. Marionette Theatre
6. Cathedral Square
7. Cathedral
8. St. Peter's
9. Franciscan Church
10. Art gallery
11. Festival Houses
12. Neutor
13. Horse Pond
14. St. Blaise's, Bürgerspital
15. Mönchsberg Lift
16. Natural History Museum
17. Carolino Augusteum Museum
18. Mozart's birthplace
19. Town Hall
20. Alter Markt, St. Florian Fountain
21. Kollegien Church
22. University
23. Residence
24. Residence Fountain
25. St. Michael's
26. Glockenspiel chimes
27. Mozart Monument
28. Paracelsus House
29. Chiemseehof
30. Kajetaner Church
31. Old town walls
32. Nonnberg Abbey
33. Erhard Church
34. Ursuline Church
35. Town gate
36. Müllner Church
37. Roof Café
38. Capuchin Monastery
39. St. Sebastian's Cemetery
40. Loreto Church
41. Mirabell Palace
42. Theatre
43. Holy Trinity Church
44. Mozarts dwellinghouse
45. Mozarteum
46. Kurhaus
47. Kongresshaus
47. St. Andrew's Church

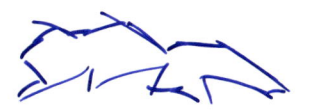

London underground

Use the map on the back cover.

Dialogues

You are at Tottenham Court Road.

46–47

46

You:	Excuse me, how do I get to Notting Hill Gate?
–	You take the Central Line from here, westbound.
You:	How many stops is it?
–	It's the sixth station.
You:	Thank you.

47

You:	Excuse me, how do I get to Covent Garden?
–	Take the Northern Line from here, southbound. Get off at Leicester Square and change to the Picadilly Line.
You:	Thank you.

When giving directions it might be useful to tell the direction.

eastbound
westbound
southbound
northbound

You are at Tottenham Court Road. Ask your partner how to get to:

- Leicester Square
- Liverpool Street
- Marble Arch
- Camden Town
- Waterloo
- St. Paul's
- Victoria
- Piccadilly Circus
- Wimbledon
- Baker Street
- West Hampstead
- Paddington

16th Lesson

Hotel Facilities

Match the room items with the numbers in the picture.

1 curtains
2 desk / chair
3 waste-basket
4 coat-hangers
5 wardrobe
6 bed
7 bedside table
8 reading lamp
9 pillow
10 blanket
11 sheet
12 TV-set
13 telephone
14 carpet
15 minibar
16 window

Hotel Info

Guest room facilities

Remote control TV

- 34 movie and satellite channels
- Direct-dial telephone, 2 lines
- 110w plug sockets
- Bathroom telephone, voice mail
- Dual voltage power points
- Data port, modem, email
- Bathrobes, minibar
- Laundry and valet service
- 24-hour room service

Hotel guests have a wide variety of needs.
In order to ensure the total well-being and relaxation of guests, good hotels provide a range of additional services, for example a fitness room, ladies hairdressing salon or a traditional gentleman's barber.
Business travellers may request secretarial support or a personal computer, printer, scanner, fax machine and manual typewriter to be delivered to their room. Fax machines can also be provided in all guest and private rooms on request.

Unsere Ziele

Nach Bearbeitung dieses Kapitels sollten Sie

- Gegenstände im Hotelzimmer benennen können;
- dem Gast verschiedene Angebote im Hotel nennen können;
- die unterschiedlichen Zimmerkategorien erklären können;
- wichtige Dienste erklären sowie
- eine Bestellung aufnehmen können.

16. Lektion

A Bathroom

Match the bathroom items with the numbers in the picture.

- ○ toothpaste
- ○ toilet paper
- ○ razor socket
- ○ shower
- ○ plug
- ○ wash basin
- ○ toothbrush
- ○ toilet
- ○ towel
- ○ mirror
- ○ bath
- ○ soap
- ○ taps

Practise

Form sentences with a partner with the words in the tables below. Think of other words.

Student 1

There's no There are no	toilet paper soap towels sheets telephone directory room service menu television coathangers etc.	in on	the	room. washbasin. bed. desk. bathroom. bedroom. wardrobe. etc.

Student 2

Sorry, sir / madam, I'll	bring	one some	up for you.

Present perfect

to check on jobs done

e.g.: Have you replaced the missing bulb?

Going to

for intended actions

e.g.: I'm going to report it now.

Will

for promises

e.g.: I'll send someone up immediately.

Need + ...ing

to describe requirements

e.g.: The plant needs watering.

each for emphasis on one particular of a group

e.g.: **Each** person gets three cards.

every for emphasis on all

e.g.: **Every** schoolchild knows that!

Find the complete list at:
www.dorchesterhotel.com

To learn

to provide
a large choice of
a wide range of
is located
to look after
requirements
to be available
equipment
arrival
departure
to arrange
accessible
use
valet
garments
extensive
to book – booking

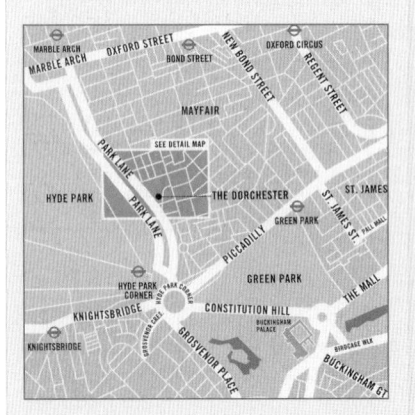

THE DORCHESTER

Air-conditioning	Individually controlled in all bedrooms. All public areas are fully air-conditioned.
Arrival Time	2pm
Barber's Shop	Our traditional men's barber shop is located near The Dorchester Spa.
Business Centre	The Boardroom Business Centre looks after all your secretarial and administrative needs.
Cancellation Policy	Any bookings cancelled after 2pm (London time) of the day before arrival will be charged one night's accommodation at the rate booked.
Car Parking	There is limited parking within the hotel. Please specify your requirements at time of booking. There is a wide choice of public car parks very close to the hotel.
Children	Children and babies are very welcome at The Dorchester. We can provide cots, baby-sitting services, high chairs and a wide range of other equipment which will make your stay with your children more comfortable. An extra bed for children up to 14 can be placed in your room at no charge.
Computer Links	Analogue and digital telephone lines for computer links are available. Alternatively, you can use the computers in the Boardroom Business Centre.
Credit Cards	The following credit cards are accepted at The Dorchester: Access, American Express, Diner's Club, Eurocard, JCB, Mastercard and Visa.
Departure Time	12 noon. Late departures can only be given by prior arrangements.
Foreign Currency Exchange	The Cashier can arrange Foreign Currency Exchange for you.
Hairdressing	Charles Worthington, twice voted British Hairdresser of the Year, runs the hairdressing salon at The Dorchester, open seven days a week.
Handicap accessible rooms	The hotel provides good public access and two handicap accessible rooms. All our restaurants are wheelchair accessible.
Laundry, dry-cleaning	Available seven days a week.
Newspapers	You will receive a complimentary copy of The Daily Telegraph every morning. Additional newspapers can be ordered.
Restaurants	We offer a wide range of dining within the hotel.
Room Service	A wide range of hot and cold dishes are available 24-hours a day.
Safe Deposit Boxes	There are safe deposit boxes in all rooms. Alternatively, valuables can be held for safekeeping in the hotel's safe.
Telephones	Three direct dial telephones in every room, with multiple lines and voicemail.
Television	We have a wide range of satellite channels available with a choice of foreign language channels.
Transportation	The Dorchester is close to many of London's main transport links – air, rail and road.

16. Lektion

ROOM TARIFF Effective 1st September 20.. to 28th November 20..					
ROOMS		SUITES		ROOF GARDEN SUITES	
Single occupancy		Junior Suite	£450	The Audley	£950
Queen/Superior	£275	Small Suite	£550	The Harlequin	£1,525
Queen/Deluxe	£295	Front Suite	£775	The Oliver Messel	£1,925
Double occupancy		Luxury Suite	£875	The Terrace	£1,925
King/Superior	£305	Park Suite	£950		
King/Deluxe	£335	Dorchester Suite	£1,075		
Breakfast Prices		Continental Breakfast	£18.50		
		English Breakfast	£22.00		
		Health Breakfast	£22.00		
		Japanese Breakfast	£28.50		

*All prices are quoted exclusive of **Value Added Tax** which is added at the standard rate of 17.5%. Room rates include service.*

VAT = Value Added Tax

Rooms at The Dorchester
No two rooms have the same design or decorative scheme. They are decorated in a cosy, comfortable 'Georgian Country House' style, characterised by the generous use of the highest quality, exclusive fabrics from Gainsborough, Percheron and Lelievre, hand mixed paint colours, original prints and oils and antique and reproduction furniture

Certain rooms have been designated for non-smokers, others for the special needs of guests with disabilities.

handicapped

Bathrooms throughout The Dorchester are fitted with Italian marble, etched glass and chrome fittings to recall the sleek style of the buildings Thirties origins. Stylishly lit, most bathrooms also enjoy natural daylight and the deepest baths in London!

precious stone

There are 53 suites, each one individual. Original wooden panelling, a generous use of the highest quality, exclusive fabrics, a wealth of pictures and accessories, fine antiques add up to a decadent experience. From our Art Deco Junior Suites to the ample proportions of The Dorchester Suites with their huge sitting / dining rooms overlooking Hyde Park, there is something for everyone.

The Dorchester Spa
Opened in October 1991, The Dorchester Spa is an oasis of cool and tranquil beauty in the heart of London, offering both male and female guests the opportunity to enjoy unqualified luxury in opulent surroundings.
Situated on the lower ground floor of The Dorchester hotel, The Spa offers excellent beauty, grooming and health facilities, including a hair salon, a barber shop, gymnasium and exercise studios, spa baths, steam and sauna rooms and private therapy rooms for a variety of specialist body treatments.

16th Lesson

Consider any of the facilities or services mentioned before. Tell other students in the class about any hotel you know or have worked in. Describe the services the hotel offers / does not offer. Think about services the hotel should offer.

Work with a partner

Think of a hotel you would like to run or own. Write your own hotel guide, listing special services and explaining how they can be obtained.

Exchange the hotel guide with another pair and look for similarities / opposites.

Exercise

Look at the guide again and tick the correct answer.

	true	false
Credit cards are not accepted.		
There is enough parking space for every hotel guest.		
The VAT is included.		
The hairdresser is open all week.		
Many different newspapers are offered every morning.		
Room service is only offered until midnight.		
Baby-sitting service is provided.		
At the departure day the room has to be cleared until 1 p.m.		
There is a safe in all rooms.		

Listen   48

Peter and Sarah have recently become manager and assistant manager of a small hotel in England. It is a little old-fashioned and they are thinking about improvements that have to be done.

Listen to their conversation and write in your exercise book.

Facilities they offer now: _____

Facilities they may offer in the future: _____

Room Service

Dialogue   49

Most hotels offer room service. Many guests like to stay in their rooms and have breakfast there. Listen and note the breakfast order.

_____
_____
_____
_____
_____
_____

16. Lektion

Room Service Menu
Available 8.00am - 11:00pm,

TOAST WITH HOMEMADE PRESERVES
Choice of brioche or five grain loaf

MUESLI
Warm dried fruits & grain with honey yoghurt

BRIOCHE FRENCH TOAST
With fresh banana, vanilla cream,
Maple syrup & home cured streaky bacon

FRUIT PANCAKE STACK
With pure Canadian Maple syrup & vanilla cream

EGGS BENEDICT
Poached eggs & grilled ham upon an English muffin,
with lemon Hollandaise

CORN & BRIE FRITTERS
Served with home cured streaky bacon & avocado

CLASSIC BREAKFAST
Farm fresh eggs, hash brown, bacon & brioche toast

VEGGIE BREAKFAST
Grilled tomato, farm fresh eggs, hash browns & beans with
brioche toast

THE BIG BREAKFAST
Farm fresh eggs, bacon, sausage, black pudding, grilled tomato,
mushrooms, hash brown & brioche toast

SOUP OF THE DAY

HUEVOS RANCHEROS
Fried eggs on refried beans, a tortilla & a spicy tomato
& cilantro salsa

BLAT SANDWICH
Bacon, lettuce, avocado & tomato with aioli & fries

TANDOORI CHICKEN SALAD
Served with lemon cumin dressing, red peppers, avocado,
onions & mini poppadoms

SPICE RUBBED LAMB FILLETS
With cherry tomatoes, black olives, cucumber,
parsley & feta cheese

ICE-CREAM SELECTION
Three ice-creams on a tuille biscuit & fruit coulis

WHITE CHOCOLATE TART
Served with homemade raspberry ripple ice-cream
& a tuille biscuit

Side Orders

SHOESTRING FRIES
MESCULIN SALAD
HASH BROWN
BACON

---

cured — smoked, salted

hash brown — potatoes

black pudding — „Blutwurst"

a tortilla — corn pancakes

aioli — mayonnaise and garlic

Call "Room Service" and make orders.

In the Kitchen

Everyone who loves a good substantial meal will be impressed by the German way of cooking. Explaining regional dishes to a foreigner is not only a matter of translation, it needs knowledge of preparation and ingredients of the dishes. Only this way the guest can get an idea what kind of dish it is and choose the one to his / her liking.

The purpose of preparing food is to make it good to eat. But careful preparation, handling and serving is important for food to be wholesome and food poisoning can also be minimized by this. Two-thirds of food poisoning outbreaks can be traced to meat, meat products and poultry, so it's especially important to handle these foods hygienically.

Unsere Ziele

Nach Bearbeitung dieses Kapitels sollten Sie

- Lebensmittel ihren entsprechenden Kategorien zuordnen können;
- die Zubereitung verschiedener Lebensmittel erklären sowie
- Rezepte lesen und schreiben können.

17. Lektion

Animal	Offal	Meat	Cuts
cow, bull, ox	kidney	beef	saddle of
calf	sweetbread	veal	neck of
pig	liver	pork	loin of
sheep	lights	mutton	rib of
lamb	tripe	lamb	leg of
	heart		breast of
	tongue		shoulder of
	brains		escalope of (cutlet, fillet of)
			steak
			chop

How to translate meat dishes:

cooking term + cut + meat

e.g.: roast saddle of pork

How to translate offal dishes:

cooking term + animal + offal

e.g.: sautéed pig's liver

Exercise

Number the cuts.

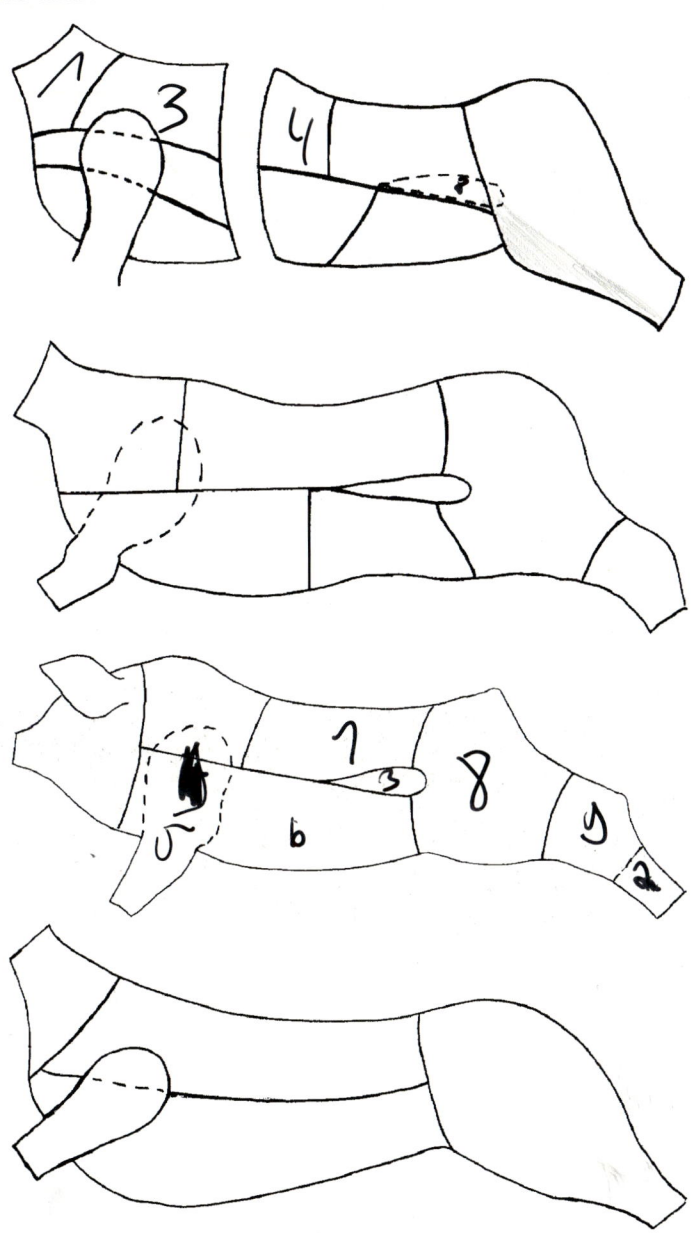

Side of beef

1 neck
2 shoulder
3,4 ribs
5 brisket
6 sirloin
7 rump
8 fillet, tenderloin
9 round and shank

Side of veal

1 leg
2 fillet, tenderloin
3 loin
4 neck
5 breast
6 shoulder
7 knuckle

Side of pork

1 hind leg, fresh ham
2 loin
3 fillet, tenderloin
4 neck
5 shoulder
6 belly
7 jowl
8 hock
9 knuckle

Side of lamb / mutton

1 leg
2 saddle
3 neck
4 shoulder
5 breast

Write / Name some dishes made from the cuts above.

17th Lesson

As soon as the dish is on the plate ready to serve, you use the past tense to translate it.

preparing food – **present** tense
prepared dish – **past** tense

To learn

to go with ....
... goes well with ....
can be ...ed
buttered
braised
creamed
cheese sauce
Dutch sauce
melted butter
à la polonaise

can be + verb pp

active:
He **peels** the potatoes.
passive:
The potatoes **are peeled**.

Form sentences.

Example:
mince / beef

The cook minces beef.
The waiter / waitress serves minced beef.

- mash / potatoes
- slice / tomatoes
- fry / scampi
- stew / lamb
- bake / ham

Dialogues 50–52

50

John: What about the vegetables?

Chef: Toady we have _____

with the roast veal and _____ with the second main course.

51

John: How can we prepare the spinach?

Chef: _____ or _____ with _____ or

_____ .

52

John: What will we do with the _____ and _____

_____ today?

Chef: Well, first we'll boil the _____ and _____

_____ . Then we can prepare _____

_____ . _____ can be served with

_____ , _____ , or _____ .

Exercise

Which verb goes with which picture?

◯ to peel   ◯ to mince   ◯ to fillet   ◯ to slice
◯ to grate ◯ to stuff   ◯ to mash

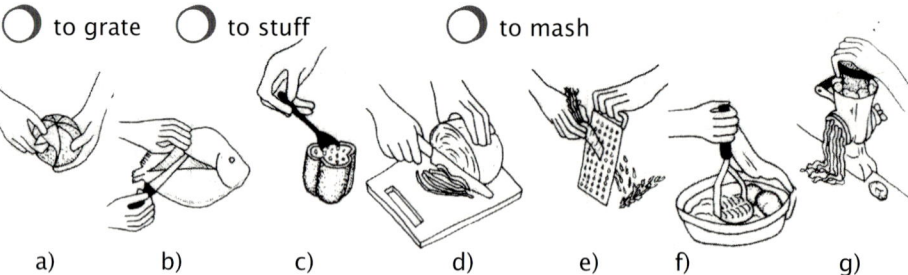

a)   b)   c)   d)   e)   f)   g)

Practise

Example:

What can you grate? I can grate carrots.

- peel   - mash   - fillet   - stuff   - mince

Example:

How can salmon be prepared? Salmon can be grilled.

- cauliflower   - veal   - chicken   - beans   - shrimps

17. Lektion

Dialogues   53–54

Steaks can be prepared:
- rare
- medium rare
- medium
- medium well
- well done (underdone)

53

Waiter: I can offer you either a _____ or a _____. Which one would you like?

Guest: I'll take the _____ .

Waiter: How would you like your steak?

Guest: I'd like it _____ .

54

Waiter: Would you like your fillet steak _____ , _____ or _____ ?

Guest: I'd like it _____ , please, and bring me a mixed salad, too.

Exercise

Correct the order of the recipes.

Fresh leek soup

- 7 [2] stir in the flour and cook
- 8 [2] finish with a little cream
- 1 [1] melt butter in a pan
- 4 [6] put in the stock
- 5 [3] bring to boil
- 2 [4] add the leeks and fry gently
- 6 [ ] simmer about 40 minutes
- 3 [9] season and add milk

Sauce verte

- [4] add the purée to the mayonnaise
- [1] boil the herbs in salted water
- [2] prepare the mayonnaise
- [6] finish with a little cream
- [5] pass the drained herbs through a strainer
- [3] also add a little boiling water

Salmon poached in champagne

- [2] marinate with lemon juice
- [1] skin the salmon and cut into pieces
- [3] poach the salmon in this stock
- [9] strain the stock
- [5] slice the onions
- [8] remove when done and put it on a hot plate
- [11] add champagne
- [6] sauté the onions in butter
- [4] season to taste
- [10] garnish with red peppercorns
- [7] finish it with fresh butter and cream

To learn

mixed salad
tossed salad

assorted salad
different kinds of salad next to each other

stock
fond

Courses of a meal

Cold appetizer
Soup
Warm Appetizer
Fish / Entree
Roast
Side dishes
Dessert
Coffee

Simple

Starters
Main courses
Side dishes
Desserts

Watch the pronounciation!

de**ss**ert
Nachspeise

de**s**ert
Wüste

17th Lesson

To learn

coating
a thin layer of something that covers

coat (noun)
something to wear

to coat (verb)
cover

yolk
the yellow part of the egg

shred
to tear apart

1 _____

2 _____

3 _____

Write your own recipe.

meal
Essen, Mahlzeit

food
Lebensmittel

Read

Guess these three Austrian specialities.

1

First take a slice of veal, dip in flour and egg. Then coat it with breadcrumbs and fry until golden brown. Garnish with a slice of lemon.

2

Beat the egg whites with sugar. Add the yolks and flour and put in some raisins. Fry and shred with a fork. Serve with powdered sugar and stewed plums.

3

Take a pot, put in water, root vegetables and parsley. Boil the beef in this stock. Season to taste. Slice the beef and garnish with parsley or chopped chives. Serve with hashed brown potatoes and apple-horseradish.

Complete and find other examples for each type of food

asparagus, beans, brains, bread, cabbage, chamois, cherry, chicken, chilli, chives, cod, corn, ginger, goose, grape, grapefruit, kidney, lamb, lemon, lobster, margarine, mussles, mustard, mutton, nutmeg, oil, oysters, parsley, peas, pheasant, pineapple, pork, pumpkin seed oil, quail, rice, salmon, salt, shrimps, spinach, strawberry, sweetbread, tunny, turbot, turkey, veal, vinegar, wheat, wild boar

Fish: trout, cod

Shellfish: crab, crab, shrimps, mussles

Meat: beef, veal, pork, mutton, lamb

Poultry: duck, chicken, goose, quail, turkey

Game: venison,

Offal: liver, kidney, brains, sweetbread

Vegetables: cauliflower,

Fats and oil: butter, margarine, pumpkin seed oil

Condiments: pepper, salt, chilli, mustard, nutmeg

Flavourings (herbs): garlic, salt

Cereals and cereal products: flour, rice

Fruits: apple, lemon, cherry, grapefruit, strawberry

18. Lektion

In the Restaurant

The range of food service found in hotel restaurants today is extensive. In the first category, there are restaurants offering the highest grade of service with a full à la carte menu. This includes dishes served by the waiter from a trolley in the dining room, and is known as gueridon service. The section captain must always be skilled, for he has to carry out procedures such as filleting, carving, and cooking speciality dishes at the table.

A second less complicated type of service is silver service where the menu can be either à la carte or table d'hôte. In this system, the food is prepared in the kitchen and then put on to silver flats and presented to the guests in the dining room.

A third form of table service, used mainly with a table d'hôte menu, is plate service. Here the waiter receives the meal already plated from the service hotplate and only has to place it in front of the guest and make sure that the correct cover is laid and the necessary accompaniments are on the table.

In a fourth type of service, called self-service, a customer collects a tray from the service counter, chooses his dishes and selects the appropriate cutlery for the meal.

Today, with ever-increasing needs for economy, many establishments usually prefer a variety of types of service. Tourist hotels, for example, frequently offer a combination of self-service and plate service for breakfast and another combination of self-service and silver service for luncheon.

Unsere Ziele

Nach Bearbeitung dieses Kapitels sollten Sie

- die verschiedenen Gänge eines Menüs erklären und dem Gast anbieten können;
- mit unterschiedlichen Speisenkarten umgehen können;
- Nationalgerichte den verschiedenen Ländern zuordnen können;
- mit der Rechnungslegung vertraut sein sowie
- Währungen umgehen können.

18th Lesson

Find a word or an expression on the menu that means:

- glazed carrots garnished with parsley
- cream of chicken with vegetables
- omelette surprise with ice cream
- small cakes
- cut asparagus in a cocktail sauce
- a clear, thin soup made by boiling meat and vegetables
- rice soufflé with chocolate and maraschino

You are the guest. Choose a three-course dinner from the menu.

55 Listen and note the orders of Mr. and Mrs. Bates.

To learn

to choose
I can offer you ...
Are you ready to order?
I'll take ...
the same for me
May I recommend ...?
I'd prefer ...
May I suggest ... ?

Menu

Parfait of Smoked Trout and Salmon
or
Asparagus Cocktail with Breast of Chicken

Cream "Franz Joseph"
or
Beef Broth with Cheese Straws

Stuffed Quail
or
Dover Sole in White Wine Sauce

Fillet of Beef, Vichy Carrots, Broccoli, Duchess Potatoes
or
Roast Vermont Turkey with Chestnut Stuffing, Cranberry Sauce

Chocolate Soufflé "Schönbrunn"
or
Baked Alaska

Mocca

Petits Fours

Wines

Grüner Veltliner, Weingut L Hagn, Mailberg
Pinot Nior, Weingut P. Schandl, Rust

Fill in

I come from	I speak	I am	I like to eat / drink
			Rösti
			Smørrebrød
			Crêpe Suzette
			Caviar
			Pörkölt
			Bird Nest Soup
			Idaho Potatoes
			Chianti
			Steak and Kidney Pie
			Gouda
			Gazpacho
			Ouzo
			Canadian Salmon
			Pilsner Beer
			Sushi
			Curry Chicken
			Döner Kebab
			Chili con carne

18. Lektion

Exercise

Write this menu in the correct order.

ROASTED TURKEY
Breast of Turkey enhanced by a Cream Sauce,
served with Carrots,
sauteed Spring Onions and Rice with Chanterelles

FILLET OF SOLE
Roasted Sole Fillet presented with a Cream Sauce,
accompanied by Spinach Tagliolini,
Yellow Root Vegetables,
Carrots and Tomato Concasse

MARBLE NUT CAKE

SEASONAL GARDEN GREENS
complemented by an Italian Dressing

SMOKED SALMON
with Creamed Horseradish

SELECTED FRUIT AND FINE CHEESE

BROILED BEEF TENDERLOIN
Broiled Tenderloin of Beef accented by a Cream Sauce,
served with Potato Noodles,
Broccoli and Vegetable Julienne

(Original Menu)

On American menus you can find "roasted", (roast – roasted – roasted) on English menus mostly "roast" (roast – roast – roast).

The following expressions have been used to make the menu more interesting:

enhanced by
seasoned with
presented with
complemented by
accented by
accompanied by

broiled
American for braised, roast or grilled

Recipe

Gazpacho

2 x 410 g	cans whole tomatoes
1	medium green pepper, de-seeded and sliced
1	small onion, sliced
1	medium cucumber, peeled and cut into chunks
50 ml	red wine vinegar
1	pepper
1 ml	sugar

Place all the soup ingredients in a liquidizer or food processor until coarsely puréed and all the large pieces are broken down. Chill overnight to develop the flavour. Serve with croutons and lemon wedges.
Serves 4.

18th Lesson

The European monetary unit is known as the euro; there are 100 cents in a euro.

Coins consist of 2 and 1 euros, then 50, 20, 10, 5, 2 and 1 cents.

Bank notes are available in 500, 200, 100, 50, 20, 10 and 5 euros.

The Bill

Currency

There are 7 euro notes in different colours and sizes. The notes are uniform throughout the Euro area. The designs are symbolic for Europe's architectural heritage. Windows and gateways dominate the front side of each banknote as symbols of the spirit of openness and cooperation in the EU. The reverse side of each banknote features a bridge from a particular age, a metaphor for communication among the people of Europe and between Europe and the rest of the world. All Euro notes are legal tender in all countries of the Euro area.

There are 8 euro coins. Every euro coin carries a common European face. On the obverse, each Member State decorates the coins with their own motifs. No matter which motif is on the coins they can be used anywhere inside the 11 member states. For example, a French citizen is able to buy a hot dog in Berlin using a euro coin carrying the imprint of the King of Spain. The common European face of the coins represents a map of the European Union against a background of transverse lines to which are attached the stars of the European flag.

Value added Tax (VAT)

While shopping in Europe keep in mind that a sales tax, or Mehrwertsteuer (MWSt), is included in all prices. Although there is one common currency within the countries participating in the monetary union the tax rates may vary sharply from country to country. In Denmark for example you pay 25 % of VAT, in Austria 20 %, in Germany or Spain 16 %, in Luxemburg only 15 %. Non-European Union residents may receive a refund of this tax. While customers in Austria can get up to 13 % back, in Germany the tax is completely refundable. After buying something in a shop which is connected to the Europe Tax Free System customers should fill in a Tax-free Cheque. The time between purchase and export should not be longer than three months, but generally, you can get a refund for tax-free shopping until three years after the purchase.

Dialogues 56–59

Listen and complete the dialogues.

56

Guest: Waiter, can I have the bill, please?
Waiter: Certainly, madam.
Guest: Why are there two different percentages? Could you kindly explain it to me?

```
*TOTAL*              € 51,00
BETRAG I             € 41,00
BETRAG II            € 10,00
10 % MWST            €  3,73
20 % MWST            €  1,67
MWST GESAMT                € 5,40
*** GESAMT TOTAL***        € 51,00
```

Waiter: _____, madam.

In Austria we have two different percentages of VAT in the hotel business:

10 per cent on food and accommodation, 20 per cent on beverages,

coffee and tea. The total amount _____

_____ .

Tipping

Restaurant bills have a service charge of 10.5–15 % already added. However, it is customary to add 5 % to 7 % to the total. At hotels, the doorman and bellhop generally receive a tip per bag.

? How much is the total amount?

How much is the VAT?

Is the service charge included?

18. Lektion

[57]

Guest: I'd like to settle my bill, please.

Waiter: _____ , sir?

Guest: In cash. Do you accept foreign currency?

Waiter: _____ have you got?

Guest: US Dollars.

Waiter: _____ , sir. The _____ is …

[58]

Guest: The bill, please.

Waiter: _____ .

Guest: I'd like to pay by credit card. You do take American Express, don't you?

Waiter: _____ , madam.

Guest: Fine, here's my card.

Waiter: Thank you. Would you _____ ?

Here's _____ , madam.

59

Guest: Waiter, the bill, please.

Waiter: Would you like to put it _____ , sir?

Guest: Yes, please.

Waiter: What's your _____ , sir?

Guest: 225.

Waiter: Thank you, sir. _____ here, please?

RESTAURANT-RECHNUNG / RESTAURANT ACCOUNT

RECHNUNG für _____
Kellner: Tisch: Datum:
10% MWSt. — € | c
20% MWSt. — € | c

Rechnungsbetrag (inkl.)

MWSt. — € | c
Nettobetrag — € | c

10% Mehrwertsteuer
20% Mehrwertsteuer
Summe

ZIMMER-NR. / ROOM NO.
NAME (Druckschrift – please print)
UNTERSCHRIFT / SIGNATURE

To learn

How are you paying?

I'd like to pay
　… (in) cash
　… in foreign currency
　… by credit card

How much is …?

The total amount / exchange rate is …

Service and value-added tax are included.

Would you like to put it on your hotel bill?

Would you sign here, please?

Here's your receipt.

How do you say?

Example: $ 120.50
You say: one hundred and twenty dollars and fifty cents

- JPY　774
- SIT　102
- HUF　985
- CHF　 44

Make up your own bill.

Prepare and practise a conversation between a guest and a waiter in a hotel. Use a menu. Fill in the room number and ask your guest to sign the bill.

Study the exchange rates in the daily newspaper.

Dealing with Complaints

Please give us a moment to help us serve you better!

Dear Guest,

thank you for staying at our hotel.

Your opinion of our facilities and service is very important to us in order that we can continue to improve our operations. To help us better serve you, we would appreciate your taking a few minutes to let us know how we are doing.

Please visit us again soon!

OASIS BUFFET

Oasis Buffet management requests your comments and observations. So that we may serve you better please rate the following:

SAHARA Hotel and Casino LAS VEGAS

	Excellent	Good	Fair	Poor
1. Oasis Buffet appearance was:				
2. Hostess acknowledgement:				
3. Buffet selection was:				
4. The food quality was:				
5. Buffet attendents attitude was:				
6. Employee's grooming and appearance:				
7. Beverage selection:				
8. Dessert selection:				
9. Please rate your overall experience:				

Date: _____   Time: _____   Server _____

Hotel Guest: Yes _____   No _____

If so desired:
Name _____
Address _____

Please write any additional comments on the back of this form and give it to the cashier when you leave. Thank you.

When you are dealing with complaints, you should listen carefully. Be polite and don't comment until the guest has finished. Then, make a short, clear apology. After that, you should repeat the complaint. This is to make sure that you have understood the problem and that there are no misunderstandings. Next, you should decide who will deal with the complaint. Explain the guest the action you plan to take and tell him when it will be done. Most businesses take complaints very seriously. It is often the responsibility of an individual staff member to deal with the problem. Sometimes it is necessary to refer an unhappy guest to someone else, such as to the manager.

🎯 Unser Ziel

Nach Bearbeitung dieses Kapitels sollten Sie

- auf die Beschwerden eines Gastes im Restaurant richtig reagieren können.

19. Lektion

Listen and fill in 🔘 60

a) *Guest:* This coffee is cold.

   Waiter: _____ .

b) *Guest:* This glass is dirty.

   Waiter: _____ .

c) *Guest:* The wine tastes like vinegar.

   Waiter: _____ .

d) *Guest:* This meat is rather tough.

   Waiter: _____ ?

   _____ ?

e) *Guest:* I've been kept waiting for half an hour.

   Waiter: _____ ?

f) *Guest:* This fish is not fresh.

   Waiter: _____ .

Listen and complete 🔘 61–63

Three guests at the restaurant are making complaints to staff members there. While you are listening to their conversations, complete the chart below.

details of complaint	action taken
61 the meat is tough	_____
62 _____	recommend a Beaujolais
63 the tablecloth is dirty	_____
_____	speak to the chef

Exercise

Try to deal with the following complaints.

complaint	your reaction
This meat is rare. I wanted it well done.	_____
There is something wrong with the wine.	_____
This glass is dirty. There is some lipstick on it.	_____
I ordered veal, this is pork.	_____
The tablecloth is dirty.	_____

To learn

Sorry, …

Would you like to change your order?

May I take your order now?

I'll speak to the wine butler.

I'll speak to the chef.

I'll be with you in a minute.

There doesn't seem to be anything wrong with it.

Play the scenes with your partner.

If you were a head waiter, what would you say in the following situations?

- A guest wants a table but the restaurant is fully booked.
- The apprentice has spilled hot soup on a gentleman's suit.
- A guest wants roast lamb but there isn't any left.
- A guest says that the white wine isn't chilled.

In the Bar

Drinks are divided in three categories:

- *short*
- *long*
- *on the rocks*

Short is a mixture of alcoholic or not, served in small quantities and small glasses.

Long is a mixture, usually iced and served in large glasses and generous quantities, mostly composed of a spirit diluted with a fizzy non-alcoholic beverage.

On the rocks is usually a single spirit poured over ice cubes.

A small amount of alcohol is more likely to be beneficial than harmful to healthy people who enjoy a drink. Alcohol has been an integral part of parties, celebrations and other happy social gatherings for centuries. It helps people to relax, to feel cheerful and to be more sociable. As long as drinking is controlled, there's no reason why that should be changed. But staying in control and knowing when to stop is the key. That's good news for millions of men and women who like the taste of wine, spirits or beer. But how much alcohol can be taken without risk to health?

Drinking too much over a period of months or years damages far more than the nervous system. Liver, heart, glands, stomach and intestine may all suffer, even though the person concerned rarely, if ever, gets drunk. The real concern is for the increasing number of people with alcohol-related disorders. Too many deaths in road traffic accidents are associated with blood alcohol levels that are over the limit. Millions of working days are lost each year because of excessive alcohol intakes. It is an offence for anyone under the age of 18 to sell or buy alcoholic drinks. Some alcohol is enjoyable, too much may be dangerous. Make sure you know where to draw the line.

🎯 Unsere Ziele

Nach Bearbeitung dieses Kapitels sollten Sie

- *das Barpersonal und seine Tätigkeiten kennen;*
- *einige Bargegenstände nennen und deren Verwendung erklären können;*
- *einige typische Bargetränke kennen sowie*
- *einige Cocktails beschreiben und zubereiten können.*

20. Lektion

Dialogue

Listen and write the answers.

Who is responsible for the bar?
_____

Who serves the drinks and cocktails to the tables in the bar?
_____

What kinds of drinks can you get in the bar?
_____

Who prepares the drinks?
_____

When starting to mix a cocktail have all the ingredients and tools handy, so as not to have to stop proceedings to look for the missing item. Never forget oranges, lemons and have some small onions, olives and fresh seasonal fruits ready.

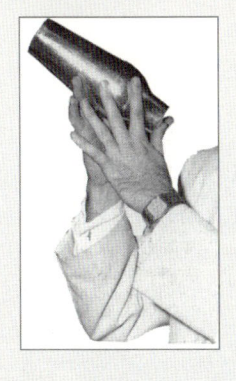

Bar Utensils

Connect

What do we need these bar utensils for?

1.	Hamilton beach		for straining ...
2.	measuring glass		for stirring ...
3.	shaker		for cutting ...
4.	mixing glass		for shaking ...
5.	strainer		for mixing ...
6.	bar spoon		for squeezing ...
7.	lemon squeezer	*1*	for blending ...
8.	bar knife		for measuring cream
9.	ice bucket		for keeping ice cubes cold
10.	small grater		for picking cherries
11.	fork		for grating nutmeg

85

20th Lesson

To learn

double Scotch
non-alcoholic
crisps and peanuts
sundries
anything else
long drinks
short drinks

Sort of beers

- a pint of bitter
- lager beer
- export beer
- strong beer
- bottled beer
- draught beer

Dialogues

Listen and complete.

65

Guest: _____, please!

Waiter: I'm sorry, sir. We only have _____ and _____.

Guest: Which is better?

Waiter: Well, the _____ is stronger, but both are _____. They are _____, not _____.

Guest: I'll take a _____ one, please.

Waiter: Of course, here you are.

66

Guest: _____, please!

Waiter: _____, sir?

Guest: No, just a _____, please.

Waiter: Anything else, sir?

Guest: Yes, a _____, please.

67

Guest: Something _____ for me.

Waiter: A tonic, fruit juice, a ginger-ale, or mineral water, perhaps?

Guest: _____. And can you bring some _____ and _____?

Waiter: Certainly, sir.

68

Guest: What cocktails do you serve?

Waiter: You can have _____, _____, _____, _____ or _____.

Guest: One Gin Fizz, and what does a Side Car consist of?

Waiter: It consists of _____, _____ and _____.

Guest: No, thanks. Bring me a _____, please.

Waiter: Anything else?

Guest: Do you sell cigarettes?

Waiter: Yes, sir. What sort?

20. Lektion

Listen

🔘 69

Fill in the missing words.

When you prepare a _____, you take a _____, put in two or three _____, add the other ingredients (_____, _____ and _____) and _____. Then you take a _____ and strain the drink into a _____ which you _____ with _____. For the preparation of _____ we need a _____ _____. We put in _____, add the _____ and perhaps _____ or _____, and _____ with a _____. Then we strain the drink _____ _____. A _____ we serve with a _____, a _____ with _____ or _____ _____.

Attention

put in ...
add ...

Exercise

Correct the order.

Martini Dry Cocktail

- [ ] Stir well.
- [ ] Serve it with an olive and lemon twist.
- [ ] Add gin and dry vermouth.
- [*1*] Take a mixing glass.
- [ ] Strain into cocktail glass.
- [ ] Put in ice cubes.

Sherry Flip

- [*1*] Put ice cubes into shaker.
- [ ] Add nutmeg.
- [ ] Add sugar, egg yolk, and sherry.
- [ ] Shake well.
- [ ] Strain into flip glass.

Alexander

- [ ] Strain into cocktail glass.
- [ ] Shake well.
- [ ] Add nutmeg if desired.
- [ ] Add cream, crème de cacao, and brandy.
- [*1*] Put ice cubes into shaker.

Young Colada

- [ ] Shake well.
- [ ] Put in pineapple juice, coconut cream, lemon juice and grenadine.
- [ ] Strain into tumbler.
- [ ] Garnish with slice of lemon.
- [*1*] Put ice cubes into tumbler.
- [ ] Take a shaker.

? How do you prepare a White Lady?

21st Lesson

www.deutschland-tourism.de
www.tiscover.com
www.info-germany.de

Sightseeing in Germany

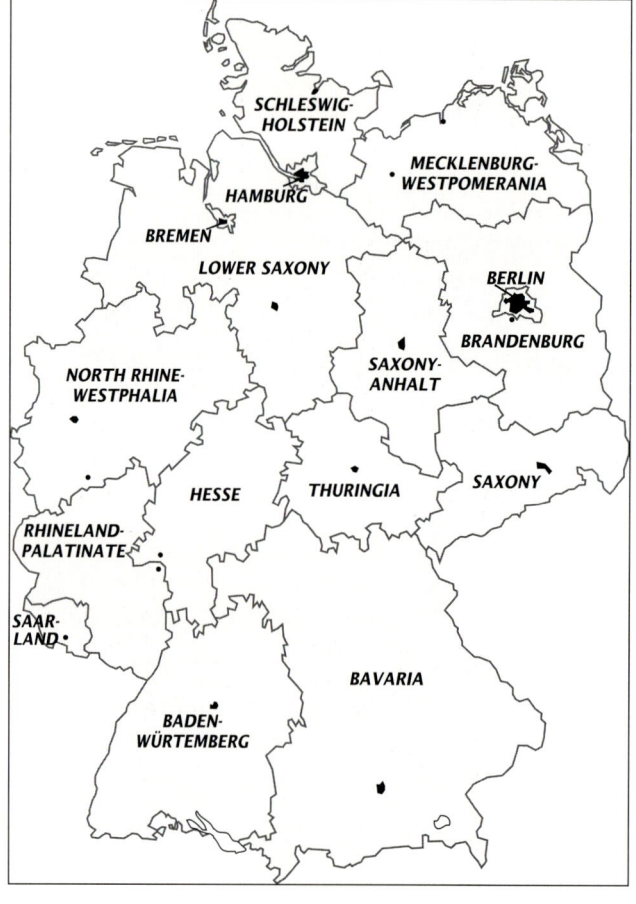

After the reunification in 1990 there are 16 federal states to choose a holiday destination from. Each has its own special appeal and its own character.

Let's begin our journey in the northernmost state, in **Schleswig-Holstein,** "cradled by the sea", it offers lively resorts along the North and Baltic Sea coasts. Sylt, Germany's only fashionable ocean bathing resort is well known as a centre of surfing. Germany's "Gateway to the World" is Hanseatic Hamburg, the city of over a million people and a world metropolis, with countless opportunities to spend your money or only your time by going window-shopping.

Surrounded by the State of Lower Saxony you will find the smallest state in the republic: **Bremen,** not only known as a Hanseatic town but also famous for the Bremen Town Musicians, who indeed never reached their destination.

Lower Saxony is the state with the strongest contrasting landscapes: from the sand dunes of the East Frisian Islands through the Lüneburg Heath to the Harz Mountains you can have fun with swimming, cycling or hiking.

Further east we come across **Saxony-Anhalt,** with its old trading and cathedral towns: the state capital of Magdeburg, Halle, Dessau, Merseburg, Naumburg and Wittenberg.

(To be continued)

Unsere Ziele

Nach Bearbeitung dieses Kapitels sollten Sie

- *Texte lesen und verstehen können;*
- *ein Besichtigungsprogramm für Gäste erstellen können;*
- *deutsche Sehenswürdigkeiten beschreiben können;*
- *die wichtigsten Verkehrsmittel kennen und beschreiben können.*

How much do you already know of the whole Germany?

Connect these sights with the places where you find them.

1. St.-Pauli-Landungsbrücken	☐	Island of Rügen
2. Königsstuhl	☐	Dresden
3. Sanssousi Castle	☐	Berlin
4. Brandenburg Gate	☐	Potsdam
5. Loreley Cliffs	☐	Bavaria and Austria
6. Lake Constance	1	Hamburg
7. Goethe's birthplace	☐	Eisenach
8. Wartburg Castle	☐	Frankfurt am Main
9. Zugspitze	☐	"Father Rhine"
10. Green Vault	☐	Island of Mainau

Read

Travelling in Germany (part two)

Brandenburg, another new state, was the heart of the old state of Prussia. Famous tourist attractions are Potsdam's Sanssousi, Frederik II's summer residence and Cecilienhof Castle, the scene of Germany's division in the year 1945. Germany's both old and new capital of **Berlin** still is a city of contradictions – today as in times past. But the wall, which has divided the city and the whole country for 28 years, has fallen.

From Berlin we turn again to the west, to **North Rhine-Westphalia,** the land of wide plains, countless lakes, and green highlands such as Teutoburger Wald or the Sauerland. "Father Rhine", leads us through the state with the largest population density. The most attractive section of the Rhine is considered to be the course of the river in the state of **Rhineland-Palatinate,** where steep cliffs, romantic castles, doll house towns at the foot of wine terraces and thousand-year-old cathedrals line the banks of the Rhine.

The **Saarland** is the smallest state in the republic. In 1955 it rejoined Germany, but the French art of "joie de vivre" is still very much alive there.

From here our trip takes us to **Hesse.** There you find old half-timbered towns and restful hilly landscapes, medieval Limburg, the old university town of Marburg as well as the European financial metropolis Frankfurt.

Hesse's neighbouring state, **Thuringia,** has got the honorary title "Green Heart of Germany", for its landscapes offer the hiker everything: lovely walks, breathtaking views from many castles, rushing waterfalls and cool grottos. Weimar, centre of German classical literature, Wartburg Castle or the capital Erfurt are worth visiting for tourists.

Our journey takes us further east, to the Free State of **Saxony,** to the trade fair city of Leipzig and to Dresden. Beautifully restored buildings, such as the Zwinger and the Semper Opera House, today evoke the old glory of the "Florence of the Elbe". Near Dresden there stretches Saxon Switzerland, known for its picturesque rock formations and bizarre stone towers.

To the south, Saxony borders the Free State of **Bavaria,** which is not only the largest of all states but also the most highly individual. White and blue skies over green meadows and wooded hills, clear lakes, prettily decorated farmhouses, cheerful baroque churches and fairy-tale castles like Neuschwanstein – all that describes one of Germany's most popular holiday destinations. Last but not least we arrive in the state of **Baden-Würtemberg** with its capital Stuttgart. It lies in a valley, surrounded by woods, vineyards and fruit orchards. Northwest we find Heidelberg, the town with the most famous castle ruins in the world and one of the oldest universities in Germany.

You will certainly agree that visitors to Germany can keep coming back year after year and still have not seen everything of this fascinating country.

(slightly adapted)

Exercise

Read the text and tick the corrct sentences.

- ☐ All German regions are very much alike.
- ☐ Schleswig-Holstein is surrounded by the sea.
- ☐ The city state of Hamburg has over one million inhabitants.
- ☐ Bremen is famous for its Town Musicians, who have lived there for a long time.
- ☐ In Lower Saxony you find a lot of different landscapes for various activities.
- ☐ Saxony-Anhalt is situated east of Lower Saxony.
- ☐ Brandenburg is the new name for the old state of Prussia.
- ☐ Berlin is the capital of Germany.
- ☐ The Saarland has not much in common with France.
- ☐ Hesse and Thuringia are neighbours in the middle of Germany.
- ☐ Dresden in Saxony is often compared with Florence in Italy.
- ☐ Bavaria is Germany's most popular holiday region.
- ☐ In Baden-Württemberg's Heidelberg visitors can see the ruins of Germany's oldest university.

Now correct the false sentences.

Look for more information:
www.hamburg-tourism.de

Work in pairs.

Ask for information.

Example:

How much is a ticket for ...?
What else can I do ...
- in St. Pauli?
- in the harbour?
- at New Year's Eve?
- if I like shopping?

Read

Imagine your first job took you to a hotel in Hamburg. While working at the reception you should be well informed about sightseeing in the city.

Hamburg – a modern metropolis with style and tradition
An overview
What are the first things that come to your mind when you think of Hamburg? Probably the city's stunning locations on the Elbe and Alster Rivers, the colourful activities in the St. Pauli entertainment district, unforgettable musicals, a night at the theatre, Michaelis Church (nickname: "der Michel") or the impressive harbour. Hamburg, 1200 years old, is loved both for its contemporary scene as well as for its cultural offerings.
Germany's second largest city offers high quality of life and international flair. In Hamburg, the word "boredom" is unknown.

Hamburg's greatest musicals and shows
Hamburg is Germany's undisputed musical capital. Do you like exciting entertainment, perfect choreographies, beautiful songs and moving plots? There you go, we have all for you, right here:

Lion King
The world's currently most successful musical opened its doors in the harbour district of Hamburg. The extravagant mega musical with music by Elton John and Tim Rice has won 25 major awards. The Disney show is a bestseller.
Prices from EUR 33 to EUR 108

MAMMA MIA!
This worldwide successful musical opens its doors in November. In London the show with hits of ABBA burst every record. First performance on November 5th. Advanced booking has just started! Prices from EUR 25,92 to EUR 99,36

Palazzo
Welcome to star chef Harald Wohlfahrt's Gourmet Theatre that combines Haute Cuisine and first class entertainment. Sit back, look, savour ... and be amazed! The show is on from November 15th to January 12th.
The menu comes with an entertainment programme of superior quality: PALAZZO presents international top-class artists and performances. There are comedy waiters who provide an enchanting atmosphere of art, amusement and pleasure.
New Year's Eve Special:
Enjoy one course extra and a fireworks show right in front of the tent. After the show the Palazzo band will entertain you. Beginning at 2 a.m. a DJ will heat up the atmosphere. No doubt, you will be dancing until dawn! Price: EUR 99 / 119

What to see and do during your stay

Hamburg by water

Grand Harbour Tour
See one of the world's greatest harbours – the Port of Hamburg. The tour takes you through the different harbour basins to give you a close-up view of giant ships, channels and canals, container terminals and shipyards. You go through a lock and also into the canals of the Speicherstadt, the historic warehouse district. English-speaking guides available upon request.
Departure: daily
Duration: 1 hour
Price: EUR 8,50 adults; EUR 6,50 children

Historic Canal Tour
Experience the harbour of Hamburg in a restaurated barge of the twenties and ship through plenty of romantic channels and canals of the beautiful city.
Departure: daily 11.30 a.m. and 2.30 p.m.
Duration: 2 hours
Price: EUR 13,50

Nocturnal boat tour of the Warehouse Complex
The century-old Speicherstadt is located in the Free Port between Deichtorhallen and Baumwall and is the world's oldest warehouse complex. It was built at the turn of the century in red brick, typical of northern Germany, with gabled roofs and small towers, which are beautifully reflected in the canals they border.
Now you can experience a very special highlight: The old Speicherstadt is getting lighted. Buildings, bridges and canals can be experienced in the dark – that makes the warehouse complex an impressing place of mystery and dream.
Departure: daily from Landungsbrücken, please call in advance if ebb and flow allows a tour and when it starts.
Duration: 1 hour
Price: EUR 10,50

Shopping arcades in Hamburg's city
(Use the following notes to explain some shopping facilities to your guests.)

Gänsemarkt Passage – The first shopping arcade
Established in 1979.
Perfect location, directly next to Gänsemarkt.
Nearly 50 shops with a wide range of international goods.
9 different food services offering gastronomical delights for every taste.

Hamburger Hof – Antique but still up to date
A building with history, fascinating facade was built over 100 years ago.
One of the most impressive buildings in Hamburg's inner city.
Over30 diverse and exclusive shops.
First-class food services available.

The shopping arcades in Hamburg's inner city are centrally located and can be comfortably reached on foot, by car, by bus: routes 36, 102, 109, 603, 604, 605 or by underground: routes U2 to Gänsemarkt and U1 to Jungfernstieg.

Exercise

**Plan a 3-night-package of your region from Friday to Monday.
Present it to your classmates.**

Answer
- How can I get to Jungfernsteig?
- What ca I do / see in the Speicherstadt?
- Are there tours for English speaking guests?
- Do you offer any childrens reductions?

Getting around in Germany's capital – Berlin

www.berlin.de

You may search the web for more details of the other means of transport.

Public Transport

- Bus and Underground
- Car and Taxi
- Bicycle

An interconnected three-zone tariff system (ABC) which only requires one ticket allows you to hop from bus to underground (U-Bahn) to surface rail (S-Bahn) and tram with only one ticket, for two hours after validation. Trams are fast and convenient (in former east Berlin only) and small ferries will get you across Berlin's lakes.

Cycling is highly recommended in Berlin, as it is easy and safe. Cycle lanes are a pleasure to follow, especially around the Tiergarten Park area.

By Bus and Underground – fares and zones
Berlin is divided into transport zones A, B and C but for most travel purposes A and B will be sufficient.

Single Ticket
EUR 2.10 (2 zones) or EUR 2.40 (3 zones)
Valid for two hours on all transport systems, with as many stops as you like.

Short-Hop Ticket
EUR 1.20
Valid for three U- or S-Bahn stops and six bus or tram stops only.

Day Ticket
EUR 6.10 (2 zones) or EUR6.30 (3 zones)
Valid until 3 a.m. of the day after validation

7-Day-Ticket
EUR 22.00 (2 zones) or EUR 28.00 (3 zones)
Ticket is transferable and valid 7 days after stamping.

Berlin Walks
Most cities have only one centre – Berlin has two of them. Because of the long separation there is one "City-West" around Kurfürstendamm and one "City-East" between Pariser Platz and Alexanderplatz. You can easily explore the two of them on foot, the distances are not as huge as one could expect and the traffic is rather dense most of the time. Therefore it is the quickest way without getting stuck in a traffic jam.

City-West
When you arrive at underground and train station Bahnhof Zoo you are directly at Kurfürstendamm with the famous ruin of Emperor Wilhelm Memorial Church. Tauenziehnstraße begins behind the church and the wellknown department store KaDeWe is not far away. If you go down Ku'damm towards Adenauerplatz you can come across Käthe-Kollwitz-Museum and The Story of Berlin, an exhibition about the history of the city with 3D sound systems and touch screens and much more.

Suggest different ways of exploring the centre of Berlin to a partner.
- by underground,
- by bus,
- by tram,
- on foot.

BERLIN WelcomeCard – The best way to get around – Including Potsdam
Enjoy so much of Berlin for so little money. You can use the WelcomeCard spend three days exploring Berlin and Potsdam. We offer you a good package for combined transport and museum entry tickets. Take advantage of price reductions of up to 50 per cent for a lot of cultural highlights. It is ideal for families. It is valid for three children below the age of 14 (under 6 travel for free).
EUR 18,00

21. Lektion

Exercise

What kind of ticket for transportation would you buy?

1. You will be in Berlin for three days and would like to use the trams, underground, and busses to visit a lot of attractions and maybe you want to see Sanssoussi.

   _____

2. You are on a business trip to Berlin for one week and you have to see a lot of customers in different parts of the city, but your car broke down.

   _____

3. You want to visit the German State Opera House and you live only a short distance away, parking could be a problem there but it is too far to walk.

   _____

4. You will be in Berlin for one day, but you would like to see as much as possible.

   _____

Berlin Walks
City-East
A highlight of all sightseeing tours certainly is the glass dome of the Reichstag building. From there you can enjoy a wonderful view over the city centre. Then you should go through the lately restored Brandenburg Gate, across Pariser Platz, pass Hotel Adlon and stroll along the magnificent Unter den Linden Boulevard. To the left and to the right you will find some of Berlin's most outstanding landmarks like Comedy Opera House, Gendarmenmarkt Square with the French and German Cathedrals, Humboldt University, German State Opera, Museum Island, Red Town hall and last but not least the Television Tower, which has a restaurant on its top where you can sit back and relax from all the walking.

With bus line 100 through the city
It is a cheap alternative to the "normal" sightseeing tour. The bus 100 leaves from Bahnhof Zoo and goes across the whole city to the district Prenzlauer Berg. A single ticket – valid for two hours – is enough and you can get off and on as often as you like to see as much as your heart desires.

22nd Lesson

Hotels in Germany

Go to this pages:
http://www.travelvantage.com/ger.html
http://www.hrs.de
and open the link "Hotel Reservations".

Choose a date and a region and see which hotels have free capacities for that time in Germany.

Work with a partner. Play the telephone call to one of these hotels and ask for:

- double room / one week / half board / fully booked
- single room / 4days / b&b / only 3 days
- twin-bedded room / 10 days / full board / possible

"Travel broadens the mind", as Goethe advised the "wise man" in Wilhelm Meisters Lehrjahre, and as he explained in a letter to Schiller, who was less keen on travelling: "For someone of my disposition a journey is of immense value – it invigorates, improves and informs." Travel in Germany is only a little over one hundred years old. It was not until the revolutionary political, industrial and technical developments during the 19th century that people began to travel across the "whole Germany" – characterized by the distinctive countryside between the Alps in the south and the seas in the north.

Travel in reunited Germany, from the North Sea to the Baltic, to Mecklenburg-Westpomerania and the Island of Rügen, from Lower Saxony via Saxony-Anhalt to Brandenburg and Berlin, from Münsterland up the Rhine towards Mainz, to Hesse and Thuringia and the Free States of Saxony and Bavaria, into the Alps, into the Black Forest and to Lake Constance – all this is waiting to be discovered. There is something about all regions – different for each and everyone of us.

When you are looking for accommodation you can choose from luxury hotels, castle hotels, city hotels and country inns, private boarding houses and youth hostels.

Germany is a country which is worth visiting at any time of the year. Whether you are interested in a short holiday or a weekend break, special arrangements offer something for every taste.

Unsere Ziele

Nach Bearbeitung dieses Kapitels sollten Sie

- die verschiedenen Angebote eines Hotels verstehen sowie
- einem Gast diese Angebote erklären und darüber Auskunft geben können;
- den Gast über sämtliche Einrichtungen (zB Öffnungszeiten von Restaurants und Geschäften) im Hotel informieren können.

22. Lektion

Welcome to the Four Seasons Hotel Berlin

As the world's leading operator of luxury hotels and resorts, Four Seasons currently manages 56 properties in 25 countries, primarily under the Four Seasons and Regent brands. The Company also offers a growing network of branded vacation ownership properties and private residences.

A city steeped in history, alive with artistic tradition and rich in cultural significance, seat of government, multicultural metropolis, magnet for global business, the vibrant capital of the nation. Germany's first FOUR SEASONS HOTEL rises above the famed Gendarmenmarkt Square, in the richly historical Friedrichstadt district. Travellers from the corners of the world meet here to work, explore and unwind, in the heart of the new Berlin.

Business centres are fully equipped, the room service never sleeps. A friendly, knowledgeable staff and a 24-hour concierge provide every wished-for amenity. The hotel is built on an intimate scale within a stylish multi-use complex. Opposite the hotel there are the French and German Cathedrals, the Brandenburg Gate, the renowned State Opera and Museum Island are only steps away.

Charlottenstraße 49
Berlin, Germany 10117

Telephone: 49 (30) 20 33 8
Guest Fax: 49 (30) 20 33 61 19
Room Reservation:
49 (30) 20 33 66 66

Administrative Fax:
49 (30) 20 33 60 09
Guest e-mail:
ber.guest@fourseasons.com

FOUR SEASONS HOTEL
Berlin

Accommodation

Number of rooms: 204, including 42 suites
Number of floors: 8
Guest Rooms: **Standard and Superior Rooms** (at least 40 to 45 sqm) on the lower and middle floors
Deluxe Rooms, located throughout the hotel with panoramic views

Suites: **One-Bedroom Suites** (80 to 86 sqm), large living/dining area, guest powder room
Deluxe One-Bedroom Suites (96 sqm)
Two Bedroom Suites, on the top two floors

Presidential Suite (219 sqm), on the top floor, convertible into one-, two-, three-bedroom suite

Standard Rates: **Superior Room** EUR 315,00 / 280,00
Deluxe Room EUR 345,00 / 310,00
Executive Suite EUR 380,00

Rates listed above are per room, per night, based on single or double occupancy. Service charges and taxes are additional. For breakfast EUR 25,00 are added.

Answer

- Where is the Four Seasons Berlin situated?
- How many rooms / suites does it offer?
- What are the room rates?
- What do they include?
- Which sights of the city are near the hotel?

Look for more information about hotels in your federal province.

(http://www.tiscover.com)

Ask your partner.

- Where can guests park their cars?
- Which services do you offer for families with children?
- If a performance of the State Opera is sold out, what possibilities do the guests have to get tickets?
- Is it possible to use a computer in a guest room?
- Are there non-smoking rooms?
- How many people can be hosted for meetings?
- Is it possible to organize a private party for 30 guests without being seen by other guests?
- Can you translate working papers from English into French?
- Where can guests leave their valuables?

Small talk.

- Offer your guest different guest-room facilities and explain them.
- Use 3 special features.

Read and translate this text using your dictionary.

Amenities and services

- 24-hour business service
- 24-hour in-room dining
- 24-concierge service
- Airline ticketing service
- Air conditioning
- Babysitting services available
- Complimentary children's amenities / services
- Complimentary overnight shoeshine
- Complimentary newspaper with breakfast

- Express check-in / check-out
- Elegant bar
- Limousine service
- News-stand and sundries
- Non-smoking rooms
- On-site parking
- One-hour pressing
- Overnight laundry / dry-cleaning
- Portable phones and fax machines
- Restaurant with open fireplace
- Umbrellas
- Valet parking

Guest room facilities

- 100 % cotton oversized bath towels
- 100 % wool blankets
- Thick terry bathrobes
- Complimentary toiletries
- Down pillows
- Duvets available
- Non-allergenic foam pillows available
- DVD player

- 24-hour room service
- Private stocked bar / refrigerator
- In-room dining for all meals at any time
- Twice-daily housekeeping service
- Two or more multi-line telephones
- In-room safe
- Hair dryer

Business Services

At the hotel
- Audiovisual equipment available
- Portable computer units available
- Secreterial services
- Translation services
- Japanese services
- Wired or wireless, high-speed e-mail and internet access in meeting rooms

In your room
- All-news cable network
- AM/FM clock radio
- Computer / Fax available
- Computer / Fax hook up
- Modem phone jack
- Multi-line telephone
- Speaker phone
- Voice mail

High-profile meetings and international conferences unfold smoothly and efficiently in the experienced hands of Four Seasons staff. The hotel accommodates gatherings of all kinds, from award galas to multi-media presentations, from 10 to 120 people.

For conferences, cocktails and dinner parties for up to 50 people, the Salon Langhans provides beautifully panelled space fitted with windows. Aglow with elegance, the Salon Gontard hosts social events and banquets.

Two additional boardrooms, each with a foyer, salon and fully equipped business centre are discreetly located on guest room floors, ensuring complete privacy for confidential meetings.

Four Seasons Hotel Berlin – Dining

Seasons

Enjoy a dining experience as cosmopolitan as Berlin and as traditionally as Germany, too. Seasons restaurant offers a warm and intimate atmosphere, enhanced by the fireplace and seats 64.
Reservations are recommended.

Specialities
The restaurant's menu varies seasonally and chef Drew Deckman creates daily specialities. Seasons also provides an exclusive dinner menu, which will change every month and a special children's menu.

News
Seasons has been recognized with 15 points in the 2001 issue of Gault Millau. Feinschmecker magazine nominated Four Seasons Hotel Berlin as the best Ambience Hotel of the Year 2001.

Hours of operation
Breakfast	6.30 am	to	11.30 am
Lunch	12.00 noon	to	2.00 pm
Dinner	6.30 pm	to	11.00 pm

The Bar

The bar offers lunch, snacks, light dishes and desserts in a warm, graceful and intimate atmosphere of beige and brown. Gather to deepen friendships over wine or coffee, to toast successful negotiations, or simply to sample some of Germany's outstanding beers.
It has 30 seats and is open from 11.00 am to 1.00 am.
Afternoon tea is served from 3.00 pm to 6.00 pm.

In-Room Dining

The breakfast menu includes an inspired selection of healthy options such as fresh fruit juices, Swiss muslin and Munich style white sausages with sweet mustard and poached eggs Benedict.
Lunch and dinner include home cooking, salads, pasta, sandwiches and desserts. Nutritionally balanced options and vegetarian selections are available.
In-Room Dining also offers an extensive selection of wines and other alcoholic beverages.
The overnight selections include salads, sandwiches, pizza with prosciutto, Berlin mini veal burgers and a variety of desserts.
A children's menu offers breakfast, main courses and desserts, as well as special children's amenities.
In-Room Dining also provides special lunch, vegetarian and deluxe picnic baskets. Please, allow 12 hours' preparation time.
The Seasons restaurant menu is available through In-Room Dining from 6.00 am to 11.30 pm.

Ask your partner.
- When does the restaurant open in the morning?
- How long can we have dinner at night?
- What can we do if we want to have lunch after 2.00 pm?
- Are there any vegetarian / children's dishes on the menu?

Find some more questions a guest could ask you and give information. Then change roles.

22nd Lesson

For that Personal Touch
We want to ensure that our service is a hundred per cent right for you; carried through with that all-important personal touch. As our honoured guest you can expect the right answers to all questions – at any time without ifs and buts.

The 142 elegant rooms and suites are fitted with all the modern facilities you could require.

While the choice of cuisine ranges from world renowned Thuringian specialities to enticing variations on international delicacies.

The DORINT offers the perfect combination of recreational, conference and banqueting facilities to suit a wide variety of public and private functions.

www.dorint.de

Imagine you phone the DORINT to ask some questions.

- How much do you charge for a single / double room?
- Are the taxes included? Is the breakfast included?
- Are there any special rates for groups / children?
- Could you arrange dinner for 200 persons?
- What kind of fitness facilities do you provide?

Dorint Erfurt

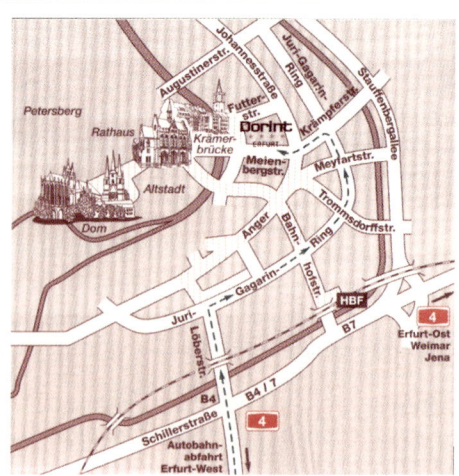

Rates 2002
With publication of this price-list all previous price-lists expire

Single Room	from	EUR	93,00	to	133,00
Double Room	from	EUR	51,50	to	71,50
Suite (1 or 2 persons)	from	EUR	163,61	to	194,29
Breakfast buffet / person		EUR	14,00		
Extra bed		EUR	25,00		
Half-board / person		EUR	20,00		
Full-board / person		EUR	38,00		
Pets		EUR	7,00		

Rates are including service charge and VAT. The use of the RELAX SPA is also included in the room rate.
Reservations will be held until 6.00 p.m. unless stated differently. Check-in time 2.30 p.m., check-out time 11.00 a.m.

Children accommodated in their parents' room:
Until 6 years   free of charge
Aged 7–11 years   EUR   17,90

Group rates
Special room rates for groups are available during certain periods:
January / February, July / August, November / December
Per person in a double room   EUR 39,00
Supplement for a single room   EUR 16,00

Restaurant & Bar
"Zum Rebstock": Breakfast and lunch buffet, afternoon coffee, dinner à la carte, Thuringian specialities
Wintergarden: Breakfast buffet, afternoon coffee
Lobby Bar: Light meals, drinks and cocktails

Function Rooms
All together 9 conference rooms are available, including one multi-purpose conference hall with a maximum seating capacity of 180. A choice of other private meeting and dining rooms for banquets, cocktails, conventions and social funtions can be provided.

22. Lektion

Explanation of symbols and abbreviations

Match each symbol and abbreviation with the correct explanation.

1 2 3 4 5 6 7 8 9 10
11 12 13 14 15 16 17 18 19 20
21 22 23 24 25 26 27 28 29 30

☐ Price for single room, incl. breakfast
☐ Price for double room, incl. breakfast
☐ Number of rooms
☐ Restaurant open all year round
☐ Closing-day, holiday close-down, restaurant
☐ Terrace / Garden
☐ Tips on leisure and cultural activities
☐ Centrally situated
☐ Quiet location
☐ Apartments / Suites
☐ Non-smoking rooms available on request
☐ Indoor swimming-pool
☐ Outdoor swimming-pool
☐ Indoor parking

☐ Outdoor parking
☐ Credit cards accepted
☐ Dogs allowed
☐ Minibar in the room
☐ TV-set in the room
☐ Suitable for use by the disabled
☐ Golf
☐ Tennis
☐ Indoor tennis courts
☐ Fitness facilities
☐ Children welcome
☐ Bicycle hire
☐ Massage treatments
☐ Beauty
☐ Conference and event facilities
☐ Audio-visual facilities

Form dialogues.

- one double room / one single for a handicapped person / parking / telephone
- one single room / diet cooking
- one double room with shower / two weeks / eat in the restaurant every evening

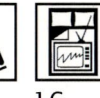

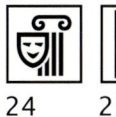

Brunch

Ask your partner:
What are the advantages of brunch?
Can you think of any disadvantages?

"Brunch" comes from America. It is a meal which combines "breakfast" and "lunch". It is usually on weekends and is served between ten o'clock in the morning and three o'clock in the afternoon. This gives guests a chance to sleep longer, without missing breakfast or lunch.

Brunch can be served in the form of a buffet, à la carte, or as a combination of both. Many restaurants vary theme and cuisine from season to season. The possibilities are virtually endless. Almost any dish can be served as long as it isn't too heavy.

The brunch buffet can simply be a table with hearty breakfast and light lunch dishes or it can be spread over a dozen semi-connected tables holding chafing dishes and action stations where cooks in uniform make omelets, fry up fajitas, carve roasts or dish out hot entrées. There can be beautifully composed salads, decadent cheese spreads, luscious breakfast breads, beautiful fruit displays, different kinds of salmon as well as smoked seafoods and big dessert spreads. For the most part, guests can heap their plates with breakfast staples like eggs Benedict, homefries or biscuits with sausage and gravy, or go for more lunchy items like roast meats and peel 'n' eat shrimp. More deluxe brunch buffets are served in a ballroom at Easter, on Mother's Day and other holidays. Simpler brunches are set up right in the kitchen. The possibilities are unlimited.

Brunch à la carte is only limited to the chef's fantasy. The menu can include any breakfast and lunch dishes. These are also served from late morning until early afternoon.

A combination of buffet and brunch offers the guests unlimited breakfast staples such as champagne, juices, breakfast breads, pancakes … at a buffet table and then the choice of an entrée.

All in all, brunch can be an exciting and different eating experience.

Unsere Ziele

Nach Bearbeitung dieses Kapitals sollten Sie

- die verschiedenen Arten von Brunch kennen;
- die Möglichkeiten kennen, mit den unterschiedlichen Arten von Brunch zu arbeiten.

23. Lektion

Dialogue

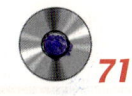

Listen and complete the conversation.

Head waiter: This morning we are going to set up _____ in the dining-room.

Apprentice waiter: What is brunch?

Head waiter: Brunch is a meal which combines _____ _____.

First of all we'll set up the buffet table. We'll need _____ and _____, _____, _____, coffee _____, dessert _____, and _____.

Apprentice waiter: And how will the tables be set?

Head waiter: We'll set them for an _____.

Now start bringing out the food: _____, _____ products, _____ and _____ fruit, _____ and _____ juices, _____, _____ and _____, bread, butter, marmalade, honey, _____.

Apprentice waiter: I think I have everything on the table now.

Head waiter: Yes, it looks very nice, but you forgot the _____ _____.

Apprentice waiter: I'm sorry, I'll get it at once.

Exercise

Fill in the numbers of the serving utensils.

1 bowls	5 dessert plates	9 warm plates	13 saucers *untertassen*
2 dessert spoons	6 spoons	10 cups	14 dessert knives
3 milk jug *Milchkrug*	7 salad forks	11 coffee / teaspoons	15 dessert forks
4 glasses	8 knives	12 serving spoon	16 nutcracker *Nussknacker*

Brunch Buffet

cereals	fruit juices	bread butter	chafing dishes for meat, eggs, fish	soup	cold cuts salads desserts pastries	breakfast beverage
16	4	14	8	12	5	11
2	15	13	9	6	5	
6	11		12	1	14	
7	10			10	15	
11					7	

Toasted Oat and Raisin Muffins

Using a ready-mixed crunchy cereal and a food processor speeds up the preparation of these muffins which can be served with bacon and eggs for breakfast.

Ingredients (for 8 to 12 muffins):

50 g (2 oz)	raisins
250 g (8oz)	crunchy toasted oat cereal
150 g (5oz)	selfraising superfine cake flour
1/2	teaspoon bicarbonate of soda
75 g (3oz)	butter
1	egg
250 ml (8fl oz)	buttermilk or fresh milk soured with
2	tablespoons lemon juice

Method:

Preheat the oven to gas mark 5/ 190C/375F. You will need a tray of 12 individual muffin tins. Grease and flour the tins. Sprinkle a few raisins in the base of each tin.
Put the crunchy cereal into the food processor and add the flour. Pulse for ten seconds, remove 2 tablespoons for the topping. Add the butter and bicarbonate of soda and pulse until the mixture is like fine breadcrumbs. Add the egg and buttermilk and pulse for a few seconds. It should form a soft batter. Spoon into the muffin tins. Sprinkle over the crunchy topping. Bake for 15 to 20 minutes. Cool for 5 minutes in the tin and serve warm.

23rd Lesson

Put together a brunch. Write a menu, or plan a buffet.

Eggs Benedict
are the perfect brunch food, requiring both skill in their preparation and a touch of decadence in their enjoyment.
The dish has two competing creation myths, but both agree that eggs Benedict originated in New York City just over a century ago. Today, eggs Benedict can be found across the world, with a number of universal and regional variations.

(http://www.brunch.org/eggsbenedict/)

Brunch Menu

Saturdays & Sundays between 11:30am and 3:30pm.

Champagne Brunch
Your champagne brunch includes the following:
A bottomless glass of champagne or Mimosa
Fresh-squeezed orange juice
Muffins
Country-style potatoes
Fresh sliced fruit
Ice cream sundae
Espresso or cappuccino
and your choice of entree

Old Fashioned Waffles
Served with butter and real maple syrup

Sirloin Tips & Eggs
3 eggs any style served with generous portion of tips, homefries & choice of toast

Traditional Eggs Benedict
Crispy English muffins are topped with Canadian bacon, poached eggs and homemade hollandaise, served with homefries

Omelet
Served with homefries & choice of toast
Choose 2: caramelized red onion, roasted peppers, mushrooms, zucchini, salsa, guacamole, tomato, sausage, Canadian bacon, cream cheese, American, Swiss, Montery Jack cheese, grilled chicken, sautéed shrimp, smoked salmon

Steak Burger
Served on a crusty roll with your choice of American, Swiss, or Montery Jack cheese, lettuce, tomato, red onion, pickle and a pile of fries

Chef's Veggie Burger
Grilled veggie burger served with your choice of American, Swiss or Montery Jack cheese, lettuce, tomato, red onion, pickle & fries

BBQ or Buffalo Chicken Sandwich
Double breast of chicken grilled and coated with our honey-garlic BBQ or Buffalo sauce served with your choice of American, Swiss or Montery Jack or Blue cheese, lettuce, tomato, red onion, pickle & fries

Breakfast Pasta
spaghetti tossed with tomatoes, goat cheese, scrambled eggs, garlic and herbs

23. Lektion

Dialogue

Listen and complete the dialogue.

Head waiter: Good afternoon!

Mr. Nelson: Good ... Oh, it's 12.30! I suppose we've missed breakfast this morning, haven't we? We were at the opera last night and we overslept.

Head waiter: Normally we don't serve breakfast at this time, but today we have a _____ .

Mr. Nelson: No, thank you. I really wanted some _____, _____, and a cup of _____ .

Head waiter: Sir, you can have that and a variety of other _____ at the brunch buffet.

Mr. Nelson: Could we take a look at the brunch buffet?

Head waiter: Yes, of course, just follow me. Here we are. As you can see, we have _____, _____, _____, _____ and rolls, _____, roast _____ and _____. Salads and _____ are over there. At this end of the table you'll find many _____ and _____.

Mr. Nelson: I don't know where to begin.

Head waiter: May I suggest a _____ and perhaps a _____ ? Then the excellent poached eggs. Just try a little of everything and don't miss the delicious pastries. Take your time, the buffet is open until two and _____ .

Mr. Nelson: We didn't miss breakfast after all, we're just combining it with lunch.

Find out the words.

LEECRAS — cereals

EAGREVEB — Beverage

FAGNICH SIHD — chafing dish

REISTPAS —

GRINVES ONOSP — Serving spoon

RLTUF — fruit

SERCUSA — sauces

ASDAL — salad

FKEARBTSA —

OCDL SCTU — cold cuts

Connect

1. Chicken à la King — cold cereal
2. omelette — 7 — breakfast beverage
3. cornflakes — vegetable
4. bananas — pastry
5. toast — soup
6. beef broth — egg dish
7. tea — warm cereal
8. tomatoes — bread
9. porridge — fruit
10. haddock — meat
11. bacon, ham — poultry
12. apple pie — fish

Dinner

Eat a variety of vegetables! To increase variety, try some that might be new to you, such as those from the cabbage family (broccoli, Brussels sprouts, cauliflower, and cabbage) dark-green leafy vegetables (spinach and kale), and yellow-orange vegetables (winter squash and sweet potatoes). For old favourites, like peas and green beans, skip the butter and sprinkle with lemon juice or herbs. Or, how about a baked potato with the skin and topped with low-fat yoghurt and chives, tomato salsa, or a small amount of low-fat cheese?

Try whole wheat pasta and casseroles made with brown rice and other grains. If you are careful with preparation, these dishes can be excellent sources of fiber and low in fat. For example, when milk and eggs are ingredients in a recipe, try using skim milk, reduce the number of egg yolks and replace with egg whites. Substitute whole-grain breads and rolls for white bread.

Choose main dishes that call for fish, chicken, turkey or lean meat. Don't forget to remove the skin and visible fat from poultry and trim the fat from meat.

Choose desserts that give you fiber but little fat such as baked apples or bananas, sprinkled with cinnamon, fresh fruit cup, brown bread or rice pudding made with skim milk, oatmeal cookies (made with margarine or vegetable oil; add raisins).

So you can reduce your risk of heart disease and cancer. Keep in mind that staying healthy requires more than just good nutrition. Regular exercise, getting enough rest, learning to cope with stress, and having regular physical checkups are important ways to help ensure good health.

What healthy dishes are offered in your restaurant / hotel? Do you have any special dishes for vegetarians on your menu?

Talk about the advantages / disadvantages of low fat food.

Unsere Ziele

Nach Bearbeitung dieses Kapitals sollten Sie

- internationale Speisen nennen und erklären können;
- eine Weinempfehlung abgeben können;
- Speisen mit den dazu passenden Weinen anbieten können.

24. Lektion

Menu

Starters

Lobster Medaillons in Champagne Jelly

Pike-Perch Terrine on Watercress Sabayon

Raw Ham with Pickled Wild Vegetables

Scottish Smoked Salmon with Parfait of Caviar

Homemade Goose Liver with Jelly of "Gewürztraminer"

Gourmet Salad (Salad Leaves with Quail Praline, Goose liver, Quail Egg, Fillet of Rabbit)

Beluga Caviar on Ice with Blinis and Sour Cream

Soups

Consommé with Vegetable Strudel and Marrow

Viennese Potato Soup

Lobster Bisque with Aniseed Bread

Cold Melon Soup with Portwine Sorbet

Fish and Crustaceans

Salmon Fillet with Chive Cream

Variations of Fish of the Region on Vegetable Stripes

Sole Spirals with Zucchini Butter

Main Courses

Veal Fillet in Morel Sauce, Buttered Noodles and Vegetables

Lamb in Crust of "Fines Herbes" and Glazed Shallots

Beef Medaillons in Merlot Sauce, Bouquet of Vegetables

Beef Fillet "Mignons" with Pepper Sauce, Noodles "Fines Herbes"

Fillet of Pork on Mustard Seedlings, Potato Noodles

Breast of Duck with Apples "Confit"

Breast of Chicken on Morels and Leeks, Potato Galettes

Main Courses for two Persons

Double Fillet of Beef, Vegetable Garnish, Béarnaise Sauce

Roast Guinea-Fowl with Savoy Cabbage and Corn Pancakes

Desserts

Flamed Strawberries with Green Peppercorns

Ice Cream or Sherbet

Honey Parfait with Raspberry Sauce

French Chocolate Mousse with Gooseberries

Fresh Fruit

Baked Pancakes with Morello Sauce

Cheese from the Cheese Bar

Scottish Salmon

Ingredients

whole salmon or salmon steaks
black pepper
salt
a little butter

Method

Make sure the salmon is clean then rub butter sparingly into the skin of the whole fish or dot the steaks with a little butter. The fish can be gently poached in just enough water to cover it, allowing 15 minutes per pound.

If you want to bake the fish, wrap the whole fish in foil (making sure that there are no leakage points) or place the steaks in an oven-proof glass dish and cover with foil. The fish will take about 15 minutes per pound in a moderate conventional oven, or 5 minutes per pound in a medium microwave. If you are using a microwave, remember to cover the tail of the salmon with foil until the last 10 minutes, since it will cook much faster than the body of the fish. The whole fish will not need to be wrapped as the skin acts as a natural cling film; a dish of salmon steaks to be cooked in a microwave should be covered in cling film, not foil.

Salmon steaks are ideal cooked for 7 hours in the slow-cooker covered with just enough water and a dash of milk.

Now that salmon has become a luxury dish, it seems strange to think that it was once so plentiful that it frequently formed part of farmworkers' wages and featured in the rural diet with monotonous regularity.

Enjoy it served hot or cold, with fennel and baked potatoes, or with salad.

Dialogue 73

Listen and note the orders.

Mr. Wilson

Mrs. Wilson

24th Lesson

To learn
dry
medium dry
medium sweet
sweet
fruity
heavy
light
full-bodied
refreshing

Choose wines from the wine list corresponding to the dishes.

- Lobster Medallions in Champagne Jelly (dry, light wine)
- Raw Ham with Pickled Wild Vegetables (light, dry, refreshing wine)
- Salmon Fillet with Chive Cream (medium dry wine)
- Lamb in Crust of "Fines Herbes" and Glazed Shallots (dry, heavy wine)
- Breast of Duck with Apples "Confit" (heavy wine)
- Honey Parfait with Raspberry Sauce (sweet wine)

Aperitifs

Sherry (Dry, Medium, Sweet)
Portwine (White)
Campari
Vermouth Martini
(Extra Dry, Dry, Rosso)
Kir Royal

Wines

French wines

White Burgundy
Chablis
Grand Cru Valmur
Paul Dorin, Chablis
Dry, Light

White Bordeaux
Château d'Yquem
Grand Premier Cru Classé
Château d'Yquem, Sauternes
Sweet, Heavy

Château Olivier
Grand Cru Classé Blanc
Château Olivier, Léognan
Medium Dry

Red Burgundy
Clos de Vougeot
Appellation Clos de Vougeot Côntrollé
Domaine Tortochot, Côte de Nuits
Dry, Heavy

Moulin-à-Vent
Appellation Moulin-à-Vent Côntrollé
Georges Duboeuf, Beaujolais
Light, Medium Dry

Red Bordeaux
Château Lafite-Rothschild
Premier Grand Cru Classé

Pauillac/Médoc
Heavy, Full-bodied

Château Pétrus
Appellation Pomerol Côntrollé
Pomerol
Heavy, Full-bodied

German wines
(Hock & Mosel)
Liebfrauenmilch Q. b. A.
Weingut Scholl & Hillebrand,
Rüdesheim am Rhein
Medium Sweet

Kröver Herrenberg Q. b. A.
Weingut Rudolf Müller,
Kröv-Kövenig/Mosel
Medium Sweet

Austrian wines
Grüner Veltliner
Ried Hinter der Burg
Weingut Prager, Weißenkirchen/Wachau
Light, Dry, Refreshing

Blauer Burgunder
Weingut Stiegelmar,
Gols/Neusiedler See
Dry, Heavy

Digestifs

Cognac
Armagnac
Grand Marnier
Cointreau
Barack Palinka
Calvados

Dialogue

Listen and note the orders.

Mr. Wilson

Mrs. Wilson

74

24. Lektion

Which wine goes well with ...?

Hors d'œuvres, salads, cold meats:	Strong white wine: *Traminer*, the medium-sweet German wines, white *Burgundy* or *Rosé: Cabernet, Rosé d'Anjou*
Soups:	*Sherry* or a light *Madeira* with consommé or any dry white wine
Shellfish (served in rich sauce or garnished):	Dry white: *Graces, Chablis*, white *Burgundy* or *Champagne*, or Rhine wine or *Moselle*.
Shellfish (plain or grilled):	Mellow white, like *Sauternes* for sweeter sauces
Fish (plain):	Dry, light white: *Chablis* (traditional with oysters), *Riesling*, especially *Moselles*, young white *Burgundy Aligoté*
Fish (with cream or wine-based sauces):	Light dry white as above
Grilled and roasted dark meats:	Fairly fruity, robust: *Traminer*, white *Bordeaux*, *Valpolicella, Riesling, Hermitage blanc*
Casseroles and stews (dark meats):	Medium, not-to-heavy reds: any good *Bordeaux*, or *Burgundy*, Californian *Cabernet Sauvignon*
Poultry (plain cooked or roasted):	Heavy, full-bodied reds: *Burgundy, Rhône, Beaujolais, Chianti*
Poultry with rich garnish or stuffing):	Heavy white: white *Burgundy*, Alsatian or Hungarian *Riesling, Traminer*
White meat:	Light, dry red: *Beaujolais, Barolo, Bardolino* (particularly good with fatty birds like duck and goose)
Game birds:	Full bodied dry or medium-dry white wine: white *Rioja*, *Graves*, white *Burgundy* or Light-bodied red: *Entre-Deux-Mers, Côtes du Rhône*, or *Rosé* (for pork and ham): *Côtes de Provence, Tavel*
Game:	Full-bodied red: *Chianti*, red *Burgundy, Bordeaux, Rhône*
Soft cheese, like Brie:	Strong, robust red: mature red *Rhône, Rioja, Burgundy*
	Fine, light red: *Bordeaux*
Hard and medium cheese, like Cheddar	Light, fruity red: *Beaujolais*, or Strong white: *Soave, Alsace, Loire*

Attention

"some" with affirmative verbs:
e.g. I'll have **some** fish.

"any" with negatives and questions:
e.g. We havn't **any** sole.

Do you have **any** vegetarian dishes?

But for questions with polite forms use "some":
e.g. Would you like **some** fish?

Dialogue 🖸 75

Listen to the waiter reading orders to the sous-chef and fill in the table below.

Table number	17	6	11
Fish dish			
Meat dish			
Side dish			

25th Lesson

Austrian and German Cooking

? *Which countries do the dishes in your restaurant come from?*

German dishes can be found everywhere in Germany – however, a specific German cuisine does not exist. For a nation existing throughout centuries within constantly changing borders and being influenced by foreign elements this is not very much astonishing. According to eating habits the foreign borders of Germany are less important than the inner-German partition into culinary regions.

But there certainly is one joint basis which was also kept during the 40 years of division. The national menu is a composition of various types of regional cuisines. Each region has developed its own delicious specialities, which are based upon the climate and the main products – plants and animals as well – of that particular region.

Especially in the border regions close relations to neighbouring eating and cooking preferences can be met. If you look to the Saarland and Alsace or Bavaria and Austria, you can find some similarities in the ingredients.

? *Do you know the origin of the German specialities you offer in your restaurant?*

Unsere Ziele

Nach Bearbeitung dieses Kapitals sollten Sie

- bekannte deutsche und österreichische Spezialitäten auf Englisch übersetzen können;
- dem Englisch sprechenden Gast deutsche und österreichische Regionalspeisen erklären können.

25. Lektion

Dialogues
Listen and complete the dialogues.

🔘 76–79

To learn
I'd / May I recommend ...
I can offer you ...
Our speciality is ...
Today we have ...
I'd suggest ...

76

Waiter: Good afternoon! _____?

Guest: Good afternoon! Perhaps you can help me. I'm staying in Austria _____ and I would like to try some of the _____ I've heard so much about.

Waiter: I'd be pleased to help you, madam. Let me see. There is _____ _____.

77

Waiter: Would you like to start with _____ or _____?

Guest: I'd like to have _____ .

Waiter: I would recommend a "Leberknödelsuppe", that is _____ _____.

Guest: I've never had anything like that before. _____

78

Guest: What Austrian speciality would you recommend for _____ today?

Waiter: A "Wiener Schnitzel" is the most _____.

Guest: What is a "Wiener Schnitzel"?

Waiter: It is a _____ usually served with _____.

79

Waiter: We have a reasonably priced table d'hôte meal. Today it is "Frittatensuppe", _____ with _____ _____ , and "Tafelspitz", which is _____ _____ with _____ and _____ _____. For dessert there is _____ _____ .

Guest: That sounds good. Thank you!

= set meal / daily special
meal at a fixed price

set lunch
set dinner

25th Lesson

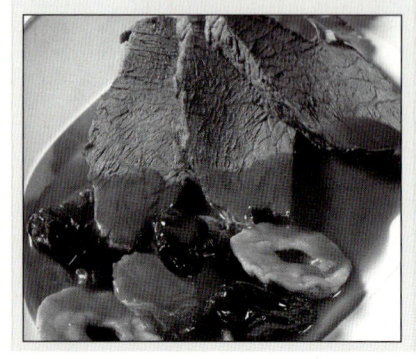

Exercise

Imagine you and your partner want to open a new restaurant with famous German specialities.
Discuss your menu. Which dishes would you choose as starters, soups, main courses, children's dishes and desserts? You can add any new ideas yourself.

Baden-Württemberg

Käsespätzle	cheese spaetzli	Badischer Hecht	pike Baden style
Maultaschen	kind of ravioli	Schwarzwälder Kirschtorte	Black Forest cake

Bavaria

Leberknödelsuppe	liver dumpling soup	Weißwürste	white sausages
Schweinshaxe mit Sauerkraut	knuckle of pork with sauerkraut	mit süßem Senf	with sweet mustard
Nürnberger Lebkuchen	Nuremberg ginger-bread	Pichelsteiner	beef stew Pichelstein

Hamburg and Schleswig-Holstein

Hamburger Aalsuppe	eel soup Hamburg style	Lübecker Marzipan	marchpane from Lübeck
Rote Grütze	red grit		

Bremen and Lower Saxony

Grünkohl mit Pinkel	green cabbage with smoked sausage	Labskaus	salted meat and herring

Hesse

Frankfurter Würstchen	Frankfurt sausages	Handkäs mit Musik	Harz cheese marinated with onions, oil, vinegar
Grüne Soße	green (herb) sauce		

Thuringia

Thüringer Klöße	Thuringian potato dumplings	Rotkohlroulade	red cabbage roll
Thüringer Rostbratwurst	Thuringian fried sausage		

Saxony and Saxony-Anhalt

Leipziger Allerlei	Leipzig hotchpotch	Halberstädter Birnenklöße	pear dumplings
Dresdner Christstollen	Christmas yeast cake	Eierschecke	curd cake with egg mousseline

Berlin and Brandenburg

Kartoffelsuppe mit Bockwurst	potato soup with sausage	Berliner (Pfannkuchen)	doughnut Berlin style
Kalbsleber Berliner Art	calf's liver Berlin style	Teltower Rübchen	Teltow turnips
		Spreewälder Gurken	salted gherkins from Spreewald

Mecklenburg-Westpomerania

Schnippelbohnen	French beans	Tollatschen	sweet mash of pork's blood and raisins
Hering in Sahnstipp	herring in cream sauce		

Saarland and Rhineland-Palatinate

Gefüllter Pfälzer Saumagen	stuffed stomach of pork	Gefillte Knepp (gefüllte Kartoffeln)	potato dumplings stuffed with minced beef

North Rhine-Westphalia

Westfälischer Pfeffer-Potthast	beef stew with pepper and herbs	Rheinischer Sauerbraten	beef soaked in vinegar with raisins
Himmel und Erde	mashed potatoes, apples with black pudding		

110

25. Lektion

Exercise

An American guest wants to try some dishes from your region. Offer him or her "Specialities of the day" from your menu. Explain the different dishes to him or her.

Which dish is it?

1. Dumplings made of raw and cooked potatoes, filled with croutons, eaten with roast any style and a lot of gravy.

2. Vegetable mix of carrots, peas, asparagus tips, cauliflower, kohlrabi, morels, freshwater-crayfish tails in a sauce of butter and flour with nutmeg, side dish for steaks or escalopes etc.

3. A soup with eel and vegetables in season, fruits like prunes, apples or pears, traditionally flavoured with 7 different herbs: a choice of parsley, thyme, marjoram, basil, tarragon, chervil, sage or savory.

4. Old seamen's dish with pickled beef, potatoes, beetroot and herring – everything mashed and served with a fried egg.

5. A cold sauce of sour and sweet cream, mayonnaise and curd with onions and herbs: chives, dill, chervil, basil, cress, burnet, a bit of tarragon.

6. Kind of ravioli, noodle paste stuffed with spinach and minced meat, can be served in bouillon or cut into stripes and fried in butter.

7. A mix of spicy and sweet ingredience: breadcrumbs, flour, lard, pork's blood, apples, raisins – flavoured with sugar, cinnamon, thyme, cardamom, anise.

8. Calf's liver with onion rings and apples, served with mashed potatoes.

9. Stomach of pork stuffed with dices of pork, beef, smoked bacon, potatoes – pot herbs, nutmeg, marjoram and pimento as flavourings, served with sauerkraut and farmer's bread.

10. Beef stew with a lot of pepper, cooked with bay leaves, pimento, lemon and onions served with boiled potatoes.

11. Kind of soup or stew with different types of meat (beef, pork, mutton) and vegetables like potatoes, leek, carrots, celery and parsley.

Where does the dish come from?

1.
2.
3.
4.
5.
6.
7.
8.
9.
10.
11.

Which Austrian and German specialities do you offer at your restaurant?

Make up your own dialogue: Offer a 3-course-dinner and German wines.

26th Lesson

Cooking all around the World

The world is a fascinating mosaic of landscapes, climates, peoples, cultures and ways of life. But no matter where in the world, there is one inexhaustible aspect of everyday life that never dulls, namely the simple pleasure of eating and drinking.

Unsere Ziele

Nach Bearbeitung dieses Kapitels sollten Sie

- internationale Menüs zusammenstellen und übersetzen können,
- Rezepte ausländischer Spezialitäten erstellen bzw. übersetzen können,
- die wichtigsten Mitglieder der Brigade einer internationalen Küche benennen können.
- die Anforderungen an Sie als Mitarbeiter bei Banketten sowie Konferenzen und Tagungen nennen können.

Read

Do you remember the kitchen staff?
The chef (chef de cuisine), the assistant chef (sous chef), the sauce cook (saucier), the larder cook (garde-manger), the fish cook (poissonnier), the vegetable cook (entremetier), the pastry cook (patissier), the kitchen assistant (aide de cuisine) and the apprentice cook (apprenti) work in international kitchens.

Do you remember their duties?

What kitchen staff is in your restaurant / hotel?

Recipe

Chinese chicken

360 g	Chinese lettuce leaves	
2 sticks	celery, washed and sliced	
2 medium	oranges	
2	cooked chicken joints	
6	spring onions	

For the dressing:

1 clove of	garlic, peeled and crushed
25 ml	soy sauce
5 ml	castor sugar
12.5 ml	grated fresh root ginger

Shred the Chinese lettuce leaves and place in a bowl. Add the celery. Peel the oranges with a sharp knife and then cut into segments. Remove the skin and bones from the chicken joints and cut the chicken into shreds. Toss into the salad with the orange pieces. Cut the spring onions into quarters lengthways and add to the chicken. Spoon into a serving bowl or individual serving dishes.
To make the dressing: Whisk all the dressing ingredients together and spoon over the salad just before serving.

To learn

lettuce leaves
to slice
spring onion
a clove of garlic
to peel
to crush
castor sugar
to grate
ginger
to shred
to toss
to whisk

Write down your favourite recipe.

Then tell your classmates which ingredients you need and how you prepare it. Don't tell them what it is. They should be able to guess what you are talking about.

British specialities

Due to the climate, British cooking tends to be warming and filling. Breakfast, afternoon tea and high tea are examples of meals peculiar to Britain. Selections of some British foods and dishes are given below.

English

Potted shrimps
Fried cod and chips
Fish cakes
Roast beef and Yorkshire pudding with horseradish sauce
Roast lamb with mint sauce

Steak and kidney pie	– a pie covering of short or puff pastry
Steak and kidney pudding	– a suet pastry meat pudding
Cornish pastry	– a pastry containing potatoes, vegetables and meat
Apple pie	– apples covered with short pastry
Trifle	– layers of fruit, sponge, custard and cream
Treacle pudding	– a steamed sponge pudding
Fool	– a purée of mixed fruit with whipped cream
Chelsea buns	– a yeast bun containing dried fruit
Worcestershire sauce	– a bottled spicy sauce used with meat dishes

Make up short dialogues. Use some of the British specialities and the explanations.

26th Lesson

A Taste of McDonald's Around the World

Internationally, the restaurants offer standard menu items, and occasionally develop other items which appeal to the host country's cultural preferences. For example, some McDonald's restaurants serve rice dishes and fried chicken in Japan; beer in Germany; Kiwi burgers in New Zealand; spaghetti in the Philippines; salmon sandwiches, called "McLaks", in Norway; and in Islamic countries, like Saudi Arabia, the restaurants offer a "Halal" Menu.

Translate these two special dinners with your classmate.

Fill in

Fill in the missing countries. The text will help you.

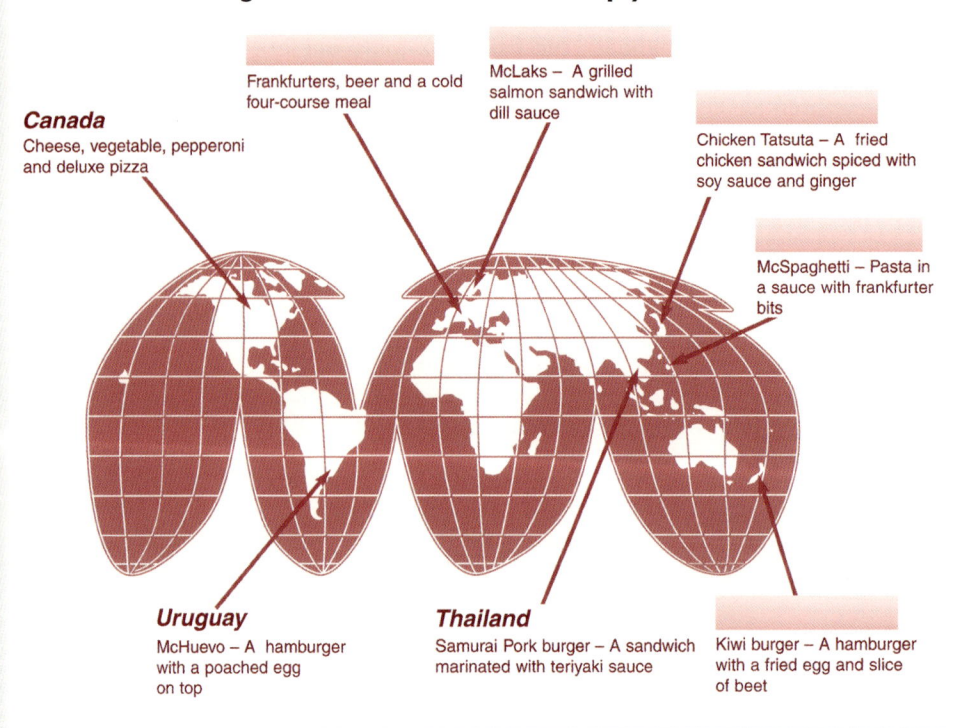

Canada
Cheese, vegetable, pepperoni and deluxe pizza

Frankfurters, beer and a cold four-course meal

McLaks – A grilled salmon sandwich with dill sauce

Chicken Tatsuta – A fried chicken sandwich spiced with soy sauce and ginger

McSpaghetti – Pasta in a sauce with frankfurter bits

Uruguay
McHuevo – A hamburger with a poached egg on top

Thailand
Samurai Pork burger – A sandwich marinated with teriyaki sauce

Kiwi burger – A hamburger with a fried egg and slice of beet

New Year's Dinner for Two

Brie and Mushroom Tartlets

Chablis
Grand Cru Valmur
Paul Dorin, Chablis

Beef, Chicken and Vegetable Fondue
Curry and Chutney Sauce
Roasted Red Pepper Sauce

Wild Rice with Carrots and Onions, Spinach, Fennel, and Pink Grapefruit Salad

Raspberry Oatmeal Lace Cookies
Chocolate Mint Truffles

A Midnight Supper

Cocktails

Paprika Shrimp Butter
Salmon and Green Peppercorn Butter
Crackers
Fennel Crudités

Staton Hills Vineyard
Yakima Valley
Johannisberg Riesling

Apricot-Glazed Ham
Maple Mustard Sauce

Moet & Chandon White Star
Extra Dry Champagne

Orzo Parsley Gratin
Coleslaw with Hot Caraway Vinaigrette
Corn and Molasses Rolls

Lemon Lime Mousse
Cinnamon Crisp Pecans

Menu

Starters

Fresh Oysters on the Half Shell
Lobster or Shrimp Cocktail
Fresh Fruit Cocktail Supreme
(Supreme of Fresh Fruits and Berries)
Scotch Salmon
(Smoked and Cured to our Specifications)
The Menu Grazers' Combination
(Lobster Medallions, Oysters, Sevruga Caviar and our own Smoked Salmon)
Chef's Pâté Selection
(With Cumberland Sauce)

Soups

Soup of the Day
(Our Chef's Special Preparation from the Freshest Ingredients)
Onion Soup
(Topped with Cheddar Cheese)
Clear Oxtail Soup

From the Sea

Key West
(Shrimp, Mussels, Snapper in Spicy Coconut Sauce)
Steamed Lobster
(With Parsley Potatoes and Drawn Butter)
Fillet of Dover Sole
(Sautéed and Served with Lemon Butter Sauce)
Snapper Lafayette
(Gulf Red Snapper, Panfried and Topped with Crab meat)
Grilled Salmon Steak
(Grilled with Garden Herb or Hollandaise Sauce)

From the Land

Broiled Baby Chicken Mercado
(Accompanied with Sautéed Onions and Peppers)
Roast Duckling
(Crispy Duckling with Orange Sauce, Red Cabbage and Potato Croquette)
Center Cut Pork Chops
(Mashed Potatoes, Gravy)
Veal Zurichoise
(Veal Tips, Sautéed with Shallots, Mushrooms in a Cream Sauce)
New York Steak 10 oz
(Choice of Steak, Butter Sauce)
Rib Eye Steak
(Center Cut Prime Rib with Choron Sauce)
Medaillons of Beef
(Three Little Fillets with Bordelaise Sauce)

Desserts

Classic Apple Pie
Vanilla Cheese Cake
Fresh Fruit Tart
Chocolate Mousse
Black Forest Cake
Caramel Custard
Peppermint Ice Cream
Soufflé Grand Marnier
Cheese from the Trolley

Arrange a 5-course-dinner for a special event. Use the menu.

26th Lesson

Role and Function of Personnel of a Traditional Kitchen

In many establishments it is necessary for staff to be working to provide meals throughout the day and, in some cases, split shifts. The split-shift system is operated so that most staff are available for both lunch and dinner. With this system the working hours will be, for example, from 9.30 a.m. to 2.30 p.m. and 6 p.m. to 10 p.m. Some establishments operate two shifts to cover the lunch and dinner service, with one shift working from 8 a.m. to 4 p.m. and the other from 4 p.m. to 11 p.m. Under the two-shift system the **partie** will have a **chef de partie** in charge of one shift and a **demi chef de partie** responsible for the other shift.

Head chef (le chef de cuisine)

In large establishments the duties of the executive chef, chef de cuisine, head chef or person in charge, are mainly administrative. The function of the chef is to:
a) organize the kitchen,
b) compile the menus,
c) order the foodstuffs,
d) show the required profit,
e) engage the staff,
f) supervise the kitchen (particularly at service time),
g) advise on purchase of equipment,
h) be responsible, in many cases, either wholly or partially, for the stores, still-room and the washing up of silver, crockery etc.

Second chef (le sous chef)

The second chef is the chef's "right hand", whose main function is to supervise the work in the kitchen so that it runs smoothly and according to the chef's wishes. In large kitchens there may be several souschefs with specific responsibility for separate services such as banquets and grill room.

Chef de partie

The chefs de partie organize their own sections, delegate the work to assistants and are, in fact, the "backbone" of the kitchen.

Assistant cooks (les commis chefs)

The chefs de partie are assisted by commis or assistants. The first commis is usually capable of taking over a great deal of the responsibility, and in some cases will take charge of the party when the chef is off duty.

Sauce party (le saucier)

The sauce cook prepares the entrées, i.e. all the meat, poultry and game dishes which are not roasted or grilled. This includes all made-up dishes, such as vol-au-vents, stews, and braised, boiled, poêled and sautéed dishes. The sauce cook will prepare certain garnishes for these dishes and make the meat, poultry and game sauces.

Roast party (le rôtisseur)

All roasted and grilled meat, poultry and game are cooked by the roast cooks. All grilled and deep-fried fish and other deep-fried foods, including potatoes, are also cooked by this party, as well as many savouries. The work of the rôtisseur includes the garnishing of the grills and roasts.

Fish party (le poissonnier)

Except for grilled and deep-fried fish, all the fish dishes and fish sauces and garnishes are cooked by this party, as well as béchamel, hollandaise sauce and melted butter.

Vegetable party (l'entremetier)

All the vegetables and potatoes, other than those which are deep-fried, and the egg and farinaceous dishes are the responsibility of the vegetable party as well as the vegetable garnishes to the main dishes. Such things as soups, savoury soufflés and, in some places, pancakes will be cooked by this party.

Apprentice (l'apprenti)

The apprentice is learning the trade and is moved to each of the parties to gain knowledge of all the sections in the kitchen.

Baker (le boulanger)

The baker makes all the bread, rolls, croissants etc., but few hotels today employ their own bakers.

Relief cook (le chef tournant)

The chef tournant usually relieves the chefs of the sauce, roast, fish, and vegetable parties on their day off. The first commis in the larder and pastry usually relieves his own chef. In some places a commis tournant will also be employed.

26. Lektion

Soup party (le potager)

In large establishments there is a separate party to make the soups and their garnishes.

Larder party (le garde-manger)

The larder is mainly concerned with the preparation of food which is cooked by the other parties. This includes the preparation of poultry and game and, in smaller establishments, the preparation of meat. The fish is prepared by a fishmonger in the larder by cleaning, filleting and portioning, although most establishments now order ready prepared fillets of fish.
All the cold soups, egg, fish, meat, poultry and game dishes are decorated and served by this party. Cold sauces, sandwiches and certain work for cocktail parties, such as canapés and the filling to bouchées, are done here.

Pastry party (le pâtissier)

All the sweets and pastries are made by the pastry cooks, as well as items required by other parties, such as vol-au-vents, bouchées, noodles etc. and also the covering for meat and poultry dishes.
The bakery goods, such as croissants, brioche etc., may be made by the pastry cook, when there is no separate bakery.

Duty cook (le chef de garde)

The duty cook is employed where split duty is involved. This chef does any orders in the kitchen during that time when most of the staff is off duty and also for the late period when the other staff has gone home.

Night cook (le chef de nuit)

A night cook is employed to be on duty part of the night and all night if necessary to provide late meals.

Staff cook (le communard)

The staff cook provides the meals for the employees.

Crossword puzzle

Across:
1. He prepares the entrées and sauces.
2. She makes all vegetables and potatoes.
3. He works in the dining and grill room.
4. Her job is to provide the meals for the employees.
5. His job is to make all cuts ready for cooking.
6. She prepares the soups.
7. Her job is to prepare the fish dishes.

Down:
8. All sweets and pastries are made by this cook.
9. He cooks all roasted meat, poultry and game.
10. His job is to relief the chefs de partie on their day off.
11. She is on duty when most of the staff is off.
12. Bread and rolls are made by him.
13. Cold dishes (sauces, eggs, fish etc.) are made by this cook.
14. He is on duty in the night.

Organizing a Banquet

Listen and fill in the function sheet

🔊 80

FUNCTION SHEET

Kind of catering / room: _____

_____

Date: _____

Time: _____

Persons: _____

Name of host, firm, note to: _____

Address: _____

Telephone / E-mail / Fax: _____

Order: _____

      Drinks: Menu:

_____

_____

_____

_____

_____

_____

Extras: _____

_____

Price per person: _____

Rent for room: _____

Specials:

Decoration: _____

Table figure: _____

Music: _____

Sitting order / Table cards: _____

Before dinner drinks: _____

After dinner drinks: _____

Technical equipment: _____

_____

(Loudspeaker, computer / internet, flip-chart, overhead projector, film projector, video, television, lectern, camera)

    Signature of the host: **For the hotel:**

_____

Deposit in €: _____ in words: _____

Issued to: kitchen, store, purchase, restaurant, laundry, wardrobe, concierge, personnel management, management, housekeeping

---

👥 **Plan two five-course-dinners for the wedding reception. Suggest the corresponding wines.**

👥 **Take the part of the banquet manager and organize a birthday party / a conference / a business meeting. Play the scene with your classmate.**

26. Lektion

Fill in

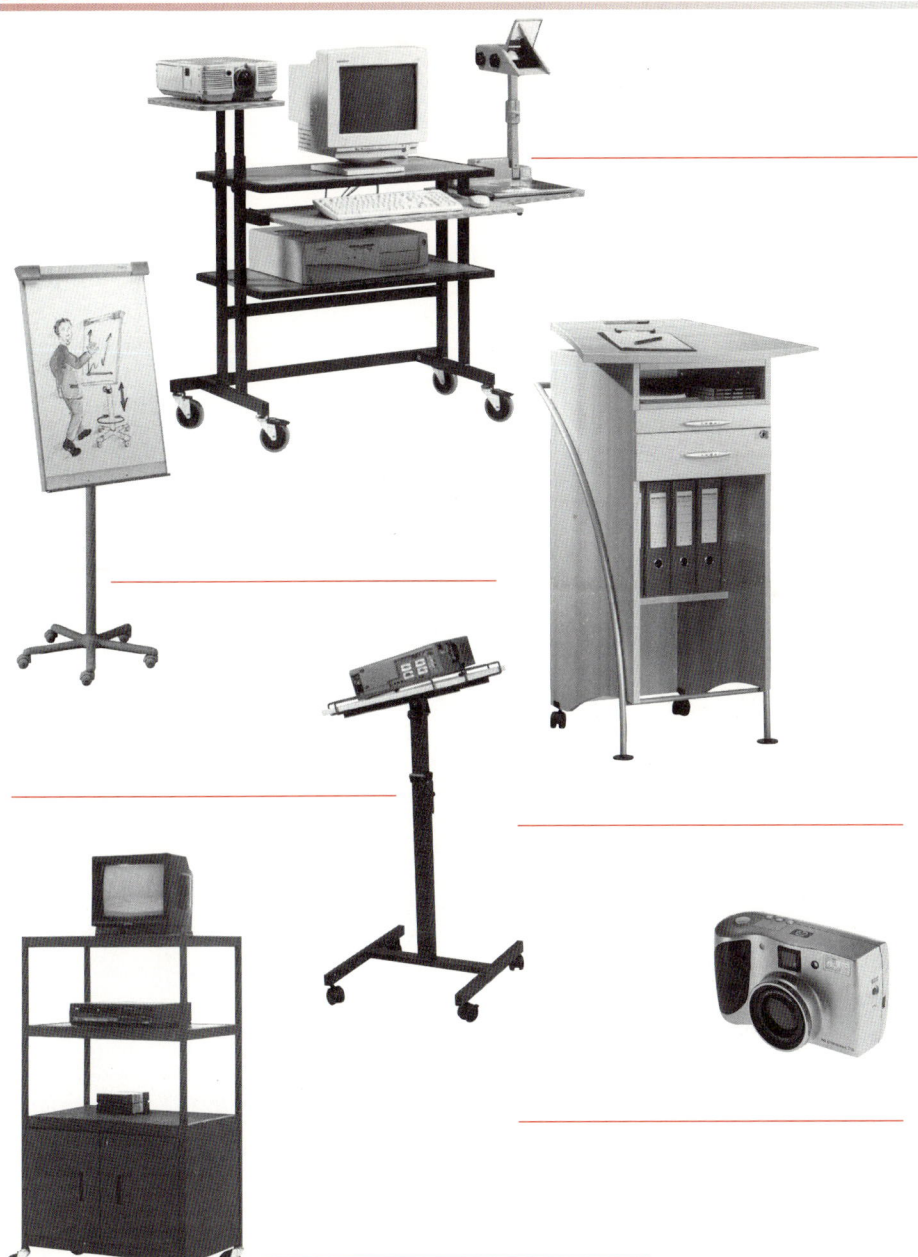

To learn

flip-chart
slide projector
video
computer / internet
overhead projector
digital camera
public address system
lectern

types of meetings

workshop
product launch
formal dinner
press conference
seminar
speech
lecture
wedding reception

Look at these plans of seating arrangements. What type of meeting are they suitable for? Make a list of meetings and suitable arrangements. Discuss them with your classmate.

schoolroom-style

boardroom-style

banqueting-style

E-shape-style

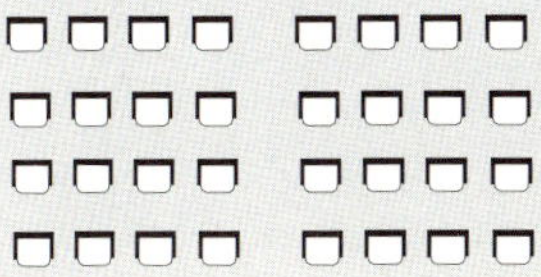

theatre-style

Meeting room requirements / facilities

horseshoe

27th Lesson

Eating Habits

Travelling in foreign countries always shows us, how different people live and eat. Each country has its own eating habits and favourites. In areas where the people's life is influenced strongly by religion, many dishes are not allowed to be eaten or they have to be prepared in a special way. Working in the tourism trade it is necessary to be aware of foreign customs and habits to satisfy the guests.

Unsere Ziele

Nach Bearbeitung dieses Kapitels sollten Sie

- *die verschiedenen Verbote der einzelnen Religionen nennen können;*
- *Menüs für verschiedene Bedürfnisse zusammenstellen können;*
- *europäische Essgewohnheiten beschreiben können.*

27. Lektion

Dialogue 81

Ann Taylor, a tour group leader, is discussing the eating arrangements for the farewell dinner of her group with Michael York, the assistant chef at the Palace Hotel.

Listen to the dialogue and complete.

farewell dinner on	
group coming back from	
special meals for	members of the group
	four two one
set dinner without	

Explain these expressions to your partner. Do you know other expressions like these?

vegetarian
diabetic

Read

Religion forbids

All customers of a hotel must be satisfied of whatever religion or state of health they are. There are many problems involved in preparing meals for Muslims, Hindus or Jews.
All **Muslims** are forbidden to eat pork, bacon, ham or any food containing pork in any form. **Hindus** do not eat beef or veal, which unfortunately cuts out some of Europe's most superb dishes. **Jewish cooking** ("kosher" food) is much more complicated. It follows the strict dietary laws and traditions laid down according to the Jewish religion. These laws control the origin and preparation of a dish and lay down whether they are "kosher" and so allowed to be eaten or not. Blood must not be eaten, and that means that animals have to be slaughtered in a way that blood is completely drained out of the animal. This is done with a special, very sharp knife. Pork, shark, eel and shrimps are also forbidden as well as the hindquarters of animals (that cuts out oxtail soup, for example).
Another prohibition is the use of milk and meat together. Staff is not allowed to mix meat and milk equipment either in the kitchen or in the service area. They also have to be cleaned separately. Very religious Jews even have their own dishwashers for each equipment in their private households. For the preparation of food you must not use lard, you have to take vegetable oil.

kosher
Jewish expression for pure or clean

Practise

Classify the following foodstuff into the religion that forbids it.

	Muslims	Jews	Hindus
pork			
beef			
ham			
shellfish			
blood			
animals' hindquarters			
milk and meat together			
lard			
bacon			
veal			
eel			

Where do your guests come from? Do they have any special wishes for their meals?

Plan a three-course set meal for each regarding the religion rules:

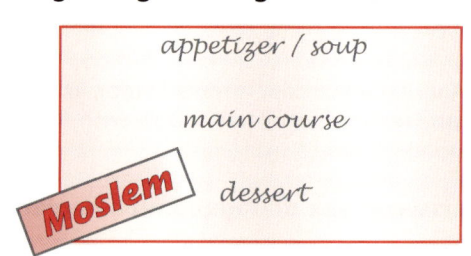

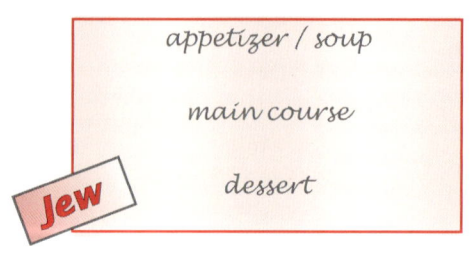

Hindu
- appetizer / soup
- main course
- dessert

Moslem
- appetizer / soup
- main course
- dessert

Jew
- appetizer / soup
- main course
- dessert

Read

Eating in Europe

Belgium

For small meals visit one of the cafés. They serve rich soups and sandwiches. For dinner seafood or meat is eaten (especially beef steak). With nearly all meals chips are served and beer is often used for cooking. Belgium is famous for its many sorts of beer.

Italy

Many popular dishes are based on pasta. They are very substantial. Very famous is "Minestrone", an excellent vegetable soup. The appetizers (antipasti) are delicious.

Spain

For the preparation of many dishes olive oil is used and rice is the main ingredient of many dishes (paella, for example). Tortillas are also very popular.

France

In French cuisine a much wider range of meat is used than in all other European cuisines. This includes poultry such as duck, goose, turkey, then lamb (but not as much as in Great Britain) and a lot of game like hare, wild boar, roe, but also domesticated rabbit. Except for nouvelle cuisine, the sauces are considered the essence of French cuisine. They bring the characteristic taste to a specific dish. French sauces in general are more elegant in taste than sauces in the rest of the world. They essentially owe their elegance to two ingredients: cream and wine. Other common ingredients are a meat or fish stock, butter, flour, tomatoes, carrots, onions, bacon, thyme, and bay leaf.

Great Britain

In the last years many foreign dishes have become popular in Great Britain. Britain itself is famous for its English breakfast. Visitors from abroad will find it terrific. After having had a good English breakfast in a hotel or at a bed and breakfast accommodation, you only will need a sandwich for lunch.

Another British speciality is "High tea". To enjoy it you must visit the countryside. Tea is served strong and with milk and sugar. It comes with ham, cheese, cucumbers, fried chicken and sandwiches, and there may also be served an assortment of pies, fruit cakes, muffins and scones with jam and cream. It is often eaten instead of a dinner.

For dinner the English like to eat lamb or roast beef. Among the fish dishes, Dover sole is eaten very often. One of the specialities is steak and kidney pie.

A cheap and very popular dish is fish and chips. The fish is deep-fried after being dipped into flour, beaten egg and breadcrumbs. Fish and chips very often are sprinkled with vinegar. For this dish cod is mainly used. It is often sold wrapped up in paper.

Explain the characteristics of the German kitchen to your partner.

27. Lektion

Tick the correct answer

	True	False
In Belgium full meals are served in the cafés.		
Chips are served with nearly all meals in Belgium.		
There are not many sorts of beer in Belgium.		
Pasta meals are very substantial.		
Antipasti are appetizers.		
Olive oil and rice is used in the Spanish kitchen.		
The French cuisine does not use much game.		
Cream and wine are the most important ingredients of French sauces.		
The English breakfast is famous around the world.		
"High Tea" is a full meal.		
The English do not like roast lamb.		
Fish and chips are eaten with vinegar.		

Alfred's Steakhouse

Since 1928, Alfred's has served the finest, mouth-watering, aged mesquite broiled steaks from the very best Midwestern corn-fed cattle. Such specialties as the kingly porterhouse, the magnificent chateaubriand, the flavourful Chicago rib steak, as well as fresh salmon fillets, and the broiled rack of lamb offer our guests a true culinary treat.
Alfred's is the best place for your next event!

Pompei's Grotto is a casual, intimate, family-style and family-operated restaurant located in San Francisco's Fisherman's Wharf area. The Pompei family is celebrating their 50th year personally serving locals and visitors their favourite seafood and Italian specialties at reasonable prices. Offerings include fresh, local fish, shellfish and pasta dishes.
Parking, small banquet room, full bar; reservations accepted. All major credit cards accepted.

Read the advertisements and discuss where you would like to have dinner and why.

L'Olivier

L'Olivier celebrates with traditional French favourites at a real value. For dinner, choose from either the A La Carte menu or Prix Fixe menu, which includes choices of appetizers, soup or salad, entree and dessert.
"A soothing place to eat and talk, invisible service, and dependably good French food."

What would an advertisement for your restaurant look like? Create one.

the Mandarin

Today, the exquisite flavours of Northern China are conjured up to titillate your palate, whether you are an epicure of fine food or trying Chinese food for the first time. Since 1968, Dignitaries and Celebrities from around the world have come to the Mandarin to dine on sumptuous meals of Peking Duck and authentically prepared Beggar's Chicken. The menu is enhanced with the additional of such dishes as sweet mango Shrimp that melts in your mouth, and delicately seasoned Salt & Pepper Calamari dipped in a paper-thin batter. The fine wine list features varietals and sparkling wines from around the globe.

28th Lesson

Payment

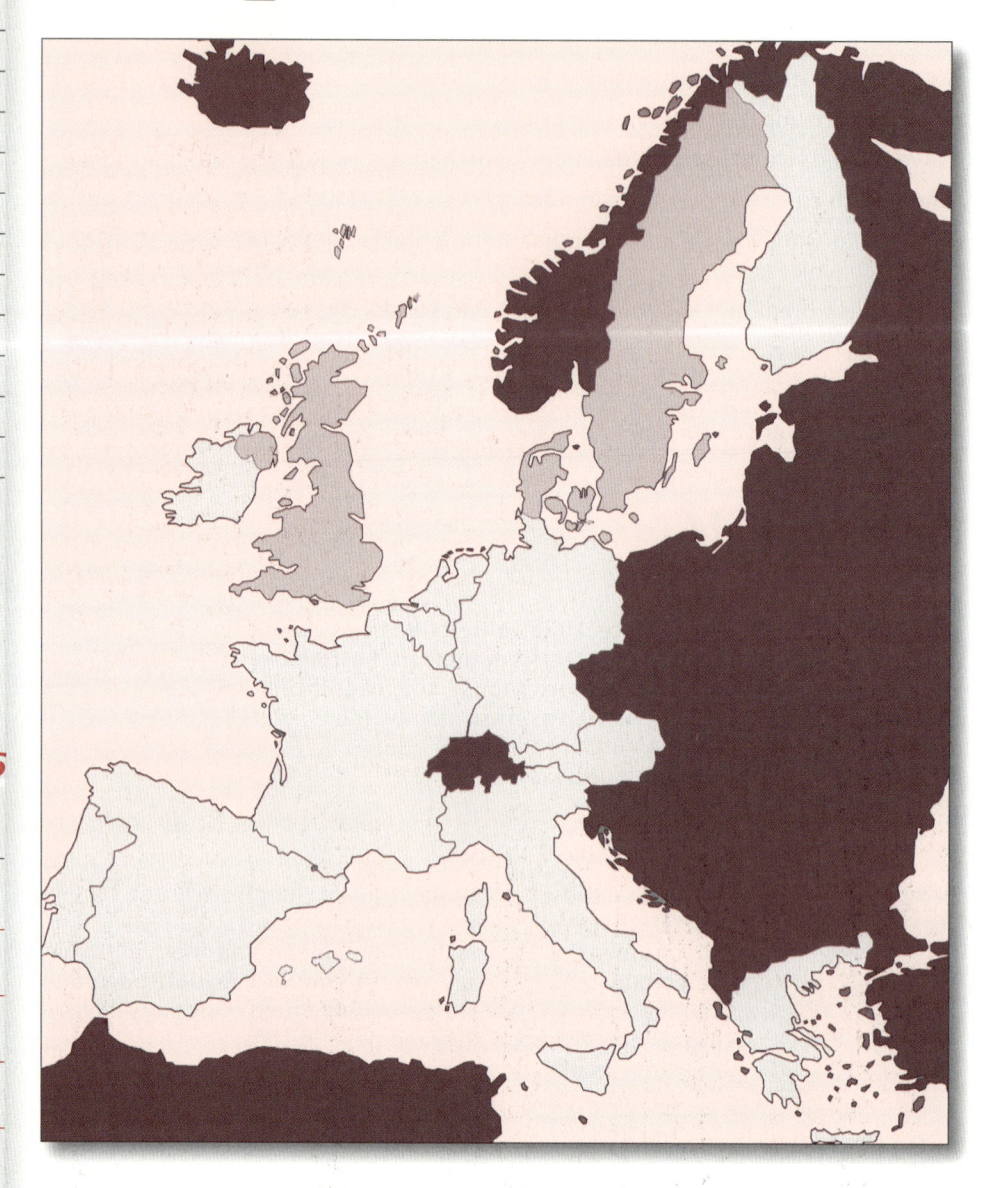

Find the 12 member states of the European Union which are participating in the common currency in the map.

They are:
1. Belgium
2. Germany
3. Greece
4. Spain
5. France
6. Ireland
7. Italy
8. Luxembourg
9. The Netherlands
10. Austria
11. Portugal
12. Finland

Denmark, Sweden and the United Kingdom are members of the European Union but are not participating in the common currency currently.

🎵 82–86

Listen and try to find out how the guests paid their bills.

82

83

84

85

86

To learn

I want to check out.

I'd like to settle my bill.

I'd like to pay by cheque / credit card / traveller's cheque

We accept ...

I'm sorry, we don't accept ...

It's the policy of the hotel.

Do you have a cheque card / banker's card?

Have you got any identification (means of identification)?

I hope you enjoyed your stay.

Since 1 January 2002 payment has become much easier in twelve European countries. These countries have changed their currency to the EURO, making travelling much more enjoyable. No more changing money before going on holiday, no need to spend all of the foreign coins, because they can also be used at home. This common currency has brought the European countries a little closer together.

🎯 **Unsere Ziele**

Nach Bearbeitung dieses Kapitels sollten Sie

- die Länder, in denen mit Euro bezahlt wird, nennen können;
- verschiedene andere Zahlungsmittel erklären
- sowie ein Gespräch mit dem zahlenden Gast führen können.

Traveller's Cheques

Traveller's cheques offer a safe and easy way to protect your travel money. They are accepted at millions of financial institutions and merchants all over the world, and are offered in a variety of currencies and denominations.
Unlike cash, traveller's cheques are safe and convenient. If lost or stolen, they can be replaced, with a single phone call, usually within 24 hours protecting you against inconvenience of losing cash. They also do not expire, so you could use your unused traveller's cheques for your next trip.
You can purchase traveller's cheques at thousands of financial institutions and other locations around the world.

How to accept traveller's cheques
- Watch your guest countersign the cheque.
- Compare the signatures.
- Check the identification (passport).

Credit Cards

A card that could be used repeatedly to borrow money or buy any products and services on credit is known as credit card. Banks, savings and loans, retail stores and other businesses issue credit cards. It is a convenient tool for purchases. When you purchase a product or service on credit you need to payback the amount to your bank. If you do not pay the balance full, then you would need to pay with an interest.

Types of Credit Cards
Bank Cards – These cards are issued by banks. Most prominent cards in this category are Visa, MasterCard and Discover. Barclaycard and Access are the two largest schemes in Great Britain.
Travel and Entertainment Cards – The most prominent cards in this category are American Express and Diners. These cards were originally aimed at upscale market. They are accepted by merchants though not as popular as Visa or MasterCard.
House Cards – These cards are issued by major chain stores and hold good only in them. Sears is the largest credit card issuer in this category. Oil companies, phone companies and local department stores also issue house cards.

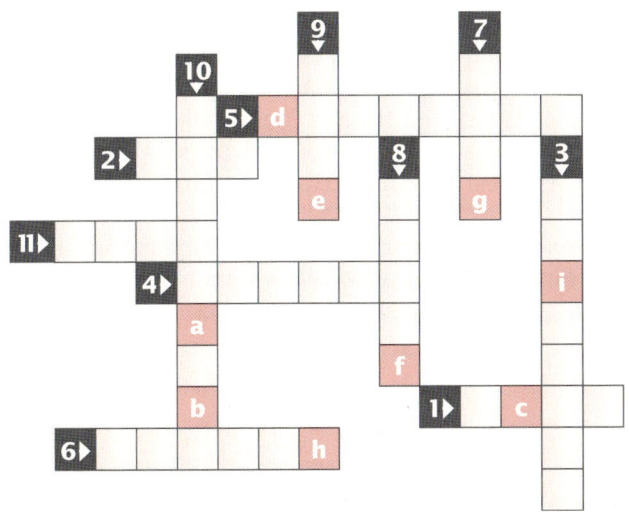

Solution: a b c d e f g h i

Form dialogues.

- 10.00 a.m. / Mr. Wilson / room 112 / bill EUR 89,40 / drinks from the minibar / hotel accepts traveller's cheques and credit cards
- 8.00 a.m. / Mrs. Sanders / room 224 / bill $ 280,00 / cash / telephone $ 45,00
- 11.30 a.m. / Mr. Baker / room 110 / £ 130,00 / American Express / laundry £ 12,00
- 10.30 a.m. / Miss Scheel / room 225 / CHF 550,00 / cash / dog CHF 30,00
- 8.30 a.m. / Mr. and Mrs. Marones / room 104 / EUR 540,00 / garage EUR 30,80

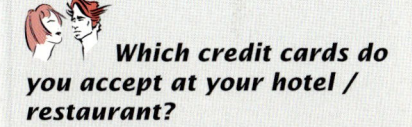

Which credit cards do you accept at your hotel / restaurant?

Find the hidden word.

Across
1. a place where you can receive or lend money
2. a small present of money to a waiter
4. to add up to a sum
5. the fact of being valid
6. a written order to pay an amount of money
11. a piece of metal issued as money

Down
3. the money in any country
7. a statement of charges for goods and services
8. a building providing accommodation
9. a locking metal container
10. a person's name written by himself

The Bar

origin unknown

The origin of the word "cocktail" is by no means universally agreed, most dictionaries simply give "orig. unk". The first use in print of the word cocktail (the drink) was in Hudson, New York, where on 13 May 1806 the editor of the Balance and Columbian Repository defined "Cock tail" as "a stimulating liquor, composed of spirits of any kind, sugar, water and bitters".

Over the last two centuries at least a dozen stories have emerged to explain the term's origin. Most involve cockerels or beautiful young women with a name which sounds like cocktail. The mire credible explanations are:

1. **Coquetier** is the French name for an egg-cup, in which a Frenchman in New Orleans is said to have served mixed drinks to his guests. In time they came to ask for his **coquetiers** and the name was corrupted to cocktails.
2. An old French recipe containing mixed wines, called **coquetel,** was perhaps carried to America by General Lafayette in 1777.
3. One Bets Flanagan of Virginia is believed to have served a handsome soldier a mixed drink containing all the colours of a cock's tail. He named it a "cock-tail".
4. In 1769 the term "cock-tailed" appeared a racing term used to describe a non-thoroughbred horse. It was the usual practice to dock the tails of such animals, causing the tail to look like that of a cockerel. According to the journals of the time, a "cock-tailed" horse was one of mixed blood. It is a short step to accept that cock-tail(ed) would soon become accepted as a term to describe anything containing mixed fluids.
5. The centuries-old expression "cocked tail" describes a horse or person displaying high spirits. It naturally follows that a beverage seen to raise people's spirits would be called a cocktail.

Answer the following questions.

- Which journal did first describe the drinks called cocktail?
- What year was it?
- What French word is another legend?

Cocktails were a small group of recipes mostly based on the 1806 formula, until the 1880s when cocktail began to develop into a generic term for an ever widening class of mixtures.

The actual root of the term is most likely to have come from a two-word expression. The last two remain the only plausible explanations, but with number 5 favourite because it alone accounts for the use of "stimulating" in the original definition.

Unsere Ziele

Nach Bearbeitung dieses Kapitels sollten Sie

- die Bargeräte und -gläser beschreiben können;
- einige Cocktails zubereiten können
- sowie verschiedene Bargetränke beschreiben können.

29. Lektion

Fill in the right number

○ ice bucket
○ nutmeg grater
○ measuring glasses
○ bottle opener
○ ice shovel

○ dash bottle
○ corkscrew
○ blender (Hamilton beach)
○ ice tongs
○ drinking straws

Dialogue   87

Listen and complete the conversation.
B = bar waiter, A = apprentice

B: Have a look at the bar list.

A: Where are the _____ ?

B: Here they are, on the left side. On the right you see the _____ .

A: Is that right, there are _____ ?

B: Yes, we offer _____ , _____

and _____ as well as _____

and _____ .

A: What _____ do we serve?

B: We offer _____ , _____ , _____ ,

and _____ .

To learn
stir well
strain
muddle
pour
spear
shake
garnish
mix
ice cubes
crushed ice
lemon twist
lemon peel
on the rocks
float

127

29th Lesson

To learn
bitter
charge
cider
half
pint

Create, describe and prepare your own cocktail. Use the I.C.C. Rules & Regulations (page 180).

very polite
Could I have a beer?
May I have your key card?
Would you like ice?

less formal
What'll you have? (will)
Can I have my key?

offering a service
Shall I charge this to your room?

Exercise

Match the bar utensils with their functions.

	Bar utensils		Functions
1.	Hamilton beach		squeezing lemons
2.	bottle opener		cutting fruits
3.	wine cooler		drinking cocktails
4.	bar knife		cooling wine
5.	straws		measuring spirits
6.	lemon squeezer		opening tins or bottles
7.	corkscrew	1	blending cocktails
8.	measuring glass		keeping ice cubes cold
9.	ice bucket		opening wine bottles

Exercise

Correct the order.

Old-Fashioned
5 cl Canadian whisky
1 piece of sugar
1 dash Angostura bitter

	stir to blend bitter and sugar
1	muddle sugar in glass
	add whisky
	add ice cubes and bitter
	garnish with cherry or an orange slice
	stir well

Manhattan
4 cl Canadian whisky
2 cl Vermouth red
1 dash Angostura bitter

	put in ice cubes
	add the ingredients
1	take a mixing glass
	pour into a chilled cocktail glass
	spear a cherry on a fruit spear
	garnish with the cherry spear
	stir well with the bar spoon

Dialogue

Listen and take the orders.

88

Tim: _____

Denise: _____

Michael: _____

Jill: _____

Practise

Work in pairs (guest and barman).
could, would, may, shall

29. Lektion

Example:

gin and tonic - Guest: Can I have a gin and tonic?
ice and lemon - Barman: Would you like ice and lemon?

a) sherry
   sweet / dry

b) beer
   pint / half

c) port
   small / large

d) whisky
   water / soda

e) lager
   draught / bottled

f) vodka and tonic
   ice

Dialogues 🎵 89

Listen and note the prices of the drinks the guests bought.
How much is the charge for each guest? The prices are in pence (£1 = 100 p).

	Pint / half			large / small	
Beer (bitter)	90	45	Whisky	130	65
Beer (lager)	96	48	Vodka	120	60
Cider	80	40	Gin	120	60
			Rum	120	60
			Lemonade	40	20
			Tonic	40	20

a) 1st guest: _____

b) 2nd guest: _____

c) 3rd guest: _____

d) 4th guest: _____

e) 5th guest: _____

Glassware

Cocktail (C)
14 cl/5 fl oz

Rocks, Old-Fashioned;
Whisky (R)
23 cl/8 fl oz

Highball (H)
28 cl/10 fl oz

Collins (CO)
34 cl/12 fl oz

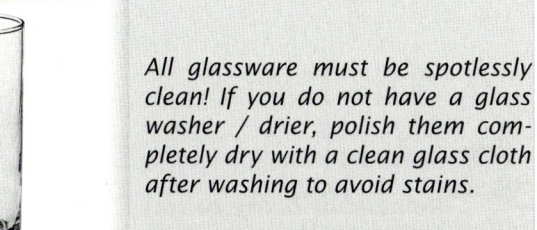

Pilsner (Pi)
28 cl/10 fl oz

Fluted
champagne
(F) 14 cl/5 fl oz

Goblet (G)
34 cl/12 fl oz

Wine (W)
20 cl/7 fl oz

Snifter or
brandy
balloon (B)
31 cl/11 fl oz

Double
cocktail (D)
23 cl/8 fl oz

Champagne
saucer (CS)
14 cl/5 fl oz

Poco or
Pina Colada (P)
40 cl/14 fl oz

Cordial or
liqueur (L)
8 cl/3 fl oz

Shot
glass (S)
5.7 cl/2 fl oz

All glassware must be spotlessly clean! If you do not have a glass washer / drier, polish them completely dry with a clean glass cloth after washing to avoid stains.

Test each type of glass to see how many measures it will hold. This will allow you to adjust your quantities to fit the glass exactly.

❓ What kind of garnishings would you prepare for different cocktails?

Complaints

5 steps to customer recovery:
- Be accessible.
- Listen and empathize.
- "Make it right" for the customer.
- Thank the customer for the feedback.
- Fix the problem.

Remember being polite when dealing with complaints! (Lesson 19)

L.A.S.T
Listen
Apologize
Solve
Thank

Welcome complaints, they are important to our success! Studies show that 80 % of guests will not say anything; they just will not return. In other words, for every guest that complains, four other guests are walking out the door, never to return again. The feedback from the "difficult" guest can help us to avoid trouble in future. In another study, 70 % of the customers polled said they were loyal to a particular company because something went wrong and they were impressed with the way the situation was handled. If we handle the situation right, they will come back again and again.

Handling stressful situations:
- Recognize that the complaint is not an attack.
- Do not take the complaint personally.
- Recognize that the customer is unhappy about the situation, not about you personally.
- Realize that the customer may be having a bad day and be in a bad mood.
- If you do not know how to deal with the situation, ask for help.
- Take a deep breath.
- Count to 10.
- Listen carefully to be sure you understand the situation before reacting.
- Focus on the problem, and fix it.

Unser Ziel

Nach Bearbeitung dieses Kapitels sollten Sie

- auf Beschwerden von Gästen im Hotel richtig reagieren können.

30. Lektion

Dialogues

🔘 90–95

Listen to the dialogues. First find out the guests' problems. Listen again and find out the reaction of the receptionist.

What's the guest's problem?   Reaction of the receptionist:

90 _____   _____

91 _____   _____

92 _____   _____

93 _____   _____

94 _____   _____

95 _____   _____

To learn

I'm very / extremely / terribly sorry

I'll send someone to deal with it / to fix it / to repair it / to replace it

I'll have it repaired / replaced / fixed

immediately / as soon as possible / at once

Deal with the guest's problem. Ask for the room number.

- light bulb is broken / 704
- no towel / 318
- bath is dirty / 221
- alarm clock doesn't work / 401
- likes an extra pillow / 512
- wanted a single room with balcony (there is no balcony) / 624
- the window doesn't close / 534

Exercise

🔘 96

Put into the right order. Then listen and check.

◯ Receptionist: We usually check every room before the guest arrives. I'll get the chambermaid to sort it out immediately.

◯ Guest: No, but hurry up, please. I'd like to take a shower.

◯ Receptionist: I'll send someone to check the air-conditioning. Is there anything else?

◯ Guest: I hope so. I've just checked in and the room you've given me is in a horrible condition.

◯ Receptionist: Good morning, madam. Can I help you?

◯ Guest: And I need an extra blanket. It's awfully cold in the room.

◯ Receptionist: I'm very sorry to hear that. What's wrong?

◯ Guest: There are no towels. The bath needs cleaning. One light bulb is broken. Did you have the room checked before?

◯ Receptionist: Yes, of course, madam. I'll send the chambermaid along right away.

What would you say to the guest in the following situations? (Remember the 5 steps!)

- A famous pop star is disturbing other guests by having a noisy party in his room.
- A guest wants to come to the night club wearing a T-shirt and jeans.
- A guest wants to take his dog into the restaurant (no dogs allowed there).
- A guest is complaining about the slow service in the restaurant.
- A guest is complaining that the indoor pool is closed.
- A guest is complaining that the toilets in the pool area are dirty.

131

Looking for a Job

Southampton Princess

CHEFS DE PARTIE
CHEFS DE PARTIE/PASTRY
CHEFS DE PARTIE/BAKERS

All applicants must be 21 years of age – all positions are subject to immigration approval and position availability.

Living accommodations provided.

Please apply in wirting with full resume references and photograph with **English translations** to:

Human Resources Administrator
Human Resources Department
Southampton Princess Hotel
P.O. Box HM 1379
Hamilton HM FX, Bermuda

At the interview:

1. Arrive early. Phone if you are held up.
2. Try to smile.
3. Show interest in the job and ask questions.
4. Be polite.
5. Don't panic, even if faced by more than one person.
6. Don't slouch around and look bored.
7. Don't smoke or chew.
8. Don't give one word answers.

Tourism industry covers a wide spectrum of activities. Therefore the range of information sources on employment opportunities is very broad. Career advisers, newspapers and magazines, contact with companies, the internet, employment agencies are some possibilities to find a job in tourism industry.

The internet is an up-to-date medium. There are many links for recommendations. The number of internet users has risen abruptly. On the one hand the charges (e.g. telephone charges) for the use of the internet or the appropriate services are being constantly lowered. And on the other hand owning a PC and in association with this a connection to the internet, has reached the same "must-have" factor as, for example, a television. It has been predicted in studies that in 2003 there will be more PCs than televisions throughout the world. If anyone does not have access to the internet at home, he can use it at internet cafes or bars.

Unsere Ziele

Nach Bearbeitung dieses Kapitels sollten Sie

- Stellenanzeigen in englischer Sprache verstehen können;
- Qualifikationen für einen Job aus Ihrer Branche definieren können;
- eine Stellenbewerbung und den Lebenslauf in englischer Sprache verfassen können
- sowie einen Bewerbungsbogen in Englisch ausfüllen können.

Dialogue 97

Listen to the interview and fill in the table below.

Record sheet	Dialogue	You
Position applied for		
Name		
Address		
Marital status		
Date of birth		
Education		
Practical experience		
Qualifications (languages)		

Now answer the questions. Tell your classmate about yourself.

Take the role of a personnel manager and interview your classmate.

To learn

skills
apply for a job
application
experience

Read

Many positions may be obtained by way of introduction or simply by applying for a job. Letters of application are usually written in reply to an advertisement (newspaper, internet). Read the following advertisements and note the jobs offered.

Relais and Chateaux, Canada
May 6th to October 20th, 2002
The Inn at Manitou
★★★★★

A small Luxury Golf, Tennis and Spa resort on a beautiful Lake North of Toronto.

Looking for skilled, experienced, young professionals with good communication skills and who enjoy dealing with sophisticated clientele.

Salary plus accommodation and meals. We arrange work visas. London interviews – Nov. 16-20, 2001.

Front Desk / Receptionists / Concierge / Maitre D' / Chefs de Rang / Sous Chef / Chefs de Partie / Pastry Chef

Email CV including your phone number and mailing address: inn@Manitou-online.com
or fax to: (705) 389-3818

Check out our website: www.manitou-online.com

Cunard Line & Seabourn Cruise Line are the World's Leading Luxury Cruise Lines

Waiters * Assistant Waiters
Demi * Chef de Parties
Pastry Chefs
Wine Waiters
Cocktail Bar Staff
Cabin Stewardesses

If you are seeking an interesting challenging position with career opportunities, we offer the following year-round positions to experienced professionals:

Successful applicants will have at least 3 years experience from a variety of first class hotels, restaurants or ships that cater to international guests. All applicants must be fluent in English.

Cunard/Seabourn offers competitive salaries, free transportation to our ships and incentive bonuses. Please send your CV in English with copies of reference letters and recent passport photo.

We regret that all applications received may not receive a reply.

Cunard Seabourn Limited
Hotel Recruitment
Mountbatten House, Grosvenor Square
Southampton, U.K. SO15 2BF
job@cunardmail.com
www.cunard.com   www.seabourn.com

BERMUDA requires the following:-
- Head Chefs, Sous Chefs, Chefs de Partie, Commis Chefs
- Pastry chefs and Bakers
- Waiters/Waitresses/Chefs de rang
- Sommeliers
- Front Desk Receptionists
- Butchers
- Grocery Store Managers/Assistant Managers

Applicants must be single, over 21 years of age and have a minimum of 2 years' experience. Must be willing to commit to a one-year contract. Our clients are seeking enthusiastic, professional and dedicated team players who are interested in relocating and experiencing island life.
Please send resume (with permanent and current addresses), photo and letters of reference to:
Tempest Employment Agency
P.O. Box HM 3024
Hamilton HM NX, Bermuda
Tel (441)-295-8329 * Fax (441)-296-1224.
E-mail: temps@northrock.bm

31st Lesson

Search the internet for the job of your dreams. Find out which qualifications are required and write them down in your notebook. Discuss / compare your list with your classmate.

What do you like / not like about your job? Interview your classmates.

What qualifications are required for ...
- a waiter / waitress?
- a cook?
- a pastry chef?
- a bartender?
- a chambermaid?
- a receptionist?
- a manager?

Strengths and interests:
- ambitious
- flexible
- tactful
- being creative
- a pleasant appearance
- a good speaking voice
- organizing
- dealing with people
- listening to people
- speak at least one foreign language
- working accurately
- working irregular hours
- working at weekends
- taking orders from others

Find other skills and qualifications you need in your job.

Position (job)	Which qualifications are required?

Practise

It is up to you which job you choose. Which would you like best? What qualifications do you need for your job?

Exercise

Try to find the opposite using your dictionary.

young ___
ill ___
angry ___
lazy ___
slow ___
poor ___
diligent ___
clean ___
tidy ___
polite ___
clever ___
skilled ___
important ___
neat ___

Letter of application

Heading

Date

Addressee

Ref:

Salutation: Dear Sir / Madam,

> With reference to your advertisement in the ... I wish to apply for the position of a ... I wish to offer you my services.
> I have read your advertisement in the ... and would like to apply for the post of a ...
> I am interested in the position of a ...
> I have learned you have a vacancy for a ...
> I would like to get a position in ...

I am Austrian.
I was born on ...
I attended a vocational school. I have had a good general education. During my apprenticeship I attended courses of the Chamber of Commerce.
I am an excellent cook / waiter / waitress.
I have good knowledge of English / French / Italian.
For ... years I have been working with ... / For the past two years I have been ... I finished my apprenticeship as a ... when I was ... years old / last ...
I think your firm offers me better opportunities.
I think my qualifications enable me to meet your expectations.
The enclosed CV gives further information of my education and experience.
Enclosed please find copies of my examination certificate.
As reference I have permission to give you ...
I can give you the following names as references:
I refer to ...
My present employer knows of my application / agreed to give you information.
My present employer will be pleased to answer any inquiries as to my character and my abilities.

> I would appreciate the opportunity of a personal interview.
> I could come for an interview at any time you like / begin work any time after ...
> I hope you will consider my application favourably and grant me an interview.
> Please send me an application form.
> I should appreciate the opportunity of meeting you.
> May I please have an interview?

Closing: Yours faithfully / sincerely,

Signature

Enclosures
Curriculum vitae (CV)
Passport photo
Certificates

Write a letter of application. Apply for the job you would like. Use the pattern sentences and copy them to your situation.

31st Lesson

Application for employment

Heading

Date

The Manager
The Wharf Restaurant
P.O. Box 1555
Grand Cayman
Cayman Islands B.W.I.

Ref: Application

Dear Sir,

I refer to your advertisement in the "Caterer and Hotel Keeper" and wish to apply for the position of a bartender.

I am 23 years old and married. From 1994 to 1997 I attended the vocational school in Salzburg. After my apprenticeship I worked as a wine waiter. Since July I have been employed with Scanworld Maritime Services, Norway. I would like to get a position with opportunity for further experience and responsibility. Full details of my education and past experience are set out in the enclosed CV.

As references I am allowed to give you my former teacher and my present employer.

I could begin work any time after the end of next month and hope you consider my application favourably.

Yours faithfully,

Signature

Enclosures

Exercise

Write your curriculum vitae (CV).

Curriculum vitae / Personal data sheet

Name: _____

Age: _____

Address: _____

Nationality: _____

Education: _____
_____
_____
_____

Previous experience: _____
_____

References: _____

Qualifications: _____

31. Lektion

BEWERBUNGSBOGEN
APPLICATION FOR EMPLOYMENT

An/to

Foto

ICH BEWERBE MICH
I HEREBY APPLY FOR THE FOLLOWING POSITION

*) um die Position als
*) position applied for

Ihre Position derzeit
Your position at the moment

Familienname	Vorname	☐ männlich	☐ weiblich
surename	firstname	male	female

Jetzige Anschrift / present address — Telefon / Tel. no.

Ständige Anschrift / permanent address — Telefon / Tel. no.

Geburtsdatum			Geburtsort
date of birth	Tag/day Monat/month Jahr/year		place of birth

Staatsangeh. / citizenship — Personalausweis oder Paß-Nr. / Id. card or passport no. — Gültig bis / valid until

Name und Adresse Ihres gegenwärtigen Arbeitgebers
Name and location of your present employer

Mindestgehalt (netto) / min. salary (net) — Nettogehalt derzeit / Net salary at the moment

Warum wollen Sie sich verändern
Why do you wish to change

Wer hat Sie an uns verwiesen
Who referred you to us

Vorstrafen / previous convictions   ☐ ja / yes   ☐ nein / no

Familienstand	☐ ledig	☐ verheiratet	☐ verwitwet	☐ geschieden	☐ getrennt lebend
marital status	single	married	widowed	divorced	separated

Kinder unter 18 Jahren (mit Altersangabe)
Children under 18 years (state ages)

Sonstige abhängige Angehörige — Religion
Other dependents — religion

---

oscar's
TOP Verlag GmbH
P.O. Box 588
A-6800 Feldkirch
Tel. 0043(0)5522/76 563
Fax 0043(0)5522/82 134
Internet: www.oscars.at
E-MAIL: oscars@cable.vol.at

SCHULBILDUNG*)
EDUCATION*)

Name und Anschrift der Lehranstalten	Von	Bis	Zeugnis oder Diplom	Hauptfächer
Name and address of school/university	from	to	Degree or certificate	major course of study

*) Volkschule/Elementary School · Hauptschule/Junior High School · Allgemeinbildende Höhere Schule/High School · Hotelfachschule/Hotel Mgmt. School · Berufsschule/Vocational School

Nehmen Sie auch jetzt noch Unterricht?
Are you now studying?   Worin? / If so, what?

Voraussichtlicher Abschluß
When will you be finished?

Wo / where

Welche EDV-Programme (z.B.: "Word...")?
What computer programs?

Für welche Aufgabe sind Sie besonders geeignet?
What kind of work are you most qualified to do?

SPRACHKENNTNISSE
LANGUAGE QUALIFICATIONS

Welche Sprachen beherrschen Sie?	Sprechfertigkeit speaking proficiency			Schreibfertigkeit writing proficiency			Verstehvermögen understanding		
What languages do you know?	sehr gut excellent	gut good	genügend fair	sehr gut excellent	gut good	genügend fair	sehr gut excellent	gut good	genügend fair

ANGABEN ÜBER IHREN GESUNDHEITSZUSTAND / PHYSICAL INFORMATION

Wie ist Ihr Gesundheitszustand? ☐ ausgezeichnet / excellent ☐ gut / good ☐ durchschnittlich / fair ☐ schlecht / poor   Größe / height   Gewicht / weight

Sind Sie kriegs- oder zivilgeschädigt? Wenn ja, wieviel Prozent?   ☐ Ja / yes   ☐ Nein / no   Wenn ja, wann / If so, when?
Have you had any serious illnesses, injuries or operations?

Haben Sie Beschwerden an: Füßen / feet   Händen / hands   Sicht / sight   Gehör / hearing   Sprache / speech
Do you have any problems with:

ALLGEMEINE ANGABEN / GENERAL INFORMATION

Wurden Sie zum Wehrdienst eingezogen?   Haben Sie noch künftige Verpflichtungen?
Have you performed military service?   Do you have any future military obligation?

In welchem Lande   Rang
In which country?   rank

31st Lesson

Im Notfalle Benachrichtigung an
In case of emergency notify

Keine Verwandten aufführen
Do not list relatives

REFERENZEN
PERSONAL REFERENCES

| Name | Adresse | Beruf |
Name	Address	Occupation

Ich unterzeichne meine Bewerbung um Einstellungen und versichere dabei, daß meine Angaben der Wahrheit entsprechen und bin mir bewußt, daß irreführende Angaben oder wichtige Auslassungen zu einer Auflösung des Dienstverhältnisses führen können.

In signing this application I hereby affirm that the preceding statements are true to the best of my knowledge and belief, and that any misrepresentation of facts or material omission thereof shall be cause for termination of employment.

Zeugniskopien anbei
Copies of certificates enclosed

Datum   Unterschrift
Date   Signature

Der Bewerber muß zum Zwecke der Einstellung Aufenthalts- und Arbeitsgenehmigung erlangen können.
Employment is subject to applicants ability to secure residence permit and work permit.

EINTRAGUNG FÜR DEN PERSONALCHEF
RECORD FOR THE PERSONNEL MANAGER

Betrieb   Abteilung   Position
Company   Department

Arbeitsbeginn   Gehalt
Date employed   Salary

Bemerkungen
Remarks

BEURTEILUNG UND KOMMENTARE DES ARBEITSGEBERS
EMPLOYER EVALUATION AND COMMENTS

STELLENNACHWEIS
EMPLOYMENT RECORD

Geben Sie alle Ihre bisherigen Stellungen an und beginnen Sie mit Ihrer letzten Position. Machen Sie bitte möglichst genaue Angaben.
Please list the positions you have held in the space below, showing last position first. Be as specific and thorough as possible.

| Unternehmen | Beschäftigt employed | | Art des Unternehmen | Ihr Aufgabenbereich | Nettogehalt | Kündigungsgrund |
Company	Von from	Bis to	Nature of Business	Position & Duties	net salary	reason for leaving

Hobbies

Welche Erwartungen haben Sie von der gewünschten Stelle?
What expectations do you have from your desired position?

Was sind Ihre beruflichen Ziele?
What are your career goals?

32. Lektion

Corres- pondence

1 heading

2 date

3 addressee

4 subject matter / reference

5 opening (formulae) salutation

6 text

7 closing

8 signature

9 enclosures

Translate

1 Briefkopf
2
3
4
5
6
7
8
9

Unsere Ziele

Nach Bearbeitung dieses Kapitels sollten Sie

- die Form eines englischen Briefes kennen;
- Redewendungen betreffend Reservierung und Stornierung eines Zimmers übersetzen und in Briefen anwenden können;
- auf die elektronische Post eines Englisch sprechenden Gastes korrekt antworten können.

32nd Lesson

Where would you like to spend your holidays? And your classmates? Ask them, too. Read and compare the following offers.

Postal card – Request of an English guest

Dear Sir,

My wife and I are going to tour Europe this summer, spending two weeks in Austria.

We require a nice double room with bath from 28 July to 11 August 20..

Please inform us of your present rates and send us a brochure of your hotel.

Confirm the booking

The guest, Mr. Knight, 129 Bayswater Road, London W2 4RJ, wants to spend his holidays in Austria. Confirm his booking.

Dear Mr. Knight,

Thank you for your letter of ...

We are pleased to confirm your reservation of

**one double room with bath
from 28 July to 11 August 20..**

For further details concerning our hotel, please see the enclosures.

We are looking forward to your definite booking.

Yours sincerely,

Managing Director

Enclosures

Dear Madam,

In reply to your letter of ..., we are pleased to confirm your booking for

**a single room with shower
from ... to ...**

The rate for half board is € 45.00. The room has colour TV with video channel.

We assure you, we will do everything to make your visit enjoyable.

Yours faithfully,

Managing Director

I hope you can make up your mind. Write a letter asking for accommodation.

Letter of refusal

Dear Sir,

We regret to inform you that we are fully booked for the coming season.

Unfortunately we cannot accommodate you from 28 July to 11 August 20... Our hotel is fully booked at this time. Perhaps you can postpone your visit, otherwise we will forward your letter to the Tourist Office.

We should appreciate your reply.

Yours faithfully,

Managing Director

Pattern sentences – Confirming a booking

Dear Sir / Madam,
Gentlemen / Ladies and Gentlemen
Dear Mr. (Mrs., Miss) Baker,

Thank you for your letter of ...
In reply to your letter / telephone call / fax / e-mail of ...
In response to your ...
With reference to your ... / Referring to your ...

We are pleased to confirm your reservation of ... We are able to offer you ...
I am pleased to book a ... for you.
We are glad to confirm your reservation of ...

... a nice single room (double room, twin-bedded room) with bath (shower, balcony, extra bed etc.) overlooking the lake (garden, city) / on the south side / with view to the mountains.
... from 28 July to 11 August 20..
... for three weeks from the beginning of September 20..
... from arrival on 5 June until departure 10 June 20..

The rate for half board is EUR ... per person and day.
The price for bed and breakfast is ...
... with full board, taxes and service included, for two persons at the rate of ...
The terms for ... will be ... everything included.
The rate for the room is ... per person and day, three meals and all extra charges included.
Children under 15 are free of charge in extra-bed in the apartment of parents.
Only for thermal baths, there will be an extra charge of ...
All these terms are fully inclusive.

Please see the enclosures.
For further details concerning the hotel, please see the enclosed brochure.
We enclose a prospectus with information regarding the excellent location, accommodation, and events for the coming season.

We look forward to hearing from you at your earliest convenience.
May we look forward to receiving your definite booking.
We should appreciate your reply.
We assure you of our best service during your stay in our house.
We look forward to welcoming you.
I look forward to your arrival and wish you a pleasant journey.

Confirm the reservation

J. S. Black, 52 Ashford Court, London NW 2, from 4 March 20..
one quiet single room, nice view, on the top floor, bathroom, from 2 June to 9 June 20.., half board

A. Ashley, 17 Tottenham Court Road, London W. 1, from 15 May 20..
two double rooms with connecting door, bathroom, balcony, from 3 September to 14 September 20.., bed and breakfast

Refuse the reservation

Florence Feather, 130 East 57th Street, New York, NY 10017, from 2 October 20..
6 twin-bedded rooms, bathroom or shower, conference facilities, from 20 to 25 November 20.., bed and breakfast

32nd Lesson

Planning for your next trip?

Online hotel bookings offer you direct and easy access to a range of hotels in several countries, complete with up-to-date availability information. You will find brochures of the hotels, room rates, hotel packages, special offers and last minutes, including real-time booking facilities.

Online booking offers a simple, advanced and secure booking service worldwide. You can plan your travels with guaranteed accommodation.

Search for more information in the www.

Name of guest(s):

___

___

Number of guests:

___

___

Room(s) required:

___

___

Dates:

___

___

Special requirements:

___

___

Pattern sentences – Refusal

We regret to inform you that we are fully booked for the coming season.
I am sorry to inform you that we are closed during the winter.
All our rooms have been reserved for the dates requested.
Unfortunately we are unable to offer you the room you require / we cannot accommodate you from ... to ...
We have forwarded your letter to ...
Perhaps you can postpone your visit.
We hope that you will be able to come to some other arrangement.
We should be obliged to receive an early reply.
An early reply would be appreciated.

Exercise

1. For the greater part of hotels, fax / E-mail / online bookings are the most common. Read this example of a reservation and complete the chart below:

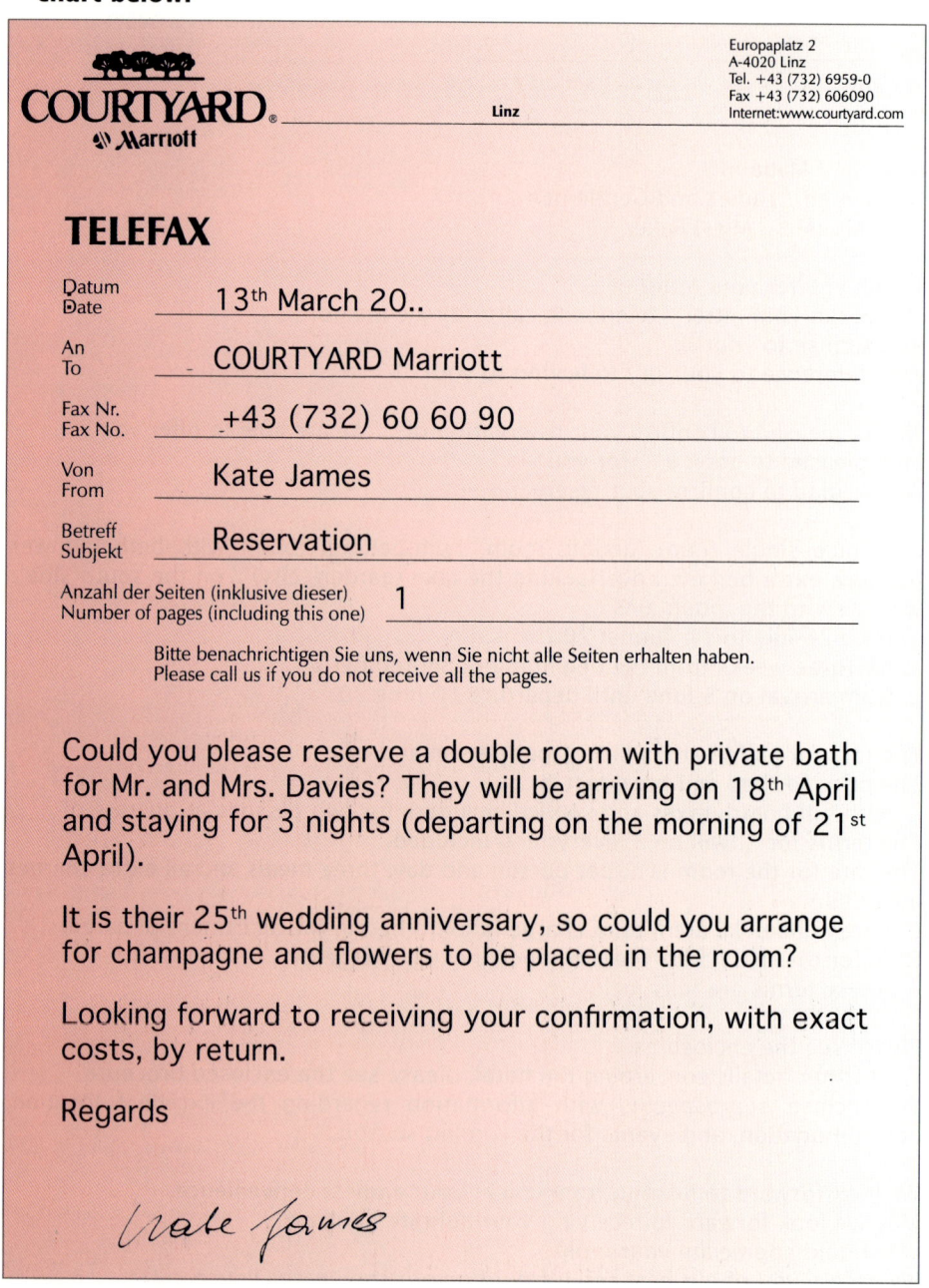

COURTYARD Marriott
Europaplatz 2
A-4020 Linz
Tel. +43 (732) 6959-0
Fax +43 (732) 606090
Internet: www.courtyard.com

TELEFAX

Datum / Date	13th March 20..
An / To	COURTYARD Marriott
Fax Nr. / Fax No.	+43 (732) 60 60 90
Von / From	Kate James
Betreff / Subjekt	Reservation
Anzahl der Seiten (inklusive dieser) / Number of pages (including this one)	1

Bitte benachrichtigen Sie uns, wenn Sie nicht alle Seiten erhalten haben.
Please call us if you do not receive all the pages.

Could you please reserve a double room with private bath for Mr. and Mrs. Davies? They will be arriving on 18th April and staying for 3 nights (departing on the morning of 21st April).

It is their 25th wedding anniversary, so could you arrange for champagne and flowers to be placed in the room?

Looking forward to receiving your confirmation, with exact costs, by return.

Regards

Kate James

---

2. Reply to the reservation by fax or e-mail, asking for any additional information you require.

32. Lektion

COURTYARD Marriott

Europaplatz 2
A-4020 Linz
Telefon +43 (732) 6959-0
Telefax +43 (732) 606090
Internet: www.courtyard.com

Linz

TELEFAX

An / To _____ Fax No. _____

Von / From _____ Datum / Date _____

Betrifft / Subject _____

Seitenanzahl (inkl. Deckblatt) / No. of Pages (incl. This Coversheet) _____
Bitte benachrichtigen Sie uns, wenn Sie nicht alle Seiten erhalten haben. / Please call us if you did not receive all the pages.

> Mr. Adams left a message for Mrs. Curtis, room 204, that he would not be able to meet her in the bar at 9 p.m. this evening.

COURTYARD Marriott

MITTEILUNG / MESSAGE

Für Hr./Fr.
To Mr./Mrs.

Zimmer Nr.
Room No.

Von Hr./Fr.
From Mr./Mrs.

Telefon Nr.
Phone No.

☐ rief Sie an / called   ☐ ruft wieder an / will call again   ☐ war im Haus / came to see you
☐ erbittet Ihren Anruf / please return the call   ☐ möchte Sie treffen / would like to meet you   ☐ wichtig / urgent

Mitteilung
Message
_____
_____
_____
_____

Aufgenommen von
Message received by

Zeit   Datum
Time   Date

Exercise

Use your notebook.

You work in Reservations at the COURTYARD Marriott. The manager gives you the following instructions. Read them and complete the fax above.
Could you send a fax to Imperial Chemicals? Thank them for the two bookings and say that'll be fine. You'd better quote the standard prices first, including half board, service charges, and taxes – that's £ 165.00 and £ 85.00 a night. I think we usually give them 10 % discount, so work out what it comes to and put the total at the end.

COURTYARD Marriott

Date: _____

From: Reservations

To: _____

Attention: _____

Thank you for ...

Fill in

Fill the gaps in the fax with the words listed next to the sentences. The first one has been done for you.

IMPERIAL CHEMICALS

Date: 24 May
From: Miranda Smith
             Marketing and Promotions
To: COURTYARD Marriott
Attention: Reservations

Could you please *reserve* the _____ rooms:

1 A single _____ room for our Sales Director, Mr. Henry Green, for two nights from August 18.

2 A standard _____ room with _____ bathroom for our Sales Manager, Miss Caroline Lamb, for three nights from August 18.

Please confirm _____ and send _____ of prices of rooms, _____ half board and our normal _____.

_____,

Miranda Smith
Manager

- *reserve*
- *details*
- *en suite*
- *following*
- *Regards*
- *availability*
- *discount*
- *executive*
- *including*
- *single*

143

Weather

Berlin
Sunny skies 29/24
Thursday: Sunny skies 25/7
Friday: Sunny skies 34/6

Brussels
Sunny skies 38/11
Thursday: Abundant sunshine 38/13
Friday: Partly cloudy 45/32

Paris
Increasing clouds 47/25
Thursday: Sun returns 47/32
Friday: Clouds early, then partly sunny 50/42

London
Increasing clouds 43/31
Thursday: Clearing by noon 44/38
Friday: Increasing clouds 47/38

Madrid
Showers 49/40
Thursday: Overcast 50/43
Friday: Partly sunny 51/40

Rome
Sunny skies 47/31
Thursday: Sunny skies 45/38
Friday: Sunny skies 43/29

Stockholm
Plenty of sunshine 25/11
Thursday: Mostly sunny 34/9
Friday: Abundant sunshine 36/24

Munich
Partly sunny 31/18
Thursday: Sunny skies 24/19
Friday: Sunny skies 36/9

To learn
degrees
clouds
rain
fog
storm
snow
thunderstorm
light / heavy showers
sunny intervals
sleet
hail
partly cloudy

Today's temperatures, forecasts around the world

c cloudy — r rain — sh showers
pc partly cloudy — s sun — sn snow
i ice — sf snow flurries — t thunderstorms

°Fahrenheit: Below 10 | 10s | 20s | 30s | 40s | 50s | 60s | 70s | 80s | 90s | 100s
°Fahrenheit: 10 | 20 | 30 | 40 | 50 | 60 | 70 | 80 | 90 | 100
°Celsius: -12 | -7 | -1 | 4 | 10 | 16 | 21 | 27 | 32 | 38

Rain/showers — Thunderstorm — Snow — Ice

Europe

Reykjavik 47/42s
Aberdeen 45/29s
Bergen 40/33c
Oslo 24/7s
Stockholm 25/11s
Goteborg 25/11s
Helsinki 22/11s
St. Petersburg 20/9s
Riga 20/9s
Minsk 16/4pc
Belfast 50/45pc
Galway 56/49c
Shannon 56/50c
Dublin 52/47c
Edinburgh 45/29s
Newcastle 46/31s
Manchester 47/32s
Birmingham 47/34pc
London 43/31c
Amsterdam 40/18s
Hamburg 31/20s
Copenhagen 27/22s
Berlin 29/24s
Warsaw 22/20s
Brussels 38/11s
Bonn 42/18s
Kraków 25/24sf
Le Havre 49/32pc
Frankfurt 40/20s
Prague 29/24c
Paris 47/25pc
Munich 31/18s
Bratislava 35/25c
Vienna 35/29c
Zürich 36/14s
Salzburg 28/20pc
Lyon 42/24s
Venice 45/20s
Budapest 35/27c
Bordeaux 54/45pc
Milan 45/22s
Florence 47/25s
Belgrade 34/29s
Santiago de Compostela 58/50sh
Marseille 49/32s
Dubrovnik 49/31s
Rome 47/31s
Skopje 29/6pc
Sofia 29/15pc
Lisbon 62/52sh
Madrid 49/40sh
Ajaccio 56/34pc
Naples 45/29s
Tirana 42/24c
Barcelona 50/42pc
Cagliari 50/38s
Faro 61/53pc
Seville 63/50s
Valencia 58/45sh
Palma 61/43pc
Palermo 50/36s
Athens 47/36s
Rabat 74/50s
Algiers 67/49s
Tunis 52/45s

Unsere Ziele

Nach Bearbeitung dieses Kapitels sollten Sie

- die wichtigsten Begriffe in Bezug auf das Wetter können;
- Auskunft über das Wetter geben können.

33. Lektion

Exercise

What's the weather like ...?

in Berlin _____

in Brussels _____

in Paris _____

in London _____

in Madrid _____

in Rome _____

in Stockhom _____

in Munich _____

Fill in

Example:

sun ☀ *sunny*

clouds

rain

fog

storm

snow

Prepare a weather forecast. What's the weather like in London?

Look for more information:
http://www.bbc.co.uk/weather

Fahrenheit and Celsius temperature scales

212 Boiling point of water
98.4 Normal body temperature
32 Freezing point of water

$°C = (°F - 32) \times 5/9$
$°F = °C \times 9/5 + 32$

London, United Kingdom — BBC WEATHER CENTRE

5-Day Forecast	Thursday	Friday	Saturday	Sunday	Monday
	☁	☁	☀	☁	☁
Temperature (°C / °F)	Max: 11 / 51 Min: 2 / 35	Max: 8 / 46 Min: 8 / 46	Max: 12 / 53 Min: 8 / 46	Max: 11 / 51 Min: 9 / 48	Max: 12 / 53 Min: 7 / 44
Air Pollution Index	3	3	3	3	3
Sun Index	1	1	1	1	1
Sunrise (GMT)	7:59	7:58	7:57	7:56	7:55
Sunset (GMT)	16:22	16:23	16:25	16:26	16:28

Current Nearest Observations	☁
Temperature (°C / °F)	10 / 50
Relative Humidity	78 %
Wind Speed (mph)	10 (SW)
Pressure (mB)	1015, Falling
Visibility	Very good

- Set London to be my hometown Why?
- Go to the BBC Weather Centre.
- Go to Europe Continental Weather

Nearest weather station located at Lat: 51.517, Long: -0.127. Observed at 0900 17/1/2002.   CLOSE

Read

It is true that we can be 'under the weather'. Weather has short and long term effects on our bodies and this is studied by scientists called biometeorologists. It affects the death rate and is linked to seasonal illnesses such as winter flu, sunstroke, or hay fever. Some people claim that they can feel changes in the weather with aches and pains worsening and the onset of headaches. Some sufferers of rheumatism or arthritis even notice changes in atmospheric pressure affecting the fluid around their joints.

Our bodies react differently to the weather depending on our age, sex, or general state of health as well as where we actually live. These reactions are linked to our endocrine system, the system of glands which regulates the production of hormones in our bodies, and which is affected by pain, stress and the weather. One in three people are thought to be sensitive to the changing weather but the old, young and the chronically ill suffer more, and women are generally more sensitive than men.

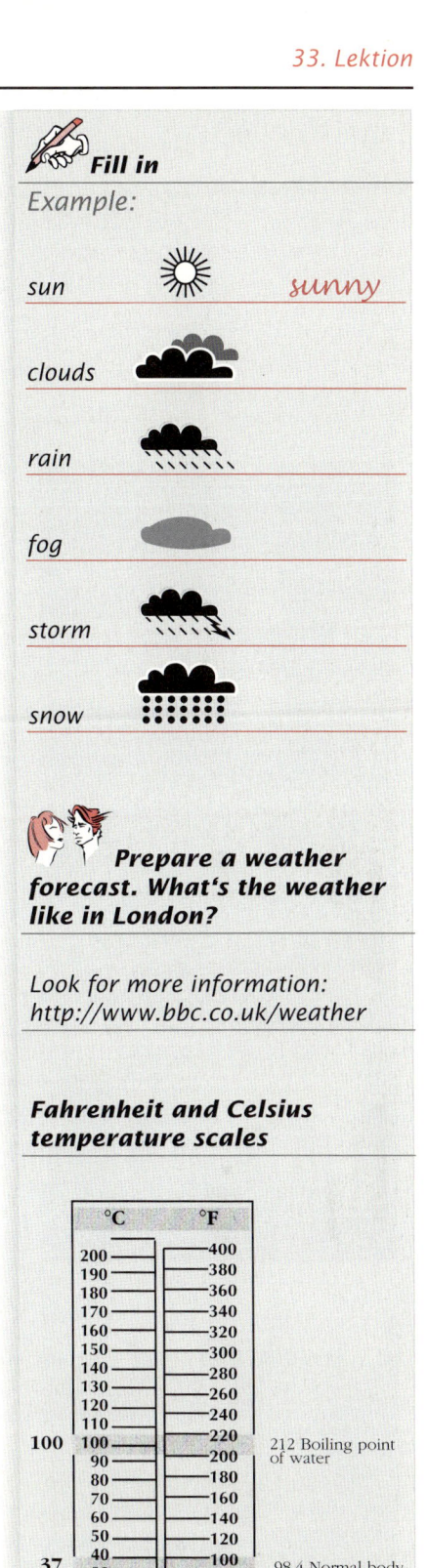

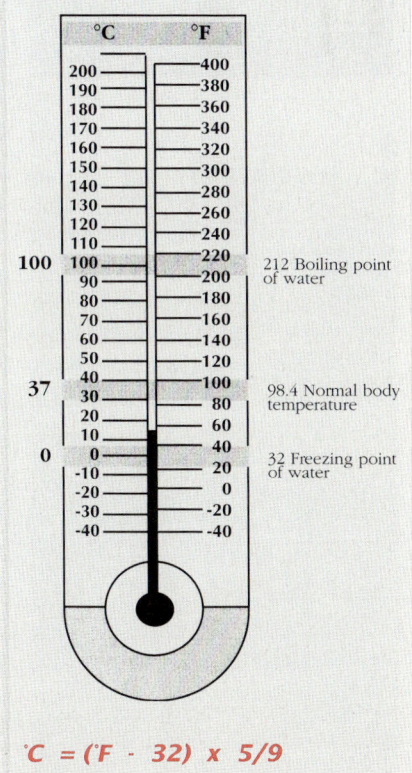

Regional Studies

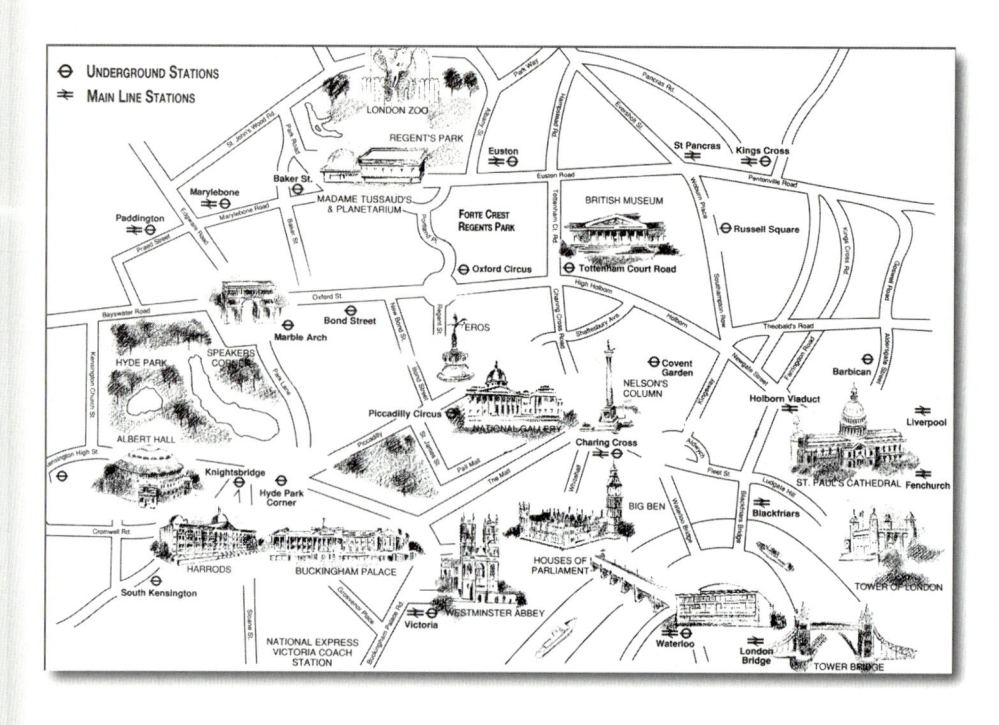

Many roads lead to London – whether you take the Eurostar underneath the English Channel, a ferryboat, or travel by plane in great comfort and directly from Vienna Airport to Heathrow, Gatwick and Stansted.
Despite reservations concerning a united Europe and non-participation in the European Monetary Union, London is still the secret capital of Europe. Nowadays, the conqueror's spirit of the former British Empire has found a different way to express itself: always a trailblazer, always ahead of zeitgeist, London sets trends in arts, culture and fashion. In recent years, Tory grey suits and bowler hats have been exchanged for elegant designer suits and chic fashion of New Labour. There is one thing, however, that will never change: Style! They always pour the milk first and then the tea, and the Gregorian houses still have a stronger influence on the appearance of the city than the fast-lived pop glamour of certain girly bands. Despite techno and house rhythms, the computer-generated sounds in London still carry more melody in their core than anywhere else in our cyber-oriented world, and everything else in good old London makes you somehow happy.

Original Text

Unsere Ziele

Nach Bearbeitung dieses Kapitels sollten Sie

- die wichtigsten Sehenswürdigkeiten von London kennen;
- sehenswerte Orte außerhalb Londons kennen sowie
- eine Besichtigungstour für einen Urlaub in den USA planen können.

The Sights of London

Buckingham Palace
London Palace of Her Majesty Queen Elizabeth II. When she is in residence, the Royal Standard flies from the mast. Changing of the Guard takes place at 11.30 a.m., alternate days in winter. Built by the Duke of Buckingham in 1703, Buckingham Palace was bought by George III in 1761, was rebuilt again by George IV and became Queen Victoria's London home. Refaced in 1913. The Queen's Gallery, which forms part of the private chapel destroyed in the Second World War, contains a varying exhibition of master pieces and works of art from the royal art treasures.
Queen's Gallery Admission Charge. Open: Tuesday to Saturday 11.00 a.m. to 5.00 p.m. Sundays 2.00 p.m. to 5.00 p.m. Royal Mews Admission Charge. Open: Wednesday and Thursday (except during Royal Ascot Meeting) 2.00 p.m. to 4.00 p.m. No advance bookings. Station: Green Park J.P.V., St. James's Park Cir.D., Victoria Cir.D.V.

Covent Garden, Southampton Street, WC2
Originally "Covent Garden", the area was laid out by Inigo Jones for the Earl of Bedford 1635, with a central square enclosed by two covered walks, and the "Actors Church" St. Paul's on the west side. The square is now pedestrianized with the central market hall restored and open as an environment of shops, studios, cafés, promenades and landscaped areas. The Flower Market now houses the London Transport Museum. The market, given Royal Charter in 1671, grew into London's largest wholesale fruit, vegetable and flower market and has moved to a new site off Nine Elms Lane.
Station: Covent Garden P. (closed Sundays).

Houses of Parliament, Parliament Square
Stand throughout the world as a symbol of democratic government. Rebuilt in 1840 on the site of the old Palace of Westminster, which was destroyed by fire, this is the largest building erected in England since the Reformation. When Parliament sits, a flag flies from Victoria Tower by day, and by night a light in the Clock Tower burns above the famous Big Ben. The statue of Winston Churchill is by Mr. Oscar Nemon.
Open: (a) Conducted tours start from Victoria Tower on Saturdays; also Mondays, Tuesdays and Thursdays in August, and Thursdays in September (subject to security).
(b) For admission to hear debates apply in advance to an MP, or join the public queue for the Stranger's Gallery outside St. Stephen's Entrance.
Station: Westminster Cir.D.

Hyde Park
This Royal Park covers 341 acres. On the south side from Hyde Park Corner westwards, many people take an early morning ride in Rotten Row before going to business. On Sundays the park is crowded, and it is then that the famous "tub-thumping" public orators on rostrums and soap boxes near Marble Arch air their views to groups of listeners. The Serpentine, a large lake in the centre of the park, provides boating, and is one of London's Lidos, where, from the last Saturday in April until the second Sunday in October mixed bathing is allowed.
Station: Hyde Park Corner P., Knightsbridge P., Lancaster Gate Cen., Marble Arch Cen.

St. Paul's Cathedral, Ludgate Hill
This is Sir Christopher Wren's masterpiece, built to replace the much larger Old Cathedral on the same site after its destruction in the Great Fire of 1666. The most prominent of London's buildings, this is an immense Renaissance structure, its exterior length being 515 ft., its width across transepts 250 ft., and the height from pavement to the top of the cross 365 ft. Together with other chapels in St. Paul's there is the American Chapel which was dedicated in the presence of Queen Elizabeth II and the then Vice-President Nixon of the United States. Among the many famous people buried here are Christopher Wren, Nelson, Wellington, Jellicoe, Reynolds and Turner. 627 steps lead to the Galleries and to the Great Hall.
Open: Summer 9.00 a.m. to 6.00 p.m. Winter 9.00 a.m. to 5.00 p.m. East End, Crypt and Galleries on Weekdays only 10.00 a.m. to 4.15 p.m. (3.15 Winter); from 11.00 a.m. Saturdays. Visiting subject to services.
Admission Charge to Crypt, Galleries and East End.

34th Lesson

Tower of London
Built in part by William the Conqueror in 1078 as a fortress to guard the river approach to London, this is the most perfect example of a medieval castle in England, the outer walls being added later. The White Tower contains, besides its collection of firearms and execution relics, the finest early-Norman chapel in this country. The Crown Jewels are housed in Waterloo Block. Heralds Museum shows history and development of heraldry. Anne Boleyn, Katherine Howard, Lady Jane Grey, Margaret Countess of Salisbury, Jane Viscountess Rochford, Robert Devereux Earl of Essex were executed on Tower Green.
Admission Charge: extra charge for the Jewel House. Weekdays March to end October 9.30 a.m. to 5.00 p.m. November to end February 9.30 a.m. to 4.00 p.m. Sundays 2.00 p.m. to 5.00 p.m. March to end October. Closed Good Friday, Christmas Day and Boxing Day. Jewel House closed all February for cleaning.
Station: Tower Hill Cir.D.

Trafalgar Square
Laid out as a war memorial and named after the victory of Trafalgar, the square was completed in 1841. In the centre raises Nelson's Column, 170 ft. high overall, allowing Nelson a view of the sea. The lions at the base are by Landseer. Fountains and pigeons delight on lookers. Facing Whitehall is a 17th century equestrian statue of Charles I, the Martyr King. On the north side are the standard measures of length: inch, foot etc.
Station: Charing Cross B.J.N. & SR.

Westminster Abbey, Parliament Square
One of the most interesting and historic religious buildings in England; and architecturally one of the masterpieces of the Middle Ages. Founded about 800 AD, the present edifice was planned and erected as a Royal Mausoleum by Henry III in memory of Edward the Confessor; and until George II most of the Kings of England were buried with its precincts. Almost all, too, have been crowned here; the only two exceptions being Edward V, who was murdered before he could be crowned, and the Duke of Windsor Edward VIII, who renounced the throne before his coronation. The famous Coronation Chair is in Edward the Confessor's Chapel. Many famous men are buried in the Abbey; there is the well-known Poets' Corner and the grave of the Unknown Warrior.
Open daily 8.00 a.m. to 6.00 p.m., Wednesday to 8.00 p.m.; Sundays Nave only (between services).
Admission Charge to Royal Chapels, Poets' Corner, Chapter House and Museum.
Station: Westminster Cir.D., St. James's Park Cir.D.

Westminster Bridge, 1D79
The second bridge to be built over the Thames in London, it was not even begun until 1739. The present bridge dates from 1862.
Station: Westminster Cir.D.

Original Text

London's Tate Gallery
Celebrate the beguiling, cockeyed world of surrealism at major exhibitions at London's Tate Modern gallery. Across from St. Paul's Cathedral, on the other side of the Thames, you can marvel at modern art in an impressive building, and the entrance is free. To call the Tate Modern an art gallery is pure understatement, because the former power station, which supplied the city's energy well into the fifties, offers spectacular insights and views. Permanent exhibitions show works from all the important epochs of the 20th century.
Open: daily 10 AM–5:50 PM.
Admission charge: Admission to the rest of the gallery is free, but tickets for exhibitions are $12 for adults and $9 for seniors and educators
Station: The gallery is located at Bankside, London SE1 The nearest Tube stop is Southwark

Millennium Dome
The Millennium Dome, clearly visible from the riverside at Greenwich and from the upper parts of Greenwich park, opened to the public on January 1, 2000.
The Dome was completed at a total cost of something approaching £800 million. Designed by Richard Rogers (of Lloyd's Building and Pompidou Centre fame), the Dome's geodesic dome is by far the world's largest – 1km in circumference and

50m in height – held up by a dozen, 90m-tall, yellow steel masts. The interior is divided into twelve themed zones, each replete with interactive and virtual reality gadgetry. At the centre a high-tech, live, multi-media extravaganza is performed at regular intervals.

Getting to the Dome is an experience in itself. The site has its very own Jubilee line tube station designed by Norman Foster. There are also several options of arriving by boat and an aerial cable car link with East India DLR station on the north bank of the Thames

Original Text

Exercise

Working in pairs answer the following.

Buckingham Palace

English Queens and Kings _____

Opening hours of Queen's Gallery _____

Why is it called Buckingham Palace? _____

Covent Garden

What was it in the last century? _____

What is it now? _____

What happened to the flower market? _____

Houses of Parliament

What was on the site of the Houses of Parliament before 1840?

_____

Which statue can be seen? _____

Where can you find Big Ben? _____

Hyde Park

Where can people take a ride? _____

What's the name of the lake? _____

Underground stations: _____

St. Paul's Cathedral

Who was the architect? _____

Which event caused the reconstruction? _____

People buried here: _____

Find the way to the sights by underground. Your hotel is at Earl's Court. Use the maps on page 146 and on the back cover.

Ask for each of the sights. Describe the sight asked for (underground station, built when …).

34th Lesson

A Day out of London

Canterbury / Kent
58 miles from central London.
22 St. Peter's Street (Mon–Sat, all year). (0227) 66567.
Ancient city, with more than 2,000 years of history. One of the earliest centres of Christianity in England – the magnificent cathedral, 12th to 15th century, stands on the site of the first cathedral founded by St. Augustine on his mission to England in 597. After the murder in the cathedral of Archbishop Thomas Becket, in 1170, it became one of the main centres of pilgrimage in Europe. About half of the medieval city walls remain, on the eastern side. Several interesting museums. Shopping centre rebuilt after bomb damage in last war. Shops close early Thursday.
Travel from London.
Two trains per hour from Victoria, fastest journey time 1 hour 18 minutes; also hourly from Charing Cross and Waterloo East, journey time 1 hour 30 minutes.
Triple Ticket Destination.
National Express: Two-hourly, daily from Victoria Coach Station, journey time 1 hour 50 minutes.
A2, M2.

Cambridge / Cambridgeshire
54 miles from central London.
Wheeler Street (Mon–Sat, all year, daily, May–Sept). (0223) 358977, weekends 353363. Guided tours of city available throughout year.
Beautiful county town with one of the oldest universities in England. There are 31 colleges, of which Peterhouse was the first to be founded in 1284. King's College Chapel contains Rubens' famous painting
"The Adoration of the Magi" Cambridge has a wide variety of good shops, lovely parks, Botanic Garden, riverside walks. Punts or rowing boats can be hired for a trip past the "Backs" – lawns sloping down to the riverside. Most shops open Mon–Sat.
Travel from London.
Hourly from Liverpool Street, journey time 1 hour. Triple Ticket Destination.
National Express: Hourly from Victoria Station, journey time 1 hour 50 minutes.
A10; or A1, then A505, A10; or M11, then A10.

Greenwich / South-East London
51 miles from central London.
Cutty Sark Gardens (daily, Apr–Oct; Sun afternoons, Nov–Mar). (01) 8586376.
Greenwich and Blackheath Trail leaflet available from Tourist Information Centre, Victoria Station, London SW1.
Intimately connected with British sea power. Near the pier in dry dock is the famous clipper, Cutty Sark, launched 1869, also Gipsy Moth IV, in which Sir Francis Chichester sailed around the world 1966 – 67. Royal Naval College, formerly Greenwich Hospital, was rebuilt largely by Sir Christopher Wren for William III on the site of an earlier palace. The Painted Hall is well worth a visit. Nearby Queen's House (1635), by Inigo Jones, is the earliest example of English Palladian architecture. The National Maritime Museum is now housed in this and a range of adjoining buildings. Greenwich Park rises behind to the former Royal Observatory, on Greenwich Meridian. Several fine 17th- and 18th-century houses on western side of park. Many other places to visit, including Ranger's House, former home of the Ranger of Greenwich Park. Shops close early Thursday.
Travel from London.
Two trips per hour from Westminster and Charing Cross piers, journey time 45 minutes.
Hourly from Cannon Street, journey time 11 minutes; also three trains per hour from London Bridge, journey time 8 minutes.
Triple Ticket Destination.
London Transport bus: Route 53 from Piccadilly Circus to Greenwich Park, journey time approx. 50 minutes. Routes 177, 188 from Waterloo to Greenwich, journey time approx. 35 minutes.
A200.

34. Lektion

Dover / Kent
74 miles from central London.
Burlington House, Townwall Street (daily, all year).
(0304) 205108.
Town Hall (Mon–Fri, all year; Mon–Sat, Jun–Aug).
(0304) 206941.
Since Roman times, Dover has been one of the most important entries to the country. It was one of the original Cinque Ports and is now the busiest passenger port in England. The castle epitomizes the history of Dover and England – Roman Pharos, or lighthouse, adjoins Anglo-Saxon church (restored) of St. Mary-in-Castro; magnificent Norman keep; additions and alterations up to present day. Good coastal walks from Dover to Folkestone in one direction, and to Walmer, passing St. Margaret's Bay with lovely Pines Garden, in the other. Shops close early Wednesday.
Travel from London.
Two trains per hour from Charing Cross and Waterloo East, fastest journey time 1 hour 30 minutes.
National Express: Two-hourly from Victoria Coach Station, journey time 2 hours 15 minutes.
A20 (M20) or M2 / A2.

Oxford / Oxfordshire
56 miles from central London.
St. Aldate's (Mon–Sat, all year; daily, May–Sept).
(0865) 726871.
Guided tours of colleges available daily during summer, Sat only in winter.
Ancient and very beautiful university town, with colleges dating from 13th century to present day. Colleges normally open to the public. University College is the oldest; Magdalen (1458) perhaps the most beautiful; Merton has the oldest library in England. Boat trips on the River Thames, here called the Isis; punting on River Cherwell; eights rowing races held from Folly Bridge to Iffley Lock. Lovely walks through Christ Church Meadow and along the river banks. Theatre, museums, excellent shops. Market day: Wed. Most shops open Mon–Sat; some close early Thursday.
Travel from London.
0935a, 0950, 1035a, 1115, 1135a, 1215 (a – change at Didcot) from Paddington, fastest journey time 60 minutes.
Triple Ticket Destination.
Oxford City Link: Half-hourly from Victoria Coach Station, route 190, fastest journey time 1 hour 40 minutes.
A40 (M40).

Ask for one of the towns (distance from London, how to get there, sights ...).

Describe the town and sights you are asked for.

Marlborough / Wiltshire
78 miles from central London.
St. Peter's Church, High Street (Easter weekend; Mon–Sat, May–Sept). (0672) 53989.
Historic town with very wide High Street, and narrow lanes leading through to a picturesque green. At one end is Marlborough College, the famous public school founded in 1843, including a fine 18th-century house which for a time became the Castle Inn – Marlborough was, in coaching days, an important stage on the London to Bath road. Around Marlborough is contrasting scenery; to the north and west open chalk downland; to the south-east the 2,300-acre Savernake Forest, once a medieval hunting chase. Market days: Wed, Sat. Shops close early Wednesday.
Travel from London.
Hourly from Paddington to Swindon, journey time 60 minutes; then local bus, 45 minutes.
A4; or M4 to Junction 12, then A4.

Anna Hathaway's Cottage

Highlight the answers to these questions in the original text.

1. What was the name of Shakespeare's wife?
2. Where was Archbishop Thomas Becket murdered?
3. What is the name of the university, where you can admire one of Rubens' paintings?
4. Where is the cathedral founded by St. Augustine in 597?
5. What is the port, where many ferryboats from the continent arrive?
6. Where do shops close early on Wednesday?
7. Which ship did Francis Chichester use to sail around the world?
8. One of the oldest universities in England is in ...
9. What is the name of the town all smokers should know?
10. In which college is the oldest library in England?
11. Eights rowing races are held in ...
12. What is the birthplace of William Shakespeare?
13. What's Cutty Sark?

Stratford-upon-Avon / Warwickshire
93 miles from central London.
Judith Shakespeare House, 1 High Street (Mon–Sat, all year; daily, Apr–Sept). (0789) 293127. Daily guided tours available.
Stratford-upon-Avon, the birthplace of 16th-century playwright and poet William Shakespeare, is a picturesque old town. Many half-timbered houses line the streets and there is a fine modern theatre on the riverside. Rother Street market on Friday. Shops close early Thursday. You can follow much of Shakespeare's life by visiting the following: Holy Trinity Church, where he was christened and buried; his birthplace in Henley Street; Anne Hathaway's cottage at Shottery (her thatched home prior to her marriage to Shakespeare); Halls Croft, Old Town, a fine Tudor house, where Shakespeare's daughter lived; New Place, Chapel Street, foundations of Shakespeare's last house; Mary Arden's house, 3 miles away at Wilmcote, a Tudor farmhouse with museum, where his mother lived. Stratford is situated in the heart of England's lovliest countryside, and has many fine historical and scenic attractions within easy reach.
Travel from London.
British Rail / Guide Friday Ltd "Shakespeare connection". Trains 0840, 1540, 1610, 1640, 1710 from Euston to Coventry, then express coach; journey time 1 hour 50 minutes; returns early evening or post theatre.
Two-hourly from Paddington (change at Reading and Leamington Spa), fastest journey time 2 hours 21 minutes. Also two trains per hour from Euston to Birmingham New Street, journey time 1 hour 42 minutes; then local train to Stratford, 57 minutes.
National Express: One trip daily from Victoria Coach Station, journey time 2 hours 45 minutes.
A40 (M40) to Oxford, A34.

Windsor / Berkshire
21 miles from central London.
Windsor & Eton Central Station (daily all year).
(95) 52010.
Guided tours of town and castle available Mon–Sat.
Attractive town on River Thames, dominated by the castle which was founded by William the Conqueror and has been a royal residence since the reign of Henry I. The town has cobbled lanes with small antique shops and tea shops; the guildhall was completed by Wren in 1689. Madame Tussaud's new "Royalty and Railways" exhibition is at the Central Station. Surrounded by good walking country in 4,800 acre- Great Park. Eton, across the Thames, has a quaint old High Street and Eton College, founded in 1440 by Henry VI. Market day: Sat. Shops close early Mon, Wed.
Travel from London.
Two trains per hour from Waterloo, journey time 48 minutes; also two trains per hour from Paddington (change at Slough), 30 minutes.
Triple Ticket Destination.
Green Line: Half-hourly (three coaches per hour in summer) from Victoria (Eccleston Bridge); route 700 (May–Sept), journey time 1 hour; route 701, journey time 1 hour 15 minutes; route 704, journey time 1 hour 30 minutes. Hourly from Eccleston Bridge, route 718, journey time 1 hour 45 minutes.
M4 (Junction 6), A308.

Original Text

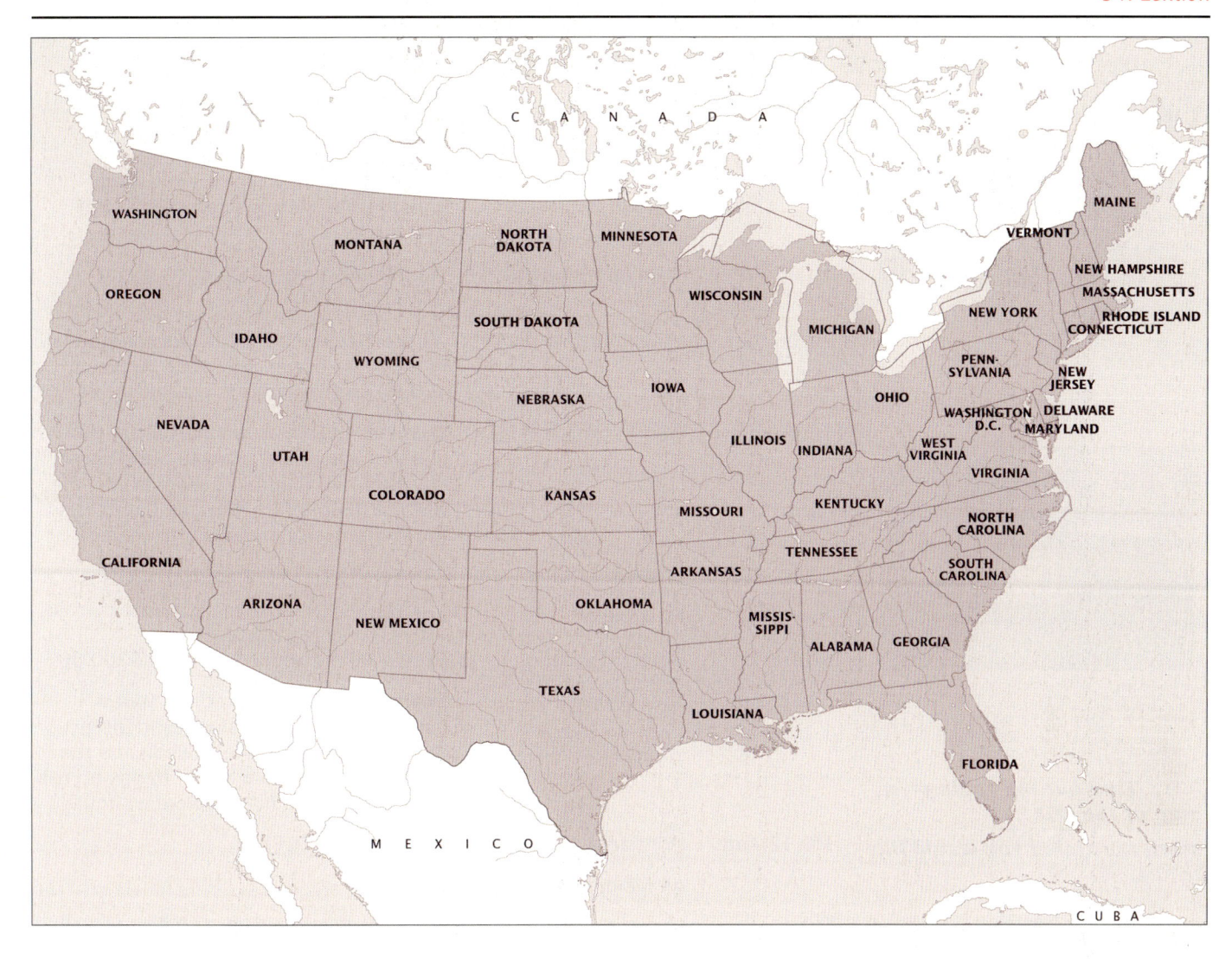

The USA in 4 Weeks

The US claims to be the greatest success story of the modern world – a nation fashioned from an incredibly disparate population who, with little in common apart from a desire to choose their own paths to wealth or heaven, rallied around the ennobling ideals of the Constitution and the Declaration of Independence to forge the richest, most inventive and most powerful country on earth.

Despite polemicists who justly cite the destruction of Native American cultures, racism and imperialism at the top of a long list of wrongdoings, half the world remains in love with the idea of America. This is, after all, the country that introduced the world to the right to the pursuit of happiness, free speech, electric light, airplanes, refrigerators, the space shuttle, computers, blues, jazz, rock & roll and movies that climax at the high school prom.

Come prepared to explore the USA's unique brand of 'foreignness' rather than stay in the comfort zone of the familiar. You'll discover several of the world's most exciting cities, some truly mindblowing landscapes, a strong sense of regionalism, a trenchant mythology, more history than the country gives itself credit for, and arguably, some of the most approachable natives in the world.

Original Text

34th Lesson

Find out the route on a map of the USA.

Mark the sights you would like to see.

Discuss the trip offered here with your partner.

What would you like to see?

What places would you like to visit that are not mentioned in the tour?

Date	Info	Details
FR 02 Aug	LV Vienna	1140A Austrian Airlines 0S87, Lunch / Snack
	AR New York/JFK	2500P
FR 02 Aug	Tour information	While in New York, see the Statue of Liberty, Wall Street, the Empire State Building, the Metropolitan Museum of Art.
TU 06 Aug	Train information	Train to Washington DC costs about $160.00
TU 06 Aug	Hotel information	A hotel like the Wyndham Washington DC in the heart of the city; costs between $79.00 and $259.00.
TU 06 Aug	Tour information	Washington DC is a wonderful city for children and adults. The Air and Space Museum, the National Gallery of Art, the Natural History Museum, the Capitol and the White House are all worth seeing.
SA 10 Aug	LV Wash / Dulles	835A Delta DL351, Breakfast
	AR Atlanta	1027A
SA 10 Aug	Hotel information	Hotels will be about $70.00 to $200.00
SA 10 Aug	Tour information	Downtown's CNN Center, the Martin Luther King Jr. National Historic District, the World of Coca-Cola Pavilion and the Underground Atlanta are all things no trip to Atlanta would be complete without.
MO 12 Aug	LV Atlanta	1015A Delta DL1779
	AR Memphis	838A
MO 12 Aug	Hotel information	Hotels here range from $60.00 to $180.00 per room per night downtown.
MO 12 Aug	Tour information	
WE 14 Aug	LV Memphis	725A Delta DL3724[1], Snack
	AR Dallas / Ft. Worth	902A
WE 14 Aug	LV Dallas / Ft. Worth	950A Delta DL691, Snack
	AR Phoenix	1030A
WE 14 Aug	Car information	Pick up an economy car with unlimited mileage for $299.99 for the week – and drive to Sedona seeing Oak Creek Canyon on the way; about a two hour drive.
WE 14 Aug	Hotel information	Hotels cost about $80.00 to $200.00
TH 15 Aug	Tour infromation	On to Lake Powell for two overnights – one full-day boat trip on the lake exploring fantastic canyons.
TH 15 Aug	Hotel information	Two nights hotel at about $90.00 per night and boat trip at about $60.00.
SO 18 Aug	Tour information	On to Bryce and Zion Park. Both are beautiful, both should be visited.
SO 18 Aug	Hotel information	Very decent accommodations here for about $60.00.
TU 20 Aug	Tour information	The Grand Canyon.
TU 20 Aug	Hotel information	Hotels will be $70.00 to $200.00.

34. Lektion

TH 22 Aug	Tour information	4 to 5 hour drive back to Phoenix – drop off car – pick up flight as follows.
TH 22 Aug	LV Phoenix	1022A Delta DL38241, Lunch
	AR Salt Lake City	100P
TH 22 Aug	LV Salt Lake City	315P Delta DL219, Snack
	AR San Fransisco	406P
TH 22 Aug	Car information	Pick up car – rate same.
TH 22 Aug	Tour information	See the Golden Gate Bridge, Chinatown, Sausalito, The Embarcadero Golden Gate Park etc.
TH 22 Aug	Hotel information	Hotels in San Francisco range from $160.00 to $200.00.
SO 25 Aug	Tour information	Two choices here. Drive along the coast – down the Big Sur on a road, that takes you between the Pacific and interesting hills.
SO 25 Aug	Tour information	Or go inland to Sequoia National Park to see the giant redwoods and up to Yosemite Park.
SO 25 Aug	Hotel information	Hotels for all the above will be in the $100.00 and $150.00 range.
WE 28 Aug	Tour information	On to Los Angeles. See Universal Studios, and Disneyland. If you have time, drive to San Diego to see the Zoo.
WE 28 Aug	Hotel information	Hotels in Los Angeles run about $160.00 per room per night.
SA 31 Aug	LV Los Angeles	820A Delta DL136, Lunch
	AR New York / Newark	440P
SA 31 Aug	LV New York / JFK	635P Austrian 0S88, Dinner
	Misc. information	I have also enclosed a river trip brochure in case you want to put some "excitement" into your trip, and a Pocket Guide for the Metro in Washington DC.

Have a pleasant trip.

Customs Form

Before arriving in the United States of America, each traveler or head of family is required to fill out a Customs Declaration Form.

*Most of the questions can be answered with a "yes" or "no". The form must be signed and dated. Please print legibly, using black or blue ink. Entries must be in **ENGLISH** and in **CAPITAL LETTERS**.*

The Customs Declaration Form will be distributed during the flight.

Immigration and Customs Forms
Before arriving in the United States of America, you are required to fill out an I-94W (green) form if you are a national of one of the countries listed in 8CFR 217 – ask your flight attendant for the current list of elilgible countries – and if either (1) you are traveling to the U.S.A., without a U.S. visa, under the "Visa Waiver Program" or (2) you are in transit to a country outside the U.S.A., without a U.S. visa, under the "Visa Waiver Program." One form is required for each family member.
This form is in two parts. Please complete both the Arrival Record (items 1 through 11) and the Departure Record (items 14 through 17). The reverse side of this form must be signed and dated. Children under the age of 14 must have their forms signed by a parent or guardian. Please print legibly, using black or blue ink.
The bottom part of the form must be kept with your passport until you leave the U.S.A.

[1] Delta Codesshare Partner

Lösungen
Solutions

Appendix

1st Lesson
INTRODUCTION

Dialogues 1–6

Dialogue 1
Mary: Hello. I'm Mary.
Gary: My name is Gary.
Mary: Nice to meet you, Gary.

Dialogue 2
Gary: Here comes my girlfriend, Anna.
Anna, I'd like to introduce you to Mary.
Mary: How do you do?
Anna: How do you do? Nice to meet you.

Dialogue 3
Mary: Where are you from?
Anna: I'm from New York.

Dialogue 4
Mary: And what do you do?
Anna: I'm a waitress in my father's restaurant. My mother is a cook. My father is a waiter and my brother is a hotel assistant. My sister is an apprentice.

Dialogue 5
Anna: What do you do?
Mary: I'm a stewardess and Gary is a travel agent.

Dialogue 6
Mary: Do you like your job?
Anna: Yes, I do.

2nd Lesson
PHONING

Fill in 7

Listening (a)
What's your telephone number?
My number is 01 - 982 77 53.

Listening (b)
Please call me. My mobile telephone number is 0664 / 259 63 48.

Listening (c)
Call Gary, his mobile number is 0676 / 180 32 43.

Listening (d)
May I give you the telephone number of our hotel?
The international dialling code is 0043, the area code is 0732, omit the 0 when dialling from a foreign country, the telephone number is 531 42 27.

3rd Lesson
WELCOMING GUESTS

Dialogues 8

Dialogue (a)
Waiter: Good evening, sir. Can I help you?
Guest: Yes, please. A table for two, please.
Waiter: Please follow me.

Dialogue (b)
Waiter: Good evening, madam. What can I do for you?
Guest (lady): A table for three, please.

Dialogue (c)
John Miller: I'm John Miller. How do you do?
Bill Brown: How do you do? I'm Bill Brown and this is my wife Ellen.
John Miller: Nice to meet you, Mrs. Brown.

Dialogue (d)
Guest (man): Goodbye.
Waiter: Goodbye. Have a nice day.

Dialogue (e)
Bill: Hello, John. How are you today?
John: Not very well. I didn't sleep last night.

Dialogue (f)
Waitress: Good evening, sir. A table for three?
Guest (man): Yes, I phoned this morning. My name is Johnson.
Waitress: This way, please.

4th Lesson
APOLOGIZING

Dialogues 10

Dialogue (a)
Guest: I'd like to book a table for two.
You: I'm afraid we're fully booked.

Dialogue (b)
Guest: I'm looking for a double room with shower for two nights.
You: I'm sorry, there are only rooms with hot and cold water at the moment.

Dialogue (c)
Guest: I'd like to change money.
You: I'm sorry, we don't take foreign money, but you can change it at the reception.

Dialogue (d)
Guest: May I speak to Mr. Duncan in room 204?
You: I'm sorry, the line is engaged. Would you like to leave a message?

Dialogue (e)
Guest: Could I reserve a table for Monday evening?
You: I'm afraid we haven't got any tables left on Monday.

Dialogue (f)
Guest: I'd like a large espresso.
You: I'm sorry, unfortunately the machine is broken.

5th Lesson
TELLING THE TIME

Dialogues 12

Dialogue (a)
When does the next train to Manchester leave?
It leaves at six thirty p.m.

Dialogue (b)
When is breakfast served?
Breakfast is served from 7 to 10 a.m.

Dialogue (c)
Excuse me, what's the time, please?
It's 24 minutes past 8.

Dialogue (d)
Let's have dinner together.
At what time?
Is half past eight all right?

Dialogue (e)
Hurry up, we'll miss the train!
Oh, it's late! It's almost ten to seven.

Dialogue (f)
Hello.
Hello, John. This is Ellen from London. How are you?
Ellen, don't you know it's 3 a.m. in New York?
Oh, I'm sorry, I forgot! It's already 8 o'clock in London.

Dialogue (g)
Excuse me, what are the opening hours of banks?
They are open from 8 a.m. to half past twelve p.m. and from half past one p.m. to 3 p.m.

Dialogue (h)
When does your train arrive?
I think it arrives at 9.50 p.m.

Dialogues 13–15

Dialogue 13
Waitress: Waldviertler Hof. Guten Morgen.
Guest: Good morning. I'd like to reserve a table for Friday lunch.
Waitress: Yes, sir. What time?
Guest: At about one.
Waitress: For how many persons, sir?
Guest: Four persons.
Waitress: Could I have your name, please?
Guest: Duncan. It's D-U-N-C-A-N.
Waitress: Yes, Mr. Duncan. A table for four persons, Friday the 7th, 1 p.m.
Guest: Goodbye.

Dialogue 14
Waiter: Good evening, Bertorelli's. Can I help you?
Guest: I'd like to book a table for six, for Tuesday evening, eight o'clock.
Waiter: Yes, what name, please?
Guest: My name's Andrews.
Waiter: Yes, Mr. Andrews, a table for six, on Tuesday the 9th, at eight o'clock. Thank you.

Dialogue 15
Waiter: Good evening, sir. Can I help you?
Guest: My name is Andrews. I've got a reservation.
Waiter: Just a moment, sir. Yes, Mr. Andrews, a table for six. Please follow me.
Guest: Thank you.
Waiter: Here you are, sir.

6th Lesson
IN THE KITCHEN

Dialogue 16

Austrian chef: I use these kitchen appliances in my restaurant, too, but I don't know their English names.
English chef: Now, this is a mixer and next to it there is the weighing-machine. That's the refrigerator and the kitchen-range is over there.
Austrian chef: And what are the names of the pots and the pans?
English chef: The big one with the two handles is a stock pot.
Austrian chef: And the low one with one handle is a frying pan, isn't it?
English chef: That's right. Here you also have a whisk. You use it for preparing whipped cream. The knife is a cook's knife. It is the most important tool for a cook.

Dialogues 17–19

Dialogue 17
Cook: Here is the Blackpool Restaurant. I'd like to order 8 kilos of trout and 8 kilos of sole.
Fish monger: Yes, fine. When do you need your order?
Cook: Friday morning at 8 o'clock.
Fish monger: Alright, we'll do our best. Thank you for your order. Bye, bye.
Cook: Bye.

Dialogue 18
Cook: Hotel Imperial calling. May I give you my order? I need 2 loins of pork, 10 kilos of veal, 2 fillets of beef, 10 chickens and 10 kilos of lamb chops.
Butcher: Fine, okay. I'll deliver on Saturday morning.
Cook: That's fine. Thank you, bye!

Dialogue 19
Cook: Good morning. Restaurant Four Seasons Calling. Please send us 4 kilos of fresh peas, 3 kilos of very fine string beans, 20 kilos of potatoes and 10 kilos of onions. We also need 5 kilos of carrots and ten heads of absolutely fresh cabbage by tomorrow at 10 o'clock.
Shop: Yes, of course. Any fruit? We have a variety of fresh fruit in season.
Cook: Yes, please deliver 2 big baskets of strawberries, 1 tray of lemons, 2 boxes of oranges and 1 box of home-grown apples.
Shop: Thank you for your order. Bye.

7th Lesson
SERVING STAFF AND SERVING UTENSILS

Dialogue 20

Waiter: Now we have to set the table for dinner this evening.
Apprentice: What shall I do?
Waiter: We have already spread out the tablecloth. On the left side we put the dinner fork. The dinner knife and the tablespoon are on the right side.

Appendix

Apprentice:	Where do I put the side plate?
Waiter:	The side plate with a side knife is on the left. When the guests are sitting, we put the butter dish with a dessert fork above the side plate.
Apprentice:	And the bread basket?
Waiter:	It's in the middle. We do that later. Now take the wine glass and put it above the dinner knife. The water glass is on its right and the napkin is in it.
Apprentice:	Shall I put the ashtray and salt and pepper in the middle of the table?
Waiter:	Yes, that's right.

8th Lesson

BREAKFAST

Dialogue 21

Waiter:	Good morning, madam!
Guest:	Good morning. May I have breakfast, please?
Waiter:	Certainly, madam! English or continental?
Guest:	English, please. I'm rather hungry.
Waiter:	Very well, madam! Would you like some juice first?
Guest:	Yes, bring me a big glass of orange juice.
Waiter:	Yes, madam. Do you want a cereal?
Guest:	No, thank you. No cereal for me. Let me have two fried eggs with ham and a roll, please.
Waiter:	Of course, madam! Coffee or tea?
Guest:	Tea, please. A small pot will do.
Waiter:	Yes, madam. Anything else?
Guest:	No, thanks. That's all for the moment.
Waiter:	Very well, madam. Thank you.

9th Lesson

IN THE RESTAURANT

Dialogues 22–26

Dialogue 22

Waiter:	Here are the menus. Would you like a before dinner drink?
Man:	Yes, bring me a Martini cocktail. What about you, dear?
Woman:	A Gin and Tonic would be fine.
Waiter:	Thank you.
...	
Waiter:	Here you are. One Gin and Tonic and a Martini cocktail. May I take your orders now?
Man:	What's the soup of the day?
Waiter:	Cream of cauliflower.
Man:	Yes, one soup for me.
Woman:	The melon with raw ham for me, please.
Waiter:	One soup of the day and one melon with raw ham. Thank you.

Dialogue 23

Waiter:	May I take your order now?
Woman:	Yes, I'd like fried mushrooms, please.
Waiter:	Yes, madam.

Dialogue 24

Woman:	The melon with raw ham for me, please.
Waiter:	I'm sorry, madam, there's no more melon. May I recommend the fresh asparagus?
Woman:	Oh, I'd love it.

Dialogue 25

Man:	What's the soup of the day?
Waiter:	Cream of cauliflower.
Man:	No soup. I'll have the shrimp cocktail.

Dialogue 26

Man:	Chicken salad for me. What about you, Jane?
Jane:	I'll have the tomato soup.
Waiter:	Right, so that's one chicken salad and one tomato soup.

Dialogue 27

Waiter:	What would you like to follow?
Woman:	I think, I'll have some fish, please. Which would you suggest?
Waiter:	The fried carp is excellent.
Woman:	Yes, and a potato salad with it.
Waiter:	And for you, sir?
Man:	I think I'll try the roast pork. What do you serve with it?
Waiter:	Sauerkraut and a bread dumpling.
Man:	That sounds good.
Waiter:	And to drink?
Man:	A pint of beer for me.
Woman:	A glass of white wine and a mineral water.
Man:	And two apple strudels for the dessert, please.

10th Lesson

HOTEL STAFF

Dialogues 28

Dialogue (a)

Receptionist:	Neptun Hotel. Good evening.
Guest:	Good evening, I'd like to book a double room for Saturday.
Receptionist:	Yes, sir. What's your name, please?
Guest:	Kontarini.
Receptionist:	How do you spell that?
Guest:	K-O-N-T-A-R-I-N-I.

Dialogue (b)

Waiter:	Restaurant "Bon Appetit". Good afternoon.
Guest:	Good afternoon. I'd like to make a reservation for Friday evening.
Waiter:	Yes, sir. What's your name, please?
Guest:	Carranantee.
Waiter:	Would you spell that, please?
Guest:	C-A-R-R-A-N-A-N-T-E-E.

Dialogue (c)

Receptionist:	Beach Hotel. Good morning.
Guest:	Good morning. I'd like a single room for tonight.
Receptionist:	Yes, sir. What's your name, please?
Guest:	Poggemayer.
Receptionist:	Would you spell that, please?
Guest:	P-O-G-G-E-M-A-Y-E-R.

11th Lesson
A DAY AT A HOTEL

Dialogues 29

Dialogue (a)
Woman: Excuse me, where can I buy a pen and some paper?
Receptionist: Over there in the stationer's shop, madam.

Dialogue (b)
Woman: I'm going out with my husband tonight. Where can I have my hair done?
Receptionist: We have a hairdresser in the hotel. Shall I make an appointment for you?

Dialogue (c)
Man: Where can I find the tennis trainer?
Receptionist: He should be on the tennis court, sir.

Dialogue (d)
Man: I have to wait half an hour for my wife. She's gone swimming. Where can I have a coffee meanwhile?
Receptionist: You can wait in the coffee shop over there or I'll let you bring a coffee to the lounge. It's not as noisy there.

12th Lesson
SHOPPING

Dialogues 30

Dialogue (a)
Man: I can't find men's wear. Can you help me?
Shop a.: Of course, sir. You have to take the stairs to the lower sales floor.

Dialogue (b)
Woman: I'm looking for some new white t-shirts for my son.
Shop a.: Right over here, madam, next to the children's underwear.

Dialogue (c)
Boy: I need a new chef's jacket. Do you also have red ones?
Shop a.: I'm not sure. Have a look downstairs, they will help you there.

Dialogue (d)
Woman: Where can I find knives?
Shop a.: They are on the upper sales floor, next to the pots and pans.

13th Lesson
FAMILY

Dialogue 31

TV moderator: Good evening, ladies and gentlemen. This is our "Family Party". First I'd like to welcome the Johnson family. Hello, Mr. Johnson, how are you?
Mr. Johnson: Hello. I'm fine, thanks.
TV moderator: Mr. Johnson, will you please introduce your family?
Mr. Johnson: Yes, of course. This is my wife Alice, she's a teacher. Next to her is our eldest son, Tom, and his wife, Kate. On my left is our son Ed, and the lady beside him is Alice's mother.
TV moderator: And who is this nice little girl?
Mr. Johnson: That's Tom's daughter Ann. She's my first grandchild.

14th Lesson
CAFÉS

Listen and connect 32

Guest: Good afternoon.
Waiter: Good afternoon, madam.
Guest: I'd like to have a cup of coffee.
Waiter: There are many kinds of coffee specialities. I can offer you a Kapuziner, a Kaisermelange, a Pharisäer, or just a large or small espresso.
Guest: Sorry, I don't know anything about the Viennese coffee specialities. Could you explain them to me?
Waiter: A Kapuziner is a coffee with a small amount of cream, a Kaisermelange is half coffee and half milk with egg liqueur, and a Pharisäer is coffee with rum and whipped cream.
Guest: I'll try the Pharisäer, it sounds interesting. And what sweets can you offer me?
Waiter: We have Gugelhupf, Sachertorte and Apfelstrudel.
Guest: What's a Gugelhupf?
Waiter: That's a Viennese yeast cake.
Guest: Oh no! Bring me an apple strudel, please.

15th Lesson
FRONT OFFICE

Dialogues 33–34

Dialogue 33
Receptionist: Good evening, sir. Welcome to Hotel Hope. Can I help you?
Guest: Yes, I phoned last week to book a double room.
Receptionist: What name is it?
Guest: Barry Benson. B-E-N-S-O-N.
Receptionist: Yes, Mr. Benson, one double room for three nights.
Guest: That's right.
Receptionist: Would you fill in this registration form, please?
Guest: Is it necessary to fill in the passport information?
Receptionist: Yes, if you would. Here is your key. It's room number 22 on the second floor. I'll ask the porter to help you with your luggage.
Guest: By the way, what time's breakfast?
Receptionist: Breakfast is served from 7.30 to 10.30 a.m.

Dialogue 34
Receptionist: Good evening, madam. May I help you?
Guest: I have a booking for tonight. The name is Jones.
Receptionist: One moment, madam. Yes, that was a single room with shower.
Guest: That's right.

Appendix

Receptionist: Would you like to register, please? Just put your surname here on the first line, then your first name below. Here, put your date of birth, and next to that, put your nationality. Write your home address on the next line, and please sign here. Could I see your passport, please?
Guest: Here you are.
Receptionist: Thank you. You have room number 12 on the first floor. The porter will show you to your room. Have a nice evening, madam.

Exercise 35–42

Dialogue 35
Receptionist: Good evening, sir. May I help you?
Guest: I'd like to book a single room.
Receptionist: How long will you be staying, sir?
Guest: Two nights.
Receptionist: Would you like a room with bath or shower?
Guest: With shower, please.
Receptionist: Can you give me your name, please?
Guest: Robert James. J-A-M-E-S.
Receptionist: Mr. Robert James. A single room with shower for two nights.

Dialogue 36
Receptionist: Good afternoon. May I help you?
Guest: Yes, we have a booking for tonight. My name is Dickson.
Receptionist: Just a moment, please. Yes, that was a double room with bath.
Guest: That's right.
Receptionist: Would you fill in this registration form, please? Thank you. May I see your passport, please?
Guest: Here you are.
Receptionist: Thank you. Here's your key. You have room number 20 on the second floor. The porter will carry your luggage up to the room.

Dialogue 37
Guest: Have you got any vacancies?
Receptionist: What kind of room would you like?
Guest: Er ... a twin-bedded room with bath, please. How much is bed and breakfast?
Receptionist: 40.00 euros per person and day.

Dialogue 38
Guest: The travel agency reserved a room for me.
Receptionist: Who's the reservation for?
Guest: Wilson. W-I-L-S-O-N.
Receptionist: Would you fill in this registration form, please?

Dialogue 39
Guest: I'd like a double room for one night.
Receptionist: Do you have a reservation, sir?
Guest: Yes, my name is Swanley.

Dialogue 40
Guest: Do you have a double room for one week?
Receptionist: Sorry, we're fully booked. Would you like me to get you a room in another hotel?
Guest: No, thank you.

Dialogue 41
Guest: Do you have a single room for this weekend?
Receptionist: Yes, sir. A single with bath.
Guest: How much is the room?

Dialogue 42
Guest: Could I book a family room for next week?
Receptionist: I'm afraid we haven't got any rooms left.

Dialogues 43–45

Dialogue 43
Guest: Have you got a map of the city centre?
Porter: Yes, madam. Here you are.
Guest: I'd like to go to the cathedral this morning. Is it within walking distance?
Porter: Take a look at the map. We are here. When you go out of the hotel, go over the bridge, go down to the traffic lights, then turn right. Go across the Mozartplatz. You'll see the cathedral straight ahead of you.
Guest: Fine, thank you very much.

Dialogue 44
Guest: Excuse me, could you tell me how to get to the zoo, please?
Porter: Well, it's too far to walk. You can take the bus number 55. You get off right outside the zoo.
Guest: And where's the bus stop?
Porter: It's just across the street, madam.
Guest: That sounds easy. Thank you.

Dialogue 45
Guest: Excuse me, can you tell me if the theatre is far from here?
Receptionist: It's only a few minutes walk.
Guest: How do I get there?
Receptionist: Turn right outside the hotel, go straight across at the traffic lights, follow this street, and go down to the roundabout. You'll see the theatre in front of you.
Guest: Thank you.

16th Lesson
HOTEL FACILITIES

Listen 48

Sarah: One thing we ought to have is a baby-listening service with a microphone in each room. Even though guests can arrange for someone to come and stay with their baby while they are away, we should offer a listening service from the central switchboard as well.
Peter: Well, let's find out the possibilities. But before we should really modernize our telephone system. At present we only have direct-dialling for local calls, to make a long-distance call you have to be connected by the receptionist. There should be modern equipment for all in- and out-going calls, where the charge would appear on the bills automatically, too.
Sarah: You're right. Most hotels have that nowadays, and business people certainly want to be able to dial directly. There should also be computer links in each room.
Peter: Talking about business facilities, we should provide better photocopying facilities. Now guests must hand in their papers at the reception, but we could provide a photocopier with public access, so that guests could do their own photocopying.
Sarah: I agree. How about placing a fax machine next to it?

Peter: Good idea! There are other facilities we don't offer like shoe-cleaning machines. They are quite useful and we could put one on each floor next to the elevator, so guests can shine their shoes while waiting for the elevator. Things like that can make all the difference …

Dialogue 49

Waiter: Room service, good morning. What can I do for you?
Guest: This is Mr. Moore in room 295. We would like to order breakfast.
Waiter: Yes, sir.
Guest: We would like to start with a glass of orange juice and a glass of grapefruit juice, not canned or frozen.
Waiter: Of course, sir.
Guest: Then I'll have the Classic Breakfast, but can I have ham instead of bacon?
Waiter: No problem, sir.
Guest: My wife would like a muesli and then toast with homemade preserves. Which ones are served with the toast?
Waiter: Would orange and strawberry be alright?
Guest: Fine.
Waiter: Very well, sir. Tea or coffee?
Guest: We'll both have coffee, one decaffeinated.
Waiter: Thank you for your order. Breakfast will be brought up soon. That was room 295?

17th Lesson
IN THE KITCHEN

Dialogues 50–52

Dialogue 50
John: What about the vegetables?
Chef: Today we'll have buttered green peas and carrots with the roast veal, and braised cabbage with the second main course.

Dialogue 51
John: How can we prepare the spinach?
Chef: Buttered or baked with cheese sauce or as creamed spinach.

Dialogue 52
John: What will we do with the string beans and the asparagus today?
Chef: Well, first we'll boil the beans and the asparagus. Then we can prepare buttered string beans. The asparagus can be served with melted butter, Dutch sauce or à la polonaise.

Dialogues 53–54

Dialogue 53
Waiter: I can offer you either a porterhouse steak or a T-bone steak. Which one would you like?
Guest: I'll take the porterhouse steak.
Waiter: How would you like your steak?
Guest: I'd like it medium, please.

Dialogue 54
Waiter: Would you like your fillet steak rare, medium or well done?
Guest: I'd like it medium rare, please, and bring me a mixed salad, too.

18th Lesson
IN THE RESTAURANT

Listen 55

Waiter: Good evening. Tonight we have a special five-course dinner with two choices of each course. Here are the menus. Would you like an apéritif? I can offer you a Martini, a sherry, a Campari, a Manhattan or fresh orange juice.
Mr. Bates: One dry sherry and a glass of orange juice for me.
Waiter: Thank you.
…
Waiter: Here are your apéritifs. Are you ready to order now?
Mr. Bates: Well, we've chosen two parfaits.
Waiter: Yes, and which soup?
Mrs. Bates: What is the "Cream Franz Joseph" soup?
Waiter: It's a chicken cream soup with vegetables.
Mr. Bates: No soup for me.
Mrs. Bates: I'll take the beef broth. Then we will both have the Dover sole.
Waiter: Very well. And for the main course?
Mrs. Bates: I would like the fillet of beef.
Mr. Bates: I don't like turkey with chestnut stuffing. I think I'll take the beef, too.
Waiter: May I recommend the Grünen Veltliner with the fish and the Pinot Noir with the main course?
Mr. Bates: That's fine.
Waiter: And for the dessert?
Mrs. Bates: I'll have the soufflé.
Mr. Bates: I'd prefer the baked Alaska.
Waiter: Thank you very much.

Dialogues 56–59

Dialogue 56
Guest: Waiter, can I have the bill, please?
Waiter: Certainly, madam.
Guest: Why are there two different percentages? Could you kindly explain it to me?
Waiter: That's the value-added tax, madam. In Austria we have two different percentages of VAT in the hotel business: 10 per cent on food and accommodation, 20 per cent on beverages, coffee and tea. The total amount includes service and tax.

Dialogue 57
Guest: I'd like to settle my bill, please.
Waiter: How are you paying, sir?
Guest: In cash. Do you accept foreign currency?
Waiter: What kind have you got?
Guest: US Dollars.
Waiter: Of course, sir. The exchange rate is …

Dialogue 58
Guest: The bill, please.
Waiter: Yes, madam.
Guest: I'd like to pay by credit card. You do take American Express, don't you?
Waiter: Certainly, madam.
Guest: Fine. Here's my card.
Waiter: Thank you. Would you sign here, please? Here's your receipt, madam.

Appendix

Dialogue 59
Guest: Waiter, the bill, please.
Waiter: Would you like to put it on your hotel bill, sir?
Guest: Yes, please.
Waiter: What's your room number, sir?
Guest: 225.
Waiter: Thank you, sir. Would you sign here, please?

19th Lesson
DEALING WITH COMPLAINTS

Listen and fill in 60

Dialogue (a)
Guest: This coffee is cold.
Waiter: I'm sorry, I'll bring you a hot one.

Dialogue (b)
Guest: This glass is dirty.
Waiter: Sorry, I'll bring you a clean one.

Dialogue (c)
Guest: The wine tastes like vinegar.
Waiter: Sorry, I'll speak to the wine butler.

Dialogue (d)
Guest: The meat is rather tough.
Waiter: I'm sorry. Would you like to change your order?

Dialogue (e)
Guest: I've been kept waiting for half an hour.
Waiter: I'm sorry, may I take your order now?

Dialogue (f)
Guest: This fish is not fresh.
Waiter: Sorry, I'll speak to the chef.

Listen and complete 61–63

Dialogue 61
Manager: You asked to see me, sir?
Guest: I certainly did.
Manager: Perhaps you could tell me what the problem is?
Guest: It's the meat. It's tough. I told the waiter, but he didn't take any notice.
Manager: I'm extremely sorry. He should have taken it back.
Guest: Well, why didn't he?
Manager: A misunderstanding. I'll have it taken care of immediately.

Dialogue 62
Wine butler: Can I help you, sir?
Guest: This wine is corked. Taste it yourself.
Wine butler: There doesn't seem to be anything wrong with it. Perhaps it's a little dry. I'd recommend you to try the Beaujolais.

Dialogue 63
Waiter: Is everything alright, sir?
Guest: No, it isn't. The tablecloth is dirty and the fish is not fresh.
Waiter: I'll change the tablecloth straight away and then I'll speak to the chef.

20th Lesson
IN THE BAR

Dialogue 64
John: This is our bartender.
Bill: What drinks does he prepare?
John: He prepares long and short drinks and various cocktails. You know, the bartender or barkeeper and the barman as well as the barlady can be in charge of the bar area. We have two barwaiters and three barwaitresses.
Bill: Are they also in charge of the bar area?
John: No, they serve the drinks which are prepared by the barkeeper or barlady.

Dialogues 65–68

Dialogue 65
Guest: A pint of bitter, please!
Waiter: I'm sorry, sir. We only have lager and export beer.
Guest: Which is better?
Waiter: Well, the export beer is stronger, but both are light. They are bottled, not draught.
Guest: I'll take a bottle of the stronger one, please.
Waiter: Of course, here you are.

Dialogue 66
Guest: A double Scotch, please!
Waiter: On the rocks, sir?
Guest: No, just a little water, please.
Waiter: Anything else, sir?
Guest: Yes, a Martini Dry Cocktail, please.

Dialogue 67
Guest: Something non-alcoholic for me.
Waiter: A tonic, fruit juice, a ginger-ale, or mineral water, perhaps?
Guest: Grape juice. And can you bring some crisps and peanuts?
Waiter: Certainly, sir.

Dialogue 68
Guest: What cocktails do you serve?
Waiter: You can have a Martini Cocktail, a Bloody Mary, a Gin Fizz or a Side Car.
Guest: One Gin Fizz, and what does a Side Car consist of?
Waiter: It consists of brandy, Cointreau and lemon juice.
Guest: No, thanks. Bring me a Bloody Mary, please.
Waiter: Anything else?
Guest: Do you sell cigarettes?
Waiter: Yes, sir. What sort?

Listen 69

When you prepare a Gin Fizz, you take a shaker, put in two or three ice cubes, add the other ingredients (lemon juice, sugar and gin) and shake well. Then you take a strainer and strain the drink into a tumbler which you fill up with cold soda water.

For the preparation of a Martini Dry Cocktail we need a mixing glass. We put in two or three ice cubes, add the ingredients (gin, dry or sweet vermouth) and perhaps Angostura or orange bitter, and stir well with a mixing spoon. Then we strain the drink into a cocktail glass. A sweet Martini we serve with a cherry, a dry Martini with an olive or a little slice of lemon peel.

21st Lesson
SIGHTSEEING IN AUSTRIA

"Der liebe Augustin" 🔘 70

Diese Hörübung ist nur in der Österreichausgabe dieses Buches. Aus produktionstechnischen Gründen ist dieser Text auch auf der CD bzw. Kassette enthalten.

23rd Lesson
BRUNCH

Dialogue 🔘 71

Head waiter:	This morning we are going to set up brunch in the dining-room.
Apprentice waiter:	What is brunch?
Head waiter:	Brunch is a meal which combines breakfast and lunch in buffet form. First of all we'll set up the buffet table. We'll need water and milk glasses, stacks of small plates, bowls, coffee spoons, dessert forks, and knives.
Apprentice waiter:	And how will the tables be set?
Head waiter:	We'll set them for an American breakfast. Now start bringing out the food: cereals, milk products, fresh and stewed fruit, fruit and vegetable juices, meat, egg and fish dishes, bread, butter, marmalade, honey, salads.
Apprentice waiter:	I think I have everything on the table now.
Head waiter:	Yes, it looks very nice, but you forgot the bread basket.
Apprentice waiter:	I'm sorry, I'll get it at once.

Dialogue 🔘 72

Head waiter:	Good afternoon!
Mr. Nelson:	Good … Oh, it's 12.30! I suppose we've missed breakfast this morning, haven't we? We were at the opera last night and we overslept.
Head waiter:	Normally we don't serve breakfast at this time, but today we have a brunch buffet.
Mr. Nelson:	No, thank you. I really wanted some eggs, rolls, and a cup of strong black coffee.
Head waiter:	Sir, you can have that and a variety of other breakfast and lunch dishes at the brunch buffet.
Mr. Nelson:	Could we take a look at the brunch buffet?
Head waiter:	Yes, of course, just follow me. Here we are. As you can see, we have cereals, fruit, bread, muffins, and rolls, poached eggs, roast chicken and sausage. Salads and vegetables are over there. At this end of the table you'll find many desserts and cheeses.
Mr. Nelson:	I don't know where to begin.
Head waiter:	May I suggest a fruit juice and perhaps a roll and butter? Then the excellent poached eggs. Just try a little of everything and don't miss the delicious pastries. Take your time, the buffet is open until two and you can eat as much as you like.
Mr. Nelson:	We didn't miss breakfast after all, we're just combining it with lunch.

24th Lesson
DINNER

Dialogue 🔘 73

Waiter:	Good evening.
Mr. Wilson:	Good evening. My name is Wilson. I booked a table for eight o'clock.
Waiter:	That's right, a table for two. Would you come this way, please?
Mr. Wilson:	Thank you.
Waiter:	May I bring you an apéritif before you order?
Mr. Wilson:	Yes, I'll have a sherry. The same for you, Jill?
Mrs. Wilson:	No, I'd rather have a Campari.
Waiter:	Your menus.
Mr. Wilson:	Thank you.
Waiter:	May I take your order now?
Mrs. Wilson:	I haven't decided yet. What would you recommend for the main course?
Waiter:	The beef medallions in Merlot sauce is very good. It is served with a bouquet of vegetables.
Mrs. Wilson:	Fine, I'll have that.
Waiter:	And for you, sir?
Mr. Wilson:	I'll have the fillet "mignons" with pepper sauce. Rare, please.
Waiter:	And to start with?
Mr. Wilson:	I'll have the pike-perch terrine and then the consommé with vegetable strudel. What about you, Jill?
Mrs. Wilson:	I don't like pike-perch. What is the gourmet salad?
Waiter:	It is lettuce with quail praline, goose liver, quail egg, fillet of rabbit.
Mrs. Wilson:	That sounds good. I'll start with that, followed by the lobster bisque.
Waiter:	Very well, madam.
Wine butler:	Good evening. Here is our wine list.
Mr. Wilson:	What about a "Grüner Veltliner" to start with?
Mrs. Wilson:	Yes, that's fine.
Mr. Wilson:	Bring us a bottle of "Veltliner" from the Wachau to begin with and then we'll have the Austrian burgundy.
Wine butler:	Fine, sir.

Dialogue 🔘 74

Waiter:	Are you ready for the dessert now?
Mrs. Wilson:	Yes, I'll have the French chocolate cake.
Waiter:	With whipped cream?
Mrs. Wilson:	Why not?
Waiter:	Have you tried our delicious white chocolate mousse, sir?
Mr. Wilson:	No, I haven't. But I'd rather have some fresh fruit.
Waiter:	I'll bring you the dessert trolley. Perhaps you'll also find a pastry to your liking.
Mr. Wilson:	Yes, thank you.
Waiter:	May I offer you some coffee and an after dinner drink?
Mrs. Wilson:	Some coffee for me, please.
Mr. Wilson:	The same for me and a cognac, please.
Waiter:	Thank you.

Appendix

Dialogue 75

Waiter:	... and for the main course they'd like ...
Sous-chef:	That's table 17 you mean?
Waiter:	Yes, one sole spirals with zucchini butter and one breast of duck with apples confit.
Sous-chef:	Fine, any others?
Waiter:	Yes, table 6 beef fillet "mignons", pepper sauce and noodles "fines herbes".
Sous-chef:	Okay.
Waiter:	Table 11, Saskia.
Sous-chef:	Yes.
Waiter:	A lamb in crust "fines herbes" and glazed shallots, one salmon fillet with chive cream.

25th Lesson
AUSTRIAN COOKING

Dialogues 76–79

Dialogue 76

Waiter:	Good afternoon! What can I do for you?
Guest:	Good afternoon! Perhaps you can help me. I'm staying in Austria for a few days and I would like to try some of the Austrian specialities I've heard so much about.
Waiter:	I'd be pleased to help you, madam. Let me see. There is quite a lot to choose from.

Dialogue 77

Waiter:	Would you like to start with a soup or an appetizer?
Guest:	I'd like to have a soup.
Waiter:	I would recommend a "Leberknödelsuppe", that is a clear soup with a liver dumpling.
Guest:	I've never had anything like that before. I'll try it.

Dialogue 78

Guest:	What Austrian speciality would you recommend for lunch today?
Waiter:	A "Wiener Schnitzel" is the most typical Austrian dish.
Guest:	What is a "Wiener Schnitzel"?
Waiter:	It is a deep-fried breaded veal cutlet, and it's usually served with an assorted salad.

Dialogue 79

Waiter:	We have a reasonably priced table d'hôte meal. Today it is "Frittatensuppe", a clear soup with sliced pancakes, and "Tafelspitz", which is boiled round of beef with spinach and hashed brown potatoes. For dessert there is apple strudel.
Guest:	That sounds good. Thank you!

26th Lesson
COOKING ALL AROUND THE WORLD

Listen and fill in the function sheet 80

Banquet manager:	Good morning. Hotel "Kärntner Hof". Banquet service. May I help you?
Mr. Baker:	Good morning. My name is Baker. I'm calling from San Diego. I'd like to arrange a wedding reception for my daughter on Sunday, July the 6th for about 50 persons.
Banquet manager:	You are lucky. Our "Zirbenstube" is vacant. Just a moment, I'll note: ... wedding arrangement ... "Zirbenstube" ... Sunday, July the 6th ... beginning: 1 p.m. ... open end ... 50 persons ... Mr. Baker, Rosedrive 123, San Diego 890 ... telephone number 045/34/95617 ... five-course dinner ... EUR 50.00 per person, wine and beverages not included ... 10 double rooms, 5 single rooms ... red roses and candles ... E-figure ... live music ... table cards will be sent ... Manhattan, Screwdriver, sparkling wine, various juices ... Bénédictine, Brandy, Black Russian ... video ... deposit EUR 730.00. Thank you, Mr. Baker. I'll send you a copy of the function sheet as confirmation. Goodbye.
Mr. Baker:	Goodbye.

27th Lesson
EATING HABITS

Dialogue 81

Michael:	Hello, Ann. Any problems with your group?
Ann:	I think we've arranged our farewell dinner for the early evening on Tuesday. But we'll be back from Stratford a few hours later. Could we change the time?
Michael:	Of course, what about 10 p.m.? The hotel is nearly full, but I think I can arrange that.
Ann:	There is another problem, too. Seven members of my group will need special meals.
Michael:	What exactly?
Ann:	Four of them are vegetarians.
Michael:	That's no problem. For dinner, a number of vegetarian dishes is provided.
Ann:	That's fine. And there are two diabetics in the group.
Michael:	Ask them to see me. I'll find out their special requirements and we'll prepare special dishes for them. And the last one?
Ann:	He is Moslem. His religion doesn't allow him to eat any pork.
Michael:	OK. We'll prepare a set dinner without any pork for him.

28th Lesson
PAYMENT

Dialogues 82–86

Dialogue 82

Receptionist:	Good morning, sir. May I help you?
Guest:	Yes, I want to check out, please.
Receptionist:	What's your room number, please?
Guest:	225.
Receptionist:	Just a moment, please. Here's your bill, sir. That'll be EUR 167,20.
Guest:	Do you take traveller's cheques in dollars?
Receptionist:	Certainly, sir. Have you got any identification?
Guest:	Here's my passport.
Receptionist:	Thank you, sir. The amount in dollars is ...

Dialogue 83

Receptionist:	Good morning, madam.
Guest:	I have to pay my bill. The name is Morgan, room 115.
Receptionist:	Yes, madam. That'll be EUR 134,45.

Guest:	I don't have any more euros. Do you mind if I pay in dollars?
Receptionist:	Of course not, just let me have a look at the exchange rates. That would be $ 116,21.
Guest:	Here are $ 120,00. The rest is for you.
Receptionist:	Thank you, madam. May I call you a taxi to the airport?
Guest:	Yes, please.
Receptionist:	It was a pleasure having you here.
Guest:	Goodbye.

Dialogue 84
Receptionist:	Good morning, Mr. Barley.
Guest:	Good morning. Is my bill ready?
Receptionist:	How are you paying, sir?
Guest:	By credit card, if you don't mind.
Receptionist:	Fine, sir. We accept Diners Club.
Guest:	Is this the total amount at the bottom there?
Receptionist:	Yes, sir.
Guest:	I think there's a mistake. That's far too much.
Receptionist:	I'll check it for you. Oh, I'm sorry, sir. This isn't your bill.

Dialogue 85
Guest:	I'd like to settle my bill, please.
Receptionist:	One moment, please.
Guest:	Do you accept credit cards?
Receptionist:	I'm sorry, we don't. It's the policy of the hotel.
Guest:	I see. I'll pay in cash then. How much is it?

Dialogue 86
Guest:	Can you prepare my bill? I'll be checking out tomorrow morning.
Receptionist:	Certainly, sir.
Guest:	I'd like to pay by bank card, is that possible?
Receptionist:	Of course. Did you also have some drinks from the mini bar?
Guest:	Yes, I ticked them on the list on the desk in my room.
Receptionist:	Thank you, sir.
Guest:	I also had some long distance calls.
Receptionist:	Our computer already put them on your bill.
Guest:	Fine, thanks.

29th Lesson

THE BAR

Dialogue 87

Bar waiter:	Have a look at the bar list.
Apprentice:	Where are the alcoholic drinks?
Bar waiter:	Here they are, on the left side. On the right you see the cocktails.
Apprentice:	Is that right, there are before and after dinner cocktails?
Bar waiter:	Yes, we offer a Manhattan, a White Lady and an Old Fashioned as well as an Alexander and a Black Russian.
Apprentice:	What non-alcoholic drinks do we serve?
Bar waiter:	We offer various juices, tonic water, Coke, and mineral water.

Dialogue 88

Barman:	Good evening, sir. What can I get you?
Tim:	A pint of beer, please. What would you like, Denise?
Denise:	A gin and tonic, please.
Barman:	Would you like ice and lemon in it, madam?
Denise:	Yes, please!
Tim:	Here's Michael. What will you have, Mike?
Michael:	Oh, a dry sherry for Jill, and a larger one for me, Tim.
Barman:	Would you like a pint or a half, sir?
Tim:	Make it a pint.
Barman:	Thank you, sir. Shall I charge this to your room?
Tim:	Yes, please.
Barman:	May I have your key card, please?
Tim:	Oh yes, here you are.

Dialogues 89

Dialogue (a)
Barman:	Good evening, What can I get you?
Guest:	A large gin and tonic for my wife and a large whisky for me, please.

Dialogue (b)
Guest:	Oh, barman, could I have a half of cider and a small rum, please?
Barman:	Certainly, sir.

Dialogue (c)
Barman:	Can I help you, madam?
Guest:	Yes, I'd like a small vodka and tonic, and a double rum and lemonade.
Barman:	Would you like ice in both, madam?
Guest:	Yes, please.

Dialogue (d)
Guest:	Two pints of lager, please, and two single whiskeys.
Barman:	Yes, sir.

Dialogue (e)
Guest:	Two lemonades, two halves of bitter, a cider, and a double gin and tonic, please.
Barman:	Of course, sir!

30th Lesson

COMPLAINTS

Dialogues 90–95

Dialogue 90
Receptionist:	Good afternoon, sir. Can I help you?
Guest:	I hope so. The basin in my room is blocked.
Receptionist:	I'm very sorry about that. I'll get someone to deal with it as soon as possible. What room are you in?
Guest:	Room 217.

Dialogue 91
Receptionist:	Good morning, madam. Can I help you?
Guest:	Yes, please. It was very cold last night. Can I have an extra blanket?
Receptionist:	Certainly, madam. I'll speak to the chambermaid about it. What room is it?
Guest:	Room 624.

Dialogue 92
Receptionist:	Good evening, sir. Can I help you?
Guest:	I certainly hope so. The tap in my room is dripping. Could you do something about that?
Receptionist:	Of course, sir. I'll have it repaired immediately. What room are you in?
Guest:	Room 109.

Dialogue 93
Receptionist:	Good evening, madam. Can I help you?
Guest:	I hope so. The family in the room below me is very loud. I can't sleep.
Receptionist:	I'm extremely sorry to hear this. I'll deal with it immediately. What room are you in?
Guest:	Room 745.

Dialogue 94
Receptionist:	Good afternoon, madam. Can I help you?
Guest:	Yes. I've just checked in. I booked a room with bath, but you've given me one with a shower.
Receptionist:	I'm so sorry about this. I'll sort it out immediately. What room is it?
Guest:	307.

Dialogue 95
Receptionist:	Good morning, sir. Can I help you?
Guest:	Yes. The TV-set in my room isn't working.
Receptionist:	I'm sorry about that. I'll have it replaced as soon as possible. What room are you in?
Guest:	Room 654.

Dialogue 96
Receptionist:	Good morning, madam. Can I help you?
Guest:	I hope so. I've just checked in and the room you've given me is in a horrible condition.
Receptionist:	I'm very sorry to hear that. What's wrong?
Guest:	There are no towels. The bath needs cleaning. One light bulb is broken. Did you have the room checked before?
Receptionist:	We usually check every room before the guest arrives. I'll get the chambermaid to sort it out immediately.
Guest:	And I need an extra blanket. It's awfully cold in the room.
Receptionist:	I'll send someone to check the air-conditioning. Is there anything else?
Guest:	No, but hurry up, please. I'd like to take a shower.
Receptionist:	Yes, of course, madam. I'll send the chambermaid along right away.

31st Lesson
LOOKING FOR A JOB

Dialogue 97
Personnel officer:	Good afternoon. Come in, please.
Applicant:	Good afternoon. I have an interview at 3 p.m.
Personnel officer:	Please have a seat.
Applicant:	Thank you. I wish to apply for the position of a waitress.
Personnel officer:	Now I need some personal details. What's your full name, please?
Applicant:	Baumann, Bettina Baumann.
Personnel officer:	And your permanent address and telephone number?
Applicant:	Alpenstraße 42, 5020 Salzburg, and my telephone number is 0043-(0)662-62 88 07.
Personnel officer:	Are you married?
Applicant:	No, I'm single.
Personnel officer:	And your date of birth?
Applicant:	29th of November, 1980.
Personnel officer:	Which schools did you attend?
Applicant:	Elementary school, comprehensive school, polytechnical course, and vocational school.
Personnel officer:	What qualifications do you have?
Applicant:	I've got three years of experience in silver service in luxury hotels and full knowledge of wines. My English is fluent.
Personnel officer:	Do you speak any other foreign languages?
Applicant:	Some French and a little Italian.
Personnel officer:	Well, we are looking for somebody with your qualifications. When would you be available?
Applicant:	I have to give my present firm two weeks' notice.
Personnel officer:	Fine, then I'll give you our decision in the next few days. Thank you for coming.

Speisenkarten
Menus

Rezepte
Recipes

Menus

CONTINENTAL BREAKFAST

YOUR BREAKFAST INCLUDES

Breakfast basket with croissant, Danish pastry,
breakfast rolls and bread, butter,
jam and marmalade
orange, grapefruit or tomato juice
coffee, tea or hot chocolate

BREAKFAST BUFFET

OUR BREAKFAST BUFFET

offers a large variety of breakfast items including fruit juices,
fresh, assorted rolls and breads,
assorted cold cuts and cheeses,
breakfast cereals, scrambled eggs,
coffee, tea or hot chocolate.

Please make your selection.
(Should you like eggs other than scrambled, please ask your server.)

À LA CARTE BREAKFAST ITEMS

French toast with maple sirup

Parma ham with melon in season

Breakfast cereals with milk

Stewed prunes

Grapefruit cocktail

Omelet to order

Two eggs to order with ham or bacon

Fresh squeezed orange juice

Grapefruit or tomato juice

Coffee, tea, hot chocolate

All taxes and service charges included

Breakfast express

Your breakfast is guaranteed on time or it's on us.

*Hang on outside doorknob by midnight.
We'd be pleased to serve you a cheerful wake up breakfast.*

To be served between: ✓ Check Preference

- ○ 6:30 - 6:45   ○ 7:15 - 7:30   ○ 8:00 - 8:15   ○ 8:45 - 9:00
- ○ 6:45 - 7:00   ○ 7:30 - 7:45   ○ 8:15 - 8:30   ○ 9:00 - 9:15
- ○ 7:00 - 7:15   ○ 7:45 - 8:00   ○ 8:00 - 8:45   ○ 9:15 - 9:30

○ **The Pastry Shop $9** ─────── ☐ Add Quantity

An assortment of toast, croissant, Danish, muffins with preserves, butter or margarine.

○ **Griddle Selections $9** ─────── ☐ Add Quantity

Served with whipped butter & syrup.

Choose from: ☐ Fluffy Pancakes   ☐ Belgian Waffles   ☐ French Toasts

○ **The Healthy Start $10** ─────── ☐ Add Quantity

Hot or cold cereal topped with fresh berries or bananas and whole or skim milk. Served with toast, muffin or bagel.

Cold Cereal: ☐ Raisin Bran   ☐ Corn Flakes   ☐ Granola
 ☐ Rice Krispies   ☐ Frosted Flakes
Hot Cereal: ☐ Oatmeal
Bread: ☐ Toast Muffin   ☐ Bagel

○ **The All American $13** ─────── ☐ Add Quantity

Two eggs any style, choice of meat served with fresh breakfast potatoes, toast, muffin or croissant.

Egg Style: ☐ Fried Up   ☐ Over medium
 ☐ Over Easy   ☐ Scrambled   ☐ Egg Whites
Meat: ☐ Bacon   ☐ Sausage   ☐ Turkey   ☐ Ham
Bread: ☐ Toast   ☐ Muffin   ☐ Croissant

○ **NEW! Kid's Breakfast $7** ─────── ☐ Add Quantity

Chilled juice with your choice of:
 ☐ Scrambled eggs, bacon and toast
 ☐ Cold cereal with sliced banana and milk

○ **NEW! Seasonal Fruit Platter $9** ─────── ☐ Add Quantity

A variety of fresh seasonal fruits with choice of cottage cheese or plain yogurt.

○ **All the above include a choice of cold or hot beverage:**

Cold Beverage: ☐ Fresh Orange   ☐ Grapefruit   ☐ Tomato
 ☐ Apple   ☐ Lemon   ☐ Milk
Hot Beverage: ☐ Coffee Brewed   ☐ Decaf   ☐ Tea
 ☐ Hot Chocolate   ☐ Hot Milk

ROOM NUMBER ─────────────

SERVER (Marriott use only) ──────── **CHECK NUMBER** ────

A 17% Service Charge will be added to your check plus $2.50 trip charge.

CAPTAIN'S GALA

APPETIZERS

Iced Russian Sevruga Caviar with Traditional Condiments, Blinis and Melba Toast

Pâté de Foie Gras with Warm Brioche and Port Wine Gelée

Oysters Rockefeller

Coconut Half Filled with Tropical Fruit and Sprinkled with Armagnac

SOUPS

Consommé Elysee 1975 – Beef Essence with Truffle in a Puff Pastry Dome

Cream of Asparagus "Argenteuil"

Low sodium soups are available upon request

SALADS

Commander's Salad – Medley of Selected Crunchy Field Lettuce, Radicchio, Asparagus, Tomatoes, Artichoke, Leek Straw, and Caramelized Walnuts
Served with Sherry-Walnut Vinaigrette

Traditional favorite dressings available, plus today's specials:
Fat-Free Tomato-Basil and Low Calorie Yogurt-Basil Dressing

SHERBET

Refreshing Kir Royale Sherbet

PASTA DISH

Fettuccine Pasta e Pomodoro
Tossed with Light Creamy Sun Dried Tomato Sauce

MAIN COURSES

Broiled Alaskan Crab Legs
Served with Melted Lemon Butter or Sauce Hollandaise,
Steamed Fresh Garden Vegetables, and Saffron Pilaf Rice

Filet of Beef Wellington
Pink Roasted Tenderloin of Beef in Flaky Puff Pastry, Sauce Perigourdine,
Steamed Garden Vegetables, and Dauphine Potatoes

Grilled Wisconsin Veal Medallions
On Creamy Porcini Sauce, with Steamed Vegetables, and Angel Hair Pasta

Baked Supreme of Pheasant Breast
Stuffed with Foie Gras, with Corn Fritters, Black Currant Sauce,
Caramelized Apple Slices, and Champagne Cabbage

SIDE ORDERS

Steamed Garden Vegetables   Dauphine Potatoes   Champagne Cabbage
Fettuccine Pasta with Tomato Sauce   Corn Fritters

Upon request, dishes are available without sauce. Vegetables are also available steamed, without butter or salt.

Captain's Gala

Crystal Harmony
Dessert

Friday, October 19, 2001 • At Sea
"Caribbean Passage" Cruise

Maître d'Hôtel **Jacques Martin** Executive Chef **Günter Lorenz**
Executive Pastry Chef **Hans Kiendl**

Sweet Finale

The American Institution – Baked Alaska Flambée en Parade
Blackberry Mousse with Cassis Mirror
Sugar-Free Coffee Cake
Assortment of Truffles and Friandises
Tropical Fruit

Ice Cream
Frozen Yogurt
Sherbet

Vanilla, Rocky Road, Strawberry Cheesecake, or Cinnamon Swirl Ice Cream
with your choice of Mango, Strawberry, or Butterscotch Topping
Freshly Frozen, Nonfat Banana or Vanilla Yogurt
Refreshing Kir Royale Sherbet

From the Cheese Trolley

Gorgonzola   Reblochon   Camembert   Crottin de Chavignol   Monterey Jack
Served with Crackers and Biscuits

Beverages

Freshly Brewed Coffee   Decaffeinated Coffee   Café Latte   Cappuccino
Espresso   Selection of International Teas

After Dinner Drinks

As a Digestif, we would like to recommend:

Galliano – $3.95   Taylor Fladgate 20 yr. Port – $6.00

Bailey's Irish Cream – $4.25   Martell Cordon Bleu. – $10.00

or your favorite classic after dinner liqueur, available from your Sommelier.

Appendix

Cold hors-d'œuvres

White herring
*marinated, apple slices,
onions, sour cream*

Smoked fillet of trout
*creamed horseradish,
toast and butter*

Assorted smoked meat and sausages
*horseradish, pickled onions
and rye bread*

Home-made venison pâté
*white mushrooms, grapes,
Cumberland sauce, bread and butter*

Shrimp cocktail
*on lettuce leaves in cognac sauce
with salmon caviar on quail egg,
toast and butter*

Tartar steak
toast and butter

Soups

Beef consommé
*with semolina dumplings,
or with sliced pancakes*

Cream of garlic

Cream of herb

Chicken broth
*with ham profiteroles, vegetables
and chicken meat*

Typical local small dishes

Pan-fried dumplings
with bacon and egg, salad

Omelette "Peasant style"
with bacon, potatoes, vegetables, salad

Stewed lights
with bread dumplings

Cheese spaetzle
with cheese, bacon, sautéed onions, salad

Viennese specialities

**Viennese breaded and deep-fried chicken
with potato salad**
(20 minutes to prepare)

Veal stew in paprika cream sauce
with small dumplings

Garnished Sauerkraut
*with smoked pork, roast pork,
sausage and bread dumpling*

Wiener Schnitzel
*deep-fried breaded escalope of veal
with parsley potatoes*

Sautéed calf's liver
with buttered rice

Braised escalope of beef
with sautéed onions and home-fried potatoes

Boiled round of beef
*with hashed brown potatoes, vegetables,
chive and apple-horseradish sauce*

Grilled stuffed fillet of pork
in cream sauce, broccoli and roasted potatoes

Grilled and pan-fried dishes

Pork chop "Farmer Style"
with mushrooms, onions
and roasted potatoes

Gratinated lamb chops
served with string beans and potatoes

Councillors Special Plate
(for two or more persons)
Wiener Schnitzel, pork medallions,
lamb chops, calf's liver,
grilled tomatoes, string beans
and potato croquettes

Gratinated Sirloin steak
with mushrooms and bone marrow,
grilled tomatoes, leek onion,
and potato strudel

"Stroganoff"
sautéed sliced fillet of beef
with broccoli and noodle soufflé

Braised fillet of beef
with slices of bone marrow
in red wine sauce,
with string beans and
small potato cubes

Fish

Grilled fillet of pike-perch
with boiled potatoes

Pan-fried mountain trout
with red wine butter and
boiled potatoes

Poached fillet of salmon trout
with leek onion, and saffron rice

Salads from the trolley

A selection of seasonal fresh salads
Your choice of dressing:
French, Thousand Island, yoghurt herb,
red wine vinegar and olive oil

Cheese

Grey cheese

Goat cheese

**Cheese platter with assorted
Austrian cheeses**

Desserts

A delicious choice from the trolley

Viennese desserts

Viennese apple strudel
served hot or cold

White cheese dumplings
with plum compote

"Powidltascherln"
sweet dumplings filled with
Bohemian plum compote

Pancakes
filled with cranberries or apricot jam
or chocolate sauce

"Kaiserschmarren"
(25 minutes to prepare)
broken-up pancake
served with plum compote

Reservations: Phone number: 42 12 19
Opening hours: 11.30 a.m. to 3.00 p.m., 6.00 p.m. to 11.30 p.m.
Kitchen at disposition until 11.00 p.m.
Closed on Sundays and holidays

Appendix

Recipes

Starters

Rare Beef with Orange and Mustard Mayonnaise

- 12 thin slices of rare lean beef
- 2 cucumbers
- 7–8 small salad tomatoes

For orange garnish:

- 3 oranges
- 4 rounded tablespoons basic mayonnaise
- 1 tea spoon prepared French mustard
- salt and pepper
- 1 1/2 cups mushrooms
- 1 bunch of watercress

Arrange the beef in a circle on a round serving platter. Slice the cucumber finely and arrange around the beef and in the centre. Place whole tomatoes at regular intervals around the cucumber and one whole tomato in the centre of the platter. Divide each orange in two with a sharp pointed knife by cutting in zigzag pattern right through to the centre. Scoop out the flesh and strain through a sieve to extract the juice. Measure 1/4 cup juice, put in a pan and boil to reduce until thick. Leave to cool, then stir into the mayonnaise with the mustard and salt and pepper to taste.
Wipe the mushrooms clean with a damp cloth, but do not peel. Chop or slice finely, then stir into mayonnaise mixture.
Place the orange halves in between the tomatoes on the serving platter. Arrange a few sprigs of watercress in each orange, then top with 1–2 spoonfuls of the mayonnaise mixture.

Niçoise Salad

- 4 firm tomatoes
- 1/2 cucumber
- 225 g French beans, cooked until crisp
- 2 onions, chopped
- 1 cos or Webb's lettuce
- 75 ml French dressing
- 50 g anchovy fillets
- 200 g can tuna
- 3 hard-boiled eggs
- 2 tablespoons chopped parsley

Quarter the tomatoes, slice the cucumber, cut the French beans into short lengths and add to the onions. Wash lettuce, tear into strips and arrange in the bottom of the salad bowl. Drain the anchovy fillets and add with the vegetables to the French dressing, toss lightly and spoon over the lettuce.
Drain the tuna fish, flake and place on top of the vegetables. Cut each egg in half lengthwise and arrange around the edge of the salad. Sprinkle with parsley and serve.

Liver Pâté

- 225 g pig's liver
- 225 g calf's liver
- 500 g fat pork
- 75 g onions, peeled and chopped
- 1 garlic clove, crushed
- salt, freshly ground pepper
- 150 ml dry white wine
- 5 tea spoons brandy
- 5 tea spoons olive oil
- 1/2 tea spoon dried thyme
- 225 g streaky bacon rashers
- 2 eggs
- 125 g chicken liver, quartered
- juniper berries
- 3 bay leaves
- 150 ml liquid aspic jelly

Divide the liver and pork into small strips, discarding any skin and ducts. Place these in a bowl with the onion, garlic, seasoning, wine, brandy, oil, and thyme. Cover and marinate overnight.
Stretch the rashers of bacon, using a bluntedged knife, and use to line a 1.5 l capacity terrine dish, leaving the rashers hanging over the edge of the terrine. Drain the marinade from the other ingredients and reserve the liquid. Mince the liver mixture and return to the marinade with the eggs and chicken liver. Mix well. Turn into the lined dish. Draw the rashers over the top, cover and bake in a water bath in a preheated moderate oven (160 °C) for one hour. Lower the heat to cool (150 °C) and cook for further 1 1/2 hours or until firm.
Place a weight on the pâté and leave to cool overnight. Decorate with juniper berries, bay leaves and aspic for serving.

Soups

Fresh Leek Soup

- 50 g butter
- 700 g leek, cleaned and finely chopped
- 25 g flour
- 600 ml stock or clear soup
- 300 ml milk
- salt and pepper

Melt the butter in a large saucepan. Add the leek and fry gently stirring occasionally without browning for 5 minutes. Stir in the flour and cook for 2 minutes. Gradually add the stock, stirring continually. Add seasoning and milk, bring to the boil and simmer for 30 minutes. Season to taste. Add a little cream.

Clear Oxtail Soup

- 1 oxtail, jointed, about 1 kg in weight
- 40 g dripping
- 25 g flour
- 600 ml water
- 2 onions, chopped
- 2 carrots, chopped
- 2 sticks celery, sliced

- salt and pepper
- pinch cayenne pepper
- 1 bay leaf
- a little gravy browning

Trim any excess fat from the oxtail. Heat the dripping in a large pan and fry the oxtail quickly on all sides to brown. Remove from the pan. Stir the flour into the fat remaining in the pan and cook for a minute, then stir in the water and bring to the boil. Stir until dissolved. Return the oxtail to the pan with the vegetables, seasoning and bay leaf, cover and simmer very gently for 50 minutes until the meat can be easily removed from the bones. Skim off any surplus fat, remove the bay leaf. Adjust the seasoning and add a little gravy browning.

Main Courses

Presidential Corn Beef Hash

- 2 cups minced corn beef
- 4 medium-sized boiled potatoes
- 1/2 cup hot water
- 3 tablespoons butter
- 2 tablespoons chopped parsley
- 2 tablespoons chopped onion
- 2 tablespoons chopped green pepper
- salt and pepper to taste
- 9 bacon strips
- new potatoes
- parsley, chopped for garnish

Mix all ingredients (except bacon strips and new potatoes) thoroughly, add salt and pepper to taste. Shape into loaf form with bacon strips over the top.
Bake in greased pan in moderate oven (350 °F) 35 to 40 minutes.
Meanwhile, boil the new potatoes, use them as garnish sprinkled with chopped parsley. Pour tomato sauce over the corn beef hash.

Yorkshire Pudding

- 1 pint of milk
- 2 eggs
- 2 heaped tablespoons of flour
- salt
- dripping

Put the flour and a good pinch of salt into a basin, make a well in the centre, break in the eggs, stir gradually, mixing in the flour from the sides, and add milk by degrees until a thick smooth batter is formed. Now beat well for about ten minutes, then add the remainder of the milk, cover, and let it stand for at least 1 hour. When ready to use, cover the bottom of a pudding tin with a thin layer of dripping taken from the meat tin, and while the tin and the dripping are getting thoroughly hot in the oven, give the batter another good beating.
Bake the pudding for about 10 minutes in a hot oven partially to cook the bottom, or, if more convenient, place the hottest shelf from the oven on the meat stand, and at once put the pudding in front of the fire, and cook it until set and well browned.
Yorkshire pudding is always cooked in front of the fire. When baked in the oven, the term "batter pudding" is applied to it by the people in the country whence it derives it's name.

Roast Turkey (with Cornbread Stuffing)

- 10- to 12-pound turkey
- unsalted, melted fat
- salt, pepper
- paprika

After washing the turkey inside and out, dry with a cloth. Rub the inside with salt, and fill the body cavity loosely with the stuffing. Sew up the incision or secure with skewers.
Place the bird, breast up, in a roasting pan. Brush the breast, legs, wings with the melted fat.
Preheat oven to 300 °F, and roast the turkey, uncovered, in the oven until tender, allowing 25 minutes to the pound. Baste frequently with pan drippings.
When turkey is half cooked, season to taste with salt, pepper, and paprika.

Old Virginia Cornbread Stuffing

- turkey giblets and neck
- 2 cups boiling water
- 1 bayleaf
- celery stalks and leaves
- salt
- 5 to 6 cups dry cornbread crumbs
- 3 tablespoons finely chopped onion
- 3 tablespoons chopped parsley
- 6 tablespoons melted butter
- 1/4 tea spoon pepper
- 1 1/2 cups chopped celery butter

Cook giblets and neck in 2 cups boiling water with bayleaf, celery stalks and leaves, and salt to taste until tender.
Drain the stock and reserve. The giblets can be cut up into small pieces and used in the gravy.
Add to the cornbread crumbs and mix thoroughly, the onions, parsley, melted butter, pepper, and chopped celery. Moisten lightly with the giblet stock. Any excess stuffing can be baked separately in a buttered casserole, dotting the top of the mixture with dabs of butter.

Paprika Chicken

- 4 chicken breasts
- 2 tablespoons salad oil
- 25 g butter
- 1 onion, chopped
- 2 level tablespoons paprika
- 25 g flour
- 150 ml stock
- 150 ml dry cider
- 5 tablespoons sherry
- 1 level tea spoon tomato purée
- salt and pepper
- 175 g small button mushrooms
- 150 ml sour cream
- chopped parsley
- fried sliced mushrooms

Remove the skin from the chicken breasts. Heat the oil in a large shallow pan, add the butter and then fry the chicken quickly to slightly brown. Remove from the pan and drain on kitchen paper. Add the onion and paprika to the pan and fry for 2 minutes. Blend in the flour and cook for a further minute. Remove from the heat and stir in the stock, cider and sherry. Return to the heat and simmer until thick. Add the tomato purée and seasoning to the sauce, stir well and then return the chicken breasts to the pan. Cover and simmer gently for 30 minutes, turning once.

Appendix

Wash the mushrooms, add to the pan and simmer for further 5 minutes. When ready to serve, lift the chicken breasts onto a serving dish and stir the sour cream into the sauce, then pour over the chicken. Sprinkle with parsley and garnish the dish with fried sliced mushrooms.

Lamb Bourguignon

- 1.25 kg boned lean leg of lamb (boned weight)
- 225 g small onions
- 3 tablespoons corn oil
- 50 g margarine
- 225 g button mushrooms
- 225 ml red wine
- 300 ml brown stock
- salt and pepper
- 1 tablespoon arrowroot
- 1 tablespoon water
- chopped fresh parsley
- fried croutons to garnish

Discard all skin and fat from the lamb. Cut into large fork-size pieces. Blanch the onions in boiling water for 2 minutes, then drain and peel them.
Heat the oil in a deep-frying pan. Add the margarine and, when frothing, put in the meat to seal on all sides.
Remove the meat cubes from the pan as they brown. Add the onions and brown evenly. Drain and add to the meat. Finally, lightly fry the mushrooms.
Replace the meat and vegetables in the pan and stir in the wine, stock, and seasoning. Bring to the boil, then transfer to a flameproof casserole. Cover and cook in a preheated moderate oven (160 °C) for about 1 1/2 hours or until the meat is tender.
Dissolve the arrowroot in the water. When the lamb is cooked, put the casserole on top of the cooker and stir in the arrowroot. Cook until clear and thickened – about 2 minutes. Serve the lamb garnished with parsley and croutons.

Desserts

Walnut Cake with Coffee Cream

- 2 eggs
- 5 egg yolks
- 1/2 cup sugar
- 3/4 cup walnuts, grated
- 1/2 cup hazelnuts, grated
- 1 tablespoon almonds, grated
- 1/4 cup cake crumbs
- 5 egg whites, stiffly beaten

Filling:

- 1/2 cup butter
- 1/2 cup sugar
- 1 1/2 cups walnuts, halved
- 2 tablespoons black coffee
- coffee icing (see below)
- 1/3 cup walnuts, halved

Beat eggs, egg yolks, and sugar until fluffy. Add walnuts, hazelnuts, almonds, and cake crumbs. Fold in egg whites. Bake in buttered and floured baking tin in oven (300 °F) 35–45 minutes. When cold, split into two layers.
Preparation of the filling: Beat butter until creamy. Add sugar, walnuts, and coffee. Spread between layers. Top with coffee icing, decorate with halved walnuts.

Coffee Icing

- 1 3/4 cups confectioner's sugar
- 1/3 cup black coffee, strong
- 1 tablespoon raspberry juice
  (or few drops food colouring)

Stir ingredients until smooth. Add more liquid if needed.

Christmas Cake

- 500 g butter
- 750 g brown sugar
- 750 g flour
- 2 tea spoons nutmeg
- 1 tea spoon mace
- 1 tea spoon cloves
- 2 tea spoons cinnamon
- 1 tea spoon baking soda
- 3 tea spoons baking powder
- 750 g raisins
- 750 g currants
- 500 g citron, sliced
- 500 g dates, sliced
- 10 eggs, well beaten
- 1 cup molasses
- 1 cup cold coffee beverage
- juice and grated rind of 2 oranges
- juice and grated rind of 1 lemon
- 1 cup tart jelly
- 150 g almonds, sliced

Cream butter, gradually add sugar until fluffy. Sift dry ingredients together. Mix with fruit. Add eggs in thirds to creamed mixture, beating well. Stir in fruit mixture alternately with next ingredients. Blend well. Pour into 4 loaf pans, greased and lined. Sprinkle with almonds. Cover cakes with greased paper. Steam 2 hours, then bake at 160 °C 1 1/2 to 2 hours. Remove paper last 1/2 hour.

Special Apple Cake

- 150 g butter
- 2 large eggs
- 225 g castor sugar
- 5 ml almond essence
- 225 g self-raising flour
- 1 level tea spoon baking powder
- 350 g cooking apples, after peeling
- icing sugar

Melt the butter in a pan over a medium heat until just runny and pour into a large bowl. Add the eggs, sugar and almond essence and beat well until mixed. Fold in the flour and baking powder. Spread just under two thirds of the mixture in the cake tin. Then straight away peel, core and slice the apples and arrange roughly on top of the mixture. Spread the remaining mixture over the apples. It is difficult to get this last bit of mixture smooth, but don't worry as the blobs even out during cooking. Bake for 1 1/2 hours, until the apple is tender when propped with a skewer. Loosen the sides of the cake with a knife and carefully push the cake out.
Dust over very generously with icing sugar when slightly cooled and serve warm or cold with lots of lightly whipped or thick cream.

Mixed Drinks

Young Colada
- 10 cl pineapple juice
- 3 cl coconut cream
- 1 cl lemon juice
- 1 cl grenadine

Put ice cubes into tumbler. Take a shaker and put in pineapple juice, coconut cream, lemon juice, and grenadine. Shake well. Strain into tumbler.

Alexander's Sister
- 20 g gin
- 20 g white or green crème de menthe
- 20 g cream

Shake well with ice. Strain into pre-chilled cocktail glass.

Bombay
- 40 g brandy
- 10 g dry vermouth
- 10 g sweet vermouth
- 1 bar spoon curaçao
- 1 bar spoon Pernod
- 1 slice fresh or canned mango

Shake brandy, both kinds of vermouth, curaçao, and Pernod well with ice. Strain over rocks in pre-chilled old-fashioned glass. Add mango slice.

Bronx
- 30 g gin
- 10 g orange juice
- 10 g dry vermouth
- 10 g sweet vermouth

Shake well with ice. Strain into pre-chilled cocktail glass. For a drier Bronx, omit sweet vermouth and increase gin.

Butterfly
- 20 g dry vermouth
- 20 g sweet vermouth
- 10 g red Dubonnet
- 10 g orange juice

Shake everything well with ice. Strain over rocks in pre-chilled old-fashioned glass. This combination of orange juice and three fortified wines is extremely light.

Cardinal II
- 20 g gin
- 20 g Campari
- 20 g dry vermouth
- lemon peel

Stir gin, Campari and vermouth well with ice. Strain into pre-chilled cocktail glass. Twist lemon peel above drink and drop into glass.

Diabolo
- 40 g imported dry white port
- 20 g dry vermouth
- 1 bar spoon lemon juice
- lemon peel

Shake port, vermouth and lemon juice well with ice. Strain into pre-chilled cocktail glass. Twist lemon peel above drink and drop into glass.

Hudson Bay
- 40 g gin
- 10 g cherry liqueur
- 10 g orange juice
- 1 bar spoon lime juice
- 1 bar spoon 151-proof rum
- 1 slice lime

Shake gin, cherry liqueur, orange juice, lime juice, and rum well with ice. Strain into pre-chilled cocktail glass. Add lime slice.

Mai Tai
- 40 g light rum
- 20 g lime juice
- $1/4$ bar spoon triple sec
- $1/2$ bar spoon sugar
- 1 slice lime
- 1 mint sprig
- 1 pineapple stick

Shake rum, lime juice, triple sec, and sugar well with ice. Strain into pre-chilled double old-fashioned glass. Tear one or two mint leaves partially to release flavour. Garnish with lime slice, mint sprig and pineapple stick.

Manhattan de Luxe
- 1 part Cinzano Italian vermouth
- 5 parts bonded whisk(e)y
- 1 dash Angostura bitter
- 1 cherry

Stir well in a mixing glass with large ice cubes and pour into chilled cocktail glass. Add a cherry to each glass.

Negroni
- 20 g Campari
- 20 g gin
- 20 g sweet vermouth

Stir well with ice. Strain into pre-chilled cocktail glass. May be served on the rocks with a twist of lemon or splash of soda or both.

Planter's Punch
- 1 part sugar syrup
- 2 parts lemon juice
- 3 parts Jamaica rum
- 2 or 3 dashes Angostura

Shake vigorously with crushed ice and pour, without straining, into collins glass. Decorate with fruit as desired and serve with straws.

Santa Fe
- 20 g brandy
- 20 g grapefruit juice
- 20 g vermouth
- 1 bar spoon lemon juice

Shake all ingredients well with ice. Strain into pre-chilled sugar-rimmed cocktail glass.

Sunset
- 40 g tequila
- 10 g lime juice
- 10 g grenadine
- $1/2$ cup crushed ice
- 1 slice lime

Put tequila, lime juice, grenadine, and ice into -blender. Blend at low speed 10–15 seconds. Pour into pre-chilled old-fashioned glass. Add ice slices or cubes to fill glass. Garnish with lime slice.

Tahiti Club
- 40 g golden rum
- 10 g lime juice
- 10 g pineapple juice
- 10 g lemon juice
- 1 bar spoon maraschino liqueur
- 1 slice orange

Shake rum, lime juice, pineapple juice, lemon juice, and maraschino liqueur well with ice. Strain into pre-chilled old-fashioned glass. Add cracked ice or ice cubes to fill glass. Add orange slice.

Appendix

Serving Temperatures

5 – 7 °C	champagne sparkling wine
6 – 8 °C	non-alcoholic beer
8 °C	beer
8 – 11 °C	young, white and rosé wine
11 – 13 °C	late vintage white wine
13 – 15 °C	dessert wine, high quality wine
14 – 16 °C	light and medium, not too heavy red wine
16 – 18 °C	heavy red wine
19 – 22 °C	port, sherry

Standard measures

1 gallon (US)	128	ounces
1/2 gallon	64	ounces
1 quart	32	ounces
1 fifth ($4/5$ quart)	25.6	ounces
3/4 quart	24	ounces
1 pint	16	ounces
1 tenth	12.8	ounces
1 cup ($1/2$ pint)	8	ounces
1 jigger	$1\,1/2$	ounces
1 pony	$1/8$	ounce
1 dash	3	drops
1 fluid ounce (fl. oz) = 2.8 cl		

Example:

Manhattan

4 cl whisky	1 $1/2$	fl. oz
2 cl vermouth red	$2/3$	fl. oz
1 dash Angostura bitter		

International Cocktail Competition (I.C.C.)

Rules & Regulations

1. The International Cocktail Competition (I.C.C.) is open to member guilds of the International Bartenders Association only.
2. The International Cocktail Competition (I.C.C.) shall be formalized and prepared by the "host-country" in accordance with the I.C.C. Rules & Regulations. In accordance with the I.C.C. Rules & Regulations, the Organizing Committee of the host-country, in agreement with the I.B.A.–I.C.C. Committee, will reserve the right to reject any competitor or recipe considered unacceptable.
3. The International Cocktail Competition (I.C.C.) – in the host-country – will be supervised by an I.B.A. Committee, composed of: the IBA-President the IBA Vice Presidents, the I.B.A.–I.C.C. Committee and the President of the host-country.
4. Prior to the I.C.C., the I.B.A.–I.C.C. Committee will review all recipes for eligibility.
5. The International Cocktail Competition (I.C.C.) shall be held each year in that country so designated by the Council of the I.B.A.
6. Each member guild shall submit one recipe on a standard form of the Organizing Committee **on or before** the designated date.
7. All recipes are sole property of the I.B.A.
8. Each year, one category will be featured at the I.C.C. to create the "Best Drink" in that category. The categories will be:
   a) Before-Dinner Cocktail   – Dry or Medium
   b) After-Dinner Cocktail   – Sweet
   c) Long Drink   – Collins Type
   The "Before-Dinner Cocktail" shall not contain more than two (2) centilitres of sweetened products.

Recipes

1. All recipes shall be expressed in centilitres, with a maximum of 7 cl, divided in resp.: 5 cl, and/or: 4 -$1/2$ cl, 4 cl, 3 $1/2$ cl, 3 cl, 2 $1/2$ cl, 3 cl, 1 $1/2$ cl, 1 cl. and as smallest quantities: dashes and/or drops.
2. Competitors ingredients may be measured with a measuring cup.
3. All drinks may be: hand stirred, hand shaken or blended on an electricmixer.
4. Competitors may bring their own bar utensils.
5. Glasses will be furnished by the host-country/Organizing Committee and shall be: cocktail glasses: with a content of nine (9) centilitres,
long drink glasses: with a content of thirty (30) centilitres.

Ingredients

1. The maximum number of international marketed alcoholic and non-alcoholic ingredients shall be limited to **five (5), including dashes and drops.**
2. The alcoholic ingredients shall not exceed seven (7) centilitres.
3. Fruit juices, syrups, bitters, carbonated and non-carbonated liquids or any other condiments that are internationally marketed shall be allowed.
4. Home-made or self-made ingredients, or the blending of ingredients to count as one (1) ingredient, shall not be allowed.
5. Dairy products shall consist only of fresh milk, cream and eggs.
6. Heated ingredients shall not be allowed.
7. Any substitutions in a competitor's original recipe must be approved by the I.C.C. Committee before mixing.
8. Any questionable ingredients must be approved by the I.C.C. Committee.
9. All competitors shall have enough ingredients to make the minimum of seventeen (17) drinks.

Garnishes

1. Garnishes will be prepared (cut up) prior to going on stage. **But** the prepared garnishes shall be put together after the drinks are made on stage. These will be observed by the I.C.C. Committee.
2. Garnishes shall consist only of **edible fruit or vegetables.**
3. Basic garnishes, such as: cherries, olives, lemons, limes and oranges, will be furnished by the host-country. All other fruits and vegetables shall be provided by the competitor.
4. No artificial arrangements or food dyes shall be allowed.
5. Garnish decorations shall not be arranged so as to display any identifiable signs.
6. Condiments, such as: salt, sugar, pepper, nutmeg, cinnamon and others which are (internationally) marketed, shall be allowed.
7. Only standard long and short straws, picks and stirrers are to be used and as furnished by the host-country.
8. Any questionable garnishes must be approved by the I.C.C. Committee.

Literatur
Reading Exercises

Reading Exercises

Hotel Management and Administration

Special terms

Management:	The establishment or the carrying out of policies for an organization. The people who collectively perform this function are known as the management. An individual involved in management is a manager.
Hotelier:	A French word for hotelman that is frequently used in English. In other words, a hotelier is a professional in the hotel business.
Chain:	A business enterprise that operates at least several outlets. The Hilton, Sheraton, and Holiday Inn enterprises are examples of world-wide hotel chains.
Shift:	A work period, often for eight hours. Because hotels operate twenty-four hours a day, many jobs are scheduled on a morning-, evening-, or night-shift basis.
Posting:	An accounting term for entering charges on the appropriate financial record. Guest charges in a hotel are posted on the guest's bill as quickly as possible.
Night auditor:	An employee in the accounting office of a hotel who checks the accuracy of postings on the guest accounts. As the title indicates, the job is performed at night.
Cashier:	A hotel accounting office employee who provides financial services to the guests at the front desk. Other cashiers may be employed in the hotel's food and beverage service area.
Front desk:	The desk or counter at which guests in a hotel register, get their keys and mail, make inquiries, and pay their bills.
Credit manager:	A hotel accounting office employee who checks the financial standing of guests or other hotel customers.
Promotion:	The process of making the public aware of an enterprise. Advertising is paid promotion, while publicity is usually unpaid.
Media:	The means of mass communication and information: newspapers, magazines, radio, television, and electronic systems. Media is the plural of medium.
Travel agent:	A person who makes travel arrangements for the public. In most cases, the service he or she offers is paid for by the transportation and accommodation companies whose services will be used.

Travelling in Britain

Arrival

There are different ways to get to Britain: by sea, by air or with Eurotunnel. You come across the Channel from France or Belgium by boat or hovercraft to Dover, Folkestone or Ramsgate or across the North Sea from Holland to Felixstowe or Harwich. If you arrive by boat, you have to go through customs and then go on to London by coach or train.

If you fly to England, you will land at one of London's main airports, Heathrow, Gatwick, Luton or Stansted. The first is one of the busiest airports in the world.

Information

BTA (British Tourist Authority): Information Centre, 64 St. James's Street, London SW 1.
Railway stations: London is the hub of the British rail network with eight major terminals, all linked by tube:
Victoria: for south-east and Channel crossing.
Charing Cross: for south-east.
Paddington: for west and Wales.
Euston: for north-west, Glasgow and a ferry to Ireland.
St. Pancras: for the Midlands, Sheffield.
King's Cross: for Scotland, Edinburgh and east coast.
Liverpool Street: for eastern England and Cambridge.
Waterloo Station: for southern England.
London Tourist Board: at Victoria Station, for buying a "Go As You Please Ticket" for a stay in London or a "Travel Card" for two or more zones of the underground and bus network.

Buses and coaches: In towns people ride on buses, on tours people travel by coach. The cheapest way to get around Britain is by coach. Coaches go every-where, from John O'Groats at the north-eastern tip of Scotland to Land's End in the far south-west. Coaches offer the fare-saving "Britexpress Travelcard" for five or ten days unrestricted travel between 60 main towns.

Some Sights of Interest

Buckingham Palace: Royal main residence, Changing of the Guard takes place every summer morning at 11.30. Windsor Castle, Sandringham, and Balmoral Castle in Scotland are private residences of the Royal Family. Trooping the Colour is a military parade every year in June to officially celebrate the Queen's birthday.

London places of interest: Westminster Abbey, the Houses of Parliament, St. Paul's Cathedral, and the Tower of London are the most important historic buildings. Every tourist must go and see Madame Tussaud's exhibition of waxworks and must visit the Speaker's Corner and Soho, a district with foreign restaurants and other places of entertainment.

Some Events and Ceremonies

Oxford – Cambridge Boat Race on the Thames between Putney and Mortlake, every year in March.
Shakespeare Festival in Stratford-upon-Avon, April–January.
Grand National Steeplechase at Aintree Race-course, Liverpool, in April.
Lawn Tennis Championships at Wimbledon, London SW 19, June – July.
Edinburgh International Festival, August – September.
Veteran Car Run from London to Brighton in November.

Tourist Accommodation

Throughout Britain there is no shortage of clean, comfortable economy accommodation. Of course, it is preferable to book in advance, especially at peak holiday periods or if a special event is liable to draw large crowds of visitors. Using BTA publications, it is easy to write for reservations at hotels, pubs and inns, bed and breakfast establishments and the wide variety of other forms of accommodation Britain offers.

Normally a deposit is required with the booking. This is, of course, deducted from the final bill – but if you cancel the reservation your deposit is normally not returnable. If you want to keep your plans flexible, it is equally easy to book after you have arrived in Britain. All over the country you will find TICs (Tourist Information Centres) to help you find a bed for the night.

Large **hotels** offer all the comforts and services that discerning travellers expect. In London most hotels are in the West End, but the smaller and less expensive ones are in Kensington, Bayswater or Baker Street. Prices outside major cities are lower. And many hotels are cheaper outside the peak summer months.

In London there are groups of hotels which offer good value for money accommodation at uniform rates.

Bed and breakfast (B&B) is the alternative to hotel accommodation. For a low price you can get comfortable accommodation in a British home. You will receive a home-cooked breakfast, usually with fruit juice, cereal, eggs, bacon, sausage, bread toast, preserves and pots of tea or coffee. Guest houses are the grander version of B&Bs.

A legacy of English history are the many fascinating buildings in which tourists can spend a night. Through-out the country there are **castles, mansions and grand country houses** that combine the romantic atmosphere of past centuries with modern comfort.

Pubs and inns existed long before hotels. They have been offering hospitality since medieval times. Like the travellers of the past, you can find oak-beamed ceilings and thatched roofs. But unlike them, you will have rooms with running hot water, central heating and bedside lamps.

In getting off the beaten track, **a farmhouse holiday** provides the perfect answer. The tourist can choose from all kinds of farms. Often the guest will be welcome to watch farm activities and as a rule children are especially welcome. Farms often offer fishing and shooting facilities and ponies for trekking or riding. Children may get a reduction.

Finally, there is a well-established network of **youth hostels,** YMCAs and YWCAs throughout Britain. These establishments provide simple facilities for staying overnight and cooking meals at a reasonable price.

The British Pubs

The British pub has evolved throughout the centuries. Some pubs have old names, such as "George and Vulture", "Bag O'Nails" or "Elephant and Castle". Inside, the pubs tend to have a cosy and homey atmosphere. The log fire burning in the grate is a traditional element.

The great pub drink ist draught bitter, the British variety of beer. Most beers are matured by a process known as "lagering", but the English like their beer matured in wooden casks. Pubs also serve wines, spirits and apéritifs, but beer is the usual drink. Some famous beers are: Old Peculier (strong, dark), -Ruddles, Newcastle Brown Ale, Extra Special Bitter.

Most pubs serve simple fare at lunchtime. Visitors to Britain should try pub food in any case.

Some are typically British: ploughman's lunch (cheese, pickles, bread), shepherd's pie (minced meat covered with mashed potatoes and baked), steak-and-kidney pie, toad-in-the-hole (sausages cooked in batter), roast beef (cooked the British way: red in the centre, dark at the edges).

A pub can stay open for a maximum of nine and a half hours. Opening times vary: the usual hours are -11 a.m. to 3 p.m. and 5.30 p.m. to 11 p.m. At closing time, the landlord calls out "last orders", and ten minutes later he shouts "Time, gentlemen, please!" After that you have got another ten minutes for drinking up.

It is worth finding out about the entertainment provided by pubs. Some have theatrical perform-ances or singers at lunchtime or in the evening. But the traditional favourite is darts which originated in medieval times when archers aimed arrows at log ends. In country areas old-style bowling is a great favourite.

Dining Etiquette

Table manners play an important part in making a favorable impression. They are visible signals of the state of our manners and therefore are essential to professional success. Regardless of whether we are having lunch with a prospective employer or dinner with a business associate, our manners can speak volumes about us as professionals.

Napkin Use

The meal begins when the host unfolds his or her napkin. This is your signal to do the same. Place your napkin on your lap, completely unfolded if it is a small luncheon napkin or in half, lengthwise, if it is a large dinner napkin. Typically, you want to put your napkin on your lap soon after sitting down at the table (but follow your host's lead). The napkin remains on your lap throughout the entire meal and should be used to gently blot your mouth when needed. If you need to leave the table during the meal, place your napkin on your chair as a signal to your server that you will be returning. The host will signal the end of the meal by placing his or her napkin on the table. Once the meal is over, you too should place your napkin neatly on the table to the right of your dinner plate. (Do not refold your napkin, but don't wad it up, either.)

Ordering

If, after looking over the menu, there are items you are uncertain about, ask your server any questions you may have. Answering your questions is part of the server's job. It is better to find out before you order that a dish is prepared with something you do not like or are allergic to than to spend the entire meal picking tentatively at your food.

An employer will generally suggest that your order be taken first; his or her order will be taken last. Sometimes, however, the server will decide how the ordering will proceed. Often, women's orders are taken before men's.

As a guest, you should not order one of the most expensive items on the menu or more than two courses unless your host indicates that it is all right. If the host says, "I'm going to try this delicious sounding cheesecake; why don't you try dessert too," or „The prime rib is the specialty here; I think you'd enjoy it," then it is all right to order that item if you would like.

Appendix

"Reading" the Table Setting

Should you be attending a formal dinner or banquet with pre-set place settings, it is possible to gain clues about what may be served by „reading" the place setting. Start by drawing an imaginary line through the center of the serving plate (the plate will be placed in the center of your dining space). To the right of this imaginary line all of the following will be placed; glassware, cup and saucer, knives, and spoons, as well as a seafood fork if the meal includes seafood. It is important to place the glassware or cup back in the same position after its use in order to maintain the visual presence of the table. To the left of this imaginary line all of the following will be placed; bread and butter plate (including small butter knife placed horizontally across the top of the plate), salad plate, napkin, and forks. Remembering the rule of „liquids on your right" and „solids on your left" will help in allowing you to quickly become familiar with the place setting.

Use of Silverware

Choosing the correct silverware from the variety in front of you is not as difficult as it may first appear. Starting with the knife, fork, or spoon that is farthest from your plate, work your way in, using one utensil for each course. The salad fork is on your outermost left, followed by your dinner fork. Your soupspoon is on your outermost right, followed by your beverage spoon, salad knife and dinner knife. Your dessert spoon and fork are above your plate or brought out with dessert. If you remember the rule to work from the outside in, you'll be fine.

There are two ways to use a knife and fork to cut and eat your food. They are the American style and the European or Continental style. Either style is considered appropriate. In the American style, one cuts the food by holding the knife in the right hand and the fork in the left hand with the fork tines piercing the food to secure it on the plate. Cut a few bite-size pieces of food, then lay your knife across the top edge of your plate with the sharp edge of the blade facing in. Change your fork from your left to your right hand to eat, fork tines facing up. (If you are left-handed, keep your fork in your left hand, tines facing up.) The European or Continental style is the same as the American style in that you cut your meat by holding your knife in your right hand while securing your food with your fork in your left hand. The difference is your fork remains in your left hand, tines facing down, and the knife in your right hand. Simply eat the cut pieces of food by picking them up with your fork still in your left hand.

When You Have Finished

Do not push your plate away from you when you have finished eating. Leave your plate where it is in the place setting. The common way to show that you have finished your meal is to lay your fork and knife diagonally across your plate. Place your knife and fork side by side, with the sharp side of the knife blade facing inward and the fork, tines down, to the left of the knife. The knife and fork should be placed as if they are pointing to the numbers 10 and 4 on a clock face. Make sure they are placed in such a way that they do not slide off the plate as it is being removed. Once you have used a piece of silverware, never place it back on the table. Do not leave a used spoon in a cup, either; place it on the saucer. You can leave a soupspoon in a soup plate. Any unused silverware is simply left on the table.

The Buying Guide For Fresh Fruits, Vegetables, Herbs, and Nuts

In general, many fresh commodities must necessarily be shipped in firm condition, such as pears, avocados and tomatoes. Better retailers are conditioning these products to just the stage of ripeness the consumer likes – by the time they arrive at the point of sale.

In general, never cut a fruit or vegetable until it is ready to eat. Another general rule-off-thumb; never attempt to cause the ripening of a product while under refrigeration. Ripen first, then refrigerate.

Buy mature fruit. A green peach or nectarine, for example, will not ripen but merely soften some and wither. A cantaloupe picked too green will soften but will not be sweet and juicy. Some commodities do not gain sugar after harvest, because they have no reserve starch for conversion to sugar. On the other hand, bananas and pears gain sugar as well as tenderness after harvest.

Handle with care. Fresh fruits and vegetables, because of their perishability, require constant attention to keep their fresh appearance. The less you handle them when purchasing, or in the home, the longer their life. Don't pinch, squeeze or poke them., for bruising leads to damage and damage results in more spoilage for you or your retailer.

How To Select Fish

Fresh fish is at its very best when in season and plentiful, and the price should be cheaper then. The flesh of fresh fish should always be firm and should adhere firmly to the bone. The odor should be distinctly fresh and mild.

Fresh fish is marketed in a number of ways. They are as follows:

Whole Round – Means that the fish are exactly as they came from the water. The eyes should be clear, the gills bright red, and the skin shiny with tightly clinging scales. Allow one pound per servings.

Dressed or Pan Dressed Fish – Fish that have scales and entrails removed, and usually also with head, tail, and fins removed. Allow one-half pound per serving.

Steaks – Ready-to-cook widthwise slices of large fish. Allow one-third to one-half pound per serving.

Fillets – Ready-to-cook sides of fish cut lengthwise form the backbone. Allow one-half pound per serving.

Cooking Fish – The 10-Minute Rule:

Regardless of the fish or the cooking method, there is one uncomplicated rule of thumb that can be followed. Measure the fish, whether it be whole, in steaks, or in fillets, at its thickest point. then cook exactly ten minutes for each measured inch of thickness, fifteen minutes if it is enclosed in aluminum foil or baked in a sauce. For frozen, unthawed fish, double the cooking time.

If your are baking them in an aluminum foil package with the edges sealed, allow a little extra time for the heat to penetrate the foil – five minutes more for fresh fish, ten minutes for frozen fish.

To test for doneness, separate the fish with a fork or tip of a knife.

REMEMBER: Fish will continue to cook after it is removed from the heat source.

Factors In Quality Loss:

Seafood deteriorates much more quickly than most meats. Bacterial growth is faster and flavor falls off quickly when it is not fresh or when the frozen item is not kept below zero until ready for use. A „fishy" sharp ammonia odor means deterioration.

About 5 days is the maximum holding time for the top-quality fresh fish, even though it has been cooled quickly after being caught.

Sometimes fish caught at sea are already ten or more days old upon arrival at port, so the fish has lost „freshness" before it gets to market.

Important – When selecting fresh fish, follow these simple steps:

Only purchase fish at reputable markets

Smell the fish. It should have a „fresh sea" aroma to it – NO STRONG ODORS.

When you take the fish home, rinse it with cold water.

Frozen Fish: Did you know that fresh fish, frozen at sea, is usually fresher than so called „fresh fish" bought at your store? Most fish sold frozen is now cleaned, filleted, and frozen right on the boat within a few hours of the catch, preserving its freshness. Frozen fish in our markets come primarily from Alaska, the North Atlantic, and the Orient.

Buy frozen fish where you know the turnover is brisk. See that the packages are fresh looking and unbroken. Once frozen fish is in the distriubtuion chain, the recommended storage life is three months.

To thaw frozen fish, thaw slowly in the refrigerator for 24 hours or, if you're in a hurry, you can run the tightly wrapped fish under COLD water instead of at room temperature. Cook it as soon as possible to minimize the loss of juices. Try not to thaw frozen fish completely before cooking, or it may make them very dry and mushy.

Wine

Wine In Cooking

Never cook with any wine or spirit you **would not drink!** Cooking and the process of reducing a sauce will bring out the worst in an inferior potable.

A small quantity of wine will enhance the flavor of the dish. The alcohol in the wine evaporates while the food is cooking, and only the flavor remains. Boiling down wine concentrates the flavor, including acidity and sweetness. Be careful not to use too much wine as the flavor could overpower your dish.

Wine should never by added to a dish just before serving. It should simmer with the food or in the sauce while it is being cooked; as the wine cooks, it reduces and becomes an extract which flavors. Wine added too late in the preparation will give a harsh quality to the dish.

Serving Termperatures for Wines

More wine is ruined by being too warm than too cold. A wine that is served too cold is easily warmed, but a wine served too warm can be difficult to chill. Therefore, when in doubt, serve it colder than you might think necessary. A wine that is too warm tastes alcoholic and is not a pleasure to drink. White wines are served cooler than red wines.

Glossary Of German Wine Terms

Term	Definition
Ausbruch	Minimum sugar content 27 °KMW (138° Oechsle), naturally sweet.
Auslese	"Selection". No sugar added, minimum sugar content 21 °KMW (106° Oechsle); can be dry, is usually sweet.
Beerenauslese	"Grape Selection". No sugar added, minimum sugar content 25 °KMW (127° Oechsle); naturally sweet.
Bergwein	"Mountain Wine" from slopes of over 26 % stepth.
Blauer	"Blue", denoting red grapes.
Eiswein	"Ice Wine". Made from naturally frozen grapes; minimum sugar content, 25 °KMW (127° Oechsle).
Halbtrocken	Half Dry (4 to 9 g/l of residual sugar).
Halbsüß	Semi Sweet (9 to 18 g/l).
Kabinett	No sugar added, dry, alcohol from 10.5 to 12.7 %
Keller	Cellar.
Kellermeiser	Winemaker.
KMW	"Klosterneuburger Mostwaage"; 1 °KMW = 1 % sugar by weight in the must = 5° Oechsle.
Prädikat	All wines from the Kabinett, Spätlese, Auslese, Ausbruch, Eiswein, Beerenauslese and Trockenbeerenauslese categories. Range from dry to high natural sweetness. No sugar addition permitted.
Rheinriesling	Older name for (White) Riesling.
Ried	Vineyard site, equivalent to "Lage" in Germany or "climat" in Burgundy.
Spätlese	"Late harvest". No sugar added, natural alcohol above 12 %, usually dry, can be sweet.
Süß	Sweet. More than 18 g/l of residual sugar.
Trocken	Dry. Residual sugar less than 4 g/l.
Trockenbeerenauslese	"Dry Berry Selection". The sweetest of them all. Minimum sugar content 32 °KMW (156° Oechsle).

Jobs in Paradise

Norwegian Cruise Lines (NCL)

Miami, Florida

Year-Round

Norwegian Cruise Lines (formerly Norwegian Caribbean Lines) is one of the most successful cruise lines in the industry. The company's nine sleek vessels specialize in moderately priced, high-quality voyages to the Caribbean and Mexico. The pride of the NCL fleet ist the 2,000 plus passenger 1,035 foot long SS Norway (formerly France). The Norway is the longest ship in the world and one of the most impressive when seen at sea. However, NCL is not standing on its laurels. In 1989 the company took delivery of the brand-new Seaward, a 1,500 plus passenger vessel. NCL's smaller ships (called "the white ships" by crew members in honor of their sleek white hulls) include the Southward, Starward, Skyward, and Sunward II.

Specifics: NCL employs officers, staff, and crew for its nine ships. The Norway alone employs almost 800 personnel. Photographers are hired through the Cruiseship Picture Company, and bar, beauty salon, massage, and gift shop staff are hired through Florida Export Company (see separate listings for Cruiseship Picture Company and Florida Export Company in this chapter). NCL's "Dive In" program hires snorkeling instructors through Shallow Water Development, P. O. Box 013353, Miami, Florida 33101. Casino cashiers and croupiers should apply through the casino concessionaire Tiber Trading, 1027 Adams St., Hollywood, Florida 33019.

Insider tips: NCL's officers are all Norwegian (except the Medical Department). The crew is of mixed nationalities. Almost all staff members are American, Canadian or British.

www.ncl.com

Submitting Your Resume NCL
By Mail

Norwegian Cruise Line
Ship Personnel Dept.
7665 Corporate Center Drive
Miami, FL 33126

By Fax

(305) 436-4138

By E-mail

Send an email to webmaster@ncl.com
The subject line of your email Must Contain the words; „Shipboard Employment" followed by the position for which you would like to apply.

Snowmass Ski Area

Aspen, Colorado

Seasonal (Winter and Spring)

Snowmass rises up from the chic golden streets of Aspen like a mighty giant. Aspen's largest and most popular ski area is actually a conglomeration of six ski areas in one place.

Specifics: Snowmass hires 300 to 400 new employees each year to fill its 1,800- to 2,000-person staff. Most positions are seasonal beginning in early November and lasting through early April. The resort accepts applications for lift operators, food service staff, snowcat drivers, maids, hotel staff, ski school personnel, ski patrol members, and more. There is no application deadline. Starting pay ranges from $ 7.00 to $ 11.50 per hour depending on the position (subject to change).

Insider tips: Snowmass prides itself on its friendly staff and looks for "outgoing, people-oriented" applicants.

Perks: Most employees receive a free ski pass.

www.aspensnowmass.com

Hyatt Regency Waikiki

Honolulu, Island of Oahu, Hawaii

Year-Round

The Hyatt Regency Waikiki is one of the premier resort hotels on Oahu. Fronting Waikiki Beach, this 1,200 plus room resort boasts numerous bars and restaurants including Spats Nightclub and Trappers Jazz Club, two of the hottest night spots in the area.

Specifics: The Hyatt Regency Waikiki employs 1,100 employees and hires more than 300 people each year. Applicants can apply for entry-level line positions in all departments including housekeeping, front desk, bell, room service, bars, and food and beverage. Positions are also available for applicants with clerical or accounting skills. The hotel welcomes applicants who are interested in positions as management trainees or in entry-level management.

Insider tips: Applicants who are interested in staying for an extended period of time are more likely to land jobs.

Perks: Complimentary meals are offered in a special employee cafeteria. Uniforms are provided for managers, management trainees, and line employees.

www.waikikihyatt.com

Desert Inn Hotel & Casino

Las Vegas, Nevada

Seasonal (Limited Opportunities All Seasons) and Year-Round

The Desert Inn is an 830 room hotel complete with a health spa, eighteen-hole golf course, restaurants, lounges, and casino. Located on the world-famous Las Vegas casino strip, the Desert Inn is a landmark in Las Vegas.

Specifics: The Desert Inn employs 1,800 staff members and expects to hire approximately 800 new employees per year. Applications are accepted for a wide variety of positions in all departments including speciality shops, spa, accounting, human resources, purchasing, marketing, sales, food and beverage, hotel housekeeping, and casino.

Insider tips: "We look for friendly, courteous, and outgoing people for our staffing needs – individuals who truly enjoy their work and make our guests feel welcome."

Perks: The Desert Inn hosts special employee events such as golf tournaments, parties, and promotions. All employees are entitled to free shift meals, subsidized insurance, vacations, and holidays.

www.thedesertinn.com

Original Text

Look for more information:
www.hogastjob.com
www.job-consult.com
www.jobboerse.de
www.cruisejoblink.com
www.jobfactory.com

Grammatik
Grammar

Redewendungen
Phrases

Appendix

Grammar

THE ARTICLE

The definite article (bestimmter Artikel)

Der bestimmte Artikel ist in der Einzahl (Singular) und in der Mehrzahl (Plural) für alle drei Geschlechter (der, die, das) the [ðə], *vor Selbstlauten und stummem h* [ðı].

ZB: the [ðə] cook, waiter, waitress
          [ðı] apprentice, hour

No definite article with:

a) **meals:** Breakfast is served.
We have lunch at 12 o'clock.
but: the breakfast I had this morning

b) **days, months, seasons:** I go skiing in winter.

c) **proper nouns**
(persons, streets, towns, countries): When does the train to Manchester leave?
Ellen is from London.
but: the Tyrol, the Netherlands

d) **abstract nouns:** I have a lot of work.
He studies science.

e) **phrases:** most hotels (die meisten …)
last month, next year
to be at work
but: half the time
all the money
just the same

The indefinite article (unbestimmter Artikel)

Der unbestimmte Artikel ist a [ə], *mit Nachdruck* [eı],
vor gesprochenem Selbstlaut an [ən], *betont* [æn].

a [ə], *betont* [eı]   cook, waiter, uniform
an [ən], *betont* [æn] apprentice, Austrian, hour, uncle, aunt

Use with phrases: I am a cook.   What a shame!
I am in a hurry.   She has a headache.
three times a day   many a cook
400 a week   such a thing
a dozen eggs   half a litre
                      quite a lot

NOUNS

Das Geschlecht des Hauptwortes ist:

masculine	the waiter	he	*er*	**persons, domestic animals:**	the dog	– he is
feminine	the waitress	she	*sie*		my cat	– she is
neuter	the hotel	it	*es*	**things:**	my passport	– it is here
				animals:	the wild cat	– it bites
				the baby – it is crying		

188

Grammar

usually feminine	–	ships, countries, planes, cars
		The Queen Elizabeth and her crew.
		England – her citizens
		the moon – she (poetry) **but:** the sun – he

Different words:	masculine	feminine	masculine	feminine
	husband	wife	boyfriend	girlfriend
	nephew	niece	waiter	waitress
	sir	madam	steward	stewardess

Plural (Mehrzahlbildung)

Die regelmäßige Mehrzahl wird gebildet, indem an die Einzahl ein s angehängt wird, das nur nach stimmlosen Mitlauten stimmlos, sonst immer stimmhaft ist.

cup	cups [s]
day	days [z]
plate	plates

- *Wörter, die auf ce, ge, se, ze, s, ss, sh, ch, x und z enden, bekommen [iz] angehängt:*

glass	glasses
piece	pieces
box	boxes
dish	dishes

- *Wörter, die mit f, fe enden:*

knife	knives		**but:** roofs, chiefs, safes
wife	wives
half	halves

- *Wörter mit der Endung y nach einem Mitlaut:*

lady	ladies		**but:** days, keys
secretary	secretaries
penny	pennies

- *Wörter, die auf o enden:*

| potato | potatoes | | **but:** photos, kilos, pianos |
| tomato | tomatoes |

Irregular plural (unregelmäßige Mehrzahlbildung)

child	children	foot	feet	goose	geese
louse	lice	man	men	mouse	mice
ox	oxen	tooth	teeth	woman	women

Different meanings:

cloth	cloths	(Tücher)
	clothes	(Kleider)
custom	customs	(Sitten)
	customs	(Zoll)
colour	colours	(Farben)
	colours	(Fahne)
glass	glasses	(Gläser)
	glasses	(Augengläser)

Use singular with:	news, politics, economics, United States, United Nations, the Netherlands
	It is good news.
	The United States is ...
No plural form:	people, cattle, food, the rich, the poor, the blind (are)
Unchanged plural:	fish, sheep, deer
	one Swiss – two Swiss (Viennese, Japanese)
No singular form:	the clothes (are), the stairs, thanks, the contents
	scissors, trousers, tongs *(die aus zwei gleichen Teilen bestehen)*
Use singular or plural:	the staff works / work; family, class, crew, team ...

Appendix

PRONOUNS

Personal pronouns (persönliche Fürwörter)

1. Fall	2. Fall	allein stehend	3. und 4. Fall		rückbezüglich	
I	my hotel	mine	me	(mir, mich)	myself	(mich)
you	your ...	yours	you	(dir, dich, Ihnen, Sie)	yourself	(dich, sich)
he	his ...	his	him	(ihm, ihn)	himself	(sich)
she	her ...	hers	her	(ihr, sie)	herself	(sich)
it	its ...	its	it	(ihm, es)	itself	(sich)
we	our ...	ours	us	(uns, uns)	ourselves	(uns)
you	your ...	yours	you	(euch, euch, Ihnen, Sie)	yourselves	(euch, sich)
they	their ...	theirs	them	(ihnen, sie)	themselves	(sich)

Demonstrative pronouns (hinweisende Fürwörter)

Singular		Plural	
this	dieser, diese, dieses	these	diese
that	jener, jene, jenes	those	jene

This is an English dish and that is a French one.
These are wine glasses and those are beer glasses.

Stützwort one / ones:
Um ein und dasselbe Hauptwort nicht zu wiederholen, ersetzt man es durch one *(singular)* und ones *(plural)*.

Relative pronouns (bezügliche Fürwörter)

	Personen	*Sachen*	*Personen und Sachen*
wer?, was?	who	which	that
wessen?	whose	of which	
wem?	to whom	to which	
wen?, was?	whom / who	which	that

what = that which   This is what it costs.

Die bezüglichen Fürwörter haben in der Einzahl und in der Mehrzahl die gleiche Form.

Interrogative pronouns (Fragewörter)

Who are you?	*Wer sind Sie?*	**who**	–	}	
Whose napkin is this?	*Wessen Serviette ist das?*	**whose**	–	}	*fragen nach Personen*
Who(m) did you serve?	*Wem haben Sie serviert?*	**whom**	–	}	
Who did you see?	*Wen haben Sie gesehen?*				
What is that?	*Was ist das?*	**what**	–		*nach Sachen*
Which ist the best way?	*Welcher ist der beste Weg?*	**which**	–		*nach Personen oder Sachen*

Indefinite pronouns (unbestimmte Fürwörter)

some, somebody, someone, something
- *im bejahenden Satz:*   I'd like some coffee.
  I'd like something to eat.
  Somebody called. Someone answered.
- *im Fragesatz, wenn eine bejahende Antwort erwartet wird:* Would you like some tea? Yes, please.

any, anybody, anyone, anything
- *im verneinten Satz:*   I haven't got any money.
- *im Fragesatz, wenn die Antwort ungewiss ist:* Can I do anything for you?
  Is anybody at home?
- *im Bedingungssatz:*   If I had any time, I would visit London.

Grammar

Declension (Biegung)

Unter Biegung (declension) versteht man die Abänderung eines Wortes durch seine vier Fälle. Der 1. und 4. Fall haben dieselbe Form. Der 2. Fall wird meist mit Hilfe von „of", der 3. Fall mit „to" ausgedrückt.

Singular		*Plural*	
the / a hotel	*das / ein Hotel*	the hotels	*die Hotels*
of the / a hotel	*des / eines Hotels*	of the hotels	*der Hotels*
to the / a hotel	*dem / einem Hotel*	to the hotels	*den Hotels*
the / a hotel	*das / ein Hotel*	the hotels	*die Hotels*

Der sächsische Genetiv (besitzanzeigender Fall)

This is my father's hotel.	It is the hotel of my father.	**Singular + 's**
These are the cooks' knives.	They are the knives of the cooks.	**Plural + '**

INTERROGATIVE PRONOUNS

where?	*wo?*	why?	*warum?*	how much?	*wie viel?*
when?	*wann?*	how?	*wie?*	how many?	*wie viele?*

ADJECTIVES

Das Eigenschaftswort wird nur in der Steigerung verändert. Es behält dieselbe Form, wenn es als Beifügung vor dem Hauptwort oder als Satzaussage hinter dem Zeitwort steht.

a good dish   the dish is good

Eigenschaftswörter haben drei Steigerungsstufen:

Grundstufe	positive
1. Steigerungsstufe	comparative
2. Steigerungsstufe	superlative

Folgende Eigenschaftswörter werden mit -er, -est gesteigert:

- *einsilbige Eigenschaftswörter:*

cheap	cheaper	cheapest	
large	larger	largest	*e fällt weg*
dry	drier	driest	*y wird zu i*
hot	hotter	hottest	

Die Endbuchstaben d, g, n und t werden verdoppelt, wenn ihnen ein kurzes, betontes a, e, i oder o vorausgeht.

- *zweisilbige Eigenschaftswörter mit den Endungen le, er, y, ow und mit Betonung auf der letzten Silbe:*

dirty	dirtier	dirtiest
slow	slower	slowest
simple	simpler	simplest
polite	politer	politest

- *mehrsilbige Eigenschaftswörter werden durch Vorsetzung von „more" und „most" gesteigert:*

expensive	more expensive	most expensive
delicious	more delicious	most delicious

Die Eigenschaftswörter „common", „complete", „pleasant", „stupid" und „polite" können mit „more" / „most" oder -er / -est gesteigert werden.

Unregelmäßige Steigerungen:

good	}	better	best
well	}		

bad *(schlimm, schlecht)*	}		
ill *(krank, übel)*	}	worse	worst
evil *(übel, böse)*	}		

a few *(einige)*	}		
few *(wenige)*	}	fewer	fewest

Appendix

little *(wenig)*	} less	least		
little, small *(klein)*	} smaller	smallest		
much *(viel)*	} more	most		
many *(viele)*	}			
far	} farther *(weiter)*	farthest	It is farther to London than to Vienna. (distance)	
	} further *(ferner, weitere)*	furthest	I'll wait for further orders. (additional)	
near	} nearer	nearest *(räumlich, bildlich)*	the nearest hotel	
	}	next *(Reihenfolge)*	the next hotel	
			my nearest friend	
			(mein nächster Freund –	
			der mir am nächsten steht)	
old	} older	oldest		
	} elder	eldest		
		(nur von Personen, besonders von Geschwistern, gebraucht)		
late	} later *(später)*	latest *(späteste, neueste)*		
	} latter *(letztere)*	last *(letzte)*		

Durch „the" wird das Eigenschaftswort zum Hauptwort: the wise = der / die Weise
Nicht übersetzt wird „am" vor der 3. Steigerungsstufe: best (am besten)
the very best = *der allerbeste*
very much = *sehr viel*

Nach der 1. Steigerungsstufe „than" (als): She is younger than you.

Some more phrases:
still *(noch)*	It is still better.		
much *(viel)*	It is much more difficult.		
by far	*bei weitem*		
all the better	*umso besser*		
so much the better	*umso besser*		
as happy as	*so glücklich wie*		
not so cheap as	*nicht so billig wie*		
faster and faster	*immer schneller*	ohne „the":	
the shorter the better	*je kürzer, desto besser*	die meisten = most	Most guests come from …

CONJUNCTIONS

and	The waiter serves meals and drinks.
both … and	He serves both meals and drinks.
as well as	… meals as well as drinks.
not only … but also	… not only meals but also drinks.
neither … nor	We have neither red nor white wine.
or	Would you like orange or tomato juice?
either … or	We will either take the bus or the train.
but	Eating out is expensive, but eating there,
however	however, is more expensive.
nevertheless	I haven't got much time, nevertheless I'll go there.
therefore	You need money, therefore you have to work.
that is why	You are tired, that is why you need a rest.
when	When the guest leaves, he has to pay the bill.
as	As we were checking in, the porter carried our luggage up to our room.
since	She had not been to Vienna since her accident.
while	We had lunch while they were swimming.
as	She helps us as our mother used to.
because	Many guests visit our hotel because it is lovely.
since	Since (as) it is a lovely hotel, many guests come.
unless	We will go swimming unless it rains.
although	Although they travelled by plane, they were not early.
so	We don't have any double room, so you have to take two single rooms.

Other conjunctions:
after, before, till, until, in order to, if, though, than …

Grammar

ADVERBS

Das Umstandswort dient zur näheren Bestimmung
a) eines Zeitwortes:				He **often** works.
b) eines Eigenschaftswortes:		She is a **very** nice girl.
									In **relatively** short time ...
c) eines anderen Umstandswortes:	She does it **very** often.
									I speak English **rather** seldom.

Es gibt
- **ursprüngliche Umstandswörter**
    a) der Zeit:			now, then, always, never, often, seldom, sometimes, soon, today, yesterday, tomorrow, after ...
    b) des Ortes:			there, here, away, where
    c) der Art und Weise:	only, very, quite, rather, almost, nearly, so, therefore, thus

- **abgeleitete Umstandswörter** (durch Anhängen von -ly von den Eigenschaftswörtern abgeleitet)

quick	quickly	easy	easily
strange	strangely	true	truly
gentle	gently	dry	dryly
careful	carefully		

Gewisse Eigenschaftswörter bleiben als Umstandswörter unverändert, haben aber eine andere Bedeutung:

hardly	=	kaum
lately	=	vor kurzem
pretty	=	ziemlich
well	=	gut, wohl
directly	=	sofort

Kein Umstandswort verwenden:
to be, become, turn, get (werden), grow, feel, look (aussehen), taste, smell, seem.
I feel happy. I am careful. It looks delicious.

Stellung des Umstandswortes im Satz:
We often go to London.
I have never been to Ireland.
The guests have just arrived.

Umstandswörter, die auf -ly enden, werden mit „more" / „most" gesteigert:

slowly		more slowly		most slowly

Only:	Only I speak German.		I only speak German.
		(Nur ich spreche Deutsch))	(Ich spreche nur Deutsch)

VERBS

Es gibt regelmäßige und unregelmäßige Zeitwörter.

a) Regular verbs (regelmäßige Zeitwörter)

Die regelmäßigen Zeitwörter hängen in der Mitvergangenheit und der Vergangenheit ed oder nur d an.
In der Gegenwart wird nur die 3. Person Einzahl verändert.

Infinitive	(Grundform)	to serve	
Present tense	(Gegenwart)	I serve.	He, she, it serves.
Past tense	(Mitvergangenheit)	I served.	He, she, it served.
Present perfect tense	(Vergangenheit)	I have served.	He, she, it **has** served.
Future tense	(Zukunft)	I shall / will serve. We shall / will serve.	He, she, it will serve.
Future perfect tense	(Vorzukunft)	I will have served.	He will have served.
Present participle	(Mw. d. Gegenwart)	serving	
Past participle	(Mw. d. Vergangenheit)	served	
Imperative	(Befehlsform)	serve!	
Negation	(Verneinung)	I **do not** serve. (don't)	He **does not** serve. (doesn't)

b) Irregular verbs (unregelmäßige Zeitwörter)

to become	(werden)	became	become
to begin	(beginnen)	began	begun
to break	(brechen)	broke	broken
to bring	(bringen)	brought	brought
to burn	(verbrennen)	burnt	burnt
to buy	(kaufen)	bought	bought
can	(können)	could	–
to choose	(wählen)	chose	chosen
to come	(kommen)	came	come
to cost	(kosten)	cost	cost
to cut	(schneiden)	cut	cut
to do	(tun)	did	done
to drink	(trinken)	drank	drunk
to eat	(essen)	ate	eaten
to feed	(ernähren)	fed	fed
to forget	(vergessen)	forgot	forgotten
to freeze	(frieren)	froze	frozen
to get	(erhalten)	got	got
to give	(geben)	gave	given
to go	(gehen)	went	gone
to have	(haben)	had	had
to keep	(halten, behalten)	kept	kept
to know	(wissen)	knew	known
to lay	(legen)	laid	laid
to leave	(lassen, verlassen)	left	left
to lie	(liegen)	lay	lain
to make	(machen)	made	made
to pay	(bezahlen)	paid	paid
to put	(setzen, stellen)	put	put
to read	(lesen)	read	read
to ring	(läuten)	rang	rung
to run	(laufen)	ran	run
to say	(sagen)	said	said
to see	(sehen)	saw	seen
to sell	(verkaufen)	sold	sold
to shake	(schütteln)	shook	shaken
shall	(sollen)	should	–
to sit	(sitzen)	sat	sat
to sleep	(schlafen)	slept	slept
to smell	(riechen)	smelt	smelt
to speak	(sprechen)	spoke	spoken
to spend	(verwenden, verbringen, ausgeben)	spent	spent
to stand	(stehen)	stood	stood
to swim	(schwimmen)	swam	swum
to take	(nehmen)	took	taken
to teach	(lehren, unterrichten)	taught	taught
to tell	(erzählen, berichten)	told	told
to think	(denken)	thought	thought
will	(wollen)	would	–
to write	(schreiben)	wrote	written

Auxiliary verbs (Hilfszeitwörter)

"to be" sein

	Present	Past	Present Perfect	Past Perfect	Future
I	am	was	have been	had been	shall / will be
you	are	were	have been	had been	will be
he / she / it	is	was	has been	had been	will be
we	are	were	have been	had been	shall / will be
you	are	were	have been	had been	will be
they	are	were	have been	had been	will be

Grammar

„to have"	haben				
	Present	**Past**	**Present Perfect**	**Past Perfect**	**Future**
I	have	had	have had	had had	shall / will have
you	have	had	have had	had had	will have
he/she/it	has	had	has had	had had	will have
we	have	had	have had	had had	shall / will have
you	have	had	have had	had had	will have
they	have	had	have had	had had	will have

„to do"	tun / machen				
	Present	**Past**	**Present Perfect**	**Past Perfect**	**Future**
I	do	did	have done	had done	shall / will do
you	do	did	have done	had done	will do
he/she/it	does	did	has done	had done	will do
we	do	did	have done	had done	shall / will do
you	do	did	have done	had done	will do
they	do	did	have done	had done	will do

QUESTION AND NEGATION

Wenn die Satzaussage in Verbindung mit einem Hilfszeitwort steht, ist die Wortstellung in der Frage und der Verneinung wie im Deutschen.

S	P	O		
You	are	a cook.		
Are	you	a cook?	Yes, I am a cook. (I'm)	No, I am not a cook. (I'm not)
The chef	is	in the kitchen.		
Is	the chef	in the kitchen?	Yes, he is (in the kitchen).	No, he is not (isn't) (in the kitchen).

In den einfachen Zeiten und Formen werden die Frage und Verneinung mit „to do" gebildet:

Present tense:	I speak English.	**Do you** speak English?	Yes, I do.
			No, I do not (don't).
	He / she / it works.	**Does it** work?	Yes, it does.
			No, it does not (doesn't).
Past tense:	He paid the bill.	**Did he** pay the bill?	Yes, he did.
			No, he did not (didn't).

Kein „do" in Fragesätzen, in denen ein Fragewort selbst Satzgegenstand ist.

No „do", no „s" – Modal verbs *(unselbstständige Hilfszeitwörter)*
Sie können nicht selbstständig auftreten, stehen daher immer in Verbindung mit einem anderen Zeitwort.

Modal verb (Present tense)	Negation	Past tense	Substitute verbs (Ersatz)	
can	cannot (can't)	could	to be able to to be capable of	
may	may not must not = *Verbot*	might	to be possible to be permitted to to be allowed to	
must	need not		to have to to be obliged to	*Examples:* Can I help you?
will	will not (won't)	would	to want to to wish to	Would you like some coffee? Could you give me the menu, please? I should like a glass of red wine.
shall am to	shall not	should	to be to ought to	Who speaks German and English? What makes you think so?

Appendix

IMPERATIVE

- hat die gleiche Form wie die Nennform (Einzahl und Mehrzahl gleich)
- für Befehle und Aufforderungen

Let's have dinner!　　　　　　　　(let's = let us: *wenn sich der Sprecher mit einschließt*)
Don't open the window!　　　　　(don't = do not: *verneinte Befehlsform drückt eine Warnung oder ein Verbot aus*)

WORD ORDER

Where? When?	Subject	Predicate	Object	How?	Where?	When?
In the evening	the waitress	serves	dinner		(in the restaurant,	in the evening).
After that	she	brings	the dessert	quickly.		
(After dinner)	The guest	pays	his bill			after dinner.

GERUND (ING-FORM)

wird im Englischen sehr häufig verwendet:

Zeitwort: travel　　　　　　　　　**Gerund:** travelling *(das Reisen)*

als Satzgegenstand:　　　　　　　　**Travelling** is fascinating.
als Satzergänzung:　　　　　　　　　Would you mind **opening** the window?
steht häufig statt der Nennform:　　He likes **skiing**.
　　　　　　　　　　　　　　　　　　She hates **smoking**.

Gerund *nach* by, after, before, without, instead of, on

PROGRESSIVE FORM (DAUERFORM, VERLAUFSFORM)

- wird mit dem Hilfszeitwort „to be" und dem Mittelwort der Gegenwart (-ing) gebildet.
  Es wird eine Handlung, die gerade abläuft, noch andauert, noch nicht abgeschlossen ist, war oder sein wird, ausgedrückt:
  I am working. *(Ich arbeite gerade.)*
  I was working.
  I will be working.
  It is raining. *(Es regnet.)*

- eine beabsichtigte Handlung in naher Zukunft: „to be going to"
  I am going to travel to ...
  She is going to buy ...

- darf nicht verwendet werden für wiederholte Handlungen, allgemeine Feststellungen und bei Zeitwörtern wie:
  see　　　I am looking
  hear　　 I am listening.

PASSIVE VOICE

- wird mit der entsprechenden Form von „to be" und dem Mittelwort der Vergangenheit gebildet:
  aktiv:　　He serves the guests.
  passiv:　The guests are served (by him).

The manager offered **her a job.** She was offered a job (by the manager).
A job was offered to her (by the manager).

CONDITIONAL (IF-SENTENCES)

Es gibt drei Arten von Bedingungssätzen:

a) Die Erfüllung der Bedingung ist wahrscheinlich:
If he has time,　　　　　　　he will visit us.　　　　　　　　　　　　　　　　　　**Statt „will" im Hauptsatz:**
(Present)　　　　　　　　　　(Future)　　　　　　　　　　　　　　　　　　　　　**can, must, may**
I'll travel by train if I get a ticket. *(kein Beistrich vor „if")*

Grammar

b) Die Erfüllung der Bedingung ist unwahrscheinlich:

If I were good at English,	I would translate the letter.	*Statt „would":*
(Past)	(Conditional present = would + Nennform ohne „to")	**should, could, might**
I, he, she, it **were**.		

c) Die Bedingung ist unerfüllbar:

If I had had time,   I would have gone to the cinema.
(Past perfect)   (Conditional perfect = would + have + past participle)

Examples:

If I had time, I would / should do it.
If you asked him, he would help you.
If the weather were fine, we could go swimming.
If I had had time, I would have done it.
If the tickets had been too expensive, I would not have bought them.

No „if" after would / should, *außer es bedeutet „wollte"* – e.g.: If you would be so kind …

PREPOSITIONS

about	**um (… herum), in (… herum), über**	**below** below the head cook	**unterhalb, unter** unter dem Küchenchef stehen
the garden about the house	der Garten ums Haus	**beside** beside the knife	**neben** neben dem Messer
somewhere about	irgendwo herum	**besides** besides me	**außer, abgesehen von** außer mir
all about the hotel	im ganzen Hotel (herum)	**between**	**zwischen, unter, zusammen, neben**
to know about it	darüber Bescheid wissen	between fork and knife	zwischen Gabel und Messer
how / what about …?	wie wäre es mit …?	between you and me	unter uns
above	**über, oberhalb**	we have a room between the three of us	wir drei haben zusammen ein Zimmer
above all	vor allen Dingen, vor allem	between work and study	neben Arbeit und Studium
it's above my head	das ist mir zu hoch	**beyond**	**über, jenseits, über … hinaus, außer**
across	**über, quer durch**	beyond the Alps	jenseits der Alpen
across the road	über die Straße	until beyond next week	bis übernächste Woche
across a river	durch einen Fluss	beyond this	sonst (außer diesem, dieser)
after	**nach, hinter**	**but**	**außer**
after dinner	nach dem Essen	no one but me	niemand außer mir
after you	nach Ihnen	the first but one	der / die / das zweite
against	**gegen, wider**	**by**	**bei, an, neben, bis, mit, nach**
against payment	gegen Zahlung	by the door	bei der Tür
against the door	gegen die Tür	a holiday by the sea	ein Urlaub am Meer
against their wish	entgegen ihrem Wunsch	sit by me	setz dich neben mich
along	**entlang**	by tomorrow	bis morgen
along the street	entlang der Straße	by bus	mit dem Bus
somewhere along here	irgendwo hier (herum)	by my watch	nach meiner Uhr
among	**unter**	**down**	**hinunter, unten, entlang**
among the guests	unter den Gästen	go down the street	die Straße hinuntergehen
at	**an, bei, in, auf, um**	they were further down	sie waren weiter unten
at the window	am / beim Fenster	she was coming down the hall	sie kam die Halle entlang
at school	in der Schule	**except**	**außer**
at my party / at work	bei meiner Feier / bei der Arbeit	except me	außer mir
to look at somebody	jemanden ansehen	**for**	**für, zu, nach**
at 5 o'clock	um 5 Uhr	for you	für dich
before	**vor**	fit for nothing	zu nichts nutze / zu gebrauchen
before next week	vor nächster Woche	the train for Salzburg	der Zug nach Salzburg
ladies before gentlemen	Damen haben den Vortritt		
before our eyes	vor unseren Augen		
behind	**hinter**		
behind the door	hinter der Tür		
behind time	Verspätung		

from	*aus, von*
from London	*aus / von London*
from tomorrow	*von morgen*
from the top	*von oben*
weak from hunger	*schwach vor Hunger*
in	*in, bei*
in the room	*im Zimmer*
in the morning	*am Vormittag*
he is in the army	*er ist beim Militär*
inside	*in, innen ... in*
inside the kitchen	*in der Küche*
he went inside the hotel	*er ging ins Hotel*
into	*in ... hinein*
translate into English	*ins Englische übersetzen*
into the night	*bis in die Nacht hinein*
to divide into	*teilen*
near	*nahe an, gegen*
near the station	*in der Nähe des Bahnhofs*
near 2 o'clock	*gegen 2 Uhr*
of	*von, über, aus, vor*
a friend of ours	*ein Freund von uns*
south of	*südlich von*
free of charge	*kostenlos*
off	*von, ab von*
off the table	*vom Tisch*
off the main road	*von der Hauptstraße weg*
on	*auf, an, in, über, bei, nach*
on the table	*auf dem Tisch*
on the ground	*am Boden*
on pension	*in Rente*
on your theory	*Ihrer (deiner) Theorie nach*
on your arrival	*bei Ihrer (deiner) Ankunft*
opposite	*gegenüber*
opposite the hotel	*gegenüber dem Hotel*
out (of)	*aus, hinaus, außer*
out of the room	*aus dem Zimmer (hinaus)*
out of a glass	*aus einem Glas*
out of breath / money	*außer Atem / kein Geld mehr*
outside	*außerhalb*
outside the dining-room	*außerhalb des Speiseraumes*
over	*über*
spread the blanket over the bed	*breite die Decke über das Bett*
it is over the bed	*es ist über dem Bett*
past	*vorbei, vorüber, hinter, nach*
past the restaurant	*nach dem Restaurant*
twenty past four	*zwanzig (Minuten) nach vier*
past fifty	*über fünfzig*
round	*um (... herum)*
round the table	*um den Tisch (herum)*
round 200	*ungefähr 200*
since	*seit*
ever since 1990	*schon seit 1990*
through	*durch*
go through the hall	*durch die Halle gehen*
Monday through Friday	*von Montag bis Freitag*
till / until	*bis*
until night / then	*bis abends / dann*
to	*zu, bis, auf, vor, in*
to the cinema	*ins Kino*
to the station	*zum Bahnhof*
to the left	*nach links*
100 to 120 guests	*100 bis 120 Gäste*
to drink to your health	*auf deine Gesundheit trinken*
a quarter to three	*Viertel vor drei*
I have never been to ...	*ich war noch nie in ...*
towards	*auf ... zu, gegen*
towards the sea	*aufs Meer zu*
towards 10 o'clock	*gegen 10 Uhr*
under	*unter*
it's under there	*es ist darunter*
under 20	*unter 20*
up	*obenauf, hinauf*
up the stairs	*die Stiege hinauf*
with	*mit, bei, vor, wo*
are you pleased with it?	*sind Sie damit zufrieden?*
I'll be with you in a moment	*einen Augenblick bitte, ich bin gleich da*
with me	*bei mir*
white with snow	*weiß vom Schnee*
within	*innerhalb*
within the regulations	*im Rahmen der Vorschriften*
without	*ohne*
without passport	*ohne Pass*

Examples

Where are you going **to**?
What are you looking **for**?
to come / go from, to, into, out of (a place)
on Monday, in January, at 10 o'clock, in the evening
to go by bus / train / ship
to go into a room *(wohin?)*
to be in a room *(wo?)*
to live in Vienna *(bei größeren Städten)*
to stay at Tamsweg *(bei kleineren Städten)*
to agree on / upon / to / in / with
to live on / upon your parents
good terms with
to result from *(sich ergeben aus)*, in *(hinauslaufen auf)*
to sit at the table *(an)*, on the table *(auf)*
to start from *(abfahren von)*, for *(abfahren nach)*
a week ago   =   *vor einer Woche*
before next week   =   *vor nächster Woche*
to know about / he is known for
at the butcher's
to Rome
at the station
by day, by the way, by the time
for some weeks
into the country
to leave for Linz
to agree with somebody
from time to time
to suffer from
to prevent from
on occasion
on no account

Phrases

Guest

Hotel- or Servicestaff

In general	*Allgemein*
I'm sorry, I'm late.	Tut mir Leid, ich habe mich verspätet.
Can I have …?	Kann ich … haben?
May I …?	Darf ich …?
Yes (no), you can(not) have …	Ja (nein), Sie können (nicht) … haben.
Would you like …?	Würden (Möchten) Sie (gerne) …?
No, thank you.	Nein, danke.
Yes, please.	Ja, bitte.
I would like …	Ich möchte (gerne) …
(I beg your) pardon?	Wie bitte?
Can you understand me?	Können Sie mich verstehen?
Yes (no), I can(not) understand you.	Ja (nein), ich kann Sie (nicht) verstehen.
I am sorry. (I'm sorry.)	Es tut mir Leid.
Speak slowly, please.	Sprechen Sie langsam, bitte.
Excuse me, please.	Entschuldigen Sie (mich), bitte.
All right, OK / okay (Am.).	(Ist) in Ordnung.
Thank you (very much).	(Besten) Dank(e).
You are welcome.	Bitte sehr.
Not at all, don't mention it.	Bitte sehr, nicht der Rede wert.
Have a good time, enjoy yourself.	Gute Unterhaltung, viel Vergnügen.
Can I help you?	Kann ich Ihnen helfen?
Can you help me, please?	Können Sie mir bitte helfen?
Come and see me.	Besuchen Sie mich.
With pleasure.	Mit Vergnügen.

Greeting (a) person(s)	*Zur Begrüßung*
Ladies and gentlemen!	Meine Damen und Herren!
Good morning! (until noon)	Guten Morgen! (bis Mittag)
Good afternoon, sir!	Guten Tag, (mein) Herr!
Good evening, Mr. Brown!	Guten Abend, Herr Brown!
Good night, madam!	Gute Nacht, (gnädige) Frau!
Goodbye, Mrs. Carter!	Auf Wiedersehen, Frau Carter!
How do you do! (to each other)	Guten Tag! (Begrüßungsformel bei der ersten Begegnung)
See you later!	Bis später!

Introducing (to) a person	*Vorstellung*
What is your name, please?	Wie ist Ihr Name, bitte? Wie heißen Sie, bitte?
My name is …	Mein Name ist …
Where do you come from?	Woher kommen Sie?

Appendix

I come from ...	*Ich komme von ...*
Let me introduce you to ...	Lassen Sie mich Ihnen ... vorstellen.
What do you do / are you? = What is your profession?	Welchen Beruf haben Sie?
This is Mr. Brown!	Das ist Herr Brown!
May I introduce you to Mr. Brown?	Darf ich Sie Herrn Brown vorstellen?
Pleased to meet you.	*Sehr erfreut, Sie zu sehen.*
I'm glad to see you.	*Freut mich, Sie zu sehen.*
How are you?	Wie geht es Ihnen?
Thank you, I am (not) fine.	*Danke, mir geht es (nicht) gut.*
And how is (your) ...?	Und wie geht es (Ihrem, Ihrer) ...?
He (she) is (not) well.	*Ihm (ihr) geht es (nicht) gut.*

Having problems — **Wenn es Probleme gibt**

What's the trouble?	Welche Schwierigkeiten gibt es?
What's the matter?	Was ist los?
I am in a hurry.	*Ich bin in Eile.*
Are you in a hurry?	Sind Sie in Eile?
It is very important.	*Es ist sehr wichtig.*
That's (rather) difficult.	Das ist (ziemlich) schwierig.
I'm afraid that's not possible.	*Ich befürchte, es ist nicht möglich.*
What shall I do?	*Was soll ich tun?*
I am right.	Ich habe Recht.
You are (not) right.	Sie haben (nicht) Recht.
You are very kind.	*Sie sind sehr freundlich.*

Feeling ill — **Wenn man sich krank fühlt**

How are you feeling (do you feel)?	Wie fühlen Sie sich?
I don't feel well.	*Ich fühle mich nicht wohl.*
I feel sick.	*Mir ist schlecht.*
Headache, toothache, upset stomach	Kopfweh, Zahnweh, verdorbener Magen
Do you need a (dentist) doctor?	Brauchen Sie einen (Zahnarzt) Arzt?
Hospital, pharmacy (Am.), chemist's (shop; Br.)	Spital, Apotheke
Do you have a temperature?	Haben Sie Fieber?
Medicine, tablet, pill	Medizin, Tablette, Pille
Sticking plaster (Br.), band-aid (Am.).	Heftpflaster

Giving information — **Auskunftserteilung**

Can you show me where I am on the map?	*Können Sie mir auf der Karte zeigen, wo ich bin?*
You are here.	Sie sind hier.
Where is the ...	*Wo ist der (die, das) ...*
... information office?	*... Informationsbüro?*
... post office, telephone box?	*... Postamt, Telefonzelle?*
... station, bus stop?	*... Bahnhof, Bushaltestelle?*
... next bank, town centre?	*... nächste Bank, Stadtzentrum?*
... car ferry, (bathing) beach?	*... Autofähre, (Bade)strand?*
... main street, shopping centre?	*... Hauptstraße, Einkaufszentrum?*
... church, cathedral?	*... Kirche, Kathedrale (Dom)?*
... museum, city hall?	*... Museum, Rathaus?*
... hotel, youth hostel?	*... Hotel, Jugendherberge?*

Phrases

... swimming pool, tennis court?	... Schwimmbad, Tennisplatz?
... barber, hairdresser?	... Herren-, Damenfriseur?
... booking (ticket) office?	... Kartenbüro?
... best restaurant?	... beste Restaurant?
... cable car, chair lift?	... Seilbahn, Sessellift?
... road to Vienna?	... Straße nach Wien?
Where can I ...	Wo kann ich ...
... book an excursion to ...?	... einen Ausflug nach ... buchen?
... find a ski instructor?	... einen Schilehrer finden?
... find a tour guide?	... einen Führer finden?
... rent skis?	... Skier mieten?
Can you tell me the way to ...?	Können Sie mir den Weg zu ... erklären?
How do I get there?	Wie komme ich da hin?

Telling directions / Den Weg erklären

Which direction (way) to ...?	Welche Richtung (Weg) zu(m), nach ...?
This direction, this way.	Diese Richtung.
Straight on, right ahead.	Geradeaus.
(Right) over there.	(Direkt) dort drüben.
The first turning to the left. / Your first left.	Die erste Biegung links.
The next street to the right. / Your first right.	Die nächste Straße rechts.
In the town centre.	Im (in das) Stadtzentrum.
At the end of the village.	Am Ende des Dorfes.
Round the next corner.	Um die nächste Ecke.
Three traffic lights, then ask again.	Drei Verkehrsampeln, dann fragen Sie wieder.
Follow the overhead line of the trolley bus.	Folgen Sie der Oberleitung des Obusses.
Follow the tram.	Folgen Sie der Straßenbahn.
Opposite the church.	Gegenüber der Kirche.
(Always) keep to the right.	Halten Sie sich (immer) rechts.
There is a detour (by-pass).	Es gibt eine Umleitung.
How far is it (to ...)?	Wie weit ist es (bis ...)?
About 1 mile (= 1.6 km)	Ungefähr 1 Meile (= 1,6 km).
100 yards (= 90 m).	100 Yards (= 90 m).
How long does it take (me)?	Wie lange brauche ich?
10 minutes on foot.	10 Minuten zu Fuß.
5 minutes by car.	5 Minuten mit dem Auto.
About half (an) hour.	Ungefähr eine halbe Stunde.
Follow the signs for ...	Folgen Sie den Schildern nach ...
Where can I catch the bus to ...?	Wo hält der Bus nach ...?

Operating the telephone / Am Telefon

Lift the receiver to get the reception.	Nehmen Sie den Hörer ab, um die Rezeption zu bekommen.
Dial the number ...	Wählen Sie die Nummer ...
The number is ...	Die Nummer ist ...
Just a moment, please.	Einen Moment, bitte.
Who is speaking?	Wer spricht?
Hold on (the line).	Bleiben Sie (am Apparat).
I'll connect you.	Ich werde Sie verbinden.
(Sorry,) I cannot hear you.	Ich kann Sie (leider) nicht hören.
Can you hear me?	Können Sie mich hören?

The line (number) is busy (engaged).	Die Nummer ist besetzt.
Do you know the area code?	Wissen Sie die Vorwahl(nummer)?
We were cut off.	Wir wurden getrennt.
There is no answer.	Es meldet sich niemand.
Can you spell it?	Können Sie es buchstabieren?
Would you repeat it, please?	Würden Sie es bitte wiederholen?
Would you like to leave a message?	Möchten Sie eine Nachricht hinterlassen?

At the restaurant — Im Restaurant

Taking a reservation by phone — Telefonische Reservierung

... Restaurant, may I help you?	... Restaurant, darf ich Ihnen helfen?
We open at ...	Wir öffnen um ...
We close at ...	Wir schließen um ...
For what time?	Für welche Zeit?
For how many (people)?	Für wie viele (Leute)?
Sorry, there are no vacancies, but I can give you a table at ...	Leider, es gibt keine Plätze mehr, aber ich kann Ihnen einen Tisch um ... geben.

Receiving guests — Empfang der Gäste

Have you got a reservation?	Haben Sie eine Reservierung?
Sorry, that table is reserved.	Leider, dieser Tisch ist reserviert.
Come this way, please. / Follow me, please.	Kommen Sie weiter, bitte. / Folgen Sie mir, bitte.
Have a seat, please.	Nehmen Sie Platz, bitte.
This way, please.	Hier entlang, bitte.
Will this table be all right?	Ist dieser Tisch richtig?
I'll bring you the menu.	Ich bringe Ihnen die Speisekarte.

Taking orders — Aufnahme der Bestellung

Would you like to have lunch / supper?	Möchten Sie ein Mittagessen / kleines (spätes) Abendessen?
Dinner is served from ... to ...	Die Hauptmahlzeit wird von ... bis ... serviert.
Would you like to order now?	Möchten Sie nun bestellen?
We have got ...	Wir haben ...
Our speciality is ...	Unsere Spezialität ist ...
How would you like your ...?	Wie möchten Sie Ihr ...?
Would you like it rare, medium, well-done?	Möchten Sie es blutig, halb durch, durch?
We haven't got any ...	Wir haben kein(e) ...
There is a fixed price for ...	Es ist ein fester Preis für ...
All inclusive.	Alles inbegriffen.
Would you like (beer) or (wine)?	Möchten Sie (Bier) oder (Wein)?
Bottled or draught?	In Flaschen oder offen?
On the rocks?	Mit Eiswürfeln?
Sweet or dry?	Süß oder trocken?
I would recommend a selection of ...	Ich würde eine Auswahl von ... empfehlen.
I can offer you ...	Ich kann Ihnen ... anbieten.
May I suggest ...?	Darf ich Ihnen ... vorschlagen?
I'd suggest ...	Ich würde ... vorschlagen
May I recommend ...?	Darf ich Ihnen ... empfehlen?
May I take your order now?	Darf ich Ihre Bestellung aufnehmen?

Will that be all?	Ist das alles?
Cigarettes are in the (slot)machine.	Zigaretten sind im Automaten.
Are you ready to order?	Haben Sie schon ausgesucht?
I'll take ...	Ich nehme ...
The same for me.	Das Gleiche für mich.
I'd prefer ...	Ich würde ... bevorzugen.

Presenting the bill / Ausstellung der Rechnung

Are you paying separately?	Bezahlen Sie getrennt?
All on the same bill?	Alles auf eine Rechnung?
Item 6 is ...	Posten Nummer 6 ist ...
How are you paying?	Wie zahlen Sie?
You can pay ...	Sie können zahlen ...
... (in) cash,	... mit Bargeld, bar,
... in (foreign) currency,	... in (ausländischer) Währung,
... by credit card.	... mit Kreditkarte.
How much is ...?	Was kostet ...?
The total amount / exchange rate is ...	Die Gesamtsumme / der Wechselkurs beträgt ...
Service and value-added tax are included.	Bedienung und MwSt. sind inbegriffen.
Would you like to put it on your hotel bill?	Möchten Sie es auf Ihre Hotelrechnung setzen lassen?
Would you sign here, please?	Würden Sie bitte hier unterschreiben?
Here's your receipt.	Hier ist Ihre Quittung.

At the reception / An der Rezeption

Taking reservations / Zimmerreservierungen

We are looking for ...	Wir suchen ...
What kind of room would you like?	Welches Zimmer möchten Sie?
With breakfast, halfboard, fullboard.	Mit Frühstück, Halb-, Vollpension.
How long will you be staying?	Wie lange werden Sie bleiben?
The price is ... for ...	Der Preis ist ... für ...
There is a reduction for ...	Ermäßigung gibt es für ...
We charge ... extra for ...	Wir berechnen ... extra für ...
Sorry, we are (fully) booked but I can find you a room in another hotel.	Leider, wir sind ausgebucht, aber ich kann ein Zimmer für Sie in einem anderen Hotel finden.
What time will you be arriving?	Wann werden Sie ankommen?

Booking a room / Buchen eines Zimmers

Who's the reservation for?	Für wen ist die Reservierung?
I'd like to make a reservation.	Ich möchte gerne reservieren.
Have you got a reservation? / Do you have a reservation?	Haben Sie eine Reservierung?
What's your name (address), please?	Wie ist Ihr(e) Name (Adresse), bitte?
A single (double, twin-bedded) room.	Ein Einzel-(Doppel-, Zweibett-)zimmer.
On the first, second, third floor.	Im ersten, zweiten, dritten Stock.
With shower, (private) bath.	Mit Dusche, (eigenem) Bad.
Would you fill in this form, please?	Würden Sie bitte dieses Formular ausfüllen?
Would you fill in this registration form?	Würden Sie bitte das Gästeblatt ausfüllen?
May I have your passport, please?	Darf ich bitte Ihren Pass haben?
Your room number is ...	Ihre Zimmernummer ist ...
Here is your key.	Hier ist Ihr Schlüssel.

Appendix

Here is your key card.	Hier ist Ihre Schlüsselkarte.
Breakfast is served from ... to ...	Frühstück wird von ... bis ... serviert.
I can confirm your booking	Ich kann Ihre Buchung bestätigen.
How will you be paying? / How will you be settling your account?	Wie werden Sie bezahlen?
Can you give a deposit, please?	Könnten Sie bitte eine Anzahlung leisten?
The porter will show you to your room.	Der Kofferträger wird Ihnen Ihr Zimmer zeigen. / wird Sie auf Ihr Zimmer bringen.
The porter will carry your luggage.	Der Kofferträger wird Ihr Gepäck nehmen.
Have a pleasant stay in ... sir / madam.	Ich wünsche Ihnen einen angenehmen Aufenthalt in ..., mein Herr / Gnädige Frau.

Getting details of arrival — Einzelheiten über die Ankunft einholen

What time will you be arriving?	Wann werden Sie ankommen?
Will you be arriving before / after ...?	Werden Sie vor / nach ... ankommen?
Will you be coming by plane?	Reisen Sie mit dem Flugzeug an?
What's your flight number, please, in case the plane is late?	Wie ist bitte Ihre Flugnummer für den Fall einer Verspätung?

Getting information from the guest about a reservation — Einholung der Information vom Gast über die Reservierung

Do you have a letter or fax confirming the reservation?	Haben Sie einen Brief oder ein Fax mit der Reservierungsbestätigung?
When did you make the reservation?	Wann haben Sie die Reservierung gemacht?
When was it made?	Wann wurde sie durchgeführt?
From which country?	Von welchem Land?
Who made the reservation?	Wer führte die Reservierung durch?
I'm sorry, but I haven't got any record of that.	Es tut mir Leid, aber darüber habe ich keine Aufzeichnung.
Would you like me to get you a room in another hotel?	Möchten Sie, dass ich Ihnen ein Zimmer in einem anderen Hotel besorge?
Would you like me to call another hotel?	Möchten Sie, dass ich ein anderes Hotel anrufe?
I found you a room at ...	Ich habe für Sie ein Zimmer in ... gefunden.

Giving information about prices — Preisinformation geben

For ... the price would be ...	Für ... ist der Preis ...
... is (would be) ...	... kostet ... (würde kosten).
How much is ...?	*Wie viel kostet ..?*
The total would be ...	Die Gesamtkosten betragen ... / Der Gesamtbetrag macht ...
The price includes ...	Der Preis beinhaltet ...
... is / are included.	... ist / sind inbegriffen.
There's a reduction for ...	Es gibt eine Ermäßigung für ...
We have a special package plan for ... staying for ...	Wir haben ein besonderes Gesamtangebot für ..., ... wenn Sie ... bleiben.
We'll have to charge you ... extra.	Wir müssen Ihnen ... zusätzlich verrechnen.

Giving the guest information about the hotel — Dem Gast Information über das Hotel geben

Our hotel is located near ... / very modern etc.	Unser Hotel ist nahe ... gelegen / sehr modern etc.
We've got ...	Wir haben / bieten ...
I'm sorry, we haven't got ...	Es tut mir Leid, wir haben nicht ...
We're fully equipped for that.	Wir sind dafür vollkommen ausgestattet.
Would you like us to send you a brochure?	Wünschen Sie die Zusendung eines Prospektes?

Phrases

Registering a guest	**Einen Gast anmelden**
Would you like to register, please?	Würden Sie sich anmelden, bitte?
You'll have to register individually.	Sie müssen sich einzeln anmelden.
Would you fill in this form, please?	Würden Sie bitte diese Anmeldung ausfüllen?
Would you sign here, please?	Würden Sie hier bitte unterschreiben?
I'll need your signature.	Ich benötige Ihre Unterschrift.
Sign here, please.	Hier unterschreiben, bitte.
May I see your passport, please?	Darf ich bitte Ihren Reisepass sehen? / Können Sie sich ausweisen?
Have you got any identification?	Haben Sie irgendeinen Ausweis?

Refusing a booking	**Eine Buchung ablehnen**
Unfortunately we're fully booked for … but …	Bedauerlicherweise sind wir am … vollkommen ausgebucht, aber …
I can book you a room for the …	Ich kann Ihnen für den … ein Zimmer reservieren.
If there isn't any room, we can get you on a waiting list or we can find you a room in another hotel.	Wenn kein Zimmer frei ist, können wir Sie auf eine Warteliste setzen oder in einem anderen Hotel ein Zimmer suchen.
We won't be able to guarantee you a room for the … (date).	Wir können Ihnen für … (Datum) keine Zimmerzusage garantieren.

Extending a booking	**Eine Reservierung verlängern**
If we weren't so heavily booked, we could let you stay in the room free of charge.	Wären wir nicht so stark besetzt, könnten Sie ohne Entgelt das Zimmer behalten.
We've got a full house, so if you really want to keep your room this afternoon, we'll have to charge you 50 % of the price.	Wir haben ein voll besetztes Haus, sodass wir, wenn Sie tatsächlich Ihr Zimmer bis heute Nachmittag behalten wollen, einen Aufpreis in Höhe von 50 % des Preises verrechnen müssen.
The hotel is full and there'll be someone taking your room. We'll keep your luggage if you like.	Das Hotel ist besetzt und es gibt jemanden, der Ihr Zimmer nehmen wird. Wenn Sie es wünschen, werden wir Ihr Gepäck aufbewahren.

Room service	**Zimmerservice**
Breakfast can be served in your room.	Das Frühstück kann auf Ihr Zimmer serviert werden.
For how many (persons)?	Für wie viele (Personen)?
We begin serving at …	Wir beginnen mit dem Service um …
The waiter will be up right away.	Der Kellner wird sofort oben sein.
It will take … minutes.	In … Minuten.

At the cashier's	**An der Kassa**
What's your room number?	Wie ist Ihre Zimmernummer?
Are you Mr. (Mrs.) …?	Sind Sie Herr (Frau) …?
Here is your bill.	Hier ist Ihre Rechnung.
We accept traveller's cheques and credit cards.	Wir nehmen Reiseschecks und Kreditkarten.
The rate of exchange (exchange rate) is …	Der Wechselkurs beträgt …
Would you sign here, please?	Würden Sie hier unterschreiben, bitte?
Here is your receipt.	Hier ist Ihre Quittung.
I want to check out	*Ich möchte abreisen.*
I'd like to settle my bill.	*Ich möchte meine Rechnung begleichen.*
It's the policy of the hotel.	Das ist der Grundsatz des Hauses.
Do you have a cheque card / bankers card?	Haben Sie eine Scheck- / Bankomatkarte?
Have you got any identification?	Können Sie sich ausweisen?
I hope you enjoyed your stay.	Ich hoffe, Sie haben Ihren Aufenthalt genossen.

Appendix

Dealing with complaints	Beschwerden
I have a complaint.	Ich habe eine Beschwerde.
I'm extremely sorry (to hear that).	Es tut mir außerordentlich Leid (das zu hören).
The toilet / tap (faucet) / shower / air-conditioning does not work.	Die Toilette / der Wasserhahn / die Dusche / die Klimaanlage funktioniert nicht.
We'll attend to it right away / at once / immediately.	Wir werden sofort nachsehen.
I'll get another one.	Ich werde ein anderes (eine andere, einen anderen) besorgen.
I'll see about your order.	Ich werde mich um Ihre Bestellung kümmern.
I'll see what I can do.	Ich will sehen, was ich machen kann.
I'm sorry, that is not possible.	Tut mir Leid, das ist nicht möglich.
I'll speak to the wine butler / chef.	Ich werde mit dem Weinkellner / Küchenchef reden.
I'll be with you in a minute.	Ich komme sofort zu Ihnen.
There doesn't seem to be anything wrong with it.	Mir scheint, es ist alles in Ordnung damit.
Would you like to change your order?	Möchten Sie Ihre Bestellung ändern?
Please forgive me for not ...	Verzeihen Sie, dass ich nicht ...
I'm terribly sorry.	Es tut mir schrecklich Leid.
I really must apologize for ...	Ich muss mich wirklich für ...entschuldigen.
Can you forgive me for ...?	Können Sie mir ... verzeihen?
I greatly regret ...	Ich bedaure sehr ...
We regret to inform you ...	Es tut uns Leid, Ihnen mitteilen zu müssen, ...
Please accept our apologies.	Bitte nehmen Sie unsere Entschuldigung an.

Spelling on the Phone

	English	American	International		English	American	International
A	Andrew	Abel	Alfa	N	Nellie	Nan	Nectar
B	Benjamin	Baker	Bravo	O	Oliver	Oboe	Oscar
C	Charlie	Charlie	Coca	P	Peter	Peter	Papa
D	David	Dog	Delta	Q	Queenie	Queen	Quebec
E	Edward	Easy	Echo	R	Robert	Roger	Romeo
F	Frederick	Fox	Foxtrot	S	Sugar	Sugar	Sierra
G	George	George	Golf	T	Tommy	Tare	Tango
H	Harry	How	Hotel	U	Uncle	Uncle	Union
I	Isaac	Item	India	V	Voctor	Victor	Victor
J	Jack	Jig	Juliet	W	William	William	Whiskey
K	King	King	Kilo	X	Xmsa	X (eks)	Extra
L	Lucy	Love	Lima	Y	Yellow	Yoke	Yankee
M	Mary	Mike	Metro	Z	Zebra	Zebra	Zulu

Maße, Gewichte und Größen
Measures, Weights and Sizes

Appendix

Equivalent Measures and Weights

3 tea spoons	=	1 tablespoon
4 tablespoons	=	¹/₄ cup
16 tablespoons	=	1 cup
¹/₂ cup	=	1 gill
4 gills	=	1 pint
2 cups	=	1 pint
4 cups	=	1 quart
2 pints	=	1 quart
4 quarts	=	1 gallon
8 quarts	=	1 peck
4 pecks	=	1 bushel
16 ounces	=	1 pound
42 gallons (Öl)	=	1 barrel = 158,970 l
36 gallons (Bier)		163,565 l

Dry Measures (Trockenmaße)

2 gallons	=	1 peck	=	9,092 l
4 pecks	=	1 bushel	=	36,368 l
8 bushels	=	1 quarter	=	290,935 l

Linear Measures (Längenmaße)

1 inch	1"	=		2,54 cm
12 inches		=	1 foot (ft)	= 30,48 cm
3 feet	1'	=	1 yard (yd)	= 91,44 cm
220 yards		=	1 furlong (fur)	= 201,17 m
1760 yards		=	1 mile (m)	= 1,609 km
3 miles		=	1 league	= 4,828 km

Measures of Capacity (Hohlmaße)

Liquid measures of capacity (Flüssigkeitsmaße)			British	American
1 fluid ounce	=	2,84 cl		
1 gill	=		0,142 l	0,118 l
4 gills	=	1 pint (pt)	0,568 l	0,473 l
2 pints	=	1 quart (qt)	1,136 l	0,946 l
4 quarts	=	1 gallon (gal)	4,546 l	3,785 l
35 gallons (Öl)			159,106 l	

Weights

			British	American
1 ton	=	20 hundredweights (cwt)	1.016,05 kg	907,185 kg
1 hundredweight	=	112 pounds (lb)	50,8 kg	
		100 pounds		45,36 kg
28 pounds	=	1 quarter	1 kg = 2,2 lb	
14 pounds	=	1 stone		
1 pound	=	16 ounces (oz)	28,35 g = 1 oz	
1 ounce	=	16 drams (dr)		
1 dram	=	27 grains (gr)	0,0648 g	
1 grain				

Use with beverages:
1 l	= about 1 quart = 2 pints	a bottle of …
0,5 l	= 1 pint	a glass of …
¹/₈ l	= 1 gill	a cup of …
2 cl	= shot glass	
¹/₄	= half a pint	

American, British and Continental Sizes

Adults

Women's Dresses, Suits and Coats:

American	6	8	10	12	14	16
British	8	10	12	14	16	18
Continental	36/38	38/40	40/42	42/44	44/46	46/48

Women's Sweaters and Blouses:

American	6	8	10	12	14	16
British	8/30	10/32	12/34	14/36	16/38	18/40
Continental	36/38	38/40	40/42	42/44	44/46	46/48

Shoes:

American / British	3	4	4¹/₂	5	6	6¹/₂	7	8	9	10	11
Continental	35	36	37	38	39	40	41	42	43	44	45

Men's Suits and Overcoats:

American / British	36	38	40	42	44	46
Continental	46	48	50	52	54	56

Men's Shirts or Collar Sizes:

American / British	14	14	15	15	16	16	17
Continental	36	37	38	39	41	42	43

Colours

dark	–	dunkel	bright / light	–	hell	coloured	–	bunt
self-coloured	–	einfarbig	black	–	schwarz	white	–	weiß
beige	–	beige	blue	–	blau	blond/fair	–	blond
brown	–	braun	chestnut brown	–	kastanienbraun	gold	–	golden
silver	–	silbern	green	–	grün	yellow	–	gelb
orange	–	orange	pink	–	rosa	red	–	rot
lilac / violet / purple	–	fliederfarben / violett / lila						

Küchenfachausdrücke
Cooking Terms

Gastronomisches Fachvokabular
Gastronomic Vocabulary

Cooking Terms

Cooking utensils	Küchengeräte
baking dishes	Backgeschirr
fire-proof, oven-proof	feuerfest
heat-proof	hitzebeständig
bowl	Schüssel
casserole	Kasserolle
chopping block	Hackstock
cleaver	Hackbeil
colander	Sieb
conical strainer	Spitzsieb
cutting board	Schneidebrett
fork	Gabel
carving fork	Tranchiergabel
fish dish	Fischgeschirr
flanring	Obsttortenring
fryer	Friteuse
funnel	Trichter
grater	Reibeisen
kettle	Kochkessel
kitchen-range, stove	Herd
knife, knives	Messer
carving knife	Tranchiermesser
chopping knife	Hackmesser, Wiegemesser
cook's knife	großes Messer
meat knife	Fleischmesser
fruit knife	Obstmesser
vegetable knife	Gemüsemesser
ladle	Schöpfer
larding needle (pin)	Spicknadel
lid	Deckel
measuring jug	Messbecher
meat mincer	Fleischwolf
metal spatula	Metallspatel
microwave oven	Mikrowellenherd
mixer	Mixer
mixing bowl	Rührschüssel
oven	Backofen
oyster knife	Austernmesser
pan	Pfanne
frying pan	Bratpfanne
roasting pan	Bratenpfanne
sauté pan	Sautierpfanne
saucepan	Stielpfanne
plate	Platte, Teller
pot	Topf
refrigerator (fridge, freezer)	Kühlschrank
sieve	Sieb
skimmer	Siebschöpfer
spit	Bratspieß
skewer	Fleischspieß(chen)
spoon	Löffel
(wooden) spoon	Kochlöffel
stock pot	Suppen- / Fondtopf
strainer	Passiermaschine, Sieb, Filter
vegetable peeler	Gemüseschäler
weighing machine / scales	Waage
whisk	Schneebesen (Schaumschläger)

Activities in the kitchen	Tätigkeiten in der Küche
to add	dazugeben
to bake	backen
to baste	aufgießen (zB den Braten)
to beat	schlagen, klopfen
to beat egg whites	Eischnee schlagen
to bone	auslösen, entgräten
to braise	schmoren, im Ganzen dünsten
to bread	panieren
to brown	bräunen
to chop	hacken
to combine	zusammengeben, mischen
to cover	zudecken, bedecken, verschließen
to cream	schaumig rühren, legieren
to cut	schneiden
to deep-fry	frittieren
to dice, cube	in Würfel schneiden
to drain	abseihen, trocknen
to dress	anrichten
to fill	weich füllen (Torte)
to fold in	darunterziehen (zB Eischnee unter die Masse ziehen)
to fry	braten/backen
to garnish	garnieren
to grate	reiben (mit einem Reibeisen)
to gratinate	überbacken, gratinieren
to grease	einfetten
to heat	erhitzen
to lard	spicken
to marinate	marinieren
to mash	zerstampfen, pürieren
to melt	zerlassen
to mix, blend	mischen
to mince, grind	faschieren, klein hacken
to pan-fry	in der Pfanne braten
to peel	schälen
to place	legen, geben
to poach	pochieren, garziehen
to pour	(auf-, ein-)gießen
to powder, dust	bestäuben
to reduce	reduzieren
to remove	weggeben, entfernen
to roast	im Rohr braten
to rub	einreiben
to sauté	anschwenken
to scale	entschuppen
to sear	scharf anbraten
to season, flavour	würzen
to shred	schnetzeln, zerkleinern
to simmer	langsam kochen
to skim	abschäumen
to skin	häuten, schälen
to slice	in Scheiben (Streifen) schneiden
to smoke	räuchern, selchen
to soak	einweichen
to sprinkle	bestreuen
to steam	dämpfen
to stew	dünsten (in kleinen Stücken – Ragout)
to stir	umrühren
to strain	passieren, filtern
to stuff	fest füllen
to thicken	binden (zB mit Mehl oder Stärke)
to trim	zuputzen, parieren
to whip	aufschlagen
to wipe	abwischen

Gastronomic Vocabulary
German – English

Kalte Vorspeisen	Cold appetizers (Starters)
Aal, geräuchert	smoked eel
in Aspik	eel in jelly (aspic)
Artischocken, gefüllt	stuffed artichokes
Artischockenböden	artichoke bottoms
mit Schinken	with ham
Aufschnitt, kalte Platte	assorted cold meat (cuts)
Austern, roh	raw oysters
Beefsteak tatare	tartar steak, steak tartare
Braten, kalter	cold roast meat
Brot, belegt	open sandwich
Canapés, belegte Brötchen	canapés
Chefsalat	chef's salad
Clubsandwich	club sandwich
Cocktails	cocktails
Grapefruitcocktail	grapefruit cocktail
Garnelencocktail	shrimp (prawn) cocktail
Hummercocktail	lobster cocktail
Melonencocktail	melon cocktail
Tunfischcocktail	tunny (tuna fish) cocktail
Eier	eggs
gefüllt	stuffed eggs
in Aspik	poached egg in jelly
in Mayonnaise	eggs in mayonnaise
russische	stuffed egg, Russian style
Forelle, geräuchert	smoked trout
in Aspik	trout in jelly
Gänsebrust, geräuchert	smoked breast of goose
Gänseleber	goose liver
Gänseleberpastete	goose liver pâté
Geflügelsalat	chicken salad
Grapefruit, geeist	iced (chilled) grapefruit
gefüllt	stuffed grapefruit
Hering, geräuchert	smoked herring
mariniert	marinated herring
Heringssalat	herring salad
Huhn, gebraten	cold roast chicken
Hühnergalantine	chicken galantine
Hühnerpastete	chicken pâté
Hummer, gefüllt	stuffed lobster
Hummermayonnaise	lobster mayonnaise
Hummersalat	lobster salad
Käse	cheese
Käsesalat	cheese salad
Kaviar	caviar
Lachs, geräuchert	smoked salmon
mariniert	marinated salmon
Lachspastete	salmon pâté
Makrele, geräuchert	smoked mackerel
Melanzani, gefüllt	stuffed egg-plant (aubergine)
Melone, geeist	iced (chilled) melon
Melonensalat	melon salad
Meeresfrüchtesalat	seafood salad
Miesmuschelsalat	mussel salad
Ochsenmaulsalat	ox-muzzle salad
Ochsenzunge, geräuchert	smoked ox' tongue
Rindfleischsalat	beef salad
Roastbeef, kalt	cold roast beef
Rohkost(platte)	assorted raw vegetables (crudities)
Sardinen, in Öl	sardines in oil
Schinken, gekocht	boiled ham
geräuchert	smoked ham
roh	raw ham
Schinkenröllchen	ham rolls
Spargel(spitzen) in Sauce vinaigrette	asparagus (tips) in vinaigrette sauce
Speck	bacon
Tunfisch, garniert	tunny, garnished
Tunfischsalat	tunny salad
Waldorfsalat	celery salad with walnuts
Wildpastete	game pâté
Wildsalat	game salad
Wurst	sausage
Zungensalat	tongue salad

Suppen	Soups
klare Suppen	**clear soups**
Kraftbrühe, Consommé, Bouillon	broth, beef broth consommé, bouillon
Hühnerbrühe	chicken broth
doppelte Kraftsuppe	beef tea, warm or cold
klare Suppe mit …	clear soup (broth) with …
Backerbsen	fried batter drops
Brandteigkrapfen	profiteroles
Gemüse	vegetables
Gemüsestreifen	vegetable strips
Grießnockerl	semolina dumpling
Leberknödel	liver dumpling
Leberreis	shredded liver
Markklößchen	marrow dumpling
Milzschnitten	milt on toast
Nudeln	noodles
Pfannkuchenstreifen	sliced pancakes
Reis	rice
Schinkenknödel	ham dumpling
Schöberln, Biscuit	sponge squares
Suppennudeln	vermicelli
Tropfteig	batter (egg) drops
gebundene Suppen	**thick soups**
Püreesuppen	**purée soups**
Bohnensuppe	bean soup
Einbrennsuppe	brown soup
Gerstensuppe	barley soup
Haferflockensuppe	oatmeal soup
Hirnpüreesuppe	brain (purée) soup
Kalbspüreesuppe	veal (purée) soup
Linsenpüreesuppe	lentil (purée) soup
Wildpüreesuppe	game (purée) soup
Cremesuppen	**cream of … (soup), cream soups**
Blumenkohlcremesuppe	cream of cauliflower
Champignon-(Pilz-)Cremesuppe	cream of mushroom (soup)
Erbsencremesuppe	cream of pea
Geflügel-(Hühner-)Cremesuppe	cream of chicken
Gemüsecremesuppe	cream of vegetable

Appendix

German	English
Kartoffelcremesuppe	cream of potato
Lauchcremesuppe	cream of leek
Spargelcremesuppe	cream of asparagus
Tomatencremesuppe	cream of tomato
Wildcremesuppe	cream of venison

Spezialsuppen	**special soups**
Bouillabaisse	fish soup (French style)
Französische Zwiebelsuppe	French onion soup
Krebssuppe	bisque of crayfish
Minestrone	Italian vegetable soup
Ochsenschwanzsuppe,	
klare	clear oxtail soup
gebundene	oxtail soup
Schildkrötensuppe, falsche	mock turtle soup

Warme Vorspeisen	**Hot appetizers**
Aufläufe	soufflés
Geflügelauflauf	chicken soufflé
Käseauflauf	cheese soufflé
Schinkenauflauf	ham soufflé
Blätterteigpastetchen	patties filled with fine
mit feinen Ragouts	stews
(Kalbs-, Hühner-, Wild-,	(veal, chicken, game,
Schinken- ...)	ham ...)
Eier	eggs
pochiertes Ei mit	poached egg with
Sauce hollandaise	hollandaise sauce
Rührei mit Schinken	scrambled egg with ham
Spiegelei auf Spinat	fried egg on spinach
Omelette mit Champignons	mushroom omelette
Hühnerleber	chicken liver omelette
Spargel	asparagus omelette
Spinat	spinach omelette
Bauernomelette	country omelette
(Speck und Kartoffeln)	(bacon and potatoes)
Gemüse	vegetables
Blumenkohl, gebacken	deep-fried breaded cauliflower
Brokkoli mit Butterbröseln	broccoli with breadcrumbs and butter
Champignons, gebacken	deep-fried breaded mushrooms
Fenchel, überbacken	gratinated fennel
Spargel mit Sauce hollandaise	asparagus with hollandaise sauce
Kroketten	croquettes
Eierkroketten	egg croquettes
Fischkroketten	fish croquettes
Geflügelkroketten	chicken croquettes
Wildkroketten	game croquettes
Miesmuscheln, überbacken	gratinated mussels
Pizza	pizza
Puddings, warme	warm puddings
von Fleisch, Fisch,	from meats, fish,
Gemüsen, Hirn,	vegetables, brains,
Schinken usw.	ham etc.
Risotto	risotto
Schnecken mit Kräuterbutter	snails with herb butter
Teigwaren, italienische	Italian pasta
Törtchen	tartlets
Käse-, Morchel-, Specktörtchen	cheese, morel, bacon tartlets

Fische	**Fish**
Süßwasserfische	freshwater fish
Salzwasserfische	salt-water fish, sea fish
Aal	eel
Barsch	perch
Bückling	bloater
Dorsch	cod, codling, codfish
Forelle	trout
Bachforelle	brook trout
Regenbogenforelle	rainbow trout
Goldbarsch	dorado
Hecht	pike
Heilbutt	halibut
Hering	herring
Salzhering, getrocknet oder geräuchert	kipper (kippered herring), dried or smoked
Kabeljau	cod, codfish
Karpfen	carp
Lachs	salmon
Lachsforelle	salmon trout
Makrele	mackerel
Saibling	char
Sardelle	anchovy
Sardine	sardine
Schellfisch	haddock
Schnapper	snapper
Scholle	plaice
Seezunge	sole
Rotzunge	lemon sole
Steinbutt	turbot
Tunfisch	tunny, tuna fish
Tintenfisch	squid / octopus / cuttlefish
Wels	catfish
Zander, Schill	pike-perch

Schalen- und Krustentiere	**Shellfish and crustaceans**
Auster	oyster
Froschschenkel	frog's legs
Garnele, Krevette	shrimp, prawn
Hummer	lobster
Kammmuschel	scallop
Krabbe	crab
Krebs	crayfish
Languste	spiny lobster, crawfish
Miesmuschel	mussel
Schildkröte	turtle
Schnecke	snail
Venusmuschel	clam

Fleischgerichte	**Meat dishes**
Kalbfleisch	**veal**
Kalbsbeuschel / Lunge	calf's lights
Kalbsbraten	roast veal
Kalbsbries	calf's sweetbread
Kalbsbrust	breast of veal
Kalbsfilet, Kalbslende	fillet of veal
Kalbsgulasch	veal stew in paprika sauce
Kalbsherz	calf's heart
Kalbshirn	calf's brains
Kalbskarree	best end neck of veal (loin of veal)
Kalbskopf	calf's head

Gastronomic Vocabulary

German	English
Kalbskotelett	veal chop
Kalbsleber	calf's liver
Kalbsmedaillons	veal medallions
Kalbsnieren	calf's kidneys
Kalbsnierenbraten	roast loin of veal with kidneys
Kalbsnuss	topside of veal
Kalbsragout	veal stew, ragout of veal
Kalbsroulade	rolled stuffed veal cutlet
Kalbsrücken	saddle of veal
Kalbsschnitzel	escalope of veal, veal cutlet
Kalbsschulter	shoulder of veal
Kalbssteak	veal steak
Kalbsstelze	leg of veal
Kalbszunge	calf's tongue

Rindfleisch — **beef**

German	English
Beefsteak tatare	tartar steak
Beinfleisch	rib of beef
Beiried / flaches Roastbeef	sirloin
Chateaubriand, doppelte Lendenschnitte	double fillet steak, double tenderloin steak
Filet, Lungenbraten	fillet of beef, tenderloin
Filetsteak, Lendenschnitte	fillet steak, prime steak
klein	tournedos
Hochrippe	prime rib of beef
Ochsenschwanz	oxtail
Ochsenzunge	ox-tongue
Rinderbraten	roast beef
Rindfleisch, gepökelt	corned beef
Rindsgulasch	stewed beef in paprika sauce
Rindsherz	heart (beef)
Rindskarbonade	beef carbonade
Rindsragout	beef stew, ragout of beef
Rindsrose	aitchbone of beef
Rindsroulade	braised rolled stuffed fillet of beef
Rindsschmorbraten	braised beef
Rindsschnitzel	fillet of / slice of beef
Roastbeef	roast beef
Rumpsteak	rump steak
T-bone-Steak	T-bone steak
Porterhouse-Steak	porterhouse steak
Tafelspitz	round of beef
Zwischenrippenstück	sirloin steak
doppeltes Zwischenrippenstück	double sirloin steak

Schweinefleisch — **pork**

German	English
Pökelfleisch	salted (pickled) pork
Schinken	ham
gekocht, geräuchert, roh	boiled, smoked, raw
Schweinebraten	roast pork
Schweinekeule	leg of pork
Schweinsbrust	breast of pork
Schweinsfilet	fillet of pork
Schweinsgehacktes	ground / chopped / minced pork
Schweinshaxe	leg of pork
Schweinsherz	pig's heart
Schweinskarree	loin of pork
Schweinskotelett	pork chop
Schweinsleber	pig's liver
Schweinsnieren	pig's kidneys
Schweinsnierenbraten	loin of pork with kidneys
Schweinsragout	pork stew, ragout of pork, stewed pork
Schweinsrippe	rib of pork
Schweinsrücken	saddle of pork
Schweinsschnitzel	escalope of pork
Schweinszunge	pig's tongue
Spanferkel	sucking-(suckling-)pig
Speck	bacon
geräucherter Speck	smoked bacon

Hammel-, Lamm-, Schaffleisch — **mutton, lamb**

German	English
Hammel-(Lamm-)Braten	roast mutton (lamb)
Hammel-(Lamm-)Brust	mutton (lamb) breast
Hammel-(Lamm-)Karree	rack of mutton (lamb), loin of mutton (lamb)
Hammel-(Lamm-)Keule	leg of mutton (lamb)
Hammel-(Lamm-)Kotelett	mutton (lamb) chop
Hammel-(Lamm-)Ragout	mutton (lamb) stew
Hammel-(Lamm-)Rippenstück	mutton rib (chop)
Hammel-(Lamm-)Rücken	saddle of mutton (lamb)
Hammel-(Lamm-)Schulter	shoulder of mutton (lamb)
Lammeingemachtes	white lamb stew
Lammviertel	quarter of lamb

Geflügel — **poultry, fowl**

German	English
Ente	duck
Gans	goose
Gänseleber	goose liver
Geflügelauflauf	chicken soufflé
Geflügelklein	giblets of chicken
Geflügelkroketten	chicken croquettes
Geflügelleber	poultry liver
Geflügelragout	chicken stew
Geflügelsalat	chicken salad
Huhn, Junghuhn	chicken, spring chicken
Hühnerbrust	breast of chicken
Hühnercurry	chicken curry
Hühnerflügel	chicken wings
Hühnerkeule	leg of chicken
Hühnerleber	chicken liver
Kapaun	capon
Masthuhn	pullet, fattened chicken
Perlhuhn	guinea fowl
Suppenhuhn	boiling fowl
Taube	pigeon
Truthahn	turkey
Truthahnbrust	breast of turkey
Truthahnschnitzel	turkey fillets

Wild — **game, venison**

German	English
Frischling	young wild boar
Gämse	chamois
Hase	hare
Hasenkeule	leg of hare
Hasenrücken	saddle of hare
Hirsch	deer, venison
Hirschkeule, Hirschschlegel	leg of deer
Hirschkotelett	deer chop
Hirschragout	deer stew, ragout of deer
Hirschrücken	saddle of deer
Hirschschnitzel	escalope of deer, fillet of deer
Hirschschulter	shoulder of deer
Hirschsteak	deer steak
Kaninchen	rabbit

Appendix

Rehfleisch, Hirschfleisch Rotwildfleisch	venison
Reh	roe / roe buck (male)
Wildschwein	wild boar
Wildschweinschinken	ham of wild boar

Wildgeflügel, Federwild — game birds, wildfowl

German	English
Fasan	pheasant
Rebhuhn	partridge
Schnepfe	snipe
Wachtel	quail
Waldschnepfe	woodcock
Wildente	wild duck
Wildgans	wild goose
Wildhuhn	grouse

Fonds — Stocks

weiße Fonds — white stocks

German	English
Fischfond	fish stock
Geflügelfond	chicken stock
Gemüsefond	vegetable stock
Kalbsfond	veal stock

braune Fonds — brown stocks

German	English
Bratensaft, Fleischfond	gravy
Kalbsfond	veal stock
Wildfond	game stock

Saucen — Sauces

German	English
Bordelaiser Sauce	bordelaise sauce
Braune Saucen	brown sauces
Estragonsauce	tarragon sauce
Italienische Sauce	Italian sauce
Jägersauce (Sauce chasseur)	hunter sauce
Madeirasauce	Madeira sauce
Pfeffersauce	pepper sauce
Provenzalische Sauce	provençale sauce
Rahmsauce	cream sauce
Sauce demi-glace	basic brown sauce, demi-glace sauce
Senfsauce (Sauce Robert)	mustard sauce
Teufelssauce	devil sauce
Tomatensauce	tomato sauce
Trüffelsauce (Sauce Perigueux)	truffle sauce
Zigeunersauce	gipsy sauce, zingara sauce

warme Buttersaucen — warm butter sauces

German	English
Béarner Sauce	béarnaise sauce
Choronsauce	Choron sauce
Foyotsauce	Foyot sauce
Holländische Sauce	hollandaise sauce, Dutch sauce
Malteser Sauce	maltese sauce
Schaumsauce	mousseline sauce

kalte Saucen — cold sauces

German	English
Mayonnaisesauce	mayonnaise (sauce)
Grüne Sauce (Sauce verte)	green sauce
Kräutersauce (Sauce ravigote)	ravigote sauce (herb sauce)
Remouladensauce	remoulade sauce
Tatarensauce	tartar sauce
Tiroler Sauce (Sauce tyrolienne)	Tyrolean sauce
Vinaigrettesauce (Essigkräutersauce)	vinaigrette sauce
Norweger Sauce Fischersauce (à la pêcheur)	Norwegian sauce fisher sauce

warme Spezialsaucen — special warm sauces

German	English
Apfelsauce	apple sauce
Brotsauce	bread sauce
Sauerrahmsauce	sour cream sauce
Senfsauce	mustard sauce
Zwiebelsauce (Sauce soubise)	onion sauce, soubise sauce

kalte Spezialsaucen — special cold sauces

German	English
Cumberlandsauce	Cumberland sauce
Meerrettichsauce	horseradish sauce
Minzsauce	mint sauce
Preiselbeersauce	cranberry sauce
Sahnemeerrettich	creamed horseradish

weiße Saucen — white sauces

German	English
Velouté (weiße Grundsauce)	velouté (basic white sauce)
Béchamelsauce (weiße Grundsauce)	Béchamel sauce, milk sauce (basic white sauce)
Aurorasauce	Aurore sauce
Mornaysauce	Mornay sauce, cheese sauce
Rahmsauce	cream sauce
Deutsche Sauce (Sauce allemande)	German sauce (with veal stock)
Champignonsauce	mushroom sauce
Currysauce	curry sauce
Estragonsauce	tarragon sauce
Kapernsauce	caper sauce
Schnittlauchsauce	chive sauce
Sauce suprême (Geflügeleinmachsauce)	suprême sauce (with chicken stock)
Champignonsauce	mushroom sauce
Estragonsauce	tarragon sauce
Weißweinsauce (Fischeinmachsauce)	white wine sauce (with fish stock)
Austernsauce	oyster sauce
Garnelensauce	prawn sauce
Hummersauce	lobster sauce
Kapernsauce	caper sauce
Kräutersauce	herb sauce
Sardellensauce	anchovy sauce

Butter und Buttermischungen — Butter and savoury butters

German	English
braune Butter	brown (black) butter
geklärte Butter	clarified butter
zerlassene Butter	melted butter

Buttermischungen — savoury butters

German	English
Erdnussbutter	peanut butter
Estragonbutter	tarragon butter
Hummerbutter	lobster butter
Knoblauchbutter	garlic butter
Kräuterbutter	herb butter
Krebsbutter	crayfish (crab) butter

Krenbutter	horseradish butter
Nuss-(Mandel-)Butter	nut (almond) butter
Sardellenbutter	anchovy butter
Schneckenbutter	snail butter
Schweineschmalz	lard
Senfbutter	mustard butter
Zitronenbutter	lemon butter

Gemüse	**Vegetables**
Artischocke	artichoke
Artischockenböden	artichoke bottoms
Artischockenherzen	artichoke hearts
Blau-(Rot-)Kraut	red cabbage
Blumenkohl	cauliflower
Bohnen	beans
grüne	green, French, string beans
rote	red beans
weiße	white beans
Brokkoli, Spargelkohl	broccoli
Brüsseler Spitzen, Chicorée	chicory
Eierfrucht, Aubergine	egg-plant, aubergine
Endivie	endive
Erbsen (frische, getrocknete, grüne)	peas (fresh, dried, green)
Essiggurken	gherkins (Br.), pickles (Am.)
Fenchel	fennel
Frühgemüse	spring vegetables
Gurke	cucumber
Kopfsalat	lettuce
Karotten, gelbe Rüben	carrots
Kartoffeln (Erdäpfel)	potatoes
Knoblauch	garlic
Kohl, Wirsing	savoy cabbage
Kohlrabi	kohlrabi
Kraut, Weißkraut	white cabbage
Rotkraut	red cabbage
Kren, Meerrettich	horseradish
Kürbis	pumpkin
Lauch, Porree	leek
Linsen	lentils
Mais	corn, sweet corn
Maiskolben	corn on cob
Morchel	morel
Olive	olive
Paprikaschote (grüne, rote)	pepper (green, red)
Pastinak	parsnip
Pfifferling, Eierschwammerl	chanterelles
Radieschen	red radish
Rettich (weiß, schwarz)	radish (white, black)
Rosenkohl	Brussels sprouts
Rote Rübe	beetroot (Br.), red beet (Am.)
Sauerkraut	sauerkraut
Schalotte	shallot
Schwarzwurzel	salsify
Sellerie, Stangensellerie	celery, stalk celery
Sellerieknolle	celeriac
Spargel	asparagus
Spargelspitzen	asparagus tips
Spinat	spinach
Steinpilz	yellow boletus
Tomate	tomato
Trüffel	truffle
Zucchini, Zwergkürbisse	baby marrows, zucchini, courgettes
Zwiebel	onion

Kartoffel-(Erdäpfel-) Gerichte	**Potato dishes**
Auflaufkartoffeln	soufflé potatoes
Bouillonkartoffeln	bouillon potatoes
Bratkartoffeln	pan-fried potatoes
Dampfkartoffeln	steamed potatoes
Duchesse-(Herzogin-) Kartoffeln	duchess potatoes
Folienkartoffeln	baked potatoes
Gefüllte Kartoffeln	stuffed potatoes
Kartoffelbällchen	potato balls
Kartoffelfladen	galettes
Kartoffelknödel	potato dumpling
Kartoffelkroketten	potato croquettes
Kartoffelnudeln	potato noodles
Kartoffelpuffer	potato fritters
Kartoffelpüree	mashed potatoes
Kartoffelscheiben, gebacken	crisps chips
Neue Kartoffeln	new potatoes
Pariser Kartoffeln	parisienne potatoes
Petersilienkartoffeln	parsley potatoes
Pommes frites, Kartoffelstäbchen	chips (Br.), French fried potatoes (Am.)
Rahmkartoffeln	creamed potatoes
Röstkartoffeln	hashed brown potatoes
Salzkartoffeln	boiled potatoes, plain potatoes
Schlosskartoffeln	château potatoes, castle potatoes
Schnittlauchkartoffeln	chive potatoes
Strohkartoffeln	straw potatoes
Waffelkartoffeln, Gitterkartoffeln	wafer potatoes
Würfelkartoffeln	diced potatoes
Zündholzkartoffeln	matchstick chips, matchstick potatoes

Getreide und Teigwaren	**Cereals and pasta**
Blini, Buchweizen-pfannkuchen	blini, buckwheat pancake
Brösel	crumbs
Brot (schwarzes, weißes, Roggenbrot)	bread (brown, white, rye bread)
Brötchen, Semmel	roll
Cornflakes	cornflakes
Gerste	barley
Grieß	semolina
Hafer	oat
Haferbrei	oatmeal, porridge
Haferflocken	oat flakes, rolled oats
Kipferl	crescent (croissant)
Knusperreis, Müslireis	puffed rice, rice crispies
Mehl	flour
Nudeln	noodles
Bandnudeln	ribbon noodles
Hörnchen	elbow macaroni
Lasagne	lasagne
Makkaroni	macaroni
Ravioli	ravioli
Spagetti	spaghetti
Polenta, Sterz	polenta
Pumpernickel	pumpernickel
Roggen	rye
Weizen	wheat

Appendix

Knödel	Dumplings
Grießknödel	semolina dumpling
Käseknödel	cheese dumpling
Kartoffelknödel	potato dumpling
Leberknödel	liver dumpling
Markknödel	marrow dumpling
Semmelknödel	white bread dumpling
Schinkenknödel	ham dumpling
Speckknödel	bacon dumpling

Reis	Rice
Curryreis	curry rice
Langkornreis	long grain rice
Perlreis	short grain rice
Reis, braun	brown rice
Reis, gedünstet	steamed rice
Reis, gekocht	boiled rice
Reis, weiß	white rice
Reis, wild	wild rice
Risipisi	rice with peas
Risotto	risotto (Italian rice dish)
Safranreis	saffron rice

Würzmittel (Gewürze) und Kräuter	Seasonings (spices) and herbs
Anis	aniseed
Cayenne(-pfeffer)	cayenne (pepper)
Chili, Chilli	chili, chilli
Curry(-pulver)	curry (powder)
Essig	vinegar
Fenchel	fennel seed
Ingwer	ginger
Kapern	capers
Knoblauch(-zehe)	garlic (clove)
Kümmel	caraway seed, cumin
Kürbiskernöl	pumpkin seed oil
Majoran	marjoram
Mohn	poppy seed
Muskatnuss	nutmeg
Nelke, Gewürznelke	clove
Neugewürz, Piment	allspice, pimento
Öl	oil
Oregano	oregano
Paprika, rot	paprika
Pfeffer(-körner), schwarz, weiß, rot, grün	pepper(corns), black, white, red, green
Pfeffer, ganz, geschrotet, gemahlen	pepper, whole, crushed, ground
Salz	salt
Senf(-körner)	mustard (grains)
Senfpulver	dry mustard
Vanille	vanilla
Wacholder(-beeren)	juniper (berries)
Zimt	cinnamon
Zucker	sugar
Karamellzucker	caramel sugar
Kristallzucker	castor sugar
Rohzucker	brown sugar
Staubzucker	powder sugar
Würfelzucker	lump sugar
Zuckersirup	molasses

Kräuter	herbs
Bärlauch	wild garlic
Basilikum	basil
Bohnenkraut	savoury
Brunnenkresse	watercress
Dillkraut	dill
Estragon	tarragon
Gewürzfruchtpaste	chutney
Kerbelkraut	chervil
Kresse	cress
Lorbeer(-blatt)	bay (leaf)
Majoran	marjoram
Minze, Pfefferminze	mint, peppermint
Petersilie, Petersilwurzel	parsley, parsleyroot
Rosmarin	rosemary
Salbei	sage
Schnittlauch	chives
Thymian	thyme

Früchte, Obst	Fruits
Ananas	pineapple
Apfel	apple
Aprikose	apricot
Banane	banana
Birne	pear
Beeren	berries
Brombeeren, Schwarzbeeren	blackberries, brambleberries
Heidelbeeren	blueberries
Himbeeren	raspberries
Erdbeeren, Walderdbeeren	strawberries, wild strawberries
Johannisbeeren (rot, schwarz)	currants (red, black)
Preiselbeeren	cranberries
Stachelbeeren	gooseberries
Datteln	dates
Feigen	figs
Früchte der Saison	seasonal fruits
Grapefruit, Pampelmuse	grapefruit
Kastanie	chestnut
Kirsche(n)	cherry (cherries)
Kiwi	kiwi
Konfitüre	jam
Limone	lime
Mandarine	mandarin, tangerine
Melone	melon
Honigmelone	honey dew melon
Wassermelone	water melon
Zuckermelone	cantaloup melon
Nüsse	nuts
Cashewnüsse	cashew nuts
Erdnüsse	peanuts
Haselnüsse	hazelnuts
Kokosnüsse	coconuts
Mandeln	almonds
Pekannüsse	pecan nuts
Walnüsse	walnuts
Orange	orange
Orangenmarmelade	orange marmalade
Pfirsich	peach
Pflaume, Zwetschke	plum
Dörrpflaume	prune
Reneklode	greengage
Rhabarber	rhubarb

Gastronomic Vocabulary

German	English
Rosinen	raisins
Sultaninen	sultanas
Trauben (blau, weiß)	grapes (blue, white)
Weichseln, Sauerkirschen	morellos (morello cherries)
Zitrone	lemon

Desserts und Süßspeisen — Desserts and sweets

warm — **warm**

German	English
Aufläufe	soufflés
Aprikosenauflauf	apricot soufflé
Reisauflauf	rice soufflé
Schokoladenauflauf	chocolate soufflé
Früchte in Backteig	fruits in batter (fritters)
Apfelspalten	apple fritters
mit Ananas	pineapple fritters
mit Bananen	banana fritters
Knödel	dumplings
Germknödel	yeast dumplings
Obstknödel	fruit dumplings
Quarkknödel	white cheese dumplings
Krapfen	Austrian doughnuts
Pfannkuchen, Palatschinken	pancakes
Puddings, warm	warm puddings
Grießpudding	warm semolina pudding
Nuss-(Mandel-)Pudding	nut (almond) pudding
Mohr im Hemd	steamed chocolate pudding
Waffeln	wafers, waffles
Weinschaum (Chaudeau)	sabayon

kalt — **cold**

German	English
Cremen	creams
Bayerische Creme	Bavarian cream
Eiscremen	ice creams
Erdbeereis	strawberry ice cream
Haselnusseis	hazelnut ice cream
Vanilleeis	vanilla ice cream
Eisomelette (Omelette surprise)	ice omelette, baked Alaska
Früchte, Obst	fruits
Früchte, frisch	fresh fruit
Früchtecocktails	fruit cocktails
Früchtekompott	stewed fruit, compote
Früchtesalate	fruit salads
Gebäck, Backwerk	pastry
Blätterteig	puff pastry
Brandteig	choux pastry
Hefeteig	yeast pastry
Mürbteig	short crust pastry
Dessertgebäck	dessert pastry
Schaumgebäck	meringue
Gelees	jellies
Früchtegelees	fruit jellies
Weingelee	wine jelly
Golatschen	sweetrolls
Halbgefrorenes, Parfait	parfait
Kekse	biscuits (Br.), cookies (Am.)
Kipferl	crescent, croissant
Kuchen, Torten	cakes
belegte Kuchen (Torten)	tarts
Biskuitroulade	rolled sponge cake, Swiss roll
Biskuittorten	sponge cakes
Hefekuchen	yeast cakes
Mürbteigkuchen	short cakes
Obsttorte	flan
Rührteigkuchen	creamed cakes
Mousse	mousse
Muffin, kleiner, runder Kuchen	muffin
Pasteten, Obstpasteten	pies, fruit pies
Petits fours	petits fours
Puddings, kalt	cold puddings
Grießpudding	cold semolina pudding
Reispudding	cold rice pudding
Schnitten	slices
Sorbet	sherbet
Strudel	strudel
Apfelstrudel	apple strudel
Quarkstrudel	curd cheese strudel
Rahmstrudel	cream strudel
Törtchen	tartlets
Vanillesauce	custard

Österreichische Spezialitäten — Austrian specialities

German	English
Bauernschmaus	roast pork, smoked pork and sausage with sauerkraut and bread dumpling
Beinfleisch	boiled ribs of beef
Blutwurst	black pudding
Bratwurst mit Sauerkraut	fried pork sausage with sauerkraut
Geselchtes	smoked pork
Gulasch (Rinds-, Kalbsgulasch)	goulash (stewed beef or veal in paprika sauce)
Faschierter Braten	meat loaf
Kalbsbeuschel	stewed calf's lights
Kalbsbrust, gefüllt	roast stuffed breast of veal
Kalbsnierenbraten, gerollt	roast rolled loin of veal with kidneys
Kalbsschnitzel, Wiener Art	Wiener Schnitzel (deep-fried breaded escalope of veal)
Kalbsstelze, gebraten	roast leg of veal
Paprika, gefüllt	braised stuffed green peppers
Presskopf	brawn, headcheese
Rinderschmor(saft)braten	braised beef
Rindsroulade	braised rolled stuffed fillet of beef
Schopfbraten	roast best end neck of pork
Steirisches Masthuhn	Styrian fattened pullet (chicken)
Steirisches Wurzelfleisch	boiled shoulder of pork with carrots, leeks, celeriac and horseradish
Tafelspitz	boiled round of beef
Tiroler Gröstl	fried potatoes with pork and beef
Zwiebelrostbraten	braised fillet of beef with onions

Appendix

Getränke	Beverages
alkoholfreie Getränke	**non-alcoholic drinks**
Fruchtsäfte	fruit juices
Apfelsaft	apple juice
Himbeersaft	raspberry juice
Johannisbeersaft	currant juice
Orangensaft	orange juice
Orangensaft, frisch gepresst	orange squash
Gemüsesäfte	vegetable juices
Karottensaft	carrot juice
Tomatensaft	tomato juice
Limonade, Orangenlimonade	lemonade, orangeade
Mineralwasser	mineral water
Nektar	nectar
Sirup	syrup
Sodawasser	soda water, sparkling water
Tonic	tonic water
warme Getränke	**warm beverages**
Kaffee	coffee
Espresso	espresso coffee
Filterkaffee	filtered coffee
Kaffee mit Milch	coffee with milk
Kaffee mit Sahne	coffee with cream
Kaffee, schwarz	coffee black
Kakao	cocoa
Milch	milk
Magermilch	skim milk
Schokolade, heiß	hot chocolate
Tee	tea
Kamillentee	camomile tea
Pfefferminztee	mint tea
Tee mit Milch	tea with milk
Tee mit Rum	tea with rum
Tee mit Zitrone	tea with lemon
Tee Natur	tea plain
alkoholische Getränke (geistige)	**alcoholic drinks (liquors)**
Aperitif	apéritif, before-dinner-drink
Bier	beer
dunkel	dark beer
hell	light (pale) beer
in Dosen	tinned beer
in Flaschen	bottled beer
offen, vom Fass	draught beer
Lagerbier	lager (beer)
Branntwein, Schnaps	brandy
Cocktail	cocktail
Likör	liqueur
Rum	rum
Spirituosen	spirits
Wein	wine
Bordeauxwein, rot	red Bordeaux, claret
Bordeauxwein, weiß	white Bordeaux
Burgunder (rot, weiß)	(red, white) Burgundy
Champagner	champagne
Cognac	cognac
Flaschenwein	bottled wine
Glühwein	mulled wine
herb, trocken	dry
Heuriger	young, new wine
leicht	light
mild	mild, mellow
offen	per glass, in carafe, from the cask
Rheinwein	Rhine wine, hock
Roséwein	rosé wine
Rotwein	red wine
Schaumwein, Sekt	sparkling wine
Südwein	dessert wine, fortified wine
Madeira	Madeira
Marsala	Marsala
Portwein	port(wine)
Sherry	sherry
süß, halbsüß	sweet, semi-sweet
Vermouth	vermouth
vollmundig, schwer, üppig	heavy, full (rich) bodied
Weißwein	white wine
Whisky, Whiskey	whisky, whiskey

Gastronomic Vocabulary
English – German

Cold appetizers (Starters)	**Kalte Vorspeisen**
artichoke bottoms with ham	Artischockenböden mit Schinken
asparagus (tips) in vinaigrette sauce	Spargel(spitzen) in Sauce vinaigrette
assorted cold meat (cuts)	Aufschnitt, kalte Platte
assorted raw vegetables (crudities)	Rohkost(platte)
beef salad	Rindfleischsalat
boiled ham	Schinken, gekocht
canapés	Canapés, belegte Brötchen
caviar	Kaviar
celery salad with walnuts	Waldorfsalat
cheese	Käse
cheese salad	Käsesalat
chef's salad	Chefsalat
chicken galantine	Hühnergalantine
chicken pâté	Hühnerpastete
chicken salad	Geflügelsalat
club sandwich	Clubsandwich
cocktails	Cocktails
cold roast beef	Roastbeef, kalt
cold roast chicken	Huhn, gebraten
cold roast meat	Braten, kalter
eel in jelly (aspic)	Aal in Aspik
eggs	Eier
eggs in mayonnaise	Eier in Mayonnaise
poached eggs in jelly	Eier in Aspik
stuffed eggs, Russian style	Eier, russische
stuffed eggs	Eier, gefüllt
game pâté	Wildpastete
game salad	Wildsalat
goose liver	Gänseleber
goose liver pâté	Gänseleberpastete
grapefruit cocktail	Grapefruitcocktail
ham rolls	Schinkenröllchen
herring salad	Heringssalat
iced (chilled) grapefruit	Grapefruit, geeist
iced (chilled) melon	Melone, geeist
lobster cocktail	Hummercocktail
lobster mayonnaise	Hummermayonnaise
lobster salad	Hummersalat
marinated herring	Hering, mariniert
marinated salmon	Lachs, mariniert
melon cocktail	Melonencocktail
melon salad	Melonensalat
mussel salad	Miesmuschelsalat
open sandwich	Brot, belegt
ox-muzzle salad	Ochsenmaulsalat
raw ham	Schinken, roh
raw oysters	Austern, roh
salmon pâté	Lachspastete
sardines in oil	Sardinen in Öl
sausage	Wurst
seafood salad	Meeresfrüchtesalat
shrimp (prawn) cocktail	Garnelencocktail
smoked bacon	Speck, geräuchert
smoked breast of goose	Gänsebrust, geräuchert
smoked eel	Aal, geräuchert
smoked ham	Schinken, geräuchert
smoked herring	Hering, geräuchert
smoked mackerel	Makrele, geräuchert
smoked ox-tongue	Ochsenzunge, geräuchert
smoked salmon	Lachs, geräuchert
smoked trout	Forelle, geräuchert
stuffed artichokes	Artischocken, gefüllt
stuffed egg-plant (aubergine)	Auberginen, gefüllt
stuffed grapefruit	Grapefruit, gefüllt
stuffed lobster	Hummer, gefüllt
tartar steak, steak tartare	Beefsteak tatare
tongue salad	Zungensalat
trout in jelly	Forelle in Aspik
tunny (tuna fish) cocktail	Tunfischcocktail
tunny salad	Tunfischsalat
tunny, garnished	Tunfisch, garniert

Soups	**Suppen**
clear soups	**klare Suppen**
batter (egg) drops	Tropfteig
beef tea, warm or cold broth, beef broth	doppelte Kraftsuppe, Kraftbrühe,
chicken broth	Hühnerbrühe
clear soup (broth) with …	klare Suppe mit …
fried batter drops	Backerbsen
ham dumpling	Schinkenknödel
liver dumpling	Leberknödel
marrow dumpling	Markknödel
milt on toast	Milzschnitten
noodles	Nudeln
profiteroles	Brandteigkrapferln
rice	Reis
semolina dumpling	Grießnockerl
shredded liver	Leberreis
sliced pancakes	Frittaten
sponge squares	Schöberln
vegetables	Gemüse
vegetable strips	Gemüsestreifen
vermicelli	Suppennudeln
consommé, bouillon	Consommé, Bouillon
thick soups	**gebundene Suppen**
purée soups	Püreesuppen
barley soup	Gerstensuppe
bean soup	Bohnensuppe
brain (purée) soup	Hirnpüreesuppe
brown soup	Einbrennsuppe
game (purée) soup	Wildpüreesuppe
lentil (purée) soup	Linsenpüreesuppe
oatmeal soup	Haferflockensuppe
veal (purée) soup	Kalbspüreesuppe
cream of … (soup), cream soups	**Cremesuppen**
cream of asparagus	Spargelcremesuppe
cream of cauliflower	Blumenkohlcremesuppe
cream of chicken	Geflügel-(Hühner-) Cremesuppe
cream of leek	Lauchcremesuppe
cream of mushroom (soup)	Champignon-(Pilz-)Cremesuppe

Appendix

English	German
cream of pea	Erbsencremesuppe
cream of potato	Kartoffelcremesuppe
cream of tomato	Tomatencremesuppe
cream of vegetable	Gemüsecremesuppe
cream of venison	Wildcremesuppe

special soups	**Spezialsuppen**
bisque of crayfish	Krebssuppe
clear oxtail soup	Ochsenschwanzsuppe, klare
oxtail soup	gebundene
fish soup (French style)	Bouillabaisse
French onion soup	französische Zwiebelsuppe
Italian vegetable soup	Minestrone
mock turtle soup	Schildkrötensuppe, falsche

Hot appetizers	**Warme Vorspeisen**
croquettes	Kroketten
chicken croquettes	Geflügelkroketten
egg croquettes	Eierkroketten
fish croquettes	Fischkroketten
game croquettes	Wildkroketten
eggs	Eier
fried egg on hollandaise sauce	Spiegelei auf Sauce hollandaise
poached egg with	pochiertes Ei mit
scrambled egg	Rührei
spinach	Spinat
with ham	mit Schinken
gratinated mussels	Miesmuscheln, überbacken
Italian pasta	Teigwaren, italienische
omelette	Omelette
mushroom omelette	Omelette mit Champignons
asparagus omelette	Spargelomelette
chicken liver omelette	Omelette mit Hühnerleber
country omelette (bacon and potatoes)	Bauernomelette (Speck und Kartoffeln)
spinach omelette	Spinatomelette
patties filled with fine stews (veal, chicken, game, ham ...)	Blätterteigpastetchen mit feinen Ragouts (Kalbs-, Hühner-, Wild-, Schinken- ...)
pizza	Pizza
risotto	Risotto
snails with herb butter	Schnecken mit Kräuterbutter
soufflés	Aufläufe
chicken soufflé	Geflügelauflauf
cheese soufflé	Käseauflauf
ham soufflé	Schinkenauflauf
tartlets	Törtchen
cheese, morel, bacon tartlets	Käse-, Morchel-, Specktörtchen
vegetables	Gemüse
asparagus with hollandaise sauce	Spargel mit Sauce hollandaise
broccoli with breadcrumbs and butter	Brokkoli mit Butterbröseln
deep-fried breaded cauliflower	Blumenkohl, gebacken
deep-fried breaded mushrooms	Champignons, gebacken
gratinated fennel	Fenchel, überbacken
warm puddings from meat, fish, vegetables, brain, ham etc.	Puddings, warme von Fleisch, Fisch, Gemüsen, Hirn, Schinken usw.

Fish	**Fische**
anchovy	Sardelle
bloater	Bückling
carp	Karpfen
catfish	Wels
char	Saibling
codling	Dorsch
cod, codfish	Kabeljau
dorado	Goldbarsch
eel	Aal
freshwater fish	Süßwasserfisch
haddock	Schellfisch
halibut	Heilbutt
herring	Hering
kipper (kippered herring), dried or smoked	Salzhering, getrocknet oder geräuchert
mackerel	Makrele
perch	Barsch
pike	Hecht
pike-perch	Zander, Schill
plaice	Scholle
salmon	Lachs
salmon trout	Lachsforelle
salt-water fish, sea fish	Salzwasserfische
sardine	Sardine
snapper	Schnapper
sole	Seezunge
lemon sole	Rotzunge
squid / octopus / cuttlefish	Tintenfisch
trout	Forelle
brook trout	Bachforelle
rainbow trout	Regenbogenforelle
tunny, tuna fish	Tunfisch
turbot	Steinbutt

Shellfish and crustaceans	**Schalen- und Krustentiere**
clam	Venusmuschel
crab	Krabbe
crayfish	Krebs
frog's legs	Froschschenkel
lobster	Hummer
mussel	Miesmuschel
oyster	Auster
scallop	Kammmuschel
shrimp, prawn	Garnele, Krevette
snail	Schnecke
spiny lobster, crawfish	Languste
turtle	Schildkröte

Meat dishes	**Fleischgerichte**
veal	**Kalbfleisch**
best end neck of veal (loin of veal)	Kalbskarree
breast of veal	Kalbsbrust
calf's brain	Kalbshirn

Gastronomic Vocabulary

English	German
calf's head	Kalbskopf
calf's heart	Kalbsherz
calf's kidneys	Kalbsnieren
calf's lights	Kalbsbeuschel / Lunge
calf's liver	Kalbsleber
calf's sweetbread	Kalbsbries
calf's tongue	Kalbszunge
escalope of veal, veal cutlet	Kalbsschnitzel
fillet of veal	Kalbsfilet, Kalbslende
leg of veal	Kalbsstelze
roast loin of veal with kidneys	Kalbsnierenbraten
roast veal	Kalbsbraten
rolled stuffed veal	Kalbsroulade
saddle of veal	Kalbsrücken
shoulder of veal	Kalbsschulter
topside of veal	Kalbsnuss
veal chop	Kalbskotelett
veal medallions	Kalbsmedaillons
veal steak	Kalbssteak
veal stew in paprika sauce	Kalbsgulasch
veal stew, ragout of veal	Kalbsragout
beef	**Rindfleisch**
aitchbone of beef	Rindsrose
beef carbonade	Rindskarbonade
beef stew, ragout of beef	Rindsragout
braised beef	Rindsschmorbraten
corned beef	Rindfleisch, gepökelt
double fillet steak, double tenderloin steak	Chateaubriand, doppelte Lendenschnitte
fillet of beef, slice of beef	Rindsschnitzel
fillet of beef, tenderloin	Filet, Lungenbraten
fillet steak, prime steak tournedos	Filetsteak, Lendenschnitte klein
heart	Rindsherz
ox-tongue	Ochsenzunge, Rindszunge
oxtail	Ochsenschwanz
prime rib of beef	Hochrippe
rib of beef	Beinfleisch / Rippenfleisch
roast beef	Rinderbraten, Roastbeef
rolled stuffed fillet of beef	Rindsroulade
round of beef	Tafelspitz
rump steak	Rumpsteak
sirloin	Beiried / flaches Roastbeef
sirloin steak, double sirloin steak	Zwischenrippenstück doppeltes Zwischenrippenstück
stewed beef in paprika sauce	Rindsgulasch
tatar steak	Beefsteak tartare
T-bone steak porterhouse steak	T-bone-Steak Porterhouse-Steak
pork	**Schweinefleisch**
bacon	Speck
smoked bacon	geräucherter Speck
breast of pork	Schweinsbrust
chopped (minced) pork	Schweinsfaschiertes
escalope of pork	Schweinsschnitzel
fillet of pork	Schweinsfilet
ham	Schinken
boiled, smoked, raw	gekocht, geräuchert, roh
leg of pork	Schweinshaxe, (-stelze), (-schlögel)
loin of pork	Schweinskarree
loin of pork with kidneys	Schweinsnierenbraten
pig's heart	Schweinsherz
pig's kidneys	Schweinsnieren
pig's liver	Schweinsleber
pig's tongue	Schweinszunge
pork chop	Schweinskotelett
pork stew, ragout of pork, stewed pork	Schweinsragout
rib of pork	Schweinsrippe
roast pork	Schweinsbraten
saddle of pork	Schweinsrücken
salted (pickled) pork	Pökelfleisch
sucking- (suckling-)pig	Spanferkel
mutton, lamb	**Hammel-, Lamm-, Schaffleisch**
leg of mutton (lamb)	Hammel-(Lamm-)keule
mutton (lamb) breast	Hammel-(Lamm-)brust
mutton (lamb) chop	Hammel-(Lamm-)kotelett
mutton (lamb) rib	Hammel-(Lamm-)rippenstück
mutton (lamb) stew	Hammel-(Lamm-)ragout
quarter of lamb	Lammviertel
rack of mutton (lamb), loin of mutton (lamb)	Hammel-(Lamm-)karree
roast mutton (lamb)	Hammel-(Lamm-)braten
saddle of mutton (lamb)	Hammel-(Lamm-)rücken
shoulder of mutton (lamb)	Hammel-(Lamm-)schulter
white lamb stew	Lammeingemachtes
poultry, fowl	**Geflügel**
boiling fowl	Suppenhuhn
breast of chicken	Hühnerbrust
breast of turkey	Truthahnbrust
capon	Kapaun
chicken croquettes	Geflügelkroketten
chicken curry	Hühnercurry
chicken liver	Hühnerleber
chicken salad	Geflügelsalat
chicken soufflé	Geflügelauflauf
chicken, spring chicken	Huhn, Junghuhn
chicken stew	Geflügelragout
chicken wings	Hühnerflügel
duck	Ente
giblets of chicken	Geflügelklein
goose	Gans
goose liver	Gänseleber
guinea fowl	Perlhuhn
leg of chicken	Hühnerkeule
pigeon	Taube
poultry liver	Geflügelleber
pullet, fattened chicken	Masthuhn
turkey	Truthahn
turkey fillets	Truthahnschnitzel
game, venison	**Wild**
chamois	Gämse
deer	Hirsch
deer chop	Hirschkotelett
deer steak	Hirschsteak
deer stew, ragout of deer	Hirschragout
escalope of deer, fillet of deer	Hirschschnitzel
leg of deer	Hirschkeule, Hirschschlegel
saddle of deer	Hirschrücken

Appendix

English	German
shoulder of deer	Hirschschulter
hare	Hase
leg of hare	Hasenkeule
saddle of hare	Hasenrücken
rabbit	Kaninchen
roe, roebuck (male)	Reh
venison	Rehfleisch, Rotwildfleisch, Hirschfleisch
wild boar	Wildschwein
ham of wild boar	Wildschweinschinken
young wild boar	Frischling

game birds, wildfowl	**Wildgeflügel, Federwild**
grouse	Wildhuhn
partridge	Rebhuhn
pheasant	Fasan
quail	Wachtel
snipe	Schnepfe
wild duck	Wildente
wild goose	Wildgans
woodcock	Waldschnepfe

Stocks — Fonds

white stocks	**weiße Fonds**
chicken stock	Geflügelfond
fish stock	Fischfond
veal stock	Kalbsfond
vegetable stock	Gemüsefond

brown stocks	**braune Fonds**
game stock	Wildfond
gravy	Bratensaft, Fleischfond
veal stock	Kalbsfond

Sauces — Saucen

English	German
basic brown sauce, demi-glace sauce	Sauce demi-glace
bordelaise sauce	Bordelaiser Sauce
brown sauces	braune Saucen
cream sauce	Rahmsauce
devil sauce	Teufelssauce
gipsy sauce, zingara sauce	Zigeunersauce
hunter sauce	Jägersauce (Sauce chasseur)
Italian sauce	Italienische Sauce
Madeira sauce	Madeirasauce
mustard sauce	Senfsauce (Sauce Robert)
pepper sauce	Pfeffersauce
provençale sauce	Provenzalische Sauce
tarragon sauce	Estragonsauce
tomato sauce	Tomatensauce
truffle sauce	Trüffelsauce (Sauce Périgueux)

warm butter sauces	**warme Buttersaucen**
béarnaise sauce	Béarner Sauce
Choron sauce	Choronsauce
Foyot sauce	Foyotsauce
hollandaise sauce, Dutch sauce	Holländische Sauce
maltese sauce	Malteser Sauce
mousseline sauce	Schaumsauce

cold sauces	**kalte Saucen**
fisher sauce	Fischersauce (à la pêcheur)
green sauce	Grüne Sauce (Sauce verte)
mayonnaise (sauce)	Mayonnaisesauce
Norwegian sauce	Norweger Sauce
ravigote sauce (herb sauce)	Kräutersauce (Sauce ravigote)
remoulade sauce	Remouladensauce
tartar sauce	Tatarensauce
Tyrolean sauce	Tiroler Sauce (Sauce tyrolienne)
vinaigrette sauce	Vinaigrettesauce (Essigkräutersauce)

special warm sauces	**warme Spezialsaucen**
apple sauce	Apfelsauce
bread sauce	Brotsauce
mustard sauce	Senfsauce
onion sauce, soubise sauce	Zwiebelsauce (Sauce soubise)
sour cream sauce	Sauerrahmsauce

special cold sauces	**kalte Spezialsaucen**
cranberry sauce	Preiselbeersauce
creamed horseradish	Oberskren
Cumberland sauce	Cumberlandsauce
horseradish sauce	Meerrettichsauce
mint sauce	Minzsauce

white sauces	**weiße Saucen**
Béchamel sauce, milk sauce (basic white sauce)	Béchamelsauce (weiße Grundsauce)
Aurore sauce	Aurorasauce
cream sauce	Rahmsauce
Mornay sauce, cheese sauce	Mornaysauce
German sauce (with veal stock)	deutsche Sauce (Sauce allemande)
caper sauce	Kapernsauce
chive sauce	Schnittlauchsauce
curry sauce	Currysauce
mushroom sauce	Champignonsauce
tarragon sauce	Estragonsauce
suprême sauce (with chicken stock)	Sauce suprême (Geflügeleinmachsauce)
mushroom sauce	Champignonsauce
tarragon sauce	Estragonsauce
velouté (basic white sauce)	Velouté (weiße Grundsauce)
white wine sauce (with fish stock)	Weißweinsauce (Fischeinmachsauce)
anchovy sauce	Sardellensauce
caper sauce	Kapernsauce
herb sauce	Kräutersauce
lobster sauce	Hummersauce
oyster sauce	Austernsauce
prawn sauce	Garnelensauce

Butter and savoury butters	**Butter und Buttermischungen**
brown (black) butter	braune Butter
clarified butter	geklärte Butter
melted butter	zerlassene Butter

Gastronomic Vocabulary

savoury butters	**Buttermischungen**
anchovy butter	Sardellenbutter
crayfish (crab) butter	Krebsbutter
garlic butter	Knoblauchbutter
herb butter	Kräuterbutter
horseradish butter	Meerrettichbutter
lard	Schweineschmalz
lemon butter	Zitronenbutter
lobster butter	Hummerbutter
mustard butter	Senfbutter
nut (almond) butter	Nuss-(Mandel-)Butter
peanut butter	Erdnussbutter
snail butter	Schneckenbutter
tarragon butter	Estragonbutter

Vegetables	**Gemüse**
artichoke	Artischocke
artichoke bottoms	Artischockenböden
artichoke hearts	Artischockenherzen
asparagus	Spargel
asparagus tips	Spargelspitzen
baby marrows, zucchini, courgettes	Zucchini, Zwergkürbisse
beans	Bohnen
green, French, string beans	grüne
red beans	rote
white beans	weiße
beetroot (Br.), red beet (Am.)	Rote Rübe
broccoli	Brokkoli, Spargelkohl
Brussels sprouts	Kohlsprossen, Rosenkohl
carrots	Karotten, gelbe Rüben
cauliflower	Blumenkohl
celeriac	Sellerieknolle
celery, stalk celery	Sellerie, Stangensellerie
chanterelles	Pfifferling, Eierschwammerl
chicory	Brüsseler Spitzen, Chicorée
corn, sweet corn	Mais
corn on cob	Maiskolben
cucumber	Gurke
egg-plant, aubergine	Eierfrucht, Aubergine
endive	Endivie
fennel	Fenchel
garlic	Knoblauch
gherkins (Br.), pickles (Am.)	Essiggurken
horseradish	Meerrettich
kohlrabi	Kohlrabi
leek	Lauch, Porree
lentils	Linsen
lettuce	Kopfsalat
morel	Morchel
olive	Olive
onion	Zwiebel
parsnip	Pastinak
peas (fresh, dried, green)	Erbsen (frische, getrocknete grüne)
pepper (green, red)	Paprikaschote (grüne, rote)
potatoes	Kartoffeln (Erdäpfel)
pumpkin	Kürbis
radish (white, black)	Rettich (weiß, schwarz)
red cabbage	Blau-(Rot-)Kraut
red radish	Radieschen
salsify	Schwarzwurzel
sauerkraut	Sauerkraut
savoy cabbage	Kohl, Wirsing
shallot	Schalotte
spinach	Spinat
spring vegetables	Frühgemüse
tomato	Tomate
truffle	Trüffel
white cabbage	Kraut, Weißkraut
yellow boletus	Steinpilz

Potato dishes	**Kartoffel-(Erdäpfel-) Gerichte**
baked potatoes	Folienkartoffel
boiled potatoes, plain potatoes	Salzkartoffeln
bouillon potatoes	Bouillonkartoffeln
château potatoes, castle potatoes	Schlosskartoffeln
chips (Br.), French fried potatoes (Am.)	Pommes frites, Kartoffelstäbchen
chive potatoes	Schnittlauchkartoffeln
creamed potatoes	Rahmkartoffeln
crisps, chips	Kartoffelscheiben, gebacken
diced potatoes	Würfelkartoffeln
duchess potatoes	Duchesse-(Herzogin-)Kartoffeln
galettes	Kartoffelfladen
hashed brown potatoes	Röstkartoffeln
mashed potatoes	Kartoffelpüree
matchstick chips, matchstick potatoes	Zündholzkartoffeln
new potatoes	heurige Kartoffeln
pan-fried potatoes	Bratkartoffeln
Parisienne potatoes	Pariser Kartoffeln
parsley potatoes	Petersilienkartoffeln
potato balls	Kartoffelbällchen
potato croquettes	Kartoffelkroketten
potato dumpling	Kartoffelknödel
potato fritters	Kartoffelpuffer
potato noodles	Kartoffelnudeln
soufflé potatoes	Auflaufkartoffeln
steamed potatoes	Dampfkartoffeln
straw potatoes	Strohkartoffeln
stuffed potatoes	gefüllte Kartoffeln
wafer potatoes	Waffelkartoffeln, Gitterkartoffeln

Cereals and pasta	**Getreide und Teigwaren**
barley	Gerste
blini, buckwheat pancake	Blini, Buchweizenpfannkuchen
bread (brown, white, rye bread)	Brot (schwarzes, weißes, Roggenbrot)
cornflakes	Cornflakes
crescent (croissant)	Kipferl
crumbs	Brösel
flour	Mehl
noodles	Nudeln
elbow macaroni	Hörnchen
lasagne	Lasagne
macaroni	Makkaroni
ravioli	Ravioli
ribbon noodles	Bandnudeln

spaghetti	*Spagetti*
oat	*Hafer*
oatmeal, porridge	*Haferbrei*
oat flakes, rolled oats	*Haferflocken*
polenta	*Polenta, Sterz*
puffed rice, rice crispies	*Knusperreis, Müslireis*
pumpernickel	*Pumpernickel*
roll	*Brötchen, Semmel*
rye	*Roggen*
semolina	*Grieß*
wheat	*Weizen*

Dumplings	***Knödel / Klöße***
bacon dumpling	*Speckknödel, -kloß*
cheese dumpling	*Käseknödel, -kloß*
ham dumpling	*Schinkenknödel, -kloß*
liver dumpling	*Leberknödel, -kloß*
marrow dumpling	*Markknödel, -kloß*
potato dumpling	*Kartoffelknödel, -kloß*
semolina dumpling	*Grießknödel, -kloß*
(white) bread dumpling	*Semmelknödel, -kloß*

Rice	***Reis***
boiled rice	*Reis, gekocht*
brown rice	*Reis, braun*
curry rice	*Curryreis*
long grain rice	*Langkornreis*
rice with peas	*Risipisi*
risotto (Italian rice dish)	*Risotto*
saffron rice	*Safranreis*
short grain rice	*Perlreis*
steamed rice	*Reis, gedünstet*
white rice	*Reis, weiß*
wild rice	*Reis, wild*

Seasonings (spices) and herbs	***Würzmittel (Gewürze) und Kräuter***
allspice, pimento	*Neugewürz, Piment*
aniseed	*Anis*
capers	*Kapern*
caraway seed, cumin	*Kümmel*
cayenne (pepper)	*Cayenne(-pfeffer)*
chili, chilli	*Chili, Chilli*
cinnamon	*Zimt*
clove	*Nelke, Gewürznelke*
curry (powder)	*Curry(pulver)*
dry mustard	*Senfpulver*
fennel seed	*Fenchel*
garlic (clove)	*Knoblauch(zehe)*
ginger	*Ingwer*
juniper (berries)	*Wacholder(beeren)*
marjoram	*Majoran*
mustard (grains)	*Senf(körner)*
nutmeg	*Muskatnuss*
oregano	*Oregano*
paprika	*Paprika, rot*
pepper, whole, crushed, ground	*Pfeffer, ganz, geschrotet, gemahlen*
pepper(corns), black, white, red, green	*Pfeffer(körner), schwarz, weiß, rot, grün*
poppy seed	*Mohn*
pumpkin seed oil	*Kürbiskernöl*
salt	*Salz*
sugar	*Zucker*
brown sugar	*Rohzucker*
caramel sugar	*Karamellzucker*
castor sugar	*Kristallzucker*
powder sugar	*Staubzucker*
lump sugar	*Würfelzucker*
molasses	*Zuckersirup*
vanilla	*Vanille*
vinegar	*Essig*

herbs	***Kräuter***
basil	*Basilikum*
bay (leaf)	*Lorbeer(-blatt)*
chervil	*Kerbelkraut*
chives	*Schnittlauch*
chutney	*Gewürzfruchtpaste*
cress	*Kresse*
dill	*Dillkraut*
marjoram	*Majoran*
mint, peppermint	*Minze, Pfefferminze*
parsley, parsley root	*Petersilie, Petersilwurzel*
rosemary	*Rosmarin*
sage	*Salbei*
savoury	*Bohnenkraut*
tarragon	*Estragon*
thyme	*Thymian*
watercress	*Brunnenkresse*
wood garlic	*Bärlauch*

Fruits	***Früchte, Obst***
apple	*Apfel*
apricot	*Aprikose, Marille*
banana	*Banane*
berries	*Beeren*
blackberries	*Schwarzbeeren*
brambleberries	*Brombeeren*
blueberries	*Heidelbeeren*
cranberries	*Preiselbeeren*
currants (red, black)	*Johannisbeeren (rot, schwarz)*
gooseberries	*Stachelbeeren*
raspberries	*Himbeeren*
strawberries	*Erdbeeren*
wild strawberries	*Walderdbeeren*
cherry	*Kirsche*
chestnut	*Kastanie*
dates	*Datteln*
figs	*Feigen*
grapefruit	*Grapefruit, Pampelmuse*
grapes (blue, white)	*Trauben (blau, weiß)*
greengage	*Reneklode*
jam	*Konfitüre*
kiwi	*Kiwi*
lemon	*Zitrone*
lime	*Limone*
mandarin, tangerine	*Mandarine*
marmalade (orange)	*Orangenmarmelade*
melon	*Melone*
cantaloup melon	*Zuckermelone*
honey dew melon	*Honigmelone*
water melon	*Wassermelone*

Gastronomic Vocabulary

morellos (morello cherries)	Weichseln, Sauerkirschen
nuts	Nüsse
almonds	Mandeln
cashew nuts	Cashewnüsse
coconuts	Kokosnüsse
hazelnuts	Haselnüsse
peanuts	Erdnüsse
pecan nuts	Pekannüsse
walnuts	Walnüsse
orange	Orange
peach	Pfirsich
pear	Birne
pineapple	Ananas
plum	Pflaume, Zwetschke
prune	Dörrpflaume
raisins	Rosinen
rhubarb	Rhabarber
seasonal fruits	Früchte der Saison
sultanas	Sultaninen

Desserts and sweets — Desserts und Süßspeisen

warm	**warm**
Austrian doughnuts	Krapfen
dumplings	Knödel
fruit dumplings	Obstknödel
white cheese dumplings	Quarkknödel
yeast dumplings	Germknödel
fruits in batter (fritters)	Früchte in Backteig
apple fritters	Apfelspalten
banana fritters	mit Bananen
pineapple fritters	mit Ananas
pancakes	Pfannkuchen, Palatschinken
sabayon	Weinschaum (Chaudeau)
soufflés	Aufläufe
apricot soufflé	Aprikosenauflauf
chocolate soufflé	Schokoladenauflauf
rice soufflé	Reisauflauf
wafers, waffles	Waffeln
warm puddings	Puddings, warm
warm semolina pudding	Grießpudding
nut (almond) pudding	Nuss-(Mandel-) Pudding
steamed chocolate pudding	Mohr im Hemd
cold	**kalt**
biscuits (Br.), cookies (Am.)	Kekse
cakes	Kuchen, Torten
creamed cakes	Rührteigkuchen
flan	Obsttorte
rolled spongecake, Swiss roll	Biskuitroulade
short cakes	Mürbteigkuchen
sponge cakes	Biskuittorten
yeast cakes	Hefekuchen
cold puddings	Puddings, kalt
cold semolina pudding	Grießpudding
cold rice pudding	Reispudding
creams	Cremen
Bavarian cream	Bayerische Creme
crescent, croissant	Kipferl
custard	Vanillesauce
fruits	Früchte, Obst
fruit cocktails	Früchtecocktails
fresh fruits	Früchte, frisch
fruit salads	Früchtesalate
stewed fruit, compote	Früchtekompott
ice omelette, baked Alaska	Eisomelette (Omelette surprise)
ice creams	Eiscremen
hazelnut ice cream	Haselnusseis
strawberry ice cream	Erdbeereis
vanilla ice cream	Vanilleeis
jellies	Gelees
fruit jellies	Früchtegelees
wine jelly	Weingelee
meringue	Schaumgebäck
mousse	Mousse
muffin	Muffin, kleiner, runder Kuchen
parfait	Halbgefrorenes, Parfait
pastry	Gebäck, Backwerk
choux pastry	Brandteig
dessert pastry	Dessertgebäck
puff pastry	Blätterteig
short crust pastry	Mürbteig
yeast pastry	Hefeteig
petits fours	Petits fours
pies, fruit pies	Pasteten, Obstpasteten
sherbet	Sorbet
slices	Schnitten
strudel	Strudel
apple strudel	Apfelstrudel
cream strudel	Rahmstrudel
curd cheese strudel	Quarkstrudel
sweetrolls	Golatschen (kleiner gefüllter Hefekuchen)
tarts	belegte Kuchen (Torten)
tartlets	Törtchen

Austrian specialities — Österreichische Spezialitäten

black pudding	Blutwurst
boiled shoulder of pork with carrots, leeks, celeriac and horseradish	Steirisches Wurzelfleisch
boiled ribs of beef	Beinfleisch
boiled round of beef	Tafelspitz
braised beef	Rindersaftbraten
braised fillet of beef with onions	Zwiebelrostbraten
braised rolled stuffed fillet of beef	Rindsroulade
braised stuffed green peppers	Paprika, gefüllt
brawn, headcheese	Presskopf
fried pork sausage with sauerkraut	Bratwurst mit Sauerkraut
fried potatoes with pork and beef	Tiroler Gröstl
goulash (stewed beef or veal in paprika sauce)	Gulasch (Rinds-, Kalbsgulasch)
meat loaf	Faschierter Braten
roast best end neck of pork	Schopfbraten
roast leg of veal	Kalbsstelze, gebraten
roast pork, smoked pork and sausage with sauerkraut and bread dumpling	Bauernschmaus

Appendix

roast rolled loin of veal with kidneys	Kalbsnierenbraten, gerollt
roast stuffed breast of veal	Kalbsbrust, gefüllt
smoked pork	Geselchtes
stewed calf's lights	Kalbsbeuschel
Styrian fattened pullet	Steirisches Masthuhn
Wiener Schnitzel (deep-fried breaded escalope of veal)	Kalbsschnitzel, Wiener Art

Beverages	***Getränke***
non-alcoholic drinks	***alkoholfreie Getränke***
fruit juices	*Fruchtsäfte*
apple juice	*Apfelsaft*
currant juice	*Johannisbeersaft*
orange juice	*Orangensaft*
orange squash	*Orangensaft, frisch gepresst*
raspberry juice	*Himbeersaft*
lemonade, orangeade	*Limonade, Orangenlimonade*
mineral water	*Mineralwasser*
nectar	*Nektar*
soda water, sparkling water	*Sodawasser*
syrup	*Sirup*
tonic water	*Tonic*
vegetable juices	*Gemüsesäfte*
carrot juice	*Karottensaft*
tomato juice	*Tomatensaft*
warm beverages	***warme Getränke***
coffee	*Kaffee*
coffee with milk	*Kaffee mit Milch*
coffee with cream	*Kaffee mit Sahne (Obers)*
coffee black	*Kaffee, schwarz*
espresso coffee	*Espresso*
filtered coffee	*Filterkaffee*
cocoa	*Kakao*
hot chocolate	*Schokolade, heiß*
milk	*Milch*
skim milk	*Magermilch*
tea	*Tee*
camomile tea	*Kamillentee*
mint tea	*Pfefferminztee*
tea plain	*Tee Natur*
tea with lemon	*Tee mit Zitrone*
tea with milk	*Tee mit Milch*
tea with rum	*Tee mit Rum*

alcoholic drinks (liquors)	***alkoholische (geistige) Getränke***
apéritif, before-dinner drink	*Aperitif*
beer	*Bier*
bottled beer	*in Flaschen*
dark beer	*dunkel*
draught beer	*offen, vom Fass*
lager (beer)	*Lagerbier*
light (pale) beer	*hell*
tinned beer	*in Dosen*
brandy	*Branntwein, Schnaps*
cocktail	*Cocktail*
liqueur	*Likör*
rum	*Rum*
spirits	*Spirituosen*
wine	*Wein*
bottled wine	*Flaschenwein*
Burgundy (red, white)	*Burgunder (rot, weiß)*
champagne	*Champagner*
cognac	*Cognac*
dry	*herb, trocken*
dessert wine, fortified wine	*Südwein*
heavy, full (rich) bodied	*schwer, üppig, vollmundig*
light	*leicht*
Madeira	*Madeira*
Marsala	*Marsala*
mild, mellow	*mild*
mulled wine	*Glühwein*
per glass, in carafe, from the cask	*offen*
port(wine)	*Portwein*
red Bordeaux, claret	*Bordeauxwein, rot*
red wine	*Rotwein*
Rhine wine, hock	*Rheinwein*
rosé wine	*Roséwein*
sherry	*Sherry*
sparkling wine	*Schaumwein, Sekt*
sweet, semi-sweet	*süß, halbsüß*
vermouth	*Vermouth*
white wine	*Weißwein*
white Bordeaux	*Bordeauxwein, weiß*
young, new wine	*Heuriger*
whisky, whiskey	*Whisky, Whiskey*

Vokabelverzeichnis
Vocabulary

German – English
English – German

Appendix

Vocabulary German – English

A

German	English
Aal	eel
– in Aspik	eel in jelly (aspic)
–, geräuchert	smoked eel
abschäumen	to skim
abseihen, trocknen	to drain
abwischen	to wipe
alkoholfreie Getränke	non-alcoholic drinks
alkoholische Getränke (geistige)	alcoholic drinks (liquors)
Ananas	pineapple
Anis	aniseed
anrichten	to dress
Aperitif	apéritif, before-dinner drink
Apfel	apple
Apfelsaft	apple juice
Apfelsauce	apple sauce
Apfelstrudel	apple strudel
Aprikose	apricot
Aprikosenauflauf	apricot soufflé
Artischocke	artichoke
gefüllte Artischocken	stuffed artichokes
Artischockenböden	artichoke bottoms
– mit Schinken	artichoke bottoms with ham
Artischockenherzen	artichoke hearts
Aubergine	egg-plant, aubergine
–, gefüllt	stuffed egg-plant, aubergine
aufgießen (zB den Braten)	to baste
Aufläufe	soufflés
Auflaufkartoffeln	soufflé potatoes
aufschlagen	to whip
Aufschnitt	assorted cold meat (cuts)
Aurorasauce	Aurore sauce
auslösen	to bone
Auster	oyster
rohe Austern	raw oysters
Austernmesser	oyster knife
Austernsauce	oyster sauce

B

German	English
Bachforelle	brook trout
backen	to bake, to fry (deep-fry)
Backerbsen	fried batter drops
Backgeschirr	baking dishes
Backofen	oven
Backwerk	pastry
Banane	banana
Bandnudeln	ribbon noodles
Bärlauch	wild garlic
Barsch	perch
Basilikum	basil
Bauernomelett (Speck und Kartoffeln)	country omelette (bacon and potatoes)
Bauernschmaus	roast pork, smoked pork and sausage with sauerkraut and bread dumpling
Bayerische Creme	Bavarian cream
Béchamelsauce (weiße Grundsauce)	Béchamel sauce, milk sauce (basic white sauce)
bedecken	to cover
Beefsteak tatare	tartar steak, steak tartare
Beeren	berries
Beinfleisch, Rippenfleisch	boiled ribs of beef
Beiried, flaches Roastbeef	sirloin
belegte Kuchen (Torten)	tarts
bestäuben	to powder, dust
bestreuen	to sprinkle
Bier	beer
– vom Fass	draught beer
binden (zB mit Mehl oder Stärke)	to thicken
Birne	pear
Biskuitroulade	rolled sponge cake, Swiss roll
Biskuittorten	sponge cakes
Blätterteig	puff pastry
Blätterteigpastetchen mit feinen (Kalbs-, Hühner-, Wild-, Schinken- …) Ragouts	patties filled with fine (veal, chicken, game, ham …) stews
Blau-(Rot-)Kraut	red cabbage
Blini, Buchweizenpfannkuchen	blini, buckwheat pancake
Blumenkohl	cauliflower
–, gebacken	deep-fried breaded cauliflower
Blumenkohlcremesuppe	cream of cauliflower
Blutwurst	black pudding
Bohnen	beans
Bohnenkraut	savoury
Bohnensuppe	bean soup
Bordeauxwein, rot	red Bordeaux, claret
–, weiß	white Bordeaux
Bordelaiser Sauce	bordelaise sauce
Bouillabaisse	fish soup (French style)
Bouillonkartoffeln	bouillon potatoes
Brandteig	choux pastry
Brandteigkrapfen	profiteroles
Branntwein	brandy
Braten, kalter	cold roast meat
Bratenpfanne	roasting pan
Bratensaft	gravy
Bratkartoffeln	pan-fried potatoes
Bratpfanne	frying pan
Bratspieß	spit
Bratwurst mit Sauerkraut	fried pork sausage with sauerkraut
braune Butter	brown (black) butter
– Fonds	brown stocks
– Saucen	brown sauces
bräunen	to brown
Brokkoli, Spargelkohl	broccoli
– mit Butterbröseln	broccoli with bread crumbs and butter
Brombeeren	blackberries, brambleberries
Brösel	(bread) crumbs
Brot (schwarzes, weißes)	bread (brown, white)
–, belegt	open sandwich
Brötchen	roll
Brotsauce	bread sauce

Vocabulary

German	English
Brunnenkresse	watercress
Brüsseler Spitzen	chicory
Bückling	bloater
Burgunder (rot, weiß)	(red, white) Burgundy
Butter	butter
Buttermischungen	savoury butters

C

German	English
Canapés, belegte Brötchen	canapés
Cashewnüsse	cashew nuts
Cayenne(-pfeffer)	cayenne (pepper)
Champagner	champagne
Champignon-(Pilz-) Cremesuppe	cream of mushroom
Champignons, gebacken	deep-fried breaded mushrooms
Champignonsauce	mushroom sauce
Chateaubriand	double fillet steak
Chefsalat	chef's salad
Chicorée	chicory
Chili, Chilli	chili, chilli
Choronsauce	Choron sauce
Clubsandwich	club sandwich
Cocktail	cocktail
Cognac	cognac
Consommé, Bouillon	consommé, bouillon
Cornflakes	cornflakes
Cremen	creams
Cremesuppen	cream soups, cream of ... (soup)
Cumberlandsauce	Cumberland sauce
Curry(-pulver)	curry (powder)
Curryreis	curry rice
Currysauce	curry sauce

D

German	English
dämpfen	to steam
Dampfkartoffeln	steamed potatoes
darunterziehen (zB Eischnee unter die Masse ziehen)	to fold in
Datteln	dates
dazugeben	to add
Deckel	lid
Dessertgebäck	dessert pastry
Desserts	desserts
Deutsche Sauce (Sauce allemande)	German sauce (with veal stock)
Dillkraut	dill
doppelte Kraftsuppe	beef tea, warm or cold
doppelte Lendenschnitte	double tenderloin steak
doppeltes Zwischenrippenstück	double sirloin steak
Dörrpflaume	prune
Dorsch	cod, codling, codfish
Dosenbier	tinned beer
Duchesse-(Herzogin-) Kartoffeln	duchesse potatoes
dunkles Bier	dark beer
dünsten (in kleinen Stücken)	to stew
durch den „Wolf" lassen, klein hacken	to mince, grind

E

German	English
Eier	eggs
– in Aspik	poached egg in jelly
– in Mayonnaise	eggs in mayonnaise
–, gefüllt	stuffed eggs
Eierfrucht	egg-plant, aubergine
Eierkroketten	egg croquettes
Eierkuchen	pancakes
Eierschwammerl	chanterelles
Einbrennsuppe	brown soup
einfetten	to grease
einreiben	to rub
einweichen	to soak
Eischnee schlagen	to beat egg whites
Eiscremen	ice creams
Eisomelett (Omelette surprise)	ice omelette, baked Alaska
Endivie	endive
Ente	duck
entfernen	to remove
entgräten	to bone
entschuppen	to scale
Erbsen (frische, getrocknete, grüne)	peas (fresh, dried, green)
Erbsencremesuppe	cream of pea
Erdbeereis	strawberry ice cream
Erdbeeren	strawberries
Erdnussbutter	peanut butter
Erdnüsse	peanuts
erhitzen	to heat
Espresso	espresso coffee
Essig	vinegar
Essiggurken	gherkins (Br.), pickles (Am.)
Estragon	tarragon
Estragonbutter	tarragon butter
Estragonsauce	tarragon sauce

F

German	English
Fasan	pheasant
Federwild	game birds, wildfowl
Feigen	figs
Fenchel	fennel
–, überbacken	gratinated fennel
fest füllen	to stuff
feuerfest	fire-proof, oven-proof
Filet, Lungenbraten	fillet of beef, tenderloin
Filetsteak, Lendenschnitte	fillet steak, prime steak
Filter	strainer
Filterkaffee	filtered coffee
Fisch(e)	fish
Fischersauce (à la pêcheur)	fisher sauce
Fischfond	fish stock
Fischgeschirr	fish dish
Fischkroketten	fish croquettes
Flaschenbier	bottled beer
Flaschenwein	bottled wine
Fleischfond	stock
Fleischgerichte	meat dishes
Fleischmesser	meat knife
Fleischspieß(chen)	skewer
Fleischwolf	meat mincer
Folienkartoffeln	baked potatoes
Fonds	stocks

German	English
Forelle	trout
– in Aspik	trout in jelly
–, geräuchert	smoked trout
Foyotsauce	Foyot sauce
Französische Zwiebelsuppe	French onion soup
Frischling	young wild boar
Friteuse	fryer
Froschschenkel	frog's legs
Früchte, Obst	fruits
– der Saison	seasonal fruits
– in Backteig	fruits in batter (fritters)
–, frisch	fresh fruit
Früchtecocktails	fruit cocktails
Früchtegelees	fruit jellies
Früchtekompott	stewed fruit, compote
Früchtesalate	fruit salads
Fruchtsäfte	fruit juices
Frühgemüse	spring vegetables

G

German	English
Gabel	fork
Gämse	chamois
Gans	goose
Gänsebrust, geräuchert	smoked breast of goose
Gänseleber	goose liver
Gänseleberpastete	goose liver pâté
Garnele	shrimp, prawn
Garnelencocktail	shrimp (prawn) cocktail
Garnelensauce	prawn sauce
garnieren	to garnish
Gebäck	pastry
gebackene Ananas	pineapple fritters
– Apfelspalten	apple fritters
– Bananen	banana fritters
– Kartoffelscheiben	chips
gebundene Suppen	thick soups
Geflügel	poultry, fowl
Geflügel-(Hühner-) Cremesuppe	cream of chicken
Geflügelauflauf	chicken soufflé
Geflügelfond	chicken stock
Geflügelklein	giblets of chicken
Geflügelkroketten	chicken croquettes
Geflügelleber	poultry liver
Geflügelragout	chicken stew
Geflügelsalat	chicken salad
gefüllte Kartoffeln	stuffed potatoes
geklärte Butter	clarified butter
gekochter Schinken	boiled ham
Gelees	jellies
gemahlener Pfeffer	grounded pepper
Gemüse	vegetables
Gemüsecremesuppe	cream of vegetable
Gemüsefond	vegetable stock
Gemüsemesser	vegetable knife
Gemüsesäfte	vegetable juices
Gemüseschäler	vegetable peeler
Gemüsestreifen	vegetable strips
geräucherter Hering	smoked hering
– Schinken	smoked ham
– Speck	smoked bacon
Germknödel	yeast dumplings
Gerste	barley
Gerstensuppe	barley soup
Geselchtes	smoked pork
Getränke	beverages
Getreide	cereals
getrockneter Hering	dried hering
Gewürzfruchtpaste	chutney
Gitterkartoffeln	wafer potatoes
Glühwein	mulled wine
Golatschen	sweetrolls
Goldbarsch	dorado
Grapefruit, Pampelmuse	grapefruit
–, geeist	iced (chilled) grapefruit
–, gefüllt	stuffed grapefruit
Grapefruitcocktail	grapefruit cocktail
gratinieren	to gratinate
Grieß	semolina
Grießknödel, Grießnockerl	semolina dumpling
Grießpudding	semolina pudding
großes Messer	cook's knife
grüne Bohnen	green, French, string beans
– Sauce (Sauce verte)	green sauce
Gulasch (Rinds-, Kalbsgulasch)	stewed beef or veal in paprika sauce
Gurke	cucumber

H

German	English
Hackbeil	cleaver
Hackbraten	meat loaf
hacken	to chop
Hackmesser	chopping knife
Hackstock	chopping block
Hafer	oat
Haferbrei	oat meal, porridge
Haferflocken	oat flakes, rolled oats
Haferflockensuppe	oatmeal soup
Halbgefrorenes, Parfait	parfait
halbsüß	semi-sweet
Hammel-, Lamm-, Schaffleisch	mutton, lamb
– Braten	roast mutton (lamb)
– Brust	mutton breast
– Karree	rack of mutton, loin of mutton
– Keule	leg of mutton (lamb)
– Kotelett	mutton (lamb) chop
– Ragout	mutton (lamb) stew
– Rippenstück	mutton rib (chop)
– Rücken	saddle of mutton
– Schulter	shoulder of mutton
Hase	hare
Haselnüsse	hazelnuts
Haselnusseis	hazelnut ice cream
Hasenkeule	leg of hare
Hasenrücken	saddle of hare
häuten	to skin
Hecht	pike
Hefekuchen	yeast cakes
Hefeteig	yeast pastry
Heidelbeeren	blueberries
Heilbutt	halibut
helles Bier	light (pale) beer
herb, trocken	dry
Herd	kitchen-range, stove
Hering	herring
–, geräuchert	smoked herring
–, mariniert	marinated herring
Heringssalat	herring salad
Heuriger	young, new wine

German	English
Himbeeren	raspberries
Himbeersaft	raspberry juice
Hirnpüreesuppe	brain (pourré) soup
Hirsch	deer
Hirschfleisch	venison
Hirschkeule, Hirschschlegel	leg of deer
Hirschkotelett	deer chop
Hirschragout	deer stew, ragout of deer
Hirschrücken	saddle of deer
Hirschschnitzel	escalope of deer, fillet of deer
Hirschschulter	shoulder of deer
Hirschsteak	deer steak
hitzebeständig	heat-proof
Hochrippe	prime rib of beef
Holländische Sauce	hollandaise sauce, Dutch sauce
Honigmelone	honey dew melon
Hörnchen	elbow macaroni
Huhn, Junghuhn	chicken, spring chicken
–, gebraten	cold roast chicken
Hühnerbrühe	chicken broth
Hühnerbrust	breast of chicken
Hühnercurry	chicken curry
Hühnerflügel	chicken wings
Hühnergalantine	chicken galantine
Hühnerkeule	leg of chicken
Hühnerleber	chicken liver
Hühnerpastete	chicken pâté
Hummer	lobster
–, gefüllt	stuffed lobster
Hummerbutter	lobster butter
Hummercocktail	lobster cocktail
Hummermayonnaise	lobster mayonnaise
Hummersalat	lobster salad
Hummersauce	lobster sauce

I

German	English
im Backofen braten	to roast
im Ganzen dünsten	to braise
in der Pfanne braten	to pan-fry
in Scheiben, (Streifen) schneiden	to slice
in Würfel schneiden	to dice, cube
Ingwer	ginger
Italienische Sauce	Italian sauce

J

German	English
Jägersauce (Sauce chasseur)	hunter sauce
Johannisbeeren (rot, schwarz)	currants (red, black)
Johannisbeersaft	currant juice

K

German	English
Kabeljau	cod, codfish
Kaffee	coffee
– mit Milch	coffee with milk
– mit Sahne (Obers)	coffee with cream
–, schwarz	black coffee
Kakao	cocoa
Kalbfleisch	veal
Kalbsbeuschel/(Lunge)	stewed calf's lights
Kalbsbraten	roast veal
Kalbsbries	calf's sweetbread
Kalbsbrust	breast of veal
–, gefüllt	roast stuffed breast of veal
Kalbsfilet, Kalbslende	fillet of veal
Kalbsfond	veal stock
Kalbsgulasch	veal stew in paprika sauce
Kalbsherz	calf's heart
Kalbshirn	calf's brains
Kalbskarree	best end neck of veal (loin of veal)
Kalbskopf	calf's head
Kalbskotelett	veal chop
Kalbsleber	calf's liver
Kalbsmedaillons	veal medallions
Kalbsnieren	calf's kidneys
Kalbsnierenbraten	roast loin of veal with kidneys
–, gerollt	roast rolled loin of veal with kidneys
Kalbsnuss	topside of veal
Kalbspüreesuppe	veal (purée) soup
Kalbsragout	veal stew, stewed veal, ragout of veal
Kalbsroulade	rolled stuffed veal cutlet
Kalbsrücken	saddle of veal
Kalbsschnitzel	escalope of veal, veal cutlet
–, Wiener Art	deep-fried breaded escalope of veal (veal cutlet)
Kalbsschulter	shoulder of veal
Kalbssteak	veal steak
Kalbsstelze	leg of veal
–, gebraten	roast leg of veal
Kalbszunge	calf's tongue
kalt	cold
kalte Platte	assorted cold meat (cuts)
kalte Saucen	cold sauces
– Spezialsaucen	special cold sauces
– Vorspeisen	cold appetizers (starters)
Kamillentee	camomile tea
Kammmuschel	scallop
Kaninchen	rabbit
Kapaun	capon
Kapern	capers
Kapernsauce	caper sauce
Karamellzucker	caramel sugar
Karpfen	carp
Kartoffel-(Erdäpfel-)Gerichte	potato dishes
Kartoffelbällchen	potato balls
Kartoffelcremesuppe	cream of potato
Kartoffelfladen, Kartoffellaibchen	potato galettes
Kartoffelklöße, -knödel	potato dumplings
Kartoffelkroketten	potato croquettes
Kartoffeln (Erdäpfel)	potatoes
Kartoffelnudeln	potato noodles
Kartoffelpuffer	potato fritters
Kartoffelpüree	mashed potatoes
Kartoffelscheiben	crisps
Käse	cheese
Käseauflauf	cheese soufflé
Käseknödel	cheese dumpling
Käsesalat	cheese salad
Käsetörtchen	cheese tartlets
Kasserolle	casserole
Kastanie	chestnut

Appendix

Kaviar	caviar
Kekse	biscuits (Br.), cookies (Am.)
Kerbelkraut	chervil
Kipferl	crescent, croissant
Kirsche(n)	cherry (cherries)
Kiwi	kiwi
klare Suppe	clear soup
– mit ...	clear soup (broth) with ...
kleines Filetsteak	tournedos
Knoblauch(-zehe)	garlic (clove)
Knoblauchbutter	garlic butter
Knödel	dumplings
Knusperreis, Müslireis	puffed rice, rice crispies
Kochkessel	kettle
Kochlöffel	(wooden) spoon
Kohl	savoy cabbage
Kohlrabi	kohlrabi
Kokosnüsse	coconuts
Konfitüre	jam
Kopfsalat	lettuce
Krabbe	crab
Kraftbrühe	broth, beef broth
Krapfen	Austrian doughnuts
Kraut, Weißkraut	white cabbage
Kräuter	herbs
Kräuterbutter	herb butter
Kräutersauce	ravigote sauce
(Sauce ravigote)	(herb sauce)
Krebs	crayfish
Krebsbutter	crayfish (crab) butter
Krebssuppe	bisque of crayfish
Kresse	cress
Krevette	shrimp, prawn
Kristallzucker	castor sugar
Kroketten	croquettes
Krustentiere	crustaceans
Kuchen	cakes
Küchengeräte	cooking utensils
Kühlschrank	refrigerator (fridge)
Kümmel	caraway seed, cumin
Kürbis	pumpkin
Kürbiskernöl	pumpkin seed oil

L

Lachs	salmon
–, geräuchert	smoked salmon
–, mariniert	marinated salmon
Lachsforelle	salmon trout
Lachspastete	salmon pâté
Lagerbier	lager (beer)
Lammeingemachtes	white lamb stew
Lammviertel	quarter of lamb
Langkornreis	long grain rice
langsam kochen	to simmer
Languste	spiny lobster, crawfish
Lasagne	lasagne
Lauch	leek
Lauchcremesuppe	cream of leek
Leberkloß, -knödel	liver dumpling
Leberreis	shredded liver
legen, geben	to place
Likör	liqueur
Limonade,	lemonade,
Limone	lime
Linsen	lentils
Linsenpüreesuppe	lentil (purée) soup
Löffel	spoon
Lorbeer(-blatt)	bay (leaf)

M

Madeira	Madeira
Madeirasauce	Madeira sauce
Magermilch	skim milk
Mais	corn, sweet corn
Maiskolben	corn on cob
Majoran	marjoram
Makkaroni	macaroni
Makrele	mackerel
–, geräuchert	smoked mackerel
Malteser Sauce	maltese sauce
Mandarine	mandarin, tangerine
Mandeln	almonds
marinieren	to marinate
Markknödel, -kloß	marrow dumpling
Marsala	Marsala
Masthuhn	pullet, fattened chicken
Mayonnaisesauce	mayonnaise (sauce)
Meeresfrüchtesalat	seafood salad
Meerrettich	horseradish
Meerrettichbutter	horseradish butter
Meerrettichsauce	horseradish sauce
Mehl	flour
Melone	melon
–, geeist	iced (chilled) melon
Melonencocktail	melon cocktail
Melonensalat	melon salad
Messbecher	measuring jug
Messer	knife, knives
Metallpalette	metal spatula
Miesmuschel	mussel
–, überbacken	gratinated mussles
Miesmuschelsalat	mussel salad
Mikrowellenherd	microwave oven
Milch	milk
mild	mild, mellow
Milzschnitten	milt on toast
Mineralwasser	mineral water
Minestrone	Italian vegetable soup
Minze	mint
Minzsauce	mint sauce
mischen	to mix, blend, combine
Mixer	mixer
Mohn	poppy seed
Mohr im Hemd	steamed chocolate pudding
Möhren, gelbe Rüben	carrots
Möhrensaft	carrot juice
Morchel	morel
Morcheltörtchen	morel tartlets
Mousse	mousse
Muffin	muffin
Mürbteig	short crust pastry
Mürbteigkuchen	short cakes
Muskatnuss	nutmeg
Müslireis, Knusperreis	puffed rice, rice crispies

N

Nektar	nectar
Nelke, Gewürznelke	clove
neue Kartoffeln	new potatoes
Neugewürz, Piment	allspice, pimento
Norweger Sauce	Norwegian sauce
Nudeln	noodles
Nuss-(Mandel-)Butter	nut (almond) butter
Nuss-(Mandel-)Pudding	nut (almond) pudding
Nüsse	nuts

O

Obstkloß, -knödel	fruit dumplings
Obstmesser	fruit knife
Obstpasteten	fruit pies
Obsttorte	flan
Obsttortenring	flanring
Ochsenmaulsalat	ox-muzzle salad
Ochsenschwanz	oxtail
Ochsenschwanzsuppe, gebunden	oxtail soup
–, klare	clear oxtail soup
Ochsenzunge	ox-tongue
–, geräuchert	smoked ox-tongue
offener Wein	per glass, in carafe, from the cask
Öl	oil
Olive	olive
Omelett	omelette
– mit Champignons	mushroom omelette
– mit Hühnerleber	chicken liver omelette
– mit Spargel	asparagus omelette
– mit Spinat	spinach omelette
Orange	orange
Orangenlimonade	orangeade
Orangenmarmelade	orange marmalade
Orangensaft	orange juice
–, frisch gepresst	orange squash
Oregano	oregano
österreichisch(e)	Austrian

Q

Quarkknödel	curd cheese (white cheese) dumplings
Quarkstrudel	curd cheese (white cheese) strudel

P

panieren	to bread
Paprika, gefüllt	braised stuffed green peppers
–, rot (Gewürz)	paprika
Paprikaschote (grüne, rote)	pepper (green, red)
parieren	to trim
Pariser Kartoffeln	parisienne potatoes
passieren, filtern	to strain
Passiermaschine	strainer
Pasteten	pies
Pastinak	parsnip
Pekannüsse	pecan nuts
Perlhuhn	guinea fowl
Perlreis	short grain rice
Petersilie	parsley
Petersilwurzel	parsley root
Petersilienkartoffeln	parsley potatoes
Petits fours	petits fours
Pfanne	pan
Pfannkuchen	pancakes
Pfannkuchenstreifen	sliced pancakes
Pfeffer(-körner)	pepper(corns)
Pfeffer, ganz, geschrotet	pepper, whole, crushed
Pfefferminze	peppermint
Pfefferminztee	mint tea
Pfeffersauce	pepper sauce
Pfifferling	chanterelles
Pfirsich	peach
Pflaume	plum
Pizza	pizza
Platte, Teller	plate
pochiertes Ei mit ...	poached egg with ...
Pökelfleisch	salted (pickled) pork
Polenta, Sterz	polenta
Pommes frites, Kartoffelstäbchen	chips (Br.), French fried potatoes (Am.)
Porree	leek
Porterhouse-Steak	porterhouse steak
Portwein	port(wine)
Preiselbeeren	cranberries
Preiselbeerensauce	cranberry sauce
Presskopf	brawn, headcheese
Provenzalische Sauce	provençale sauce
Puddings, kalt	cold puddings
–, warm	warm puddings
Puderzucker	powerd sugar
Pumpernickel	pumpernickel
Püreesuppen	purée soups
pürieren	to mash

R

Radieschen	red radish
Rahmkartoffeln	creamed potatoes
Rahmsauce	cream sauce
Rahmstrudel	cream strudel
räuchern	to smoke
Ravioli	ravioli
Rebhuhn	partridge
reduzieren	to reduce
Regenbogenforelle	rainbow trout
Reh	roe
Rehfleisch	venison
Rehschnitzel	fillet of venison
Reneklode	greengage
Reibeisen	grater
reiben (mit einem Reibeisen)	to grate
Reis	rice
–, braun	brown rice
–, gedünstet	steamed rice
–, gekocht	boiled rice
–, weiß	white rice
–, wild	wild rice
Reisauflauf	rice soufflé
Reispudding	cold rice pudding
Remouladensauce	remoulade sauce
Rettich (weiß, schwarz)	radish (white, black)
Rhabarber	rhubarb
Rheinwein	Rhine wine, hock

Appendix

Rinderroulade	(braised) rolled stuffed fillet of beef
Rinderschmor(saft)braten	braised beef
Rindfleisch	beef
–, gepökelt	corned beef
Rindfleischsalat	beef salad
Rindsbraten	roast beef
Rindsgulasch	stewed beef in paprika sauce
Rindsherz	heart (beef)
Rindskarbonade	beef carbonade
Rindsragout	beef stew, stewed beef, ragout of beef
Rindsrose	aitchbone of beef
Rindsschnitzel	fillet of beef, slice of beef, escalope of beef
Rippenfleisch	rib of beef
Risipisi	rice with peas
Risotto	risotto (Italian rice dish)
Roastbeef	roast beef
–, kalt	cold roast beef
Roggen	rye
Roggenbrot	rye bread
roher Schinken	raw ham
Rohkost(platte)	assorted raw vegetables (crudities)
Rohzucker	brown sugar
Rosenkohl	Brussels sprouts
Roséwein	rosé wine
Rosinen	raisins
Rosmarin	rosemary
Röstkartoffeln	hashed brown potatoes
rote Bohnen	red beans
Rote Rübe	beetroot (Br.), red beet (Am.)
Rotkraut	red cabbage
Rotwein	red wine
Rotwildfleisch	venison
Rotzunge	lemon sole
Rührei	scrambled egg
Rührschüssel	mixing bowl
Rührteigkuchen	creamed cakes
Rum	rum
Rumpsteak	rump steak
russische Eier	stuffed egg, Russian style

S

Safranreis	saffron rice
Sahnemeerrettich	creamed horseradish
Saibling	char
Salbei	sage
Salz	salt
Salzhering	kipper (kippered herring)
Salzkartoffeln	boiled potatoes, plain potatoes
Salzwasserfische	salt-water fish, sea fish
Sardelle	anchovy
Sardellenbutter	anchovy butter
Sardellensauce	anchovy sauce
Sardine	sardine
–, in Öl	in oil
Saucen	sauces
Sauce béarnaise	béarnaise sauce
Sauce demi-glace	basic brown sauce, demi-glace sauce
Sauce hollandaise	hollandaise sauce
Sauce Mornay	Mornay sauce, cheese sauce
Sauce suprême (Geflügeleinmachsauce)	suprême sauce (with chicken stock)
Sauerkirschen	morellos (morello cherries)
Sauerkraut	sauerkraut
Sauerrahmsauce	sour cream sauce
Sautierpfanne	sauté pan
schälen	to peel, to skin
Schalentiere	shellfish
Schalotte	shallot
scharf anbraten	to sear
Schaumgebäck	meringue
schaumig rühren, legieren	to cream
Schaumsauce	mousseline sauce
Schaumwein	sparkling wine
Scheiben	slices
Schellfisch	haddock
Schildkröte	turtle
Schildkrötensuppe, falsche	mock turtle soup
Schinken	ham
–, gekocht	boiled ham
–, geräuchert	smoked ham
–, roh	raw ham
Schinkenauflauf	ham soufflé
Schinkenknödel	ham dumpling
Schinkenröllchen	ham rolls
schlagen, klopfen	to beat
Schlosskartoffeln	château potatoes, castle potatoes
schmoren	to braise
Schnapper	snapper
Schnaps	brandy
Schnecke	snail
Schnecken mit Kräuterbutter	snails with herb butter
Schneckenbutter	snail butter
Schneebesen (Schaumschläger)	whisk
Schneidebrett	cutting board
schneiden	to cut
Schnepfe	snipe
schnetzeln	to shred
Schnittlauch	chives
Schnittlauchkartoffeln	chive potatoes
Schnittlauchsauce	chive sauce
Schöberln	sponge squares
Schokolade, heiß	hot chocolate
Schokoladenauflauf	chocolate soufflé
Scholle	plaice
Schopfbraten	roast best end neck of pork
Schöpfer	ladle
Schüssel	bowl
Schwarzbeeren	blueberries
Schwarzwurzel	salsify
Schweinefleisch	pork
Schweineschmalz	lard
Schweinsbraten	roast pork
Schweinsbrust	breast of pork
Schweinsfilet	fillet of pork
Schweinsgehacktes	ground / chopped / minced pork
Schweinshaxe	leg of pork
Schweinsherz	pig's heart
Schweinskarree	loin of pork
Schweinskotelett	pork chop

Vocabulary

Schweinsleber	pig's liver
Schweinsnieren	pig's kidneys
Schweinsnierenbraten	loin of pork with kidneys
Schweinsragout	pork stew, stewed pork, ragout of pork
Schweinsrippe	rib of pork
Schweinsrücken	saddle of pork
Schweinsschnitzel	escalope of pork, pork cutlet
Schweinsschopf	neck of pork
Schweinszunge	pig's tongue
schwer	heavy, full (rich) bodied
schwingend rösten	to sauté
Seezunge	sole
Sekt	sparkling wine
selchen	to smoke
Sellerie	celery
Sellerieknolle	celeriac
Semmel	roll
Semmelkloß, -knödel	white bread dumpling
Senf(-körner)	mustard (grains)
Senfbutter	mustard butter
Senfpulver	dry mustard
Senfsauce (Sauce Robert)	mustard sauce
Sherry	sherry
Sieb	colander, sieve, strainer
Siebschöpfer	skimmer
Sirup	syrup
Sodawasser	soda water, sparkling water
Sorbet	sherbet
Spagetti	spaghetti
Spanferkel	suck(l)ing pig
Spargel	asparagus
– mit Sauce hollandaise	asparagus with hollandaise sauce
–(spitzen) in Sauce vinaigrette	asparagus (tips) in vinaigrette sauce
Spargelcremesuppe	cream of asparagus
Spargelspitzen	asparagus tips
Speck	bacon
Speckkloß, -knödel	bacon dumpling
Specktörtchen	bacon tartles
Spezialitäten	specialities
Spezialsuppen	special soups
spicken	to lard
Spicknadel	larding needle (pin)
Spiegelei auf ...	fried egg on ...
Spinat	spinach
Spirituosen	spirits
Spitzsieb	conical strainer
Stachelbeeren	gooseberries
Stangensellerie	stalk celery
Steinbutt	turbot
Steinpilz	yellow boletus
steirisches Masthuhn	Styrian fattened chicken (pullet)
Stielpfanne	saucepan
Strohkartoffeln	straw potatoes
Strudel	strudel
Südwein	dessert wine, fortified wine
Sultaninen	sultanas
Suppen- / Fondtopf	stock pot
Suppen	soups
Suppenhuhn	boiling fowl
Suppennudeln	vermicelli
süß	sweet
Süßspeisen	sweets
Süßwasserfische	freshwater fish

T

Tafelspitz	boiled round of beef
Tatarensauce	tartar sauce
Taube	pigeon
T-bone-Steak	T-bone steak
Tee	tea
– mit Milch	– with milk
– mit Rum	– with rum
– mit Zitrone	– with lemon
– Natur	– plain
Teigwaren	pasta
–, italienische	Italian pasta
Teufelssauce	devil sauce
Thymian	thyme
Tiefkühler	freezer
Tintenfisch	squid / octopus / cuttlefish
Tiroler Gröstl	fried potatoes with sliced beef, pork or bacon
– Sauce (Sauce tyrolienne)	Tyrolean sauce
Tomate	tomato
Tomatencremesuppe	cream of tomato
Tomatensaft	tomato juice
Tomatensauce	tomato sauce
Tonic	tonic water
Topf	pot
Törtchen	tartlets
Torten	cakes
Tranchiergabel	carving fork
Tranchiermesser	carving knife
Trauben (blau, weiß)	grapes (blue, white)
Trichter	funnel
Tropfteig	batter (egg) drops
Trüffel	truffle
Trüffelsauce (Sauce Perigueux)	truffle sauce
Truthahn	turkey
Truthahnbrust	breast of turkey
Truthahnschnitzel	turkey fillets
Tunfisch	tunny, tuna fish
–, garniert	tunny, garnished
Tunfischcocktail	tunny (tuna fish) cocktail
Tunfischsalat	tunny salad

U

überbacken	to gratinate
umrühren	to stir
üppig	heavy, full (rich) bodied

V

Vanille	vanilla
Vanilleeis	vanilla ice cream
Vanillesauce	custard
Velouté (weiße Grundsauce)	velouté (basic white sauce)
Venusmuschel	clam
Vermouth	vermouth
verschließen, bedecken, überziehen	to cover
Vinaigrettesauce	vinaigrette sauce

(Essigkräutersauce)	
vollmundig	heavy, full (rich) bodied

W

Waage	weighing machine / scales
Wacholder(-beeren)	juniper (berries)
Wachtel	quail
Waffelkartoffeln	wafer potatoes
Waffeln	wafers, waffles
Walderdbeeren	wild strawberries
Waldorfsalat	celery salad with walnuts
Walnüsse	walnuts
warm	warm
warme Buttersaucen	warm butter sauces
– Getränke	warm beverages
– Spezialsaucen	special warm sauces
– Vorspeisen	hot appetizers
Wassermelone	water melon
weggeben	to remove
weich füllen (Torte)	to fill
Wein	wine
Weingelee	wine jelly
Weinschaum (Chaudeau)	sabayon
weiße Bohnen	white beans
– Fonds	white stocks
– Saucen	white sauces
Weißwein	white wine
Weißweinsauce	white wine sauce
(Fischeinmachsauce)	(with fish stock)
Weizen	wheat
Wels	catfish
Whisk(e)y	whisky, whiskey
Wiegemesser	chopping knife
Wild	game, venison
Wildcremesuppe	cream of venison
Wildente	wild duck
Wildfond	game stock
Wildgans	wild goose
Wildgeflügel	game birds, wild fowl
Wildhuhn	grouse
Wildkroketten	game croquettes
Wildpastete	game pâté
Wildpüreesuppe	game (purée) soup
Wildsalat	game salad
Wildschwein	wild boar
Wildschweinschinken	ham of wild boar
Wirsing	savoy cabbage
Würfelkartoffeln	diced potatoes
Würfelzucker	lump sugar
Wurst	sausage
würzen	to season, flavour
Würzmittel (Gewürze)	seasonings (spices)

Z

Zander, Schill	pike-perch
zerkleinern	to shred
zerlassen	to melt
zerlassene Butter	melted butter
zerstampfen	to mash
Zigeunersauce	gipsy sauce, zingara sauce
Zimt	cinnamon
Zitrone	lemon
Zitronenbutter	lemon butter
Zucchini, Zwergkürbisse	baby marrows, zucchini, courgettes
Zucker	sugar
Zuckermelone	cantaloup melon
Zuckersirup	molasses
zudecken	to cover
Zündholzkartoffeln	matchstick chips, matchstick potatoes
Zungensalat	tongue salad
zuputzen	to trim
zusammengeben	to combine
Zwetschke	plum
Zwiebel	onion
Zwiebelrostbraten	braised fillet of beef with onions
Zwiebelsauce (Sauce soubise)	onion sauce, soubise sauce
Zwischenrippenstück	sirloin steak

Vocabulary English – German

A

(to) add	dazugeben
aitchbone of beef	Rindsrose
alcoholic drinks (liquors)	alkoholische Getränke (geistige)
allspice, pimento	Neugewürz, Piment
almonds	Mandeln
anchovy	Sardelle
anchovy butter	Sardellenbutter
anchovy sauce	Sardellensauce
aniseed	Anis
apéritif	Aperitif
apple	Apfel
apple fritters	gebackene Apfelspalten
apple juice	Apfelsaft
apple sauce	Apfelsauce
apple strudel	Apfelstrudel
apricot	Aprikose
apricot soufflé	Aprikosenauflauf
artichoke	Artischocke
stuffed artichokes	gefüllte Artischocken
artichoke bottoms	Artischockenböden
– with ham	– mit Schinken
artichoke hearts	Artischockenherzen
asparagus	Spargel
– with hollandaise sauce	– mit Sauce hollandaise
asparagus omelette	Omelette mit Spargel
asparagus tips	Spargelspitzen
asparagus (tips) in vinaigrette sauce	Spargel(-spitzen) in Sauce vinaigrette
assorted cold meat (cuts)	Aufschnitt, kalte Platte
assorted raw vegetables (crudities)	Rohkost(platte)
aubergine	Eierfrucht, Aubergine
Aurore sauce	Aurorasauce
Austrian	österreichisch(e)
Austrian doughnuts	Krapfen

B

English	German
baby marrows, zucchini, courgettes	Zucchini, Zwergkürbisse
bacon	Speck
bacon dumpling	Speckknödel/-kloß
bacon tartles	Specktörtchen
(to) bake	backen
baked potatoes	Folienkartoffeln
baking dishes	Backgeschirr
banana	Banane
banana fritters	gebackene Bananen
barley	Gerste
barley soup	Gerstensuppe
basic brown sauce	Sauce demi-glace
basil	Basilikum
(to) baste	aufgießen (zB den Braten)
batter (egg) drops	Tropfteig
Bavarian cream	Bayerische Creme
bay (leaf)	Lorbeer(-blatt)
bean soup	Bohnensuppe
beans	Bohnen
béarnaise sauce	Sauce béarnaise
(to) beat	schlagen, klopfen
(to) beat egg whites	Eischnee schlagen
Béchamel sauce (basic white sauce)	Béchamelsauce (weiße Grundsauce)
beef	Rindfleisch
beef carbonade	Rindskarbonade
beef salad	Rindfleischsalat
beef stew, stewed beef, ragout of beef	Rindsragout
beef tea, warm or cold	doppelte Kraftsuppe
beer	Bier
draught beer	– vom Fass
beetroot (Br.)	Rote Rübe
before-dinner drink	Aperitif
berries	Beeren
beverages	Getränke
biscuits (Br.)	Kekse
bisque of crayfish	Krebssuppe
black pudding	Blutwurst
blackberries	Brombeeren
(to) blend	mischen
blini, buckwheat pancake	Blini, Buchweizenpfannkuchen
bloater	Bückling
blueberries	Heidelbeeren, Blaubeeren
boiled ham	gekochter Schinken
boiled potatoes	Salzkartoffeln
boiled ribs of beef	Beinfleisch, Rippenfleisch
boiled rice	Reis, gekocht
boiled round of beef	Tafelspitz
boiling fowl	Suppenhuhn
(to) bone	auslösen, entgräten
bordelaise sauce	Sauce bordelaise
bottled beer	Flaschenbier
bottled wine	Flaschenwein
bouillon potatoes	Bouillonkartoffeln
bowl	Schüssel
brain (purré) soup	Hirnpüreesuppe
(to) braise	schmoren, im Ganzen dünsten
braised beef	Rinderschmor(saft)braten, Rindsschmorbraten
braised fillet of beef with onions	Zwiebelrostbraten
(braised) rolled stuffed fillet of beef,	Rinderroulade
braised stuffed green peppers	Paprika, gefüllt
brambleberries	Brombeeren
brandy	Branntwein, Schnaps
brawn	Presskopf
(to) bread	panieren
bread (brown, white)	Brot (schwarzes, weißes)
bread sauce	Brotsauce
(bread) crumbs	Brösel
breast of chicken	Hühnerbrust
breast of pork	Schweinsbrust
breast of turkey	Truthahnbrust
breast of veal	Kalbsbrust
roast stuffed breast of veal	–, gefüllt

Appendix

broccoli	Brokkoli, Spargelkohl	chicken, spring chicken	Huhn, Junghuhn
– with bread crumbs and butter	– mit Butterbröseln	cold roast chicken	–, gebraten
brook trout	Bachforelle	chicken broth	Hühnerbrühe
broth, beef broth	Kraftbrühe	chicken croquettes	Geflügelkroketten
(to) brown	bräunen	chicken curry	Hühnercurry
brown (black) butter	braune Butter	chicken galantine	Hühnergalantine
brown rice	Reis, braun	chicken liver	Hühnerleber
brown sauces	braune Saucen	chicken liver omelette	Omelett mit Hühnerleber
brown soup	Einbrennsuppe	chicken pâté	Hühnerpastete
brown stocks	braune Fonds	chicken salad	Geflügelsalat
brown sugar	Rohzucker	chicken soufflé	Geflügelauflauf
Brussels sprouts	Rosenkohl	chicken stew	Geflügelragout
Burgundy (red, white)	Burgunder (rot, weiß)	chicken stock	Geflügelfond
butter	Butter	chicken wings	Hühnerflügel
		chicory	Brüsseler Spitzen, Chicorée
		chili, chilli	Chili, Chilli
C		chips (Br.)	Pommes frites, Kartoffelstäbchen
cakes	Kuchen, Torten	chives	Schnittlauch
calf's brains	Kalbshirn	chive potatoes	Schnittlauchkartoffeln
calf's head	Kalbskopf	chive sauce	Schnittlauchsauce
calf's heart	Kalbsherz	chocolate soufflé	Schokoladenauflauf
calf's kidneys	Kalbsnieren	(to) chop	hacken
calf's liver	Kalbsleber	chopped (minced, ground) pork	Schweinsgehacktes
calf's sweetbread	Kalbsbries		
calf's tongue	Kalbszunge	chopping block	Hackstock
camomile tea	Kamillentee	chopping knife	Hackmesser, Wiegemesser
canapés	Canapés, belegte Brötchen	Choron sauce	Choronsauce
cantaloup melon	Zuckermelone	choux pastry	Brandteig
capers	Kapern	chutney	Gewürzfruchtpaste
caper sauce	Kapernsauce	cinnamon	Zimt
capon	Kapaun	clam	Venusmuschel
caramel sugar	Karamellzucker	clarified butter	geklärte Butter
caraway seed	Kümmel	clear soup	klare Suppe
carp	Karpfen	clear soup (broth) with ...	– mit ...
carrot	Möhre, gelbe Rübe	cleaver	Hackbeil
carrot juice	Möhrensaft	clove	Nelke, Gewürznelke
carving fork	Tranchiergabel	club sandwich	Clubsandwich
carving knife	Tranchiermesser	cocktail	Cocktail
cashew nuts	Cashewnüsse	cocoa	Kakao
casserole	Kasserolle	coconuts	Kokosnüsse
castor sugar	Kristallzucker	cod, codling, codfish	Dorsch, Kabeljau
catfish	Wels	coffee	Kaffee
cauliflower	Blumenkohl	coffee with milk	– mit Milch
deep-fried breaded cauliflower	–, gebacken	coffee with cream	– mit Sahne
		black coffee	–, schwarz
caviar	Kaviar	cognac	Cognac
cayenne (pepper)	Cayenne(-pfeffer)	colander	Sieb
celeriac	Sellerieknolle	cold	kalt
celery	Sellerie	cold appetizers (starters)	kalte Vorspeisen
celery salad with walnuts	Waldorfsalat	cold puddings	Puddings, kalt
cereals	Getreide	cold rice pudding	Reispudding
chamois	Gämse	cold roast meat	Braten, kalter
champagne	Champagner	cold sauces	kalte Saucen
chanterelles	Eierschwammerl, Pfifferling	(to) combine	zusammengeben, mischen
char	Saibling	conical strainer	Spitzsieb
château potatoes	Schlosskartoffeln	consommé, bouillon	Consommé, Bouillon
cheese	Käse	cook's knife	großes Messer, Küchenmesser, Kochmesser
cheese dumpling	Käseknödel		
cheese salad	Käsesalat	cookies (Am.)	Kekse
cheese soufflé	Käseauflauf	cooking utensils	Küchengeräte
cheese tartlets	Käsetörtchen	corn on cob	Maiskolben
chef's salad	Chefsalat	corn, sweet corn	Mais
cherry (cherries)	Kirsche(n)	corned beef	Rindfleisch, gepökelt
chervil	Kerbelkraut	cornflakes	Cornflakes
chestnut	Kastanie		

country omelette (bacon and potatoes)	Bauernomelett (Speck und Kartoffeln)	demi-glace sauce	Sauce demi-glace
courgettes	Zucchini, Zwergkürbisse	desserts	Desserts
(to) cover	zudecken, bedecken, verschließen	dessert pastry	Dessertgebäck
		dessert wine, fortified wine	Südwein
crab	Krabbe	devil sauce	Teufelssauce
cranberries	Preiselbeeren	(to) dice	in Würfel schneiden
cranberry sauce	Preiselbeerensauce	diced potatoes	Würfelkartoffeln
crawfish	Languste	dill	Dillkraut
crayfish	Krebs	dorado	Goldbarsch
crayfish (crab) butter	Krebsbutter	double fillet steak	Chateaubriand
(to) cream	schaumig rühren, legieren	double sirloin steak	doppeltes Zwischenrippen- stück
creams	Cremen		
cream of asparagus	Spargelcremesuppe	double tenderloin steak	doppelte Lendenschnitte
cream of cauliflower	Blumenkohlcremesuppe	(to) drain	abseihen, trocknen
cream of chicken	Geflügel-(Hühner-) Cremesuppe	(to) dress	anrichten
		dried hering	getrockneter Hering
cream of leek	Lauchcremesuppe	dry	herb, trocken
cream of mushroom	Champignon- (Pilz-)Cremesuppe	dry mustard	Senfpulver
		duchess potatoes	Duchesse- (Herzogin-)Kartoffeln
cream of pea	Erbsencremesuppe		
cream of potato	Kartoffelcremesuppe	duck	Ente
cream of tomato	Tomatencremesuppe	dumplings	Knödel, Klöße
cream of vegetable	Gemüsecremesuppe	(to) dust	bestäuben
cream of venison	Wildcremesuppe	Dutch sauce	Holländische Sauce, Sauce hollandaise
cream sauce	Rahmsauce		
cream soups, cream of … (soup)	Cremesuppen		

E

cream strudel	Rahmstrudel	eel	Aal
creamed cakes	Rührteigkuchen	eel in jelly (aspic)	– in Aspik
creamed horseradish	Sahnemeerrettich	smoked eel	–, geräuchert
creamed potatoes	Rahmkartoffeln	eggs	Eier
crescent, croissant	Kipferl	poached egg in jelly	– in Aspik
cress	Kresse	eggs in mayonnaise	– in Mayonnaise
crisps	Kartoffelscheiben	stuffed eggs	–, gefüllt
croquettes	Kroketten	egg croquettes	Eierkroketten
crustaceans	Krustentiere	egg-plant	Eierfrucht, Aubergine
(to) cube	in Würfel schneiden	elbow macaroni	Hörnchen
cucumber	Gurke	endive	Endivie
Cumberland sauce	Cumberlandsauce	escalope of deer, fillet of deer	Hirschschnitzel
cumin	Kümmel		
curd cheese (white cheese) dumplings	Quarkknödel	escalope of pork, pork cutlet	Schweinsschnitzel
		escalope of veal, veal cutlet	Kalbsschnitzel
curd cheese (white cheese) strudel	Quarkstrudel	deep-fried breaded escalope of veal (veal cutlet)	–, Wiener Art
currants (red, black)	Johannisbeeren (rot, schwarz)		
		espresso coffee	Espresso
currant juice	Johannisbeersaft		
curry (powder)	Curry(-pulver)		

F

curry rice	Curryreis		
curry sauce	Currysauce	fattened chicken	Masthuhn
custard	Vanillesauce	fennel	Fenchel
(to) cut	schneiden	gratinated fennel	–, überbacken
cutting board	Schneidebrett	figs	Feigen
cuttlefish	Tintenfisch	(to) fill	füllen
		fillet of beef, slice of beef, escalope of beef	Rinderschnitzel

D

		fillet of beef, tenderloin	Filet, Lungenbraten
dark beer	dunkles Bier	fillet of pork	Schweinsfilet
dates	Datteln	fillet of veal	Kalbsfilet, Kalbslende
deep-fried breaded mushrooms	Champignons, gebacken	fillet of venison	Rehschnitzel
		fillet steak, prime steak	Filetsteak, Lendenschnitte
deer	Hirsch	filtered coffee	Filterkaffee
deer chop	Hirschkotelett	fire-proof	feuerfest
deer steak	Hirschsteak	fish	Fisch(e)
deer stew, ragout of deer	Hirschragout		

Appendix

fish croquettes	Fischkroketten	goose	Gans
fish dish	Fischgeschirr	goose liver	Gänseleber
fish soup (French style)	Bouillabaisse	goose liver pâté	Gänseleberpastete
fish stock	Fischfond	gooseberries	Stachelbeeren
fisher sauce	Fischersauce (à la pêcheur)	grapefruit	Grapefruit, Pampelmuse
flan	Obsttorte	iced (chilled) grapefruit	–, geeist
flanring	Obsttortenring	stuffed grapefruit	–, gefüllt
(to) flavour	würzen	grapefruit cocktail	Grapefruitcocktail
flour	Mehl	grapes (blue, white)	Trauben (blau, weiß)
(to) fold in	darunterziehen (zB Eischnee unter die Masse ziehen)	(to) grate	reiben (mit einem Reibeisen)
fork	Gabel	grater	Reibeisen
fowl	Geflügel	gratinate	gratinieren, überbacken
Foyot sauce	Foyotsauce	gravy	Bratensaft
freezer	Tiefkühler	(to) grease	einfetten
French fried potatoes (Am.)	Pommes frites, Kartoffelstäbchen	green, French, string beans	grüne Bohnen
		green sauce	grüne Sauce (Sauce verte)
French onion soup	Französische Zwiebelsuppe	greengage	Reneklode
fresh fruit	frisches Obst	(to) grind	klein hacken
freshwater fish	Süßwasserfische	ground pepper	gemahlener Pfeffer
fried batter drops	Backerbsen	grouse	Wildhuhn
fried egg on ...	Spiegelei auf ...	guinea fowl	Perlhuhn
fried pork sausage with sauerkraut	Bratwurst mit Sauerkraut		
fried potatoes with sliced beef, pork or bacon	Tiroler Gröstl	**H**	
frog's legs	Froschschenkel	haddock	Schellfisch
from the cask	offen (Wein)	halibut	Heilbutt
fruits	Früchte, Obst	ham	Schinken
fruits in batter	Früchte in Backteig	boiled ham	–, gekocht
fruit cocktails	Früchtecocktails	smoked ham	–, geräuchert
fruit dumplings	Obstknödel, -klöße	raw ham	–, roh
fruit jellies	Früchtegelees	ham dumpling	Schinkenknödel, -kloß
fruit juices	Fruchtsäfte	ham of wild boar	Wildschweinschinken
fruit knife	Obstmesser	ham rolls	Schinkenröllchen
fruit pies	Obstpasteten	ham soufflé	Schinkenauflauf
fruit salads	Früchtesalate	hare	Hase
(to) fry (deep-fry)	backen	hashed brown potatoes	Röstkartoffeln
fryer	Friteuse	hazelnut ice cream	Haselnusseis
frying pan	Bratpfanne	hazelnuts	Haselnüsse
full (rich) bodied	schwer, üppig, vollmundig (Wein)	headcheese	Presskopf
		(to) heat	erhitzen
funnel	Trichter	heat-proof	hitzebeständig
		heavy	schwer, üppig, vollmundig (Wein)
G		herb butter	Kräuterbutter
galettes (potato)	Kartoffelfladen, Kartoffellaibchen	herbs	Kräuter
game	Wild	herring salad	Heringssalat
game (purée) soup	Wildpüreesuppe	herring	Hering
game birds	Wildgeflügel, Federwild	smoked herring	–, geräuchert
game croquettes	Wildkroketten	marinated herring	–, mariniert
game pâté	Wildpastete	hollandaise sauce	Holländische Sauce, Sauce hollandaise
game salad	Wildsalat	honey dew melon	Honigmelone
game stock	Wildfond	horseradish	Meerrettich
garlic	Knoblauch	horseradish butter	Meerrettichbutter
garlic (clove)	Knoblauch(-zehe)	horseradish sauce	Meerrettichsauce
garlic butter	Knoblauchbutter	hot appetizers	warme Vorspeisen
(to) garnish	garnieren	hot chocolate	Schokolade, heiß
German sauce (with veal stock)	Deutsche Sauce (Sauce allemande)	hunter sauce	Jägersauce (Sauce chasseur)
gherkins (Br.)	Essiggurken		
giblets of chicken	Geflügelklein	**I**	
ginger	Ingwer	ice creams	Eiscremen
gipsy sauce	Zigeunersauce	ice omelette, baked Alaska	Eisomelett (Omelette surprise)

in carafe	offen (Wein)		
Italian pasta	italienische Teigwaren		
Italian sauce	Italienische Sauce		
Italian vegetable soup	Minestrone		

J

jam	Konfitüre
jellies	Gelees
juniper (berries)	Wacholder(-beeren)

K

kettle	Kochkessel
kipper (kippered herring)	Salzhering
kitchen-range	Herd
kiwi	Kiwi
knife, knives	Messer
kohlrabi	Kohlrabi

L

ladle	Schöpfer
lager (beer)	Lagerbier
lamb	Hammel-, Lamm-, Schaffleisch
(to) lard	spicken
lard	Schweineschmalz
larding needle (pin)	Spicknadel
lasagne	Lasagne
leek	Lauch, Porree
leg of chicken	Hühnerkeule
leg of deer	Hirschkeule, Hirschschlegel
leg of hare	Hasenkeule
leg of pork	Schweinshaxe
leg of veal	Kalbsstelze
roast leg of veal	–, gebraten
lemon	Zitrone
lemon butter	Zitronenbutter
lemon sole	Rotzunge
lemonade	Limonade
lentil (purée) soup	Linsenpüreesuppe
lentils	Linsen
lettuce	Kopfsalat
lid	Deckel
light (pale) beer	helles Bier
lime	Limone
liqueur	Likör
liver dumpling	Leberknödel, -kloß
lobster	Hummer
stuffed lobster	–, gefüllt
lobster butter	Hummerbutter
lobster cocktail	Hummercocktail
lobster mayonnaise	Hummermayonnaise
lobster salad	Hummersalat
lobster sauce	Hummersauce
loin of pork	Schweinskarree
loin of veal	Kalbskarree
long grain rice	Langkornreis
lump sugar	Würfelzucker

M

macaroni	Makkaroni
mackerel	Makrele
smoked mackerel	–, geräuchert
Madeira	Madeira
Madeira sauce	Madeirasauce
maltese sauce	Malteser Sauce
mandarin, tangerine	Mandarine
(to) marinate	marinieren
marjoram	Majoran
marmalade	Orangenmarmelade
marrow dumpling	Markknödel, -kloß
Marsala	Marsala
mash	zerstampfen, pürieren
mashed potatoes	Kartoffelpüree
matchstick chips, matchstick potatoes	Zündholzkartoffeln
mayonnaise (sauce)	Mayonnaisesauce
measuring jug	Messbecher
meat dishes	Fleischgerichte
meat knife	Fleischmesser
meat loaf	Hackbraten
meat mincer / grinder	Fleischwolf
melon	Melone
iced (chilled) melon	–, geeist
melon cocktail	Melonencocktail
melon salad	Melonensalat
(to) melt	zerlassen
melted butter	zerlassene Butter
meringue	Schaumgebäck
metal spatula	Metallspatel, -palette
microwave oven	Mikrowellenherd
mild, mellow	mild
milk	Milch
milk sauce	Béchamelsauce
milt on toast	Milzschnitten
(to) mince	klein hacken
mineral water	Mineralwasser
mint	Minze
mint sauce	Minzsauce
mint tea	Pfefferminztee
(to) mix	mischen
mixer	Mixer
mixing bowl	Rührschüssel
mock turtle soup	Schildkrötensuppe, falsche
molasses	Zuckersirup
morel	Morchel
morel tartlets	Morcheltörtchen
morellos (morello cherries)	Weichseln, Sauerkirschen
Mornay sauce, cheese sauce	Mornaysauce
mousse	Mousse
mousseline sauce	Schaumsauce
muffin	Muffin
mulled wine	Glühwein
mushroom omelette	Omelett mit Champignons
mushroom sauce	Champignonsauce
mussel	Miesmuschel
gratinated mussels	–, überbacken
mussel salad	Miesmuschelsalat
mustard (grains)	Senf(-körner)
mustard butter	Senfbutter
mustard sauce	Senfsauce (Sauce Robert)
mutton	Hammel-, Lamm-, Schaffleisch
roast mutton (lamb)	– Braten

Appendix

English	German
mutton breast	– Brust
rack of mutton, loin of mutton	– Karree
leg of mutton (lamb)	– Keule
mutton (lamb) chop	– Kotelett
mutton (lamb) stew	– Ragout
mutton rib (chop)	– Rippenstück
saddle of mutton	– Rücken
shoulder of mutton	– Schulter

N

English	German
neck of pork	Schweinsschopf
nectar	Nektar
new potatoes	neue Kartoffeln
non-alcoholic drinks	alkoholfreie Getränke
noodles	Nudeln
Norwegian sauce	Norweger Sauce
nut (almond) butter	Nuss-(Mandel-)Butter
nut (almond) pudding	Nuss-(Mandel-)Pudding
nutmeg	Muskatnuss
nuts	Nüsse

O

English	German
oat	Hafer
oat flakes, rolled oats	Haferflocken
oat meal	Haferbrei
oatmeal soup	Haferflockensuppe
octopus	Tintenfisch
oil	Öl
olive	Olive
omelette	Omelett
onion sauce, soubise sauce	Zwiebelsauce (Sauce soubise)
onion	Zwiebel
open sandwich	belegtes Brot
orange juice	Orangensaft
orange squash	–, frisch gepresst
orange	Orange
orangeade	Orangenlimonade
oregano	Oregano
oven	Backofen
oven-proof	feuerfest
ox-tongue	Ochsenzunge
smoked ox-tongue	–, geräuchert
ox-muzzle salad	Ochsenmaulsalat
oxtail	Ochsenschwanz
oxtail soup	Ochsenschwanzsuppe, gebunden
clear oxtail soup	–, klare
oyster	Auster
raw oysters	–, roh
oyster knife	Austernmesser
oyster sauce	Austernsauce

P

English	German
pan	Pfanne
pancakes	Pfannkuchen, Eierkuchen
pan-fried potatoes	Bratkartoffeln
(to) pan-fry	in der Pfanne braten
paprika	Paprika (Gewürz)
parfait	Halbgefrorenes, Parfait
parisienne potatoes	Pariser Kartoffeln
parsley	Petersilie
parsley potatoes	Petersilienkartoffeln
parsley root	Petersilwurzel
parsnip	Pastinak
partridge	Rebhuhn
pasta	Teigwaren
pastry	Backwerk, Gebäck
patties filled with fine (veal, chicken, game, ham ...) stews	Blätterteigpastetchen mit feinen (Kalbs-, Hühner-, Wild-, Schinken- ...) Ragouts
peach	Pfirsich
peanut butter	Erdnussbutter
peanuts	Erdnüsse
pear	Birne
peas (fresh, dried, green)	Erbsen (frische, getrocknete, grüne)
pecan nuts	Pekannüsse
(to) peel	schälen
pepper (green, red)	Paprikaschote (grüne, rote)
pepper sauce	Pfeffersauce
pepper(corns)	Pfeffer(-körner)
pepper, whole, crushed	Pfeffer, ganz, geschrotet
peppermint	Pfefferminze
per glass, in carafe, from the cask	offen (Wein)
perch	Barsch
petits fours	Petits fours
pheasant	Fasan
pickles (Am.)	Essiggurken
pies	Pasteten
pig's heart	Schweinsherz
pig's kidneys	Schweinsnieren
pig's liver	Schweinsleber
pig's tongue	Schweinszunge
pigeon	Taube
pike	Hecht
pike-perch	Zander, Schill
pineapple	Ananas
pineapple fritters	–, gebacken
pizza	Pizza
(to) place	legen, geben
plaice	Scholle
plain potatoes	Salzkartoffeln
plate	Platte, Teller
plum	Pflaume
poached egg with ...	pochiertes Ei mit ...
polenta	Polenta, Sterz
poppy seed	Mohn
pork	Schweinefleisch
pork chop	Schweinskotelett
pork stew, stewed pork, ragout of pork	Schweinsragout
porridge	Haferbrei
port(wine)	Portwein
porterhouse steak	Porterhouse-Steak
pot	Topf
potatoes	Kartoffeln (Erdäpfel)
potato balls	Kartoffelbällchen
potato croquettes	Kartoffelkroketten
potato dishes	Kartoffel-(Erdäpfel-)Gerichte
potato dumpling	Kartoffelknödel, -kloß
potato fritters	Kartoffelpuffer
potato noodles	Kartoffelnudeln
poultry	Geflügel

poultry liver	Geflügelleber	roast pork	Schweinsbraten
(to) powder	bestäuben	roast veal	Kalbsbraten
powdered sugar	Puderzucker	roasting pan	Bratenpfanne
prawn	Garnele, Krevette	roe, roebuck (male)	Reh
prawn sauce	Garnelensauce	roll	Brötchen, Semmel
prime rib of beef	Hochrippe	rolled sponge cake, Swiss roll	Biskuitroulade
profiteroles	Brandteigkrapfen		
provençale sauce	Provenzalische Sauce	rolled stuffed veal cutlet	Kalbsroulade
prune	Dörrpflaume	rosé wine	Roséwein
puff pastry	Blätterteig	rosemary	Rosmarin
puffed rice	Knusperreis, Müslireis	(to) rub	einreiben
pullet	Masthuhn	rum	Rum
pumpernickel	Pumpernickel	rump steak	Rumpsteak
pumpkin	Kürbis	rye	Roggen
pumpkin seed oil	Kürbiskernöl	rye bread	Roggenbrot
purée soups	Püreesuppen		

Q

quail	Wachtel
quarter of lamb	Lammviertel

R

rabbit	Kaninchen		
radish (white, black)	Rettich (weiß, schwarz)		

S

		sabayon	Weinschaum (Chaudeau)
		saddle of deer	Hirschrücken
		saddle of hare	Hasenrücken
		saddle of pork	Schweinsrücken
		saddle of veal	Kalbsrücken
		saffron rice	Safranreis
		sage	Salbei
ragout of veal	Kalbsragout	salmon	Lachs
rainbow trout	Regenbogenforelle	smoked salmon	–, geräuchert
raisins	Rosinen	marinated salmon	–, mariniert
raspberries	Himbeeren	salmon pâté	Lachspastete
raspberry juice	Himbeersaft	salmon trout	Lachsforelle
ravigote sauce (herb sauce)	Kräutersauce (Sauce ravigote)	salsify	Schwarzwurzel
		salt	Salz
ravioli	Ravioli	salted (pickled) pork	Pökelfleisch, Surfleisch
raw ham	roher Schinken	salt-water fish	Salzwasserfische
red beans	rote Bohnen	sardine	Sardine
red beet (Am.)	Rote Rübe	sardine in oil	–, in Öl
red Bordeaux, claret	Bordeauxwein, rot	saucepan	Stielpfanne
white Bordeaux	–, weiß	sauces	Saucen
red cabbage	Blau-(Rot-)Kraut	sauerkraut	Sauerkraut
red radish	Radieschen	sausage	Wurst
red wine	Rotwein	(to) sauté	schwingend rösten
(to) reduce	reduzieren	sauté pan	Sautierpfanne
refrigerator (fridge)	Kühlschrank	savoury	Bohnenkraut
remoulade sauce	Remouladensauce	savoury butters	Buttermischungen
(to) remove	weggeben, entfernen	savoy cabbage	Kohl, Wirsing
Rhine wine, hock	Rheinwein	(to) scale	entschuppen
rhubarb	Rhabarber	scallop	Kammmuschel
rib of pork	Schweinsrippe	scrambled egg	Rührei
ribbon noodles	Bandnudeln	sea fish	Salzwasserfische
rice	Reis	seafood salad	Meeresfrüchtesalat
rice crispies	Knusperreis, Müslireis	(to) sear	scharf anbraten
rice soufflé	Reisauflauf	(to) season	würzen
rice with peas	Risipisi	seasonal fruits	Früchte der Saison
risotto (Italian rice dish)	Risotto	seasonings (spices)	Würzmittel (Gewürze)
(to) roast	im Backofen braten	semi-sweet	halbsüß
roast beef	Rinderbraten, Roastbeef	semolina	Grieß
cold roast beef	–, kalt	semolina dumpling	Grießknödel, Grießnockerl
roast loin of veal with kidneys	Kalbsnierenbraten		
		semolina pudding	Grießpudding
roast rolled loin of veal with kidneys	–, gerollt	shallot	Schalotte
		shellfish	Schalentiere
		sherbet	Sorbet
roast loin of pork with kidneys	Schweinsnierenbraten	sherry	Sherry
		short cakes	Mürbteigkuchen
		short crust pastry	Mürbteig
roast neck of pork	Schopfbraten	short grain rice	Perlreis

Appendix

English	German
shoulder of deer	Hirschschulter
shoulder of veal	Kalbsschulter
(to) shred	schnetzeln, zerkleinern
shredded liver	Leberreis
shrimp (prawn) cocktail	Garnelencocktail
shrimp	Garnele, Krevette
sieve	Sieb
(to) simmer	langsam kochen
sirloin	Beiried, flaches Roastbeef
sirloin steak	Zwischenrippenstück
skewer	Fleischspieß(chen)
(to) skim	abschäumen
skim milk	Magermilch
skimmer	Siebschöpfer
(to) skin	häuten, schälen
(to) slice	in Scheiben, (Streifen) schneiden
sliced pancakes	Frittaten
slices	Schnitten
(to) smoke	räuchern, selchen
smoked bacon	geräucherter Speck
smoked breast of goose	Gänsebrust, geräuchert
smoked ham	geräucherter Schinken
smoked hering	geräucherter Hering
smoked pork	Geselchtes
smoked pork and sausage with sauerkraut and bread dumpling	Bauernschmaus
snail	Schnecke
snail butter	Schneckenbutter
snails with herb butter	Schnecken mit Kräuterbutter
snapper	Schnapper
snipe	Schnepfe
(to) soak	einweichen
soda water	Sodawasser
sole	Seezunge
soufflé potatoes	Auflaufkartoffeln
soufflés	Aufläufe
soups	Suppen
sour cream sauce	Sauerrahmsauce
spaghetti	Spagetti
sparkling water	Sodawasser
sparkling wine	Schaumwein, Sekt
special cold sauces	kalte Spezialsaucen
special soups	Spezialsuppen
special warm sauces	warme Spezialsaucen
specialities	Spezialitäten
spinach	Spinat
spinach omelette	Omelett mit Spinat
spiny lobster	Languste
spirits	Spirituosen
spit	Bratspieß
sponge cakes	Biskuittorten
sponge squares	Schöberln
spoon	Löffel
spring vegetables	Frühgemüse
(to) sprinkle	bestreuen
squid	Tintenfisch
stalk celery	Stangensellerie
(to) steam	dämpfen
steamed chocolate pudding	Mohr im Hemd
steamed potatoes	Dampfkartoffeln
steamed rice	Reis, gedünstet
(to) stew	dünsten (in kleinen Stücken)
stewed beef in paprika sauce	Rindsgulasch
stewed beef or veal in paprika sauce	Gulasch (Rinds-, Kalbsgulasch)
stewed calf's lights	Kalbsbeuschel
stewed fruit, compote	Früchtekompott
stewed veal	Kalbsragout
(to) stir	umrühren
stock pot	Suppen- / Fondtopf
stock	Fleischfond
stove	Herd
(to) strain	passieren, filtern
strainer	Passiermaschine, Sieb, Filter
straw potatoes	Strohkartoffeln
strawberries	Erdbeeren
strawberry ice cream	Erdbeereis
strudel	Strudel
(to) stuff	fest füllen
stuffed egg, Russian style	russische Eier
stuffed eggplant, (aubergine)	Auberginen, gefüllt
stuffed potatoes	gefüllte Kartoffeln
Styrian fattened chicken (pullet)	steirisches Masthuhn
suck(l)ing pig	Spanferkel
sugar	Zucker
sultanas	Sultaninen
suprême sauce (with chicken stock)	Sauce suprême (Geflügeleinmachsauce)
sweet	süß
sweetrolls	Golatschen
sweets	Süßspeisen
syrup	Sirup

T

English	German
tarragon	Estragon
tarragon butter	Estragonbutter
tarragon sauce	Estragonsauce
tartar sauce	Tatarensauce
tartar steak, steak tartare	Beefsteak tatare
tartlets	Törtchen
tarts	belegte Kuchen (Torten)
T-bone steak	T-bone-Steak
tea	Tee
– with milk	– mit Milch
– with rum	– mit Rum
– with lemon	– mit Zitrone
– plain	– Natur
thick soups	gebundene Suppen
(to) thicken	binden (zB mit Mehl oder Stärke)
thyme	Thymian
tinned beer	Dosenbier
tomato	Tomate
tomato juice	Tomatensaft
tomato sauce	Tomatensauce
tongue salad	Zungensalat
tonic water	Tonic
topside of veal	Kalbsnuss
tournedos	kleines Filetsteak
(to) trim	zuputzen, parieren
trout	Forelle
trout in jelly	– in Aspik
smoked trout	–, geräuchert

Vocabulary

truffle	Trüffel	walnuts	Walnüsse
truffle sauce	Trüffelsauce (Sauce Perigueux)	warm	warm
tunny, tuna fish	Tunfisch	warm beverages	warme Getränke
tunny, garnished	–, garniert	warm butter sauces	warme Buttersaucen
tunny (tuna fish) cocktail	Tunfischcocktail	warm puddings	Puddings, warm
tunny salad	Tunfischsalat	water melon	Wassermelone
turbot	Steinbutt	watercress	Brunnenkresse
turkey	Truthahn	weighing machine / scales	Waage
turkey fillets	Truthahnschnitzel	wheat	Weizen
turtle	Schildkröte	(to) whip	aufschlagen
Tyrolean sauce	Tiroler Sauce (Sauce tyrolienne)	whisk	Schneebesen (Schaumschläger)
		whisky, whiskey	Whisk(e)y
V		white beans	weiße Bohnen
		white bread dumpling	Semmelknödel, -kloß
vanilla	Vanille	white cabbage	Kraut, Weißkraut
vanilla ice cream	Vanilleeis	white lamb stew	Lammeingemachtes
veal	Kalbfleisch	white rice	Reis, weiß
veal chop	Kalbskotelett	white sauces	weiße Saucen
veal medallions	Kalbsmedaillons	white stocks	weiße Fonds
veal (purée) soup	Kalbspüreesuppe	white wine sauce (with fish stock)	Weißweinsauce (Fischeinmachsauce)
veal steak	Kalbssteak	white wine	Weißwein
veal stew in paprika sauce	Kalbsgulasch	wild boar	Wildschwein
veal stew, stewed veal, ragout of veal	Kalbsragout	wild duck	Wildente
		wild fowl	Wildgeflügel, Federwild
veal stock	Kalbsfond	wild garlic	Bärlauch
vegetables	Gemüse	wild goose	Wildgans
vegetable juices	Gemüsesäfte	wild rice	Reis, wild
vegetable knife	Gemüsemesser	wild strawberries	Walderdbeeren
vegetable peeler	Gemüseschäler	wine	Wein
vegetable stock	Gemüsefond	wine jelly	Weingelee
vegetable strips	Gemüsestreifen	(to) wipe	abwischen
velouté (basic white sauce)	Velouté (weiße Grundsauce)	(wooden) spoon	Kochlöffel
venison	Hirschfleisch, Rehfleisch, Rotwildfleisch	**Y**	
vermicelli	Suppennudeln	yeast cakes	Hefekuchen
vermouth	Vermouth	yeast dumplings	Hefeknödel, -kloß
vinaigrette sauce	Vinaigrettesauce (Essigkräutersauce)	yeast pastry	Hefeteig
		yellow boletus	Steinpilz
vinegar	Essig	young wild boar	Frischling
		young, new wine	Heuriger
W			
		Z	
wafer potatoes	Waffelkartoffeln, Gitterkartoffeln	zingara sauce	Zigeunersauce
wafers, waffles	Waffeln	zucchini	Zucchini, Zwergkürbisse

Books Consulted

Adamson, Donald,
International Hotel English,
Prentice Hall International, 1989

Bacardi – Martini "Cocktails",
Editrice Eraclea Srl, Mailand 1998

Berry Mary,
Family Recipes,
Mac Donald & Co., London, 1984

Binham, Lampola, Murray,
Hotel English,
Pergamon Press, Oxford, 1988

Binham, Lampola, Murray,
Restaurant English,
Pergamon Press, Oxford, 1988

Breitsprecher, Roland; Terrell, Peter; Schnorr Veronika (Hrsg.),
PONS Wörterbuch für Schule und Studium,
Ernst Klett Verlag, 2001

Check in Vienna Airport Magazine,
Manstein Zeitschriftenverlag GmbH, Wien 2001

Enjoy Vienna – Willkommen in Wien,
Carl Gerald's Sohn Verlagsbuchhandlung, Wien 2001

Entertaining with good housekeeping,
Treasure Press, London WI, 1986

Fodor's 91, Austria,
Fodor's Travel Publications, Inc., New York

Harding, Henderson, High Season, English for the Hotel and Tourist Industry, Oxford University Press, 1994

Harkess, Shiona; Wherly, Michael,
You're Welcome! English for hotel reception,
Edward ARNOLD Ltd, London 1984

Horst Scharfenberg,
Die Küchen Amerikas,
Walter Hädecke Verlag, D-7252 Weil an der Stadt 1990

Hutchinson Tom,
Project English 3,
Oxford University Press, 1987

Jones, Leo; Alexander, Richard,
New International Business English: Communication Skills in English for Business Purposes,
Cambridge University Press, Student edition, Cambridge 1996

Keane Leila,
International Restaurant English,
Prentice Hall International, UK Ltd., 1990

Kinton, Roland; Ceserani, Victor; Foskett, David:
The Theory of Catering,
7. Auflage, Hodder & Stoughton, London 1998

Leith, Prue,
The Cook's Handbook,
Marshall Editions Ltd., London, 1993

Maltzman, Jeffrey,
Jobs in Paradise: The Definitive Guide to Exotic Jobs Everywhere,
Harper Perennial; Revised edition, New York 1993

Menu and Destination Guide,
O'Sullivan Menu Publishing, L.P. Carlstadt 1998

Rabley, Stephan,
Customs and Traditions in Britain,
Longman Group UK Limited 1986, 12. Auflage 1996

Revell Rod, Scott Trish,
Highly Recommended,
Oxford University Press, 1990

Rob, Gerda; Döbbelin, Hans-Joachim,
Austria, A culinary Tour,
Sigloch Edition, Blaufelden 1996

Roberts Jeremy, Northey José,
The Wines of the World,
Bounty Books, New York

Rod Revell, Christ Scott,
Five Star English for the hotel and tourist industry,
Oxford University Press 1982, 16. Auflage 1996

Scheibenpflug Lotte,
Specialities of Austrian Cooking,
Pinguin Verlag, Innsbruck

Server's Workbook Chili's Restaurant,
ChiliHeadQuarters, Tuscon 2000

The Oxford Wordpower Dictionary,
Oxford University Press 1999

The Visual Food Enzcyclopedia,
Macmillan Company, Les Éditions Québec/Amérique inc., Quebec 1996

Webster's College Dictionary,
Random House Reference Publishing, 2000

Yates,
May I help you?
Max Hueber Verlag, Ismaning 1991

Photo Credits

Seite 9: Top Hotel 11/93
Seite 13: Phonecard der Canada Telecom Network Inc.; Werbeprospekt der British Telecom
Seite 16: Werbefolder Hilton, VIEHLT 8/99 10 E
Seite 19: Stephan Rabley: Customs and Traditions in Britain, © Longman Group UK Limited 1986, 12. Auflage 1996
Seite 20: Britain's Tourism Industry, Published by the Foreign & Commonwealth Office, April 1993
Seite 24: British Airways Holidays Prospect 2000/2001
Seite 29: Randspalte: AHGZ vom 10.03.2001
Seite 30, 32 oben, 33 oben: The Visual Food Enzcyclopedia, Macmillan Company, © 1996 by Les Éditions Québec/Amérique Inc.
Seite 46: FM: Fach-Magazin für Touristik, Gastronomie, Hotellerie und Großverbrauch/Industrie, 25. Jg.
Seite 50: Hotelplan aus: You're Welcome! English for hotel reception, Shiona Harkess and Michael Wherly, Edward ARNOLD Ltd, London 1984; unten: Werbefolder Hilton, VIEHLT 8/99 10 E
Seite 51: oben: Hotel Sonne, Familie Paul Steindl, 6365 Kirchberg
Seite 52 Berufen zur Gastlichkeit. Hrsg. Schulgemeinde der Berufsschule Altmünster/OÖ
Seite 53: Gast 4/2002, Schiefer Katalog; Simon Jersey: The Uniform Company
Seite 58: Werbeprospekt der Hotel-Sacher-Kette
Seite 67: Rod Revell, Christ Scott: Five Star English for the hotel and tourist industry, © Oxford University Press 1982, 16. Auflage 1996
Seite 68, 69, 71: Werbematerial vom Hotel Dorchester, London 2002
Seite 75: Horst Scharfenberg: Die Küchen Amerikas, © Walter Hädecke Verlag, D-7252 Weil an der Stadt, 1990
Seite 77: Olau Tours England 1989, Tower Hotel
Seite 82: Sahara Hotel und Casino, Las Vegas
Seite 87: unten: Aspach Digest für gute Gastlichkeit. Nr. 17, Frühjahr/Sommer 1990
Seite 91 unten: © Citysights AG, Rietstr.31, CH-8240 Thayngau
Seite 92: Das neue Kranzlereck © BTM/Koch (www.btm.de)
Seite 93: U-Bahnhof Kurfürstendamm © BTM/Koch (www.btm.de)
Seite 94, 95, 96: Werbeprospekt der „Four seasons Hotels and Resorts Ltd."
Seite 98, 99: Prospektmaterial des Hotels Dorint, Erfurt
Seite 98: Hotelführer: Relais & Chateaux 2001
Seite 105: Rezept aus: Traditional Scottish Food, Cambers Verlag, © by Meg Cowie, 1989
Seite 112: Hauptspalte: Hotel Imperial © by pictures born, Josefstädterstr. 30, 1080 Wien; Randspalte: Horst Scharfenberg: Die Küchen Amerikas, © Walter Hädecke Verlag, D-7252 Weil an der Stadt 1990
Seite 114: Welcome to McDonald's, © 1996 McDonald's Corporation
Seite 119: unten: GastWirt 9/1993
Seite 121: Dolezalová; Jana; Krekulová, Alena: Jüdische Küche, Verlag Werner Dausien, Hanau, © 1996 Aventinum Nakladatelsvi, Prag
Seite 136: Werbefolder des Courtyard Marriott Hotels, Europaplatz 2, 4020 Linz
Seite 142, 143: Unterlagen des Courtyard Marriott Hotels, Europaplatz 2, 4020 Linz
Seite 144: USA Today, 2. Jänner 2002
Seite 145: http://www.bbc.co.uk/weather
Seite 146: Forte Leisure Breaks, 1994, 2nd Edition
Seite 147: River Thames and Houses of Parliament: Joe Cornish, © WPL 1987; St. Paul's Cathedral © J. Arthur Dixon
Seite 148: Trafalgar Square © J. Arthur Dixon; Westminster Abbey © WPL 1994; Tate Gallery. Aus: check in 5/2001
Seite 149: Millenium Dome. Aus: check in 5/2001
Seite 152: Anna Hathaway's Cottage © J. Salmon LTD

Freie Fotos:
Seite 9 Randspalte oben; Seite 10; Seite 28 Hauptspalte; Seite 44, 54, 56; Seite 72 unten; Seite 80; Seite 88, 89, 90; Seite 91 oben; Seite 93 Randspalte; 120 unten.

Quelle unbekannt:
Seite 9 Randspalte unten; Seite 10 Hauptspalte; Seite 15; Seite 20 Randspalte; Seite 22; Seite 28 Randspalte; Seite 47 Randspalte; Seite 52 unten; Seite 59 oben; Seite 60, 62, 70, 94, 102, Seite 119 oben; Seite 150.

Alle übrigen Fotos sind Eigentum des Trauner Verlages.